PUNISHMENT AND SENTENCING: A RATIONAL APPROACH

Mirko Bagaric, BA, LLB (Hons)
LLM, PhD (Monash)
Senior Lecturer
Monash University

Cavendish
Publishing
Limited

London • Sydney

First published in Great Britain 2001 by Cavendish Publishing Limited,
The Glass House, Wharton Street, London WC1X 9PX, United Kingdom
Telephone: +44 (0)20 7278 8000   Facsimile: +44 (0)20 7278 8080
Email: info@cavendishpublishing.com
Website: www.cavendishpublishing.com

©   Bagaric, M   2001

British Library Cataloguing in Publication Data

Bagaric, Mirko
Punishment and sentencing
1 Sentences (criminal procedure) – Great Britain
I Title
345.4'1'0772

ISBN 1 85941 631 4

Printed and bound in Great Britain

PUNISHMENT AND SENTENCING: A RATIONAL APPROACH

Cavendish
Publishing
Limited

London • Sydney

To my parents, Marica and Ante

PREFACE

In terms of the interests it deals with, sentencing is probably the most important area of the law. Ironically, it is also the least coherent. Nearly three decades ago, sentencing law was described as a wasteland in the law.[1] In the UK and Australia, this is still the case. Sentencing decisions are often made, not on the basis of established rules and principles, but in accordance with the idiosyncratic sentiments of sentencers. Sentencing law and practice in the US is, for the most part, more constrained, owing to the presence of widespread mandatory sentencing regimes in many States, but is no more principled.

The main reason for the rudimentary state of sentencing law is the absence of a rationale for punishment. If we do not know why punishment is justified and what is sought to be achieved by it, there is no prospect of developing meaningful sentencing objectives and principles. We should not be surprised at the ad hoc nature of sentencing law. As is noted by Walker and Padfield:

> [Judges do not undergo] training in which the fundamental principles of sentencing have been a subject of study ... and even those who took ... academic courses in law have not always included jurisprudence among their subjects; and even if they did by no means all jurisprudence courses pay attention to theories of punishment.[2]

This, of course, applies even more so in the case of legislators, most of whom do not have any formal legal education. The broad purpose of this book is to suggest a way of introducing principle into sentencing.

The main issue raised by the concept of punishment is how the deliberate infliction of pain on wrongdoers can be justified. There are two main theories of punishment: retributivism and utilitarianism. Retributivism represents the current orthodoxy of punishment; however, I argue that it is ultimately unconvincing. The shortcomings of retributivism include its inability to justify the imposition of harsher forms of criminal sanctions without resort to consequentialist considerations, and its doubtful premise that we should punish offenders even if no good comes from this.

It is also argued that the main criticisms that have been levelled against the utilitarian theory of punishment, and which have led to its demise as the prime philosophical justification of punishment, have been unduly persuasive. Utilitarianism is the soundest theory of punishment and should be adopted as the underlying rationale for sentencing. However, it is contended that the sentencing objectives which ought to be pursued against this background differ from those normally associated with a utilitarian theory of punishment. Traditionally, it is thought that the good consequences of punishment are rehabilitation, incapacitation and deterrence. The empirical evidence that is available, however, suggests that incarcerating high numbers of offenders does not lower crime and that punishment does not reform. The

---

1   Frankel, 1973.
2   Walker and Padfield, 1996, p 109.

only verifiable good consequence of punishment is that it deters a great many people from committing crime. It follows that the sole aim of criminal punishment should be to deter potential offenders from engaging in wrongdoing. Although there is a link between the crime rate and the existence of some criminal sanction, the evidence does not support a link between heavier penalties and the crime rate. Thus, the (modern) utilitarian theory of punishment advanced in this book differs markedly from conventional utilitarian jurisprudence on punishment.

This theoretical framework has several important practical implications for sentencing law and practice. The recent trend towards tougher penalties should be stopped. Further, many considerations which are currently regarded as being integral to the sentencing calculus, such as an offender's previous convictions and prospects of rehabilitation, are irrelevant. This leaves the way open for a widespread fixed penalty regime, which will assist in promoting consistency and fairness in sentencing.

Earlier versions of several chapters or parts of chapters were published elsewhere. Such sections as are reprinted, are reprinted by permission. I gratefully acknowledge permission to use the following papers here:

'Sentencing: the road to nowhere' (1999) 21 Sydney L Rev, pp 597–626.

'In defence of a utilitarian theory of punishment: punishing the innocent and the compatibility of utilitarianism and rights' (1999) 24 Australian Journal of Legal Philosophy, pp 95–144.

'The errors of retributivism' (2000) 24 Melbourne University L Rev, pp 124–89.

'Incapacitation, deterrence and rehabilitation: flawed ideals or appropriate sentencing goals' (2000) 24 Crim LJ, pp 21–45. This paper has been used with the express permission of LBC Information Services, a part of the Thomson Legal Regulatory Group Asia Pacific Ltd.

'Suspended sentences and protective sentences: illusory evils and disproportionate punishments' (1999) 22 University of New South Wales L Rev, pp 565–94.

'New criminal sanctions – inflicting pain through the denial of employment and education' [2001] Crim L Rev 184–204.

'Double punishment and punishing character – the unfairness of prior convictions' Criminal Justice Ethics, pp 10–28.

'Consistency and fairness in sentencing – the splendour of fixed penalties' (2000) 1 California Crim L Rev 1–25.

'Proportionality in sentencing: its justification, meaning and role' (2000) 12 Current Issues in Criminal Justice 142–65.

My interest in punishment was first stimulated by a series of inspirational lectures delivered by Chin Liew Ten about a decade ago. I owe an enormous amount to his writings and his many insightful suggestions on earlier drafts of this book. He assisted me in thinking through many philosophical issues and saved me from countless errors – I am, of course, responsible for any remaining errors. I am also extremely grateful to Kumar Amarasekara, who provided me with tremendous encouragement and assisted me to clarify many parts of the book, especially sentencing related issues.

John Kleinig gave me valuable critical advice on Chapter 10. Ian Dennis helped me to clarify aspects of Chapter 9. I am grateful to Coni Gargano for proofreading an earlier draft of this book and to Keith Ackers for his assistance in checking the footnotes.

Most of all I am grateful to my wife, Tanya, whose support has enabled me to complete this book.

Mirko Bagaric
Monash University
May 2001

CONTENTS

PART C

Contents

TABLE OF CASES

TABLE OF STATUTES

TABLE OF INTERNATIONAL INSTRUMENTS

PART A

CHAPTER 1

INTRODUCTION

1.1 THE NEED FOR PRINCIPLE IN SENTENCING

Sentencing is arguably the most important area of the law. Whereas many other areas of law are concerned with 'simply' regulating the transfer and adjustment of monetary sums, the sanctions available against criminal offenders target the most cherished and coveted individual interests, such as the right to liberty. Sentencing is the area of law where the State acts in its most coercive and intrusive manner. Not surprisingly, it is also 'the most controversial and politically sensitive aspect of the criminal law'.[1] Paradoxically, sentencing is also the least principled and coherent body of law. Judges have displayed a remarkable reluctance to any fetters being imposed on their sentencing discretion. This has been tacitly supported by legislatures in many jurisdictions, particularly Australia and the UK, which, on the whole, have refused pointedly to endorse specific sentencing goals: 'Our laws characteristically leave to the sentencing judge a range of choice that should be unthinkable in a 'government of laws, not of men'.[2] The failure to endorse a rationale for sentencing has led to what Andrew Ashworth labels a 'cafeteria system'[3] of sentencing, which permits sentencers to pick and choose a rationale which seems appropriate at the time with little constraint.

The independence of punishment theory and sentencing practice

The disorder in sentencing law and practice stems largely from the dissociation between it and theories of punishment. Sentencing is the system of law through which offenders are punished. The main issues which must be addressed by any sentencing system are the types of sanctions that are appropriate and the factors that are relevant to fitting the sanction to the crime.

Punishment is the study of the connection between wrongdoing and State imposed sanctions.[4] The main issue raised by the concept of punishment is the basis upon which the evils administered by the State on offenders can be

---

1 Freckelton, 1996, p ix.
2 Frankel, 1973, p 5. This comment was made in the context of the US sentencing system; however, as is discussed below, it is particularly apt to the present position in the UK and Australia.
3 Ashworth, 1995, p 331.
4 See, eg, Honderich, 1984, Chapter 1; Duff and Garland, 1994, p 1.

justified. Thus, sentencing and punishment are inextricably linked, with punishment being the logically prior inquiry. In order properly to decide how, and how much, to punish, it must first be established on what basis punishment is justified and why we are punishing. For example, the *lex talionis*, an eye for an eye theory of punishment, requires us to select a sanction which as far as possible equates with the nature of the crime, whereas a communicative theory of punishment favours sanctions which will best inform offenders of the wrongfulness of their crimes.

Philosophical discussion in the area of punishment has been largely confined to the justification of punishment. On the other hand, legal analysis has primarily focused on sentencing issues. Oceans of ink have been spilt on each issue; however, despite the logical dependence of sentencing on punishment, the spills have rarely merged and punishment and sentencing have generally evolved with only a cursory consideration of each other.

The division between punishment and sentencing has not gone by without raising at least a hint of suspicion: 'In democracies whose members are divided about [theories of punishment] legislators realise that ambiguity, not honesty, is the best policy.'[5] A similar view is held by Ashworth who, in the context of commenting on the failure of the Criminal Justice Act 1991 (UK) to provide a rational and coherent objective for sentencing, states that 'it is evident that the need to analyse sentencing from the point of view of philosophy and principle often gives way in practice to stronger political and pragmatic pressures'.[6] However, Nigel Walker is probably far closer to identifying the true reason for the gulf between punishment and sentencing:

> I have known magistrates who confused retribution with deterrence, and judges of appeal who confused it with denunciation. Reports of committees hurry past the fundamental issues because the draftsmen want to avoid dissension. Writers of textbooks on criminal law dispose of them in a few smooth paragraphs, knowing that they are skating on thin ice, with deep waters underneath. The deep waters are where moral philosophers lurk, preying like sharks on each other and on practitioners who are careless enough to put their feet through the ice.[7]

Whatever the reason for the separateness between punishment and sentencing, it is argued that there is a strong need for greater integration.

Lack of fairness and consistency in sentencing

As a result of the imprecise state of sentencing law, the rule of law virtues of consistency and fairness are often trumped by the idiosyncratic intuitions of sentencers. Recent changes in some jurisdictions[8] have gone a small way to

---

5 Walker, 1991, p 8.
6 Ashworth, 1995, p 84.
7 Walker, 1991, pp vii–viii.
8 See the discussion of guideline judgments in Chapter 2.

remedying the inconsistent nature of sentencing law, yet this does not necessarily address the more fundamental problem concerning the lack of fairness. In order for meaningful progress to be made in sentencing law, it is necessary to define and adopt a clear rationale for punishing offenders.

Absent an understanding of why sanctions are imposed and what they seek to achieve, only sheer luck or an incredible coincidence would produce an appropriate sentencing system. Luck and coincidence have their proper role in life: they are central to the enjoyment of a lottery or raffle and to the joys, or ills, of bumping into old acquaintances and friends. However, they are not appropriate variables when a person's liberty and standing in the community are at stake.

Due to the void between the philosophy of punishment and sentencing practice, sentencing has been dragged up rather than having been developed as a coherent social institution and body of knowledge. Sentencing law has essentially been developed and implemented in an *ad hoc* fashion without a real appreciation or serious commitment to fundamental principles, which are logically relevant to the punishment of offenders. The haphazard nature of sentencing is reflected in the fact that most systems incorporate an unhappy mix of different theories of punishment, and is exacerbated by the fact that even in jurisdictions where certain sentencing objectives are expressly adopted, there is usually no attempt to rank the respective, often competing, goals. The reluctance of courts and legislatures to prioritise the relevant sentencing considerations gives sentencers a free reign to exercise their mysterious intuitions. Such an approach makes it virtually impossible for progress to be made in the discipline of sentencing. If we do not know why and how a particular conclusion has been reached (that is, why a particular sanction was imposed), it is not possible to subject the decision, in any serious respect, to logical evaluation. At present, we have a process where certain factual data are entered, the data are then subjected to poorly defined variables and a conclusion is formed. But given that the relevant considerations are always, to some extent, conflicting and are not prioritised, we are normally not adequately informed of the rationale underlying the decision. Conflicting principles without weight are vacuous, since they can be used to justify any conclusion whatsoever.

'Judges ... frequently confess that the longer they perform the task of sentencing, the less confidence they have that they know what they are doing. Sentencing has been described as the most "painful" and "least rewarding" of judicial tasks.'[9] However, given the importance of sentencing, this is no reason to give up on attempting to ascertain a coherent justification for the practice. A difficult task is still worth undertaking if the potential gains are high. In order

---

9   Australian Law Reform Commission, 1980, p xxiii.

to have a coherent, transparent and justifiable sentencing system, the relevant principles must not only be articulated, but also prioritised. Although this may lead to mistakes being made along the way, the gravest mistake is not to attempt the task at all. By being open and forthright about why we punish people, the courts and legislatures would make their decisions subject to considered analysis and comment and thereby amenable to improvement and refinement, as opposed to possibly merely promulgating existing errors. This is the type of approach recommended by the Council of Europe, which stated that rationales for sentencing should be declared and where these rationales conflict, priorities should be stated, and where possible a primary rationale should be declared.[10]

It is to this end that exertion in the area of sentencing law should be put. Although all of the major contemporary theories of punishment have been heavily criticised, the attacks are not necessarily insurmountable, and certainly have not been so overwhelming as to make the prospect of convergence in this area hopeless. It is only after this task is undertaken that progressive sentencing reform will be possible and the most important consideration to the determination of a criminal sentence will not be which judge or magistrate will be hearing the matter, but rather, the state of the law.

1.2 OUTLINE, PURPOSE AND SCOPE OF BOOK

The aim of this book is to bridge the gulf between punishment and sentencing. The first step in this process is establishing the most persuasive justificatory theory of punishment. John Kleinig, in his influential book, *Punishment and Desert*, noted that 'as far back as Plato we find raised and considered most of the ethical problems relating to punishment'[11] and that 'the literature on punishment is almost endless'.[12] That was over a quarter of a century ago. Since then, the amount of literature on punishment seems to have increased almost exponentially. This makes it impossible to consider thoroughly every theory of punishment.

The theories that are examined most extensively in this book are retributivism (or the 'just deserts' theory)[13] and the utilitarian theory of punishment. These theories were selected because of their cogency and contemporary appeal. In Chapter 3, the exact nature of these theories is

---

10 Council of Europe, *Consistency in Sentencing* (Recommendation No R (92) 17) (1993) 6.

11 Kleinig, 1973, p 1.

12 *Ibid*, p viii.

13 The terms 'retributive' and 'desert' are, as is the custom, used interchangeably. Just Desert theorists have been labelled as 'new retributivists': see Duff and Garland, 1994, pp 1, 12.

considered. However, broadly, the utilitarian theory claims that punishment is an appropriate response to crime because it is necessary to prevent greater harm in the form of more crime. Retributivism is the view that a criminal act in itself justifies punishment – punishment is an end in itself rather than a means to an end.

Overview – theory and practice

This book is divided into three broad parts. Part A (Chapters 1 and 2) provides an overview of the current approach to sentencing and argues that there is a serious need for wide ranging reform in sentencing law and practice.

Part B (Chapters 3–6) is essentially philosophical in nature (with the exception of some of Chapter 6) and focuses on the issue of which theory of punishment is the most persuasive. Chapter 3 sets the background to the rest of the discussion by dealing with definitional matters and outlining the current state of the debate concerning punishment. In Chapter 4, the retributive theory of punishment is examined. The utilitarian theory of punishment is considered in Chapter 5. It is contended that at the theoretical level utilitarianism is the most persuasive theory of punishment. In Chapter 6, the practical objections to the utilitarian theory of punishment are discussed, and it is suggested that these, too, are not insurmountable.

Modern utilitarian approach

It is important to note, however, that the utilitarian theory of punishment advanced in this book differs significantly from the traditional utilitarian approach to the issue. It is a 'modern utilitarian theory of punishment' in that it brings the general utilitarian theory in line with the current empirical evidence concerning the efficacy of punishment to attain various sentencing objectives. The evidence does not support the efficacy of punishment to achieve the goals of incapacitation, rehabilitation and specific deterrence. Hence, these utilitarian favourites are discarded as considerations justifying punishment and as appropriate sentencing objectives. This leaves (absolute) general deterrence as the sole justificatory reason for punishment. Recognition of this proposition is the first step in establishing a rational theory of punishment and sentencing.

Part C takes the discussion from a theoretical, back to a practical level. It discusses the central practical implications that a utilitarian theory of punishment has for sentencing law and practice. This is the second, and final, step in developing a rational system of sentencing. For comparative purposes, the manner in which retributivism deals with key sentencing issues is also considered. There is a plethora of different sentencing issues. The focus in the book is on the broadest and most important: (a) how much to punish; (b) the form that punishment should take; (c) the factors that are relevant to determining how much to punish; and (d) the manner in which penalties should be determined (that is, should they be fixed or left to the discretion of the sentencer), in that order.

Part C commences by considering how much punishment should be imposed and it is argued that the principle of proportionality should be paramount in this regard. Chapters 8 and 9 examine the nature of criminal sanctions. As far as existing sanctions are concerned, it is suggested that a range of existing sanctions (such as the suspended sentence) should be abolished or the circumstances in which they are used substantially altered. In the process, the desirability of preventive sentences (which, it is argued, are logically the converse of suspended sentences), which incapacitate 'dangerous' offenders for anticipated future crimes, are considered. The issue of capital punishment is not considered in detail. As has been noted by Andrew Ashworth and Andrew von Hirsch: '... a civilised State ... should not have this vile sanction at all, so there should be no occasion for the courts to have to decide when and why it should be imposed.'[14]

As far as the form that criminal punishment ought to take, it is contended that the criminal justice system has been too stagnant and uncreative in developing sanctions, and that sentences imposing a wider range of social restrictions and deprivations should be available. In particular, it is argued that courts should have the power to prevent a person from working or undertaking educational courses.

Chapters 10 and 11 consider the factors that are properly relevant to determining how much to punish. Chapter 10 focuses solely on one such consideration: previous convictions (due to the importance currently attributed to them) and suggests that they are irrelevant to the sentencing calculus. In the final substantive chapter (Chapter 11), it is suggested that most of the sentencing considerations that are commonly assumed to be integral to the sentencing inquiry (such as remorse and the prospects of the rehabilitation) are also irrelevant. The main focus of Chapter 11, however, is on the desirability of introducing a widespread fixed sentencing regime. It is suggested that such a reform would promote consistency and fairness in sentencing, without any significant drawbacks, so long as the principle of proportionality is not violated. Chapter 12 provides a summary of the discussion.

This book is primarily normative in nature, focusing on the reforms that *should* occur. Given that it is not a descriptive, comparative or historical account of sentencing law, a comprehensive survey of sentencing law and

---

14 von Hirsch and Ashworth, 1998, p vi. The only discussion of the death penalty in this book is where it is incidentally relevant to other issues, such as deterrence.

practice would not be helpful.[15] Nonetheless, in relation to some of the proposed changes, it is not plausible to provide an account of what should occur without some understanding of what is presently the case. Where appropriate, existing features of sentencing law and practice in the UK, Australia and the US are discussed. In particular, there is a focus on sentencing law in the UK and Victoria. Following extensive inquiries, sentencing law in both of these jurisdictions has undergone significant reform in the past decade, thereby providing an ideal backdrop to much of the discussion.

1.3 ISSUES NOT DISCUSSED – ABOLITIONISM AND RESTORATIVE JUSTICE

This book does not closely examine the threshold issue concerning punishment: whether it can be justified at all. Some argue that we should abolish punishment altogether.[16] There are numerous reasons that abolitionists give for this view: a common theme being that a State which imposes criminal sanctions, rather than protecting society from harmful acts, usually provokes criminality, and in this way punishment is destructive to society. It has also been charged that punishment is inherently unfair because it is employed mainly against the underprivileged and deprived sectors of the community: 'rulers will never prosecute their own class associates. Or at least, it is very exceptional.'[17]

A popular proposed alternative to the institution of punishment is to treat what are presently criminal acts in a similar manner to civil wrongs. In this vein, it has been suggested that the emphasis of the sentencing system should be reconciliation and reparation,[18] not punishment. One of the main advantages of restorative theories of criminal justice is that they allow victims of crime – who are almost totally marginalised by the traditional criminal justice process – a far more central role at the sentencing stage. The advent of victim impact statements, which enable victims to detail the effects that the crime has had on them, and victim compensation schemes, have stemmed from a growing appreciation of the importance of the victim in the criminal

---

15 In any event, this exacting task has been undertaken by others: see Ashworth, 1995; and Walker and Padfield, 1996, for a discussion of sentencing law in the UK. Australian sentencing law is discussed in Freiberg, 1999. Canadian sentencing practice is detailed in Ruby, 1994.

16 See, eg, Christie, 1981, p 5; Mathiesen, 1990, p 141.

17 Bianchi, 1994, p 333.

18 For further discussion of restorative theories, see Christie, 1977; Cavadino and Dignan, 1997; Zender, 1994.

justice system. The Crime and Disorder Act 1998 (UK) further expands the role of the victim. Pursuant to ss 67 and 68 of the Act, offenders under the age of 18 may be required to make direct practical reparation (such as a letter of apology or a defined period of practical activity that benefits the victim)[19] to their victims.[20] Reforms of this nature, however, are unlikely to diminish the perceived need to punish offenders. At its highest, it can be argued that compensation and reconciliation should have a more prominent role in the process of State imposed punishment. The institution of State imposed sanctions for criminal behaviour is such an entrenched part of our social fabric that no amount of philosophical persuasion is likely to lead to its eradication. Thus, restorative justice is not a substitute for the process of criminal punishment. This being the case, it is more productive to make the system of punishment the best it can be, rather than seeking (pointlessly) to rail against it.

There are also several other intractable difficulties with restorative theories. First, they conflict with fundamental aspects of criminal law ideology. The criminal law punishes behaviour that is (supposedly) so repugnant that it is an affront to society as a whole, not merely the victim. It is for this reason that the State steps in to conduct criminal prosecutions, rather than leaving enforcement to victims. This breaks the nexus between the accused and victim. Secondly, restorative 'justice' is too arbitrary. As is noted by Wasik:

> Reparation turns both upon the differing practical abilities of offenders, and the differing predilections of victims ... [and] allowing victims to influence the form that reparation should take can lead to inconsistency and injustice.[21]

This was a point acknowledged by the Court of Appeal in *Nunn*,[22] where it was observed that the opinions of victims (in this case, the relatives of the deceased asked for a reduction in sentence) cannot be a guide to the appropriate sentence, as this would impair consistency in sentencing.

Before turning to substantive matters, the next chapter expands on what is wrong with existing sentencing law and practice.

---

19 See Dignan, 1999, p 52.

20 The Youth Justice and Criminal Evidence Act 1999 (UK), Pt 1, also introduces a mandatory new sentence of referral to a youth offending panel for most young offenders pleading guilty on their first youth court appearance. For a discussion of this, see Ball, 2000.

21 Wasik, 1999, pp 478–79.

22 *Nunn* [1996] 2 Cr App R(S) 136. See, also, *Hird* [1998] Crim LR 296; *Roche* [1999] Crim LR 339.

CHAPTER 2

SENTENCING LAW OVERVIEW – THE ROAD TO NOWHERE

2.1 THE ABSENCE OF A PRIMARY JUSTIFICATION FOR SENTENCING

Intellectually, sentencing is probably the most deficient area of the law. Decisions are often made not on the basis of binding rules and principles, but rather according to the intuistic sentiments of sentencers. As a result, sentencing law violates the rule of law virtues of consistency and fairness. To remedy this and to make constructive reform possible in sentencing law and practice, it is necessary to adopt a justification for punishing offenders. This chapter highlights the parlous state of sentencing law and practice and argues that there is a need for fundamental sentencing reform.

The sentencing codes of most jurisdictions do not expressly adopt a particular theory of punishment,[1] and where sentencing objectives are declared, they are often inconsistent. Good examples are the Sentencing Act 1991 (Vic) and the Criminal Justice Act 1991 (UK). The Sentencing Act 1991 (Vic) expressly endorses the apparently competing goals of deterrence, rehabilitation and incapacitation (which are paradigm aims of a utilitarian theory of punishment) on the one hand, while simultaneously promoting retributive objectives such as retribution and just deserts,[2] and provides that these five objectives are exhaustive of the purposes for which sentences may be imposed. However, by failing to prioritise the respective importance of these objectives, it seems that they may have been adopted in ignorance of any inconsistency or tension between them. Further, by effectively covering the field regarding virtually all of the possible objectives that one could seek to achieve through punishment, sentencers are given an almost totally unfettered discretion regarding the choice of sanction in relation to any particular offence.

---

1   However, as is discussed in Chapter 3, many jurisdictions, at least overtly, have a leaning towards a retributive theory of punishment.

2   The phrase actually used is 'to *punish* the offender ... in a manner which is just in all of the circumstances' (emphasis added): Sentencing Act 1991 (Vic), s 5(1)(a). Interpreted literally, this is either a tautology, at best, or more probably a nonsense. It serves in no way to guide sentencers – they are hardly likely to aim to impose unjust punishment. In order to give this phrase any meaningful content, it can only be interpreted to mean just deserts.

Despite initial optimism, the Criminal Justice Act 1991 (UK) fares no better. The White Paper upon which the Act is based clearly supported a retributive theory: '... the first objective of all sentencing is denunciation of and retribution for the crime.'[3] In light of this, it has been suggested that the Act gives desert and proportionality a primary role.[4] However, nowhere in the Act is this made express and, in fact, the Act makes no statement at all about the rationales for sentencing. Indeed, the only consideration which, in certain circumstances, can trump all others is incapacitation, which is clearly a utilitarian goal,[5] and matters not relevant to the just deserts principle have been invoked as important sentencing considerations.[6]

The vagueness of sentencing law is further highlighted by the fact that numerous *competing* principles have, at various times, been declared as the *most* important sentencing objective by the courts.

Deterrence

In *Walden v Hensler*, Brennan J stated that the 'chief purpose of the criminal law is to deter those who are tempted to breach its provisions'.[7] The primacy of deterrence (both specific and general) was also propounded in *Radich*:

> One of the main purposes of punishment ... is to protect the public from the commission of such crimes by making it clear to the offender and to other persons with similar impulses that, if they yield to them, they will meet with severe punishment. In all civilised countries, in all ages, [deterrence] has been the main purpose of punishment and still continues so.[8]

Community protection

However, the courts have also held that the ultimate purpose of sentencing is community protection. In *Channon*, Brennan J stated:

> The necessary and *ultimate justification for criminal sanctions is the protection of society* from the conduct which the law proscribes ... Criminal sanctions are purposive, and they are not inflicted judicially except for the purpose of protecting society; nor to an extent beyond what is necessary to achieve that

---

3   Great Britain, Home Office, White Paper, 1990, para 2.9.

4   Ashworth, 1995, p 81. *Ibid*, White Paper, Chapters 1 and 2.

5   The Criminal Justice Act 1991 (UK), s 1(2)(b) (now consolidated as the Powers of Criminal Courts (Sentencing) Act 2000, s 79(2)(b)) makes clear that the only reason for going beyond a proportionate sentence is where this is necessary to protect the public from serious harm. The Criminal Justice Act 1991, s 28(1) allows weight to be given to any relevant mitigating factor, and in this way other utilitarian objectives, such as rehabilitation, may also be relevant.

6   Eg, the prevalence of the offence: see *Cunningham* (1993) 14 Cr App R(S) 444, p 448.

7   (1987) 163 CLR 561, p 569.

8   *Radich* [1954] NZLR 86, p 87. This passage has been endorsed in many cases. See, eg, *Williscroft* [1975] VR 292, p 299; *Cooke* (1955) 72 WN (NSW) 132, pp 135–36.

purpose. In *Cuthbert* (1967) 86 WN (Pt 1) (NSW) 272 at 274 [[1967] 2 NSWR 329], Herron CJ said: all purposes [of punishment] may be reduced under the single heading of protection of society, the protection of the community from crime ... Courts have not infrequently attempted further analysis of the several aspects of punishment (*R v Goodrich* (1952) 70 WN (NSW) 42, where retribution, deterrence and reformation are said to be its threefold purposes). In reality they are but the means employed by the courts for the attainment of the single purpose of the protection of society [emphasis added].[9]

Proportionality

Further, the decisions of the High Court of Australia in *Veen (No 1)*[10] and *Veen (No 2)*[11] stamped proportionality as the predominant objective of sentencing in Australia.

To make the picture even more confusing, proportionality, deterrence and community protection do not exhaust the list of the 'most' important sentencing objectives. As Fox and Freiberg note, apart from deterrence and community protection, denunciation, rehabilitation and education have also been treated by the courts as the only or predominant purpose of criminal sentencing.[12]

The lack of a rationale for sentencing law and practice has resulted in several problems. These are perpetuated by the judicial approach to sentencing.

2.2 THE JUDICIAL APPROACH TO SENTENCING

The instinctive synthesis

The misfortune of the division between punishment and sentencing is no more evident than in Victoria, where the courts have flatly refused to adopt an analytical and open approach to sentencing and instead have opted for what they term an 'instinctive synthesis' technique:

Ultimately every sentence imposed represents the sentencing judge's instinctive synthesis of all the various aspects involved in the punitive process. Moreover, in our view, it is profitless ... to attempt to allot to the various considerations their proper part in the assessment of the particular punishments presently under consideration. ... We are aware that such a

---

9 *Channon* (1978) 20 ALR 1, p 15.
10 (1979) 143 CLR 458.
11 (1988) 164 CLR 465.
12 Fox and Freiberg, 1985, p 444.

conclusion rests upon what is essentially a subjective judgment intuitively reached by an appellate judge as to what punishment is appropriate.[13]

This is now the standard sentencing approach in most Australian jurisdictions. Recently, Hunt J stated:

> A lot of heartburn will also be saved in the Court of Criminal Appeal if the sentencing judge recognises that sentencing is largely an intuitive process. That process does not lend itself to the application of rigid formulas. The influences of the different factors to be taken into account in each case are infinitely various ... The more unnecessarily analytical the judge becomes, the greater the room for attack upon the sentence on appeal.[14]

In *Lawson*, the New South Wales Court of Criminal Appeal reaffirmed the instinctive synthesis method:

> Sentencing is not carried out by the application of formula. As I have said before, it is largely an instinctive process, and the influence of different factors are infinitely various in different cases.[15]

English courts have been equally reluctant to articulate and prioritise the aims of punishment and spell out the reasons underlying sentencing decisions. This has resulted in what Walker and Padfield describe as an eclectic approach to sentencing, which enables sentencers to 'select [their] justifications as the situation seems to dictate'.[16]

Although there are a growing number of circumstances where courts are required to give reasons for sentences,[17] the reasons are usually very superficial and mechanistic: '... such reasons as are given tend to consist of general references to factors taken into account rather than a detailed explanation of how the judge weighed these factors in arriving at the precise sentence.'[18]

Further, the Court of Appeal has expressly downplayed the importance of reasons:

> The statutory provisions [requiring reasons to be given] are not to be treated as a verbal tightrope for judges to walk ... sentencing judges must comply with their statutory duty, but if they err, this court will not interfere with the resultant sentence unless it is wrong in principle or excessive.[19]

---

13 *Williscroft* [1975] VR 292, p 300. This was followed in *Young Dickenson and West* (1990) 45 A Crim R 147, pp 151–52 and by Crockett J in *Nagy* [1992] 1 VR 637, pp 645–46.

14 Hunt, 1997, p 150.

15 (1997) 98 A Crim R 463, p 466, *per* Hunt CJ; see, also, p 475, *per* James J.

16 Walker and Padfield, 1996, p 109.

17 See *Smith* (1987) 9 Cr App R(S) 475.

18 Ashworth *et al*, *Sentencing in the Crown Court: Report of an Exploratory Study*, Oxford: Oxford Centre for Criminological Research, p 1.27; see, also, Ashworth, 1995, p 298.

19 *Baverstock* (1992) 14 Cr App R(S) 471.

Such unconstrained approaches to sentencing enable, if not encourage, judges to determine the sentence on the basis of what appears to them to be intuitively correct. A similar approach played a prominent role in moral theory – once upon a time. It was called intuitionism. Most philosophers dismissed it as a tenable moral theory about half a century ago.[20] The trouble with intuitions is that they all differ, and there is no basis to test the accuracy of intuitive 'truths': principle and expedience become readily indistinguishable. A practice which relies on intuitive sentiments leaves itself open for bias, ignorance and prejudice as the guiding lights. A century ago, it would, no doubt, have appeared intuitively correct to deny women the right to vote and a little further back, the enslavement of black Americans would also not have troubled the intuition too deeply. This is not to dismiss totally the important role that intuitions can have. No doubt, intuition, like luck, can be a good thing. It plays a big part when we decide which shirt to wear, which restaurant to dine at or even which partner to choose, but it has no role in decisions concerning all that is meaningful in people's lives.

It has been argued that even where the instinctive synthesis holds sway, the sentencing discretion is not totally unfettered, since the courts cannot ignore the fundamental principle that 'like cases should be treated alike'.[21] However, two separate studies, undertaken about 20 years ago, determined that there were between 200 and 300 factors that were relevant to sentencing.[22] Thus, it will be rare, if ever, that one will come across cases which are substantially alike. The main casualties stemming from an absence of a primary or coherent sentencing rationale have been fairness and certainty.

2.3 LACK OF CONSISTENCY IN SENTENCING

The reluctance of the courts to fetter the sentencing discretion

The preference in favour of flexibility over certainty is more marked in sentencing law than any other area of the law. The courts have adopted the approach that little guidance can be obtained from case comparisons for the purpose of determining the appropriate sentence. Such comparisons are thought almost meaningless, owing to the unique circumstances of each case.[23] Not only is there an absence of a coherent rationale, but the principle of *stare decisis* also appears to have little operation when it comes down to

---

20 See, eg, Ayer, 1936, pp 106, 118–20, 136–38; Mackie, 1977, pp 38–41.

21 *Pavlic* (1995) 5 Tas R 186, p 189.

22 Shapland, 1981, p 55 identified 229 factors, while Douglas, 1980, in a study of Victorian magistrates' courts identified 292 relevant sentencing factors.

23 See, eg, *Pavlic* (1995) 5 Tas R 186, p 202, where it was stated that 'it is impossible to allocate to each relevant factor a mathematical value, and from that, extrapolate a sum which determines the appropriate penalty'.

sentencing law. On infrequent occasions, the courts have, however, appeared to accept a meaningful role for relying on case comparisons as a means of utilising 'judicial wisdom'. In *Oliver*, Street CJ stated:

> The task of the sentencing judge ... is to pursue the ideal of even-handedness in the matter of sentencing. Full weight is to be given to the collective wisdom of other sentencing judges in interpreting and carrying into effect the policy of the legislature. The collective wisdom is manifested in the general pattern of sentences currently being passed in cases which can be recognised judicially as relevant to the case in hand.[24]

The advantages of such an approach were adverted to in *Zakaria*:

> One rule of fundamental importance in the administration of justice is that like cases should be decided alike (and unlike cases differently). This entails some knowledge of sentences imposed in previous cases. Prior sentences are not binding on courts but they do provide a yardstick against which a particular determination may be made. Indeed, earlier decisions provide a more reliable indication than the statutory maxima as to the appropriate sentence to be applied in a particular case. Ultimately, fair sentencing involves sentencing by analogy.[25]

Nevertheless, the weight of judicial opinion is firmly against curbing judicial sentencing discretion to any discernible extent. For example, in *De Havilland* it was stated that previous sentencing decisions are not binding owing to the fact that there are almost an infinite number of variables, and it was then noted that:

> As in any branch of the law which depends on judicial discretion, decisions on sentencing are no more examples of how the court has dealt with a particular offender in relation to a particular offence. As such they may be useful as an aid to uniformity of sentence for a particular category of crime, but they are *not authoritative* in the strict sense [emphasis added].[26]

The determination of the courts to not fetter the sentencing discretion is perhaps best illustrated by their reluctance in many jurisdictions to formulate guideline sentencing judgments.[27] Guideline judgments consider numerous variations of a specific offence and the importance of factors commonly raised in mitigation and aggravation for that offence and then suggest an appropriate sentencing tariff for that offence. In the UK, the Court of Appeal (at least initially) refused to develop sentencing guidelines[28] to complement the reforms introduced by the Criminal Justice Act 1991 (UK), despite

---

24 (1980) 7 A Crim R 174, p 177.
25 (1984) 12 A Crim R 386, p 388.
26 (1983) 5 Cr App R(S) 109, p 114.
27 But see the discussion below regarding the recent developments in the New South Wales Court of Appeal.
28 See Ashworth and von Hirsch, 1997.

encouragement and an expectation that it would do so.[29] It has been suggested that this reluctance was one of the catalysts for the Crime (Sentences) Act 1997 (UK) (the relevant sections of which are now consolidated in the Powers of Criminal Courts (Sentencing) Act 2000 (UK)), which re-introduced mandatory sentences in the UK after an absence of over a century.[30] Even in relation to the sentencing guidelines which have been developed by the Court of Appeal, the court has been quick to reduce its own significance by declaring that within the guidelines, there is still a *considerable degree of flexibility.*[31] In Victoria, recommendations by the Victorian Sentencing Committee for statutory provisions recognising the use of guideline judgments[32] led to a provision in the Sentencing Bill 1990 (Vic) permitting the making of such judgments. However, following opposition by the majority of Supreme Court judges to such judgments, who felt that they were unnecessary in the 'close knit' Victorian legal community, the provision was ultimately not enacted.[33]

The lack of uniformity in sentencing law also stems from the fact that, as was adverted to earlier, sentencing judgments do not necessarily detail all the considerations which were considered as being relevant to the decision, and accordingly, it is a pointless task to attempt to determine the precise factors which influenced the sentencing discretion.

Given the unwillingness by the courts to adopt techniques which may curtail the sentencing discretion, it is fair comment to charge that, in contrast to every other area of the law:

> ... appellate courts have actively sought to deny their own relevancy in sentencing decisions. Indeed they have embraced a culture of negation – they are loath to intervene, many judgments are *ex tempore* and/or unreported ... and it is the silences that ring the loudest.[34]

Study showing randomness in sentencing

In light of the above approach to sentencing, it is not surprising that a recent study has found an enormous disparity in sentencing outcomes among courts which are meant to be applying the same sentencing laws and practices. A

---

29 See Great Britain, Home Office, White Paper, 1990, para 2.20.

30 Henham, 1998, pp 232–33. This is discussed further in Chapter 10. However, for some recent guideline judgments by the Court of Appeal see: *Clark* [1998] 2 Cr App R 137 (theft by employees); *Avis* (1998) 1 Cr App R 420 (firearms offences); *Wijs* [1998] 2 Cr App R 436 (importing and supplying amphetamines).

31 *Johnson* (1994) 15 Cr App R(S) 827, p 830. See, also, Taylor, 1993, p 130, where he stated that guideline cases merely set the general tariff, but judges are free to tailor the sentence to the facts of the particular case.

32 Victorian Sentencing Committee, 1988, Vol 1, pp 217–20.

33 *Ibid*, Vol 3, A9–10.

34 Smith, J, 1997, p 170.

report by the Prison Reform Trust[35] in 1997 found a fundamental lack of consistency in magistrates' courts decisions throughout England and Wales. The report showed that the chances of an offender going to prison depend far more upon the court where he or she is sentenced than upon the crime of which he or she is charged.

The report shows that markedly different sentencing cultures have developed in cities which are in close proximity to each other. For example, defendants in Sunderland are twice as likely to be imprisoned for driving while disqualified and theft, and are over five times more likely to be imprisoned for car related thefts than defendants in nearby Newcastle.

In Brighton, the imprisonment rate (13%) was more than double that in Southampton (6%). There are also large discrepancies in relation to the length of sentence passed. The average in Southampton (4.4 months) was nearly 40% higher than in Brighton (3.2 months).

Similar discrepancies were found in the four Yorkshire cities and towns of Leeds, Bradford, Huddersfield and Wakefield. The incarceration rate for defendants in Bradford and Huddersfield was nearly twice that in Leeds and Wakefield. The average prison sentence in Bradford was 2.2 months, compared to 3.4 months in Leeds.

Magistrates in Wolverhampton were over 70% more likely to imprison offenders convicted of burglary offences, nearly 40% more likely to imprison disqualified drivers and twice as likely to impose prison sentences for actual bodily harm, than magistrates in Coventry. In Wales, the incarceration rate in Merthyr Tydfil was more than three times that in Llanelli.

Overall, offenders in London were 25% more likely to receive a prison sentence than nationwide. However, this overall figure is very crude and glosses over significant disparities across the 43 courts in London which are as pronounced as in other regions of the country. For example, defendants in Croydon were half as likely to be imprisoned as defendants in Sutton and defendants in Brent were twice as likely to be imprisoned as defendants in Ealing and Haringey.

The importance of consistency

The problem with an unfettered sentencing discretion is that it invariably leads to inconsistent sentencing,[36] and this offends the principle of equality

---

35 *Sentencing: A Geographical Lottery* (1997):
    http://www.penlex.org.uk/pages/prtlotte.html. The report used figures from the Criminal Statistics England and Wales, Supplementary Tables 1995, Vol 4, Proceedings in magistrates' courts – data for individual Petty Sessional Divisions, November 1996, London: HMSO.

36 See, eg, Frankel, 1973; Tata and Hutton, 1998; Hood, 1992, p 201.

before the law and the rule of law maxims that the law must be certain and that legal standards must be declared in advance:

> Just as consistency in punishment – a reflection of the notion of equal justice – is a fundamental element in any rational and fair system of criminal justice, so inconsistency in punishment, because it is regarded as the badge of unfairness and unequal treatment under the law, is calculated to lead to an erosion of public confidence in the integrity of the administration of justice.[37]

It may be countered that the failure of judges and legislatures to define uniform aims and goals of sentencing is no more than an illustration of the not atypical tension between the desirability for certainty and flexibility in the law; the apparent greater flexibility in sentencing law being necessary due to the larger amount of considerations which are relevant.

However, the wide discretion enjoyed by sentencers is more fundamental than a 'mere' conflict between certainty and flexibility: '... out of the rabble of case analysis of sentencing decisions, there is one principle which emerges supreme: judicial discretion. The search for the Holy Grail discovers nothing; but it is a Nothing held high.'[38] Sentencing is the one area of law where judges have attempted to steer clear not only of inflexible rules, but also of broad principles.

Sentencing law is so inexact that even where it is felt that a particular factor is relevant to the sentencing discretion, it is not uncommon that there will be confusion regarding whether it is aggravating or mitigating. Thus, 'factors such as diminished responsibility, intoxication, personal disadvantage, addiction, the public interest and even guilty pleas'[39] are capable of being either aggravating, mitigating or irrelevant.

Rules, principles and policy

In *Hayes*, Kirby J stated that:

> Cases vary infinitely, just as human experience does. Although in drug cases, as in other cases, there are common features, the variety of circumstances must be kept in mind before attempting to derive 'principles' from sentences imposed in apparently like cases.[40]

This is a remarkable concession about the arbitrariness of sentencing law. There are broadly only two different types of norm that comprise a legal system: rules and principles. Rules are narrow prescriptions, such as motorists must drive on the left hand side of the road or below a certain speed limit. They apply to resolve an issue conclusively or not all, hence rules never

---

37 *Lowe* (1984) 154 CLR 606, pp 610–11, *per* Mason J.
38 Smith, J, 1997, p 174.
39 *Ibid*, pp 175–76 (references omitted).
40 *Hayes* (1987) 29 A Crim R 452, p 466, *per* Kirby J.

clash.[41] Whereas principles (such as no person should benefit from his or her own wrongdoing)[42] are standards observed because of a requirement of fairness or justice and secure some individual or group right. These are of broader compass and carry a certain amount of weight; several principles can apply to one situation, with the most relevant or important resolving the outcome.[43]

The important thing to note is that in a *legal* system, rules and principles exhaust the type of considerations open to the courts. There is nothing else. Absent both, we have total randomness. Little wonder, sentencing has been described as the 'high point in anti-jurisprudence'.[44] Once a sentencer has purged him or herself of legal rules and principles, there can only be two other guiding lights: personal sentiments or policy considerations,[45] neither of which can legitimately fill the void. Personal sentiments obviously have no role in a community governed by the rule of law and, as Dworkin notes, there are two reasons why judges cannot decide cases on the basis of policy grounds. Judges are not elected and to invoke policy grounds is to apply retroactive law, unlike a principled decision which merely applies existing rights and duties.

There is no doubt that, owing to the limited nature of human foresight, not all future situations can be anticipated and, accordingly, in any area of the law it is necessary to maintain some degree of discretion. But, sentencing practice is so nebulous and unconstrained that even the outcome of stock in trade cases is unpredictable. As the situation presently stands, sentencing law is so indeterminate that judges are free to switch from one rationale to another as they choose, according to the case or type of case before them, and this amounts to a liberty to determine and to switch policy at a whim.[46]

The indefinite number of variables argument

The strongest argument that can be advanced in defence of the present approach is that because the factual circumstances that sentencing principles must apply to are so varied, it is not possible to develop or prioritise the principles fully beforehand.

---

41 The appearance that rules sometimes clash is explained by Dworkin on the basis that at least one of the rules (especially the exceptions to it) has not been fully stated.

42 See, eg, *Riggs v Palmer* (1889) 115 NY 506; 22 NE 188. For a good discussion of this case, see Dworkin, 1986, pp 15–20.

43 For a further discussion on the distinction between rules and principles, see Dworkin, 1977, pp 22–28, 76–77.

44 Smith, J, 1997, p 174.

45 Dworkin defines a policy as 'that kind of standard that sets out a goal to be reached, generally an improvement in some economic, political or social feature of the community: Dworkin, 1986, p 22.

46 See, also, Ashworth, 1995, p 60.

However, the infinite number of variables argument is circular. The only reason that there are so many factors is because there is no coherent justification for sentencing and hence, there is no basis upon which any factors may be excluded. Unless principles are adopted and standards set, not only is there no basis for identifying relevant considerations, but logically there are no criteria which can be invoked to exclude irrelevant factors. Thus, the safest, and only, thing to do is to 'let it all in'.

The potential application of a supposedly infinite number of variables and situations in the sentencing domain does not entail that lines cannot be drawn. A good illustration of this is the manner in which the substantive criminal law has developed. The criminal law governs every human activity and transaction, from scratching one's nose to detonating a bomb in a crowded building. Accordingly, there are literally an infinite number of variables that are potentially relevant to this field of law. Despite this, clear lines have been drawn between conduct that is relevant (that is, unlawful acts) and conduct that is irrelevant (that is, lawful conduct). And, what is more, the demarcation between conduct which is lawful and unlawful is essentially widely accepted and uncontroversial. The reason for this 'success' is that a (sound) justification for the criminal law has, effectively, been adopted.

The purpose of the criminal law is generally to prevent people committing acts which cause, or seriously threaten, harm to others.[47] By and large, the criminal law no longer aims also to enforce public standards of decency, thus offences relating to such matters as homosexuality and prostitution have, in many jurisdictions, been abolished. Even more generally, the criminal law is not concerned with regulating the self-regarding conduct of individuals. Matters such as suicide and attempted suicide are no longer offences. Notable exceptions to this are drug offences and the prohibition against euthanasia. Even so, in both these instances, there is growing community support for decriminalisation. The other significant exception is the proscription against the infliction of serious injury. One cannot consent to the infliction of bodily injury unless there is 'good reason' to justify the relevant behaviour,[48] owing to the importance the courts place on physical integrity and the unsavoury social consequences which would ensue were injurious conduct generally condoned.[49] However, the list of good reasons is becoming so extensive that this prohibition is becoming less and less material. Conduct which satisfies the good reason test includes surgery, sporting contests,[50] religious rituals (such

---

47 See Bagaric, 1998, pp 242–44, where it is argued that even regulatory or strict offences can be justified on the basis of the (indirect) harm they cause to others.

48 *Brown* [1994] 1 AC 212.

49 *Coney* (1882) 8 QBD 534, p 549; *Donovan* [1934] 2 KB 498, p 507.

50 So long as the injury occurs in the course of conduct sanctioned within the rules or within the accepted standard of the sport and the act does not inherently carry a high risk of injury: *Cey* (1989) 48 CCC 3d 480; *Ciccarelli* (1989) 54 CCC 3d 121.

as circumcision), ear and body piercing and tattooing, and it appears that these categories are not closed.[51]

The only reason that the criminal law is now in a state where it is approaching something like a coherent body of law, where rational and justifiable distinctions are capable of being drawn, is that it has adopted a primary rationale – or at least is coming close to such a position. If sentencing law is to mature and progress in a similar fashion, the same approach is necessary.

Moves to greater consistency – mandatory
sentencing and guideline judgments

Despite the inconsistent nature of sentencing, some jurisdictions have adopted measures which will no doubt improve uniformity. For example, the Northern Territory has introduced mandatory jail terms for certain property offences, such as criminal damage, stealing (but not shoplifting), unlawful entry into buildings and unlawful use of a vehicle. For adults, the penalty for a first offence is 14 days' imprisonment; 90 days for a second offence; and 12 months where the offender has two or more prior property offences.[52] In Western Australia, there is a mandatory 12 month term of imprisonment (for adults) or detention (for juveniles) for repeat offenders convicted of burglary.[53]

In a less drastic move, the New South Wales Court of Appeal finally appears to have accepted the need for greater certainty in sentencing. A specially constituted bench of the Court in *Jurisic*[54] for the first time issued a guideline judgment.[55] Spigelman CJ accepted that some limits must be imposed on the judicial sentencing discretion:

> The existence of multiple objectives in sentencing – rehabilitation, denunciation and deterrence – permits individual judges to reflect quite different penal philosophies. This is not a bad thing in a field in which 'the only golden rule is that there is no golden rule' (*Geddes* (1936) 365 SR (NSW) 554 at 555 *per* Jordan CJ). Indeed, judges reflect the wide range of differing

---

51 *Wilson* [1996] 3 WLR 125, where consent was a valid defence to body branding in the course of a marital relationship.

52 These provisions came into effect on 8 March 1997; see Sentencing Act 1995 (NT), ss 78A(1)–(3).

53 These provisions were introduced by the Criminal Code Amendment Act (No 2) 1996 (WA) and came into operation in November 1996. Mandatory sentencing regimes in other jurisdictions are discussed in Part C of this book.

54 *Jurisic* (1998) 101 A Crim R 259.

55 The offence involved was dangerous driving occasioning grievous bodily harm pursuant to Crimes Act 1900 (NSW), s 52A(3). The guideline issued was that for an offence of this nature where there is present to any material degree any aggravating factor, a custodial sentence of less than three years where death is caused, and less than two years where grievous bodily harm results should be exceptional.

views on such matters that exists in the community. *However, there are limits to the permissible range of variation.* The courts must show that they are responsive to public criticism of the outcome of sentencing processes [emphasis added].[56]

Several months later, in the case of *Henry,*[57] the Court of Criminal Appeal of New South Wales laid down another guideline judgment, this time concerning armed robbery. The benchmark period set by the court for an armed robbery of the type under consideration (that is, an armed robbery committed by a young offender with a weapon on a vulnerable victim, involving a small amount of money and a plea of guilty) was 4–5 years' imprisonment.

Sentencing statistics

In a double triumph towards greater sentencing uniformity, the New South Wales Court of Appeal, only several months prior to *Jurisic,* accepted that sentencing statistics have a meaningful role in the sentencing inquiry. While noting that caution needs to be exercised in using such data, Spigelman CJ stated that sentencing statistics may provide an indication of the general sentencing standards, and thus 'may be of assistance in ensuring consistency in sentencing'.[58]

Indeed, in *Henry,* the court closely examined the relevant sentencing statistics in a bid to discern any relevant sentencing trends. The court focused on statistics concerning the sentences imposed over nearly a four year period for armed robbery and robbery in company. During this period, there was a total of 835 cases. It noted that the 'statistics strongly suggest both inconsistency in sentencing practice and systematic excessive leniency in the level of sentences'.[59] However, the statistics did show that most offenders were imprisoned for the type of offence under consideration, and they were used as a basis for setting a guideline judgment.

Guideline judgments are a positive step forward in terms of achieving greater consistency in sentencing. But, ultimately, they do not go far enough. As was noted earlier, they have been a feature of the sentencing landscape in the UK for several decades and have not curtailed the cafeteria approach to sentencing. This is largely because they are only directory. This point was not missed in *Henry*:

---

56 *Jurisic* (1998) 101 A Crim R 259, p 267.

57 *Henry* [1999] NSWCCA 111 (12 May).

58 *Bloomfield* (1998) 101 A Crim R 404, p 408. Traditionally, the courts have been reluctant to rely on sentencing statistics: see *Ireland* (1987) 29 A Crim R 353, pp 361–62; *Zakaria* (1984) 12 A Crim R 386, p 388; *McGrath* [1999] VSCA 197 [24 November 1999].

59 *Henry* [1999] NSWCCA 111 (12 May), p 26. However, it was noted that of the 835 cases, a total of 688 (82%) resulted in a full time custodial sentence.

> A guideline judgment on the subject of sentencing should not lay down a requirement or anything in the nature of a rule. The failure to sentence in accordance with a guideline is not itself a ground of appeal. Guidelines are not rules of universal application. They may be departed from when the justice of a particular case requires such departure.[60]

Further, guideline judgments do not involve the courts taking a top down approach to sentencing. Rather than focusing on why we should punish offenders in the first place and developing suitable sentencing considerations (and penalties) to meet such objectives, typically, guideline decisions simply adopt existing sentencing practices and try to make them as coherent as possible.

Although it is unlikely that measures such as the issuing of guideline judgments and resorting to sentencing statistics will sufficiently attenuate the judicial sentencing discretion, it is apparent that Australian courts (or at least some of them) may finally be coming around to the realisation that uniformity in sentencing is an important matter.

In England and some States in the US, there seems to be a far more concerted effort to improve consistency in sentencing. Throughout the US, there are about a dozen 'sentencing commissions' and the like[61] which are charged, in part, with the responsibility of advising government of appropriate penalties for a wide range of criminal offences. The most well known of these is the Minnesota Sentencing Guidelines Commission. The Commission consists of 11 members representing the criminal justice system, the public, and victims. Its function is to develop and maintain a model that will provide for the rational and consistent sentencing of offenders. This is principally done through the implementation of a sentencing guideline grid that sets out standard penalties for criminal offences (this is discussed further in Chapters 10 and 11).

In the UK, there is a newly established 'Sentencing Advisory Panel', which was launched on 1 July 1999. The Panel's overall objective is 'to promote consistency in sentencing'.[62] This is to be done by providing researched and objective advice to the Court of Appeal, and in particular by assisting the court in framing or revising sentencing guidelines on particular offences or categories of offences. It is obviously too early to assess just how successful the panel will be in achieving its objective. In its first nine months (to 31 March 2000), the Panel completed one proposal to the Court of Appeal (in response

---

60 See *Henry* [1999] NSWCCA 111 (12 May), para 29, *per* Spigelman CJ.

61 These include the Maryland Commission on Criminal Sentencing Policy; Minnesota Sentencing Guidelines Commission; North Carolina Sentencing and Policy Advisory Commission; Oklahoma Sentencing Commission; Oregon Criminal Justice Commission, Sentencing and Research; Pennsylvania Commission on Sentencing; Utah Sentencing Commission; Washington State Sentencing Guidelines Commission.

62 Sentencing Advisory Panel, *Annual Report 1 July 1999–31 March 2000*: http://www.sentencing-advisory-panel.gov.uk/sapar99.htm#foreword.

to a direction from the Home Secretary) and issued consultation papers on three other categories of offence: offensive weapons, racially aggravated offences and the importation and possession of opium. The proposal to the Court of Appeal was in the form of a sentencing guideline on certain environmental offences. The Court of Appeal referred to the proposal in *Milford Haven Port Authority*,[63] but declined to issue a sentencing guideline. The court stated:

> We are grateful for the advice furnished by the Sentencing Advisory Panel which we have read with interest. Having received the Panel's advice we are required by s 80(2) of the Crime and Disorder Act 1998 to consider whether we should frame guidelines or revise any existing guidelines. We have given such consideration, but do not conclude that we can usefully do more than draw attention to the factors relevant to sentence to which we have already briefly alluded.[64]

2.4 LACK OF FAIRNESS IN SENTENCING

Although there are positive signs for improving the level of consistency in sentencing, there is no room for complacency. Consistency in sentencing is merely a necessary, but not a sufficient virtue towards the attainment of a just sentencing system. Inconsistent application of legal norms is a sure sign of unfairness, however, consistency of its own is not a telling indicator. Consistency is merely an external restraint on the application of substantive rules or principles. If the substantive norms are themselves unfair, consistent application of them merely perpetuates the injustice. Thus, while mandatory sentences result in greater sentencing uniformity, as is discussed in Part C, they have been almost universally condemned as being too harsh. Further, while guideline judgments and reliance on sentencing statistics by courts should lead to greater consistency, this will facilitate discernible betterment of the system only if the principles underpinning sentencing law are themselves justifiable. Unfortunately, this is not the case.

The lack of fairness in sentencing stems from the absence of a justification for punishing offenders. In order for the State to legitimately impose an unpleasantness on its citizens, it is necessary to provide a rationale for this. To this end, the Victorian Sentencing Committee noted that:

> Fairness in the sentencing process involves a mechanism by which it is ensured that like cases are treated in a like way, and that irrelevant considerations are not taken into account in determining a sentence, and neither is there any other ground giving rise to unequal treatment. The articulation of relevant factors to

---

63 (2000) unreported, 16 March.
64 *Ibid*.

be considered in the sentencing process may well result in fairness being achieved.[65]

The absence of a justification for the deprivations occasioned by criminal sanctions puts into question the legitimacy of the sentencing process and reflects a contemptuous disregard by the State towards offenders.

The danger of sentencing reform without principle

The absence of a justification for punishment also stifles progressive reform. Yet, this has not deterred the legislature from making significant sentencing change. Sentencing law in most Australian jurisdictions and the UK over the past decade or so has undergone significant change, with the common thread being to impose heavier penalties for many offences by using several different techniques, with the most visible result being a significant increase in the prison population. The recent wholesale sentencing changes in Victoria provide a good illustration of the potential unfairness that can result through *ad hoc* and unprincipled reform.

Increased penalties

The most transparent and obvious recent change to the Victorian sentencing system has been an increase in the maximum penalties of offences.[66] Most indictable offences now carry a heavier maximum penalty than they did a decade ago. The Sentencing Act 1991 (Vic) increased the maximum penalty for many indictable offences, effective from 22 April 1992. This was followed by another penalty hike for most indictable offences effective from 1 September 1997.[67] For example, in the space of about five years, the maximum penalty for culpable driving (causing death by dangerous driving) has increased from seven years to 15 years and then 20 years; rape has increased from 10 years to 25 years; manslaughter has changed from 15 to 20 years; handling stolen goods has changed from 14 years, to 10 years and now back up to 15 years; and intentionally causing serious injury from 15 to 20 years.

The maximum penalty attached to an offence is the single most relevant determinant regarding the seriousness of an offence. Accordingly, the breadth and significance of the changes constitutes a substantial change to what von Hirsch calls the ordinal proportionality of criminal offences, which is a measure of the relative seriousness of offences.[68] While there may have been a need for changes to the scaling of the relative seriousness of offences, in order

---

65 Victorian Sentencing Committee, 1988, Vol 1, p 145.

66 This is in keeping with a tougher sentencing policy in England and the US – see Chapters 6 and 10.

67 This last round of changes were pursuant to the Sentencing and Other Acts (Amendment) Act 1997 (Vic).

68 von Hirsch, 1985. See below, Chapter 7.

for such changes to be justified, they must be founded on a broader rationale; one which identifies the principles that are relevant to the determination of offence seriousness. As is discussed in Chapter 7, there is a significant amount of controversy concerning the exact nature of these principles. For present purposes, however, what is critical is that a wholesale change to the relative ranking of offence seriousness is an important matter and can be properly accomplished only through an application of the relevant considerations and standards. Otherwise, an unsatisfactory regime of offence ranking is merely being replaced with an arbitrary one.

The first set of increases, in 1992, followed a well researched and detailed report regarding the need for consistency, simplicity and coherency in the scale of maxima for criminal offences.[69] However, the only discernible impetus, and apparent basis, for the last lot of increases was the result of a 'sentencing survey', sanctioned by the government, which called for harsher sentences;[70] hardly the most satisfactory method of determining appropriate sentencing principles. Not only should the law help shape public sentiment regarding crime (rather than simply reflect existing public sentiments), but to the extent that public opinion about sentencing is relevant in assessing the degree of community outrage about crime, the law should look not to the actual feeling in the community, but rather informed public opinion:[71] '... it would be discreditable for the law to seek to give effect to extremist views of those palpably disabled from a fair judgment by reason of prejudice, ignorance or other such factors.'[72] It is only in an area of law where no guiding principle or purpose exists that such predilections could have induced such fundamental change.

Indefinite sentences

Indefinite sentences have also, relatively recently, become a feature of the Victorian sentencing landscape.[73] A key feature of the indefinite sentencing provisions is that an indefinite sentence may only be imposed where the court

---

69 See Victorian Sentencing Task Force, 1989.

70 The survey was in *The Herald Sun* (Melbourne), 'Crime & punishment insight: the sentencing', 29 July 1996. The results revealed that respondents wanted significantly tougher sentences to be imposed for numerous offences: *The Herald Sun* (Melbourne), 'Crime and punishment: your verdict', 13 September 1996, pp 1, 4, 12–15. The survey is unsatisfactory since it did not sample a random cross-section of the community (*Herald Sun* readers only) and was likely to invoke responses only from those who felt most strongly about sentencing issues.

71 Research in numerous jurisdictions has shown that when the full facts are presented to the public, they are far less likely to express the view that the actual sentence was too soft: see, eg, Ashworth and Hough, 1996, p 780; Spigelman, 1999, p 880.

72 *Dole* [1975] VR 754, p 768.

73 Sentencing Act 1991 (Vic), s 18A. The indefinite sentencing provisions are further spelt out in Chapters 7 and 10.

is 'satisfied, to a high degree of probability, that the offender is a *serious danger* to the community [emphasis added]'.[74]

Current empirical evidence reveals that there is no reliable method for predicting dangerousness and that there is a tendency greatly to over-exaggerate the probability of future dangerous behaviour. For example, studies have shown that psychiatric predictions concerning dangerousness are wrong most of the time.[75] Thus, there is no basis for confidence that a court which undertakes an inquiry into the dangerousness of an individual, using the best possible resources available, is likely to come to the correct decision. This, however, did not stand in the way of what, one assumes, must have seemed a good idea at the time when it was decided to introduce the indefinite sentence provisions.

One area where the Victorian legislature has been particularly active, is the introduction of a range of ancillary orders available against offenders. In addition to the normal unpleasantness that accused historically face as a direct consequence of criminal charges, namely, the imposition of criminal sanctions, there are now other painful new measures that may be employed against them.

Confiscation proceedings

The Victorian Parliament has enacted the toughest confiscation laws in Australia in a bid to seize the assets of those accused of criminal offences.[76] This includes provisions which allow confiscation of property or money even where an offender is not convicted of an offence[77] and reverse onus provisions whereby those convicted of certain offences face confiscation of property unless they can prove the property was acquired lawfully.[78] While it has been argued that offenders who derive profits from their criminal activities deserve to have these profits confiscated, on the basis of the principle that people should not profit from their own wrong doing,[79] it is a quantum leap then to propose that the process through which confiscation occurs should not be subject to safeguards which have evolved over centuries, such as the presumption of innocence and burden of proof beyond reasonable doubt. It may be contended that confiscation proceedings are essentially civil in nature, hence protections of this nature are not warranted, but this is a

---

74 Sentencing Act 1991 (Vic), s 18B(1).

75 Monahan, 1984. This issue is explored in detail in Chapter 8.

76 See Confiscation Act 1997 (Vic), which replaced the Crimes (Confiscation of Profits) Act 1986 (Vic).

77 This applies to 'civil forfeiture offences': Confiscation Act 1997 (Vic), s 37, Sched 3.

78 This applies in relation to 'automatic forfeiture orders': Confiscation Act 1997 (Vic), s 35, Sched 2.

79 Bagaric, 1997a.

distinction in form only. It ignores the reality that the catalyst for confiscation proceedings is supposed criminal behaviour and that the pain of deprivation of property is often every bit as severe as the imposition of some forms of traditional criminal sanctions.

Compensation to victims

Finally, victims may now be awarded damages against the accused for pain and suffering sustained as a result of an offence pursuant to s 86 of the Sentencing Act 1991 (Vic).[80] At first glance, one might think that there is nothing novel about this: victims have always had the capacity to sue offenders on the basis of tortious actions, such as battery, assault, false imprisonment, and negligence, for harm suffered as a result of crime. However unlike tortious actions, with s 86 applications, the victim is not put to the task of establishing the cause of action; this is done by the State through the criminal prosecution.

While, in substance, s 86 applications may not be objectionable, the procedure by which they are generally determined places the accused in a particularly precarious position and prevents him or her from fully defending his or her civil liability. All the material that a victim wishes to place before a court to enable it to determine the cause, nature and extent of the pain and suffering must be done before the offender is sentenced.[81] This normally means that s 86 applications are finalised at the end of the plea, but before sentence. An informed offender who is sceptical about the causal nexus between the crime and injury or feels that the victim is exaggerating the degree of suffering would be reluctant to cross-examine too vigorously on such matters, as it may be interpreted as an absence of remorse – which is regarded by the courts as an important sentencing consideration.

Without an acute understanding of what we are seeking to achieve through sentencing law, significant changes such as these will continue to be ill considered and there is a substantial likelihood that they may even be regressive. Decisions on matters that significantly affect people's lives should only be made on the basis of justifiable and clearly defined objectives.

There is a pressing need to adopt a rationale (or rationales) for sentencing. This will have considerable advantages in terms of improving the consistency of the sentencing system. It might also make way for fairer and more efficient sentencing practices. These possible benefits are examined in Part C, but before this, the justifications for punishment are considered.

---

80 As amended by the Victims of Crime Assistance Act (Vic) 1997. These changes commenced on 1 July 1997.

81 Sentencing Act 1981 (Vic), s 86(8); *Coffey* (1997) unreported, County Court of Victoria, 14 October, *per* Nixon J.

PART B

CHAPTER 3

THEORIES OF PUNISHMENT AND THE CURRENT STATE OF THE DEBATE

3.1 INTRODUCTION

The need for a justification of punishment

The central issue regarding punishment is the moral justification of the practice. Not all practices or types of behaviour call for a moral justification. We do not need to justify playing sport, visiting friends or dancing. However, punishment requires a moral justification because it involves the intentional infliction of some type of harm and hence infringes upon an important concern or interest. As such, it is not dissimilar to activities such as slavery, abortion and euthanasia. Zimring and Hawkins note that:

> The need to justify punishment is reflected in moral logic as well as history. Since penal practices are by definition unpleasant, the world is a poorer place for their presence unless the positive functions achieved by them outweigh the negative elements inherent in the policies.[1]

Before evaluating the leading justificatory theories of punishment, the threshold issue of the nature of punishment is considered. The essential features of retributivism and the utilitarian theory of punishment are then examined. This is followed by an overview of the current state of the philosophical debate on punishment and then a consideration of how utilitarianism and retributivism sit with contemporary sentencing practices.

3.2 THE DEFINITION OF PUNISHMENT

The concept of punishment raises several key issues. The most basic issue is ascertaining a definition of punishment that accords with the situations and cases in which the term is properly used in ordinary language. History has shown that generally, little practical mileage is made through pure linguistic analysis of normative concepts. The moral status of euthanasia, abortion or other morally contentious practices will not be resolved by discerning the linguistically correct meaning of such terms. Likewise in the case of punishment. Nevertheless, such an inquiry is necessary in order to diffuse attempts that have been made by proponents of certain views on punishment to advance their case on the basis of definitional arguments. In addition, it is

---

1   Zimring and Hawkins, 1995, p 5.

necessary to have a definitional framework of any practice before one can commence to evaluate it morally. As we shall see, there has been no shortage of definitions that have been proffered over the ages.

The key in defining punishment is to avoid definitional bias and, therefore, giving an unmerited head start to either side of the debate.[2] Numerous self-serving definitions have been advanced.

Punishment and guilt

For example, some commentators emphasise the requirement of guilt as being a definitional aspect of punishment. Thus, Herbert Morris defines punishment as 'the imposition upon a person who is believed to be at fault of something commonly believed to be a deprivation where that deprivation is justified by the person's guilty behaviour'.[3] And Duff defines punishment as 'the infliction of suffering on a member of the community who has broken its laws'.[4]

Ostensibly, confining punishment to the guilty might appear to be innocuous, but definitions of this nature have been used by utilitarians and its critics in attempts to secure (shallow) victories in the debate relating to punishing the innocent.[5] The most moderate position regarding the connection between punishment and guilt would appear to be that advanced by Walker, who provides that while punishment generally requires that the offender has voluntarily committed the relevant act, it is sufficient that the punisher believes or pretends to believe that he or she has done so.[6]

Punishment and blame

A clearer example of a loaded definition is advanced by von Hirsch, who states that 'punishing someone consists of visiting a deprivation (hard treatment) on him, *because* he has committed a wrong, in a manner that expresses disapprobation on the person for his conduct' (emphasis added),[7] or 'punishing someone consists of doing something painful or unpleasant to him, because he has purportedly committed a wrong, under circumstances *and in a manner that conveys disapprobation* of the offender for his wrong'

---

2   While questions of definition and questions of justification are normally separate, they are often merged: see Kleinig, 1973, Chapter 2.

3   Morris, 1971, pp 76, 83.

4   Duff, 1986, p 267. See, also, p 151, where Duff states that punishment is suffering imposed on an offender for an offence by a duly constituted authority.

5   See below, Chapter 5.

6   Walker, 1991, p 2.

7   von Hirsch, 1994, pp 115, 118.

(emphasis added).[8] The vice with such definitions is that they could be used to unduly favour a denunciatory theory of punishment.

It has been contended that there is an inextricable connection between blame and punishment, otherwise there would be no basis for distinguishing between punishment and a tax.[9] While this argument has some merit,[10] it is questionable whether the link between punishment and blame is absolute. The blame which is typically attached to punishment stems from the underlying association between the criminal law and moral culpability:

> Punishment involves a stigmatizing condemnation of the punished. It does so, because the person has been judged to be guilty *inter alia* of some moral wrong-doing, that is, of violating basic conditions of our human engagement ... Punishment is for a breach of standards that are believed to be of fundamental significance in our human intercourse.[11]

If the link between the criminal law and morality was severed, it is unlikely that the absence of any condemnatory component to a sanction would entail that it is not punishment. In such circumstances, offenders would be absolved of blame, nevertheless, a stint in prison would still appear to have all the pertinent hallmarks of punishment. This is evident from the fact that when people are, say, fined for conduct which arguably is not morally reprehensible, such as parking illegally or riding a push bike without a helmet, the fine is viewed as being no less punitive than the fine received by the offenders who commit offences which are clearly morally wrong, such as assault. In any event, the important point for the purpose of this discussion is that even if at the definitional level there is a link between punishment and blame, this is not necessarily the case at the justificatory level.[12]

Punishment as pain

Other definitions of punishment have focused on the unpleasantness it causes. Thus, Bentham simply declared that 'all punishment is mischief, all punishment in itself is evil';[13] Ten states that punishment 'involves the infliction of some unpleasantness on the offender or it deprives the offender of something valued'.[14] Others have placed somewhat emotive emphasis on the hurt that punishment seeks to bring about. Punishment has been described as

---

8 von Hirsch, 1985, p 35.
9 Eg, von Hirsch, 1994, pp 115, 118.
10 Although it is by no means unassailable: see Hart, 1961, p 39.
11 Kleinig, 1998, pp 273, 275. For a fuller account of Kleinig's definition of punishment, see Kleinig, 1973, Chapter 2, esp pp 41–42.
12 See Chapter 4.
13 Bentham, 1970, p 158.
14 Ten, 1987, p 2.

pain delivery,[15] and similarly it has been asserted that 'the intrinsic point of punishment is that it should hurt – that it should inflict suffering, hardship or burdens'.[16] Walker is somewhat more expansive regarding the type of evils which can constitute punishment: punishment involves 'the infliction of something which is assumed to be unwelcome to the recipient: the inconvenience of a disqualification, the hardship of incarceration, the suffering of a flogging, exclusion from the country or community, or in extreme cases death'.[17]

Punishment by an authority

There are also somewhat more fulsome definitions which attempt to highlight some other supposedly indispensable aspect of punishment. Apart from the alleged requirement of guilt and the tendency of punishment to condemn, another common definitional trait is the assumption that punishment must be imposed by a person in authority. For example, Hobbes provides that punishment is an:

> ... *evill inflicted by publique Authority* on him that hath done or omitted that which is judged by the same Authority to be a Transgression of the law; to the end that the will of men may thereby the better be disposed to obedience ... The aym of punishment is not revenge, but terrour [emphasis added].[18]

Honderich defines punishment as '*an authority's infliction of a penalty, something involving deprivation or distress, on an offender*, someone found to have broken a rule, for an offence, an act of the kind prohibited by the rule' (emphasis added).[19] And, in the postscript to the same book, written over a decade later, as 'that practice whereby *a social authority* visits penalties on offenders, one of its deliberate aims being to do so' (emphasis added).[20]

Hart is even more comprehensive, and in his definition he includes all of the features adverted to above, and then some. According to Hart, the features of punishment are that:

(a) it must involve pain or other consequences normally considered unpleasant;

(b) it must be for an offence against legal rules;

(c) it must be of an actual or supposed offender for his offence;

---

15 Christie, 1981, pp 19, 48.
16 Duff, 1996, pp 17, 18.
17 Walker, 1991, p 1. See discussion below regarding the more expansive definition offered by Walker.
18 Hobbes, 1968, pp 353, 355.
19 Honderich, 1984, p 15; see, also, p 19.
20 *Ibid*, p 208.

(d) it must be intentionally administered by human beings other than the offender;

(e) it must be imposed and administered by an authority constituted by a legal system against which the offence is committed.[21]

Walker asserts that there seem to be seven features of punishment, many of which overlap with Hart's elements.[22] However, Walker elaborates further in relation to some aspects. He points out that punishment involves the infliction of something which is *assumed* to be unwelcome by the recipient. Assumed, since it is the assumptions of those who order the sanction that determine whether or not it is punishment. In this regard, Walker is only partially right. It is correct to state that the attitude of the recipient of the sanction is not decisive of whether or not a certain measure constitutes punishment. The fact that an offender enjoys prison, or at least prefers it to other alternative living arrangements that are open to him or her, does not mean that a five year term is not punishment. However, where there is clear evidence that the particular offender enjoys the sanction imposed on him or her, it is questionable that he or she has been punished. The assumption of the sentencer is more critical in this regard. Nonetheless, it too is not conclusive. If a sentencer confers a clear benefit on an offender – for example, instead of fining the offender, awards him or her money – then irrespective of the sentencer's view, there has been no punishment. The views of the sentencer are only relevant to the extent that there is a tangible inconvenience, however slight, flowing from the sanction.[23]

From the above, it seems that there is consensus on two points. First, that punishment involves some type of unpleasantness, and secondly that it is on account of actual or perceived wrongdoing. The requirement that punishment must be imposed by a person in authority is less obvious. Walker takes the view that punishment can be ordered by anyone who is regarded as having the right to do so, such as certain members of a society or family,[24] not merely a formal legal authority, and that punishment stems not only from violation of legal rules, but extends to infringements of social rules or customs. This would seem to accord with general notions regarding punishment, and indeed there would appear to be many parallels between, say, family discipline and legal punishment. As Walker points out, punishment need not be by the State. It has different names, depending on the forum in which it is imposed.

When imposed by the English-speaking courts it is called 'sentencing'. In the Christian Church it is 'penance'. In schools, colleges, professional organisations. clubs, trade unions, and armed forces its name is 'disciplining' or 'penalizing'.[25]

---

21   Hart, 1968, pp 4–5.
22   Walker, 1991, pp 1–3.
23   See, further, the discussion in Chapter 8.
24   Walker, 1991, p 2.
25   *Ibid*, p 1. See, also, Kleinig, 1973, pp 17–22.

For all this, it is not productive to get weighed down on the identity of the punisher. This book is concerned with the social institution of punishment as authorised by the State and the assumption is made that punishment is confined to situations where the punisher has legal authority to inflict pain. However, for the sake of completeness, there does not appear to be any reason that the practice of punishment does not extend to other situations where the punisher is in a position of institutional dominance; for example, where the punisher is a teacher, parent or employer.

Preferred definition

To avoid definitional bias, a minimalist definition is adopted, one which is as neutral as possible and makes clear any assumptions that are incorporated within it. Of the definitions that have been advanced, the least expansive, when one cuts through the often colourful language, comes down to view that punishment is a hardship or deprivation; the taking away of something of value for a wrong actually or perceived to have been committed. The two main theories that have been advanced to justify punishment are now discussed.

3.3 RETRIBUTIVE THEORIES OF PUNISHMENT

Vast arrays of theories of punishment have been advanced that are classified as retributive.[26] Owing to the diversity of these theories, it has proven remarkably difficult to isolate a distinctive feature of theories carrying the tag. All retributive theories assert that offenders deserve to suffer, and that the institution of punishment should inflict the suffering they deserve; however, they provide vastly divergent accounts of why criminals deserve to suffer.

Punishment only for the guilty

Despite this, it has, somewhat ambitiously, been claimed that there are broadly three similarities which underlie retributive theories.[27] The first is that only those who are blameworthy deserve punishment and that this is the sole justification for punishment. Thus, punishment is only justified in cases of deliberate wrongdoing. This feature, however, does not justify the institution of punishment, rather it acts as a constraint on the circumstances in which

---

26 For an overview of many of the theories, see Ten, 1987, pp 38–65; Cottingham, 1979, p 238 (Cottingham identifies nine different theories of punishment that have been classified as retributive); Honderich, 1984, p 211.

27 Anderson, 1997.

punishment may be administered and does not even purport to justify the link between crime and punishment.[28]

The principle of proportionality

The second similarity is the proportionality thesis, which amounts to the claim that the punishment must be equivalent to the level of wrongdoing. This is a claim enthusiastically endorsed by Andrew von Hirsch, one of the main contemporary proponents of retributivism, who asserts that:

> Sentences according to this [that is, the just deserts] principle are to be proportionate in their severity to the gravity of the criminal's conduct ... In such a system, imprisonment, because of its severity, is visited only upon those convicted of serious felonies. For non-serious crimes, penalties less severe than imprisonment are to be used.[29]

However, the view that punishment should be commensurate with the seriousness of the offence, does not provide a justification for punishment; rather, it too, simply, acts as a restraint on it: 'the assertion that sanctions are commensurate with the blameworthiness of conduct does no more to legitimise the existence of penal sanctions than the fact that income tax is proportionate to revenue justifies the practice of taxation itself.'[30] Appeal to the principle of proportionality is also not distinctly retributivist. It is a virtue that has been endorsed by some utilitarians as far back as Bentham.[31] And, in Chapter 7, it is argued that utilitarianism provides the most convincing justification for the proportionality principle.

Punishment good in itself

Finally, it has been asserted that a distinctive feature of retributivism is that punishing criminals is itself just: it cannot be inflicted as a means of pursuing some other aim.[32] However, even a cursory consideration of some of the leading contemporary retributive theories reveals that few do not ultimately advert to extraneous reasons to justify punishment. Only one retributive theory (intrinsic retributivism) claims that punishment is justified because it is intrinsically good to punish wrongdoers. All other retributive theories appear to rely, at least partially, on the instrumental effects of punishment to justify the practice. These include the capacity for punishment to convey blame or

---

28 The other proposition implied in this first statement is that criminal guilt alone justifies punishment. This is made clearer in what Anderson claims is the third distinctive feature of retributivism, which is discussed below.

29 von Hirsch, 1985, p 10.

30 Canadian Sentencing Commission, 1987, p 131.

31 Bentham, 1970, pp 165–74.

32 Anderson, 1997, p 14. Some retributivists, such as Kant and Hegel, make the additional claim that punishment of wrongdoers is not only just, it is obligatory. However, it has been argued that even if punishing the guilty is an intrinsic good there is still no moral duty to bring about such a state of affairs: see Dolinko, 1997, pp 518–22.

reprobation;[33] to induce repentance, self-reform, reparation, and reconciliation;[34] or to restore the fair balance of benefits and burdens which is disturbed by crime.[35]

Accordingly, it is difficult to identify a principle which represents a retributive pedigree. The true picture seems to be that there are many different theories of punishment wearing the retributive label. There is no distinctive badge worn by, or internal unifying principle running through, all of them. Yet, they do have at least one thing in common: they are not utilitarian.[36] Thus, retributive justifications for punishment do not turn on the likely achievement of consequentialist goals: punishment is justified even when 'we are practically certain that ... attempt[s] [to attain consequentialist goals, such as deterrence and rehabilitation] will fail'.[37] This alludes to another characteristic feature of retributive theories: they are essentially backward looking – punishment is an appropriate response to a past offence, irrespective of other incidental effects of it. Future orientated considerations – such as the offender's need for treatment, his or her likelihood of re-offending, and the deterrent effect of punishment – have no role in determining the appropriate punishment. This is in contrast to utilitarianism, which is concerned only with the likely future consequences of imposing punishment. This distinction also explains why some theories which rely on factors or virtues outside the parameters of the act of punishment itself are still regarded as retributive. The virtues invoked are not, at least expressly, consequentialist in nature, but instead are those commonly associated with a deontological account of morality. Deontologists believe that morality consists of a series of rules and that the correctness of an action is not contingent upon its instrumental ability to produce particular ends, but follows from the intrinsic features of the act. Deontological theories claim that it is wrong, for example, to lie because it violates people's rights to be told the truth. This is so even if lying would produce good consequences. The most famous and influential deontological theory is that advanced by Immanuel Kant. He believed that the only actions that are morally appropriate are those done from a sense of moral duty and in accordance with what he termed the categorical imperative, which provides that agents should only act in accordance with rules which could serve as universal forms of behaviour. An example of such a universal law is that we should always act so as to treat others as ends and never merely

---

33   von Hirsch, 1993.

34   See Duff, 1986.

35   See Morris, H, 1973, p 40; Sadurski, 1985, Chapter 8.

36   However, it has been claimed that retributivism could be formulated as a consequentialist theory: Moore, 1993, pp 21–49. For a convincing criticism of this, see Dolinko, 1997, p 510.

37   Duff, 1986, p 7.

as means. Contemporary deontologists place more emphasis on the notion of rights, as opposed to duties. As is discussed later, most deontologists seek to justify the concept of rights on the basis of broad ideals, such as dignity, autonomy and concern and respect for others.

It is unclear whether this captures the full contrast between retributivism and utilitarianism. However, for the purpose of this book, the *precise* definition of retributivism is not critical, for it is argued that all of the leading retributive theories are unsound.

The hallmarks of retributivism are, however, made clearer by further contrasting it with the utilitarian theory of punishment.

3.4 THE UTILITARIAN THEORY OF PUNISHMENT

The picture is far clearer in relation to the utilitarian theory of punishment. Utilitarianism is the theory that the morally right action is that which produces the greatest amount of utility. The utilitarian theory of punishment is merely an application of the general utilitarian theory of morality to the specific issue of punishment. Utility has been defined in numerous ways.

Varieties of utilitarianism

The most popular version of utilitarianism is hedonistic act utilitarianism, which provides that the utility which should be maximised is happiness or pleasure, which is the sole intrinsic good, while pain is the sole inherent evil.

Ideal utilitarianism

Ideal utilitarianism is the theory that, in addition to happiness, there are other intrinsic goods such as knowledge, love and beauty, and accordingly, we should also attempt to maximise these virtues. Ideal utilitarianism, however, is unstable and ultimately collapses into hedonistic utilitarianism. It is true that we generally pursue other virtues, but we do not do so for their own sake. Rather, we seek them because they generally tend to generate pleasure. To the extent that we desire things such as love, knowledge and wealth, it is only because they are generally a means to happiness, but this does not change the derivative nature of their attraction.[38] This is apparent from the fact that few would choose the pursuit of, say, fame or wealth if they were certain that it would lead to unhappiness.

---

38 See Mill, 1986.

Preference utilitarianism

The most recent substitution of note, is to define utility in terms of preference or desire satisfaction. The corresponding theory is called preference utilitarianism.[39] Preference utilitarianism does not have the same degree of self-evident appeal as hedonistic utilitarianism. For example, it is unclear why we should seek to maximise desires which make people unhappy. Further, it is impossible to know which act will maximise desire satisfaction, given the overwhelming number of desires which will invariably need to be considered in any particular case. Also, it may be argued that our ultimate fundamental desire is generally, if not always, to be happy and hence that preference utilitarianism, too, collapses into hedonistic utilitarianism. That is, if happiness is defined broadly enough to include fulfilling what one desires,[40] then there is no conflict between hedonistic and preference utilitarianism.

Act and rule utilitarianism

A further distinction is made between act utilitarianism and rule utilitarianism. Act utilitarianism is simply the view that the correctness of an action is judged according to the degree of utility that it promotes. Rule utilitarianism is the view that the rightness of an act is assessed by reference to its compliance with rules established to maximise utility. For the rule utilitarian, the principle of utility is used as a guide for the rules we should follow, as distinct to the particular actions we should perform. Owing to the difficulty in performing the utilitarian calculus necessary to determine which of a number of options we should choose, it is claimed that a set of rules guiding us in our decisions would be more likely to achieve the desired goal. The main problem with rule utilitarianism is that it is inevitable that, in complying with the rules, there will be occasions when happiness will not be maximised. To refuse to break the rule in such circumstances constitutes 'rule-worship'.[41] It is no answer that in most cases it is beneficial to comply with the rule, otherwise we are putting the rule above its justification. If we do break the rule, we are still being guided by the ultimate principle: act utilitarianism, and rule utilitarianism has nothing distinctive to offer. As is discussed later, it is not that the act utilitarian does not see general rules as playing an important role in our moral decisions, but he or she will only act in accordance with the rules where it is felt that on each particular occasion, this will generate most happiness.

Although in the context of the punishment debate, it does not matter significantly which version of utilitarianism is taken up,[42] the most persuasive

---

39   Preference utilitarianism is outlined in Hare, 1981; and Singer, 1993.

40   As I believe to be the case; see, also, *ibid,* Singer, p 14.

41   See Smart, 1973, pp 3, 10.

42   Ten, 1987, p 4.

and coherent version of utilitarianism is adopted: hedonistic act utilitarianism. Henceforth, it is referred to simply as utilitarianism.

The utilitarian starting point regarding punishment is to consider the most direct and immediate effect of punishment, and from this perspective it is a bad thing because it causes unhappiness to the offender. It is only justified because of the wider contingent benefits it produces, which it is felt outweigh the bad consequences. The good consequences of punishment which are traditionally thought to outbalance the suffering inflicted on the offender, include discouraging the offender from re-offending and potential offenders from committing crimes in the first place, and once the offender is apprehended, rehabilitating him or her and, where necessary, incapacitating the offender. If there are several forms of punishment which produce the same good consequences, we must choose the one which imposes the least unpleasantness to the offender. Thus, unlike retributivism, the utilitarian theory of punishment is forward looking: the commission of a criminal act does not justify punishment, rather, punishment is only warranted if some good can come from it.

Utility as dominion (liberty)

An interesting variant of a consequential theory of punishment is the 'dominion' theory advanced by Braithwaite and Pettit.[43] Their theory is consequentialist; however, the utility that they believe ought to be maximised is not happiness, but what they term dominion. This is a republican concept of liberty where people are free from non-interference by others by virtue of the protection of the law and related social institutions and whereby people enjoy equality before the law. They believe that the objective of the criminal justice system is to maximise dominion. The only acts which should be subject to criminal punishment are those that violate the dominion of others and punishment should only be imposed in order to promote liberty. This can be done via several different means, such as incapacitation and deterrence. However, in their view, it is best done through shaming or censuring criminals. In contrast to von Hirsch's theory, reprobation is not an integral aspect of punishment, but has an instrumental role to the extent that it is useful in promoting observance of the law.

The motivation for the switch from happiness to dominion appears to be essentially twofold. They feel that hedonistic utilitarianism accords insufficient weight to individual interests (thus a measure is chosen which

---

43 Their theory is set out in Braithwaite and Pettit, 1990. They expand on the concept of dominion in Braithwaite and Pettit, 1993, where their theory is primarily restorative. For criticisms of their theory, see Ashworth and von Hirsch, 1992.

gives greater emphasis to personal choice) and they believe that their theory circumvents the problem of punishing the innocent.[44]

However, as is discussed in Chapter 5, hedonistic utilitarianism is well equipped to respond to these dilemmas. Moreover, dominion is a poor substitute for happiness as the ultimate virtue which ought to be maximized. It is implausible to suggest that all important human interests are reducible to, or derivative from, dominion.

Braithwaite and Pettit argue that interference with the dominion of an offender is only justified where he or she violates the dominion of another. Infringement of other interests (such as physical integrity) does not justify punishment unless dominion is also diminished. However, as has been pointed out by Ten, good things do not always go together. Rape and murder certainly do, incidentally, violate dominion, but expressing the wrongness of such crimes in terms of the violation of one's dominion fails to capture adequately the force of the objections to such conduct. Even more telling is that Braithwaite and Pettit are unable to explain intelligibly why it is wrong to inflict pain and suffering on sentient beings that have no concept of dominion, such as animals and mental defectives. This is in sharp contrast to the hedonistic utilitarian: 'the question is not, Can they *reason*? nor, Can they *talk*? but, Can they *suffer*?'[45]

These matters aside, the general thrust of the theory advanced by Braithwaite and Pettit is persuasive. The justification for punishment relates to forward thinking considerations which are aggregative in nature. However, the utility which should be aggregated is the broader notion of happiness, as opposed to dominion.

3.5 CURRENT STATE OF THE DEBATE AND CRITICISMS OF UTILITARIAN THEORY OF PUNISHMENT

Retributivism, under the banner of just deserts, has replaced utilitarianism, at least ostensibly,[46] as the prime philosophical underpinning of punishment in the Western world. It is also generally perceived that the philosophical leaning towards retributivism has permeated most sentencing systems,[47] despite the

---

44 Braithwaite and Pettit, 1990, pp 52–53. As has been correctly pointed out, the reasons they advance for the view that their theory does not permit such an outcome are no more persuasive than have been previously advanced by hedonistic utilitarians: see Ten, 1991b, pp 43–45.

45 Bentham, as cited in Ten, 1987, pp 44–45.

46 I have argued elsewhere that in reality, a utilitarian theory of punishment still best fits the relevant sentencing factors (at least in Victoria): see Bagaric, 1997a.

47 The revival of retributivism is due in a large part to the work of von Hirsch, particularly 1976, 1985. See, also, Kleinig, 1973.

gulf that normally exists between theories of punishment and sentencing practice and the tendency of the sentencing systems of most jurisdictions not to adopt a primary rationale for sentencing. In this regard, the comments of Andrew Ashworth about a decade ago have proved prophetic:

> Across the common law world and elsewhere, new sentencing systems are being introduced or recommended. For example, Sweden, the US federal jurisdictions and several American States have already begun to operate new sentencing schemes, and there are important proposals on the table in Canada, the State of Victoria and the Australian federal jurisdiction ... In planning a new system it is necessary to think seriously about the purposes of sentencing, and it is at this stage that the 'just deserts' approach has been influential in many of the jurisdictions mentioned.[48]

However, this has not long been the case. Only a few short decades ago, Mabbott stated that 'in the theory of punishment, retribution has been defended by no philosopher of note [for over 50 years] except Bradley. Reform and deterrence are the theories accepted in principle and increasingly influential in practice'.[49] In the 1975 Victorian decision of *Williscroft*, Starke J stated that 'retribution as an element of punishment has by now, in my opinion, disappeared, or practically disappeared from our criminal law ... Reformation should be the primary objective of the criminal law'.[50]

Reasons for the movement away from utilitarian punishment

The dominance of retributivism stems, first, from a vacancy being left in the field of a justificatory theory of punishment, owing to widespread criticisms that were levelled at the utilitarian theory of punishment since about the 1970s. Secondly, retributivism presented a neat and simple solution to many of the perceived problems that plagued utilitarianism. Utilitarianism lost many supporters owing to two broad type of attacks: one pragmatic and the other theoretical.

Pragmatic considerations

The first criticism was the perceived failure of penal practice and the treatment based goals of sentencing to measure up to the prime utilitarian objectives of deterrence and rehabilitation. As is discussed in Chapter 6, research findings relating to rehabilitation, in particular, were at one point so depressing that a 'nothing works' attitude was pervasive. Given the apparent failure to achieve such lofty and ambitious sentencing goals, the natural inclination was to set the sights on aims which were far more achievable.

---

48 Ashworth, 1989.
49 As cited in Armstrong, 1971, pp 19–20.
50 *Williscroft* [1975] VR 292, pp 303–04.

Future orientated goals of punishment, such as rehabilitation and deterrence, made way for backward looking considerations where the main goal was to ensure that criminals got what they deserved. Thus, the aim of doing more good through the prison system was replaced by the goal of doing justice, where justice broadly equated to imposing punishment that was proportionate to the severity of the crime. On this rationale, so long as the punishment fitted the crime, or was thereabouts, the sentencing system was a 'success', irrespective of the indirect consequences stemming from it. Retributivism was the clear beneficiary of such an approach. A retributive sentencer can be sure that the sentence will achieve the purpose for which it is imposed: punishing the offender for his or her wrongdoing. The simplicity and appeal of retributivism is evident in Mabbott's justification for punishing students breaking a rule compelling attendance at chapel:

> Many of those who broke this rule broke it on principle. I punished them. I certainly did not want to reform them; I respected their character and their views. I certainly did not want to drive others into chapel through fear of penalties ... My position was clear. They had broken a rule; they knew it and I knew it. Nothing more was necessary to make punishment proper.[51]

Theoretical attacks

The decline of utilitarian punishment and sentencing was also greatly accelerated by the fact that at the theoretical level, there was a move towards rights based moral theories and widespread support for arguments that utilitarianism commits us to abhorrent practices, such as punishing the innocent.

The main general argument in support of rights based moral theories is aptly stated by John Rawls, who claims that only rights based theories take seriously the distinction between human beings, and protect certain rights and interests that are so paramount that they are beyond the demands of net happiness.[52]

Charges of this nature have been extremely influential. Following the Second World War, there has been an immense increase in 'rights talk',[53] both in sheer volume and the number of supposed rights. The rights doctrine has

---

51 Mabbott, 1971, pp 44–45.

52 Rawls, 1971.

53 By rights talk I also include the abundance of declarations, charters, Bills, and the like, such as the Universal Declaration of Human Rights (1948); the International Covenant of Economic, Social and Cultural Rights (1966); and the European Convention for the Protection of Human Rights and Fundamental Freedoms (1966), that seek to spell out certain rights. There were numerous declarations, and the like, of rights prior to the Second World War, such as the Declaration of Independence of the United States (1776) and the Declaration of the Rights of Man and Citizens (1789); however, it is only in relatively modern times that such documents have gained widespread appeal, recognition and force.

progressed a long way since its original rather uncomplicated and noble aim of providing 'a legitimization of ... claims against tyrannical or exploiting regimes'.[54] As Tom Campbell points out:

> The human rights movement is based on the need for a counter-ideology to combat the abuses and misuses of political authority by those who invoke, as a justification for their activities, the need to subordinate the particular interests of individuals to the general good.[55]

There is now, more than ever, a strong tendency to advance moral claims and arguments in terms of rights.[56] Assertion of rights has become the customary means to express our moral sentiments: '... there is virtually no area of public controversy in which rights are not to be found on at least one side of the question – and generally on both.'[57] The domination of rights talk is such that it is accurate to state that 'the doctrine of human rights has at least temporarily replaced the doctrine of maximising utilitarianism as the prime philosophical inspiration of political and social reform'.[58]

The narrower theoretical objection to utilitarian punishment – that it permits punishment of the innocent – has been so persuasive that it, alone, has led many to reject utilitarianism as a general theory of morality.[59] The real force of this objection is found in the more general criticism that utilitarianism fails to protect basic individual rights and interests, and since it does not prohibit anything *per se* may lead to horrendous outcomes. This contrasts with the apparent ease that retributivism deals with this dilemma; by confining punishment only to wrongdoing, it ensures that no person is sacrificed for the good of others.

Before examining the objections that have been made against the utilitarian theory of punishment, it is first argued that the most popular contemporary theory of punishment is unconvincing and hence there is a need to look elsewhere to justify the link between crime and punishment. The next chapter, therefore, discusses the errors of retributive theories of punishment. First, a little on theories that are neither fully retributive, nor utilitarian.

---

54 Benn, 1978, p 61.

55 Campbell, T, 1996b, pp 1, 13.

56 Almost to the point where it is not too far off the mark to propose that the 'escalation of rights rhetoric is out of control': Sumner, 1987.

57 *Ibid.*

58 Hart, 1983, pp 196–97.

59 For a historical account of how punishing the innocent has accounted for the rejection of utilitarianism, see Rosen, 1997.

3.6 COMPROMISE THEORIES OF PUNISHMENT

Although only utilitarian and (some) retributive theories are considered at length in this book, it is noteworthy that a number of theories of punishment have been advanced that in some manner merge elements of retributivism and utilitarianism. Some of these theories have proved quite popular, and hence it would be remiss completely to overlook them. There is no settled terminology for these theories, but among the numerous labels ascribed to them include compromise, hybrid or teleological retributive theories.[60] A common theme of such theories is that utilitarian considerations provide the justification for punishment, while retributivism dictates how much to punish and sets limits on who can be punished. The theory of punishment advanced by HLA Hart has been the most influential mixed theory.[61]

Hart believes that it is untenable to proffer a theory of punishment which is either absolutely utilitarian or retributive; rather, a compromise is necessary. For Hart, the utilitarian aim of crime reduction provides the general justification of punishment (he terms this the General Justifying Aim of punishment); however, this is mitigated by the notion of justice (called Retribution in Distribution), which determines two aspects of punishment: who should be punished and to what extent.

This is the theory endorsed by the New South Wales Law Reform Commission, which felt that it is:

> ... impossible to identify among the varying philosophical approaches to punishment a dominant rationale which should or could rationally guide the reform of sentencing law ... The court must impose a sentence which emerges as a compromise between the competing factors, regardless of which punishment theory is currently in vogue.[62]

Hart's prime reason for invoking the principles of justice to act as side constraints on the General Justifying Aim is that he believes that the principles of justice, such as the proscriptions against sacrificing the innocent and vicariously punishing family members of offenders, cannot be derived from utilitarianism (or, for that matter, retributivism). However, ostensibly abhorrent practices such as punishing the innocent are not so shocking at the pre-philosophical level that we ought to permit the intuitive unease that stems from them to prevail over principle. The utilitarian theory soundly deals with such dilemmas (see Chapter 5). This being so, there is no reason for importing external principles or limits in order to appease our intuition. To do so would

---

60 For a discussion of such theories see Ten, 1987, Chapter 4, where he advances a similar theory to Hart. See, also, Walker, 1991, Chapter 15; Honderich, 1984.

61 Hart, 1968. In particular, see the first essay in this book: 'Prolegomenon to the principles of punishment.' Hart claims that the principles of justice are not derivative from either retributivism or utilitarianism.

62 New South Wales Law Reform Commission, 1996a, p 56.

not only result in a loss of doctrinal coherency, but also leave one with little guidance on critical matters. For example, in the case of Hart's theory, where the principles of justice conflict with utilitarianism there is nowhere to look for the answer. Despite the emphasis of Hart's theory on the virtue of justice, he accepts that in 'extreme cases'[63] it may be right to violate the principles of justice; however, no indication is given as to when such a point is reached. Preferably, a single principle should be adopted as being cardinal. In this regard, the sentiments of Braithwaite and Pettit, that a comprehensive theory is required, are persuasive:

> We object to [retributivism invoking consequentialist supplements], and not just because it is excessively complex in having a retributivist and consequentialist component. It is a theory of dubious coherence, since it is not made clear why punishment should be imposed according to retributivist constraints in cases where its imposition happens not to advance the general justifying aim of the institution.[64]

In light of this, the search for a single coherent theory of punishment should not be condemned to the 'too hard basket' just yet.

It is also notable that the compromise approach best reflects the present state of the sentencing law and practice. The parlous state of this institution provides perhaps the strongest reason why a more principled and pointed approach is necessary.

3.7 CONCLUSION

Punishment involves the imposition of pain on the offender for a wrong that the offender has (actually or purportedly) committed. This definition may appear so obvious to be almost tautologous; however, as is discussed in Chapter 8, it is a point that has been apparently overlooked in relation to some criminal sanctions.

Retributivism has replaced utilitarianism as the most widely accepted and influential justificatory theory of punishment. This is largely due to seemingly persuasive practical and theoretical objections to utilitarianism. The following three chapters discuss which of these theories is best able to justify the institution of punishment. Given that retributivism represents the current orthodoxy in punishment, it is examined first.

---

63 Hart, 1968, p 12.
64 Braithwaite and Pettit, 1990, p 206. See, also, pp 15–20.

CHAPTER 4

THE ERRORS OF RETRIBUTIVISM

4.1 INTRODUCTION

This chapter analyses the most influential retributive theories of punishment: intrinsic retributivism; the unfair advantage theory; and the theories advanced by RA Duff and Andrew von Hirsch. It concludes that none of these theories is able to provide a justification for punishment. The most pervasive flaw with retributive theories is that they are unable to substantiate the link between crime and punishment without relying on consequentialist considerations. It is argued that the shortcomings of the retributive theories are so grave that we should reject retributivism as a worthwhile legal and philosophical concept and look elsewhere for a justificatory theory of punishment. In the process, the manner in which utilitarianism deals with many of the problems plaguing retributive theories is also considered.

Most of the significant groundwork in the development of retributive theories has been undertaken in the philosophical context. While retributivism is an established legal concept, it has been subject only to superficial analysis in the legal arena. Although it is not uncommon for judges and legal commentators to advert to the concept, there is normally a pronounced lack of convergence regarding which version of retributivism is being invoked and an aversion to detailed discussion regarding the intricacies underlying the concept. In this domain, the concept is normally tossed about with enormous generality and, in the rare cases that a specific form of retributivism is considered, it often seems to be in ignorance of other competing versions. Thus, judges (and legal commentators) have contributed little of substance to the debate on retributivism. This, however, is not meant as a criticism of the judicial approach to sentencing.

Choosing a particular theory of punishment represents an (important) policy choice, and is accordingly a matter for legislatures. Given the reluctance of most legislatures to take a pointed stance in this regard, it is not surprising that the courts have at least tinkered with the issue of why it is that we do and should punish wrongdoers. Despite the relatively cursory analysis of retributivism by the courts, the judicial approach to the issue forms a useful backdrop to the foregoing discussion, if mainly to underline the nebulous and evolving nature of the concept. An overview of the judicial approach to retributivism also shows that at some point, many of the major themes running through retributivism have been recognised to some extent.

4.2 JUDICIAL APPROACH TO RETRIBUTIVISM

Retribution as vengeance and the lex talionis

The crudest form of retributivism is intrinsic retributivism, or retributivism as vengeance. This has been acknowledged by the courts, though its reception has been mixed. It has been asserted that offenders deserve harm and that there is an element of revenge in sentencing. In *Gordon*, it was said that:

> Retribution, or the taking of vengeance for the injury which was done by the offender, is ... an important aspect of sentencing ... Not only must the community be satisfied that the offender is given his just deserts, it is important as well that the victim, or those who are left behind, also feel that justice has been done.[1]

A contrary view was taken in *Wheatley*: '... the relatives of the victims ought to approach this type of case not in the spirit of Old Testament morality, seeking vengeance, but rather in light of *ordinary straightforward retribution*' (emphasis added).[2] But, in *Collins*, Tadgell J seemed to assume that revenge and retribution were equivalent:

> What are we about when we say our task is to uphold the criminal law? We mean that we must implement it; but in doing so we must be sure that we are not concerned with the exaction of revenge. The punishments that the courts impose are not primarily to be seen to be retributive.[3]

In *Sargeant*, it was suggested that the *lex talionis*, which is often used interchangeably with intrinsic retributivism, is misguided: 'The Old Testament concept of an eye for an eye and a tooth for a tooth no longer plays any part in our criminal law.'[4]

> In a similar vein, in *Roberts*, it was stated that:

> At one time punishment was regarded in the light of vengeance or retribution against the wrongdoer and offenders were sentenced to be hanged for comparatively minor offences. This was an outgrowth of old Biblical concept expressed in the words 'eye for eye and tooth for tooth'. Retributive justice has faded into comparative insignificance in the present-day administration of criminal justice.[5]

Retribution and satisfaction

The satisfaction theory of retributivism provides that punishing wrongdoers satisfies 'the feeling of hatred – call it revenge, resentment, or what you will –

---

1   (1994) 71 A Crim R 459, p 468.
2   (1982) 4 Cr App R(S) 371, p 374.
3   (1984) unreported, 26 November, Court of Criminal Appeal (Vic), *per* Tadgell J.
4   (1974) 60 Cr App R 74, p 77.
5   [1963] 1 CCC 27, p 45.

which the contemplation of such conduct excites in healthy constituted minds'[6] and thereby diminishes the prospect of harmful vendettas by victims and their associates, who may be tempted to exact their own revenge. It, too, has occasionally been endorsed by the courts:

> One of the objects of punishment, and by no means the least important object of punishment, is to prevent, so far as possible, the victims of crime from taking matters into their own hands. It is no great step from private vengeance to vendetta, and there is no knowing where the vendetta will stop.[7]

Retribution and denunciation

The version of retribution which has possibly received the greatest judicial support is denunciation. Denunciation is a mark of public disapproval of criminal conduct, and is a means by which the courts can maintain public confidence in the administration of justice and reflect the moral sense of the community in the sentence. In *Nichols*, Lee AJ stated that in the case of serious crime, the court must show its denunciation of the crime committed: '... the moral outrage of the community must be taken into account.'[8] English courts have expressed similar sentiments, in holding that one of the purposes in sentencing is 'to mark the disapproval of society'[9] or 'to mark the abhorrence which society feels for this type of attack'.[10]

As we saw in Chapter 2, in assessing the degree of community outrage, the courts look to informed public opinion, not actual community feeling – which may be influenced by prejudice or ignorance.[11] The public is assumed to have knowledge of the circumstances of the case and an appreciation of the range of penalties imposed in previous similar cases.[12]

The irrelevance of actual community sentiment to denunciation is highlighted by the fact that evidence of community feeling is not even admissible:

> The evaluation of the criminality of the offence and whether imprisonment is called for is for the judge to determine upon the relevant evidence in relation to the crime. It is not a matter to be determined by reference to the views of others given directly in evidence or as hearsay, which views in any event may be

---

6   Stephen, JF, *Liberty, Equality, Fraternity*, 1873, London: Smith, Elder, 161–62, as cited in Honderich, 1984, p 49.

7   *Darby* (1986) 8 Cr App R(S) 487, p 490; *Amituanai* (1995) 78 A Crim R 588, p 596.

8   (1991) 57 A Crim R 391, p 395. See, also, *Channon* (1978) 20 ALR 1; *Dixon* (1975) 22 ACTR 13; and *Williscroft* [1975] VR 292.

9   *Hitchcock* (1982) 4 Cr App R(S) 160, p 161.

10 *Hay* (1982) 4 Cr App R(S) 392, p 394. See, also, *Milne* (1982) 4 Cr App R(S) 397. In Canada, a similar view is expressed in *Clayton* (1983) 69 CCC (2d) 81, p 82.

11 *Dole* [1975] VR 754, p 768. See, also, *Causby* [1984] Tas R 54, pp 59–60.

12 See *Inkson* (1996) 6 Tas R 1, p 16.

based on wrong facts or facts not in evidence ... The extent of community abhorrence of a crime or a type of crime is not a matter of evidence.[13]

A recent illustration of this principle is the case of *Secretary of State for the Home Department ex p Venables and Thompson*,[14] where the House of Lords considered the case of two boys aged 10, who were convicted of the murder of a two year old boy (James Bulger). In sentencing the accused, the trial judge imposed the mandatory sentence of detention during Her Majesty's pleasure provided for by s 53(1)(a) of the Children and Young Persons Act 1933 (UK). In his report to the Home Secretary, the judge recommended that the tariff period of their sentence be eight years' detention. The Lord Chief Justice then advised the Home Secretary that the tariff period should be 10 years.

The perceived leniency of this sentence led to much disquiet in the community, resulting in a petition containing some 278,300 signatures, a campaign of over 20,000 coupons organised by *The Sun* newspaper and over 5,000 letters demanding that the accused should remain in detention for life. The former Home Secretary, Michael Howard, then exercised his discretion (under s 35b of the Criminal Justice Act 1991 (UK)) and increased the sentences to 15 years. In doing so, the Home Secretary stated that he had regard to the public concern about the case.

The House of Lords ultimately upheld the decision of the Court of Appeal to quash the Home Secretary's decision. It observed that in fixing a tariff, the Home Secretary was exercising a power akin to a judge's sentencing power and, therefore, he was required to disregard public opinion. The public protests were legally irrelevant and should not have influenced his decision in fixing the tariff. As a result of giving weight to public opinion, it was held that the Home Secretary had acted in a procedurally unfair way.[15]

Other objectives of denunciation

Support for a denunciatory theory of punishment has not always coincided with an endorsement of retributivism. Denunciation has often been backed because it is felt that it will promote more fundamental objectives of sentencing, many of which sit more comfortably in a utilitarian ethic.

For example, it has been contended that denunciation prevents crime by publicly declaring that criminal activity will not be tolerated. In *McKenna*, it was stated that:

---

13 *H* (1980) A Crim R 53, p 65, but cf *Miller* [1995] 2 VR 348.

14 [1997] 3 All ER 97.

15 The House of Lords also held that in setting the tariff, the Home Secretary failed to take sufficient account of the welfare of the accused (children) as he was required to do pursuant to the Children and Young Persons Act 1933 (UK), s 44(1)(c).

A non-custodial sentence ... lacks the element of denunciation of the crime which is of vital importance in the case of laws designed to protect young persons and thus necessary if deterrence is to be achieved.[16]

Denunciation has also been regarded as a means of satisfying victims[17] and maintaining public confidence in the criminal justice system.[18] It is also said to have a strong educative role. In *Collins*, Tadgell J, quoting the words of Sir John Barry, stated that punishment:

... serves by its solemn procedures as a teacher of minimal standards of morality and behaviour; as an agency for the expression of public indignation and condemnation; and as a force operating to produce cohesion within society.[19]

This point was also emphasised by the English Court of Appeal in *Sargeant*:

There is however another aspect of retribution ... it is that society, through the courts, must show its abhorrence of particular crime ... The courts do not have to reflect public opinion. On the other hand the courts must not disregard it. Perhaps the main duty of the court is to lead public opinion.[20]

Retributivism and reform bodies

Reports by sentencing committees and the like have, on the whole, been far less supportive of the retributive cause than the judiciary. This may be largely due to the sweeping manner in which retributive theories have been considered by such bodies. The Victorian Sentencing Committee provided that:

Retribution is a justification which provides that a person is to be punished for his or her wrongful acts simply because he or she deserves it. It is based on the ancient principle of an eye for an eye and a tooth for a tooth. Retribution in its pure form has very little application today.[21]

More recently, the New South Wales Law Reform Commission also failed to distinguish between different retributive theories and simply provided that 'retribution is the notion that the guilty ought to suffer the punishment which they deserve'.[22] A little further it stated that 'just deserts [of the type adopted in some Australian jurisdictions] is merely a reflection of the common law principle of proportionality which places limits, in terms of the gravity of the offence in issue, on the severity of the punishment'.[23] The Canadian

---

16 (1992) unreported, CCA (NSW) 16 October, *per* Lee AJ, p 9.
17 *Williscroft* [1975] VR 292, p 300.
18 *Dixon* (1975) 22 ACTR 13, p 19.
19 *Collins* (1984) unreported, Court of Criminal Appeal (Vic), Tadgell J, 26 November.
20 (1974) 60 Cr App Rep 74.
21 Victorian Sentencing Committee Report, 1988, p 88.
22 New South Wales Law Reform Commission, 1996a, p 45.
23 *Ibid*.

Commission on Sentencing was quick to conclude that retributivism must borrow utilitarian arguments to address the issue of the justification of punishment convincingly.[24]

Such dismissive remarks lack persuasion due to the all-embracing treatment of retributivism. A convincing rejection of any theory requires, at the minimum, an exploration of its distinctive features and supposed advantages and, where relevant, important modifications and subtleties.

This task is now undertaken. This requires a detailed consideration of the philosophical debate in this area, where dozens of different retributive theories have been advanced. It is not possible to consider each of them meaningfully. With one exception, the focus is on the retributive theories which have proved to be the most influential. Thus, von Hirsch's theory, which is widely acknowledged as being largely responsible for the revival of retribution, is considered. This is followed by a consideration of Duff's theory which picks up many of the themes discussed by von Hirsch. Finally, the unfair advantage theory of punishment which George Sher has recently attempted to revive is discussed.

The starting point is the crudest and most straightforward version of retributivism: intrinsic retributivism. This has few contemporary adherents – retributive theories are now more intricate. Although most have written intrinsic retributivism off the 'tenable theories of punishment list', it merits detailed consideration because, with a little re-posturing, it is ultimately the most persuasive retributive theory.

4.3 DESERT AS A NATURAL RESPONSE – INTRINSIC RETRIBUTIVISM

4.3.1 Outline of the theory

The paradigm and most basic retributive theory has been dubbed intrinsic retributivism. This is the simple claim that punishment is justified because there is intrinsic good in making wrongdoers suffer: 'The principle that wrongdoers deserve to suffer seems to accord with our deepest intuitions concerning justice':[25]

> As individuals we have a wholly proper desire to seek revenge when wrongs are inflicted on us: as a society we demand that constituted authority punish those who unjustifiably inflict injury on others or otherwise act in ways we

---

24 Canadian Sentencing Commission, 1987, pp 141–42, 144. As was noted in Chapters 1 and 2, an exception to this trend was the White Paper forming the basis of the Criminal Justice Act 1991 (UK), which enthusiastically endorsed a retributive theory of punishment.

25 Kleinig, 1973, p 67.

think are wrong. If other benefits are incidentally derived from making the wicked suffer, well and good; but those benefits must not be sought for their own sake.[26]

Intrinsic retributivism is commonly associated with the lex talionis: an eye for an eye, a tooth for a tooth, and so on. This, however, is not necessarily the case, since intrinsic retributivism says nothing about the amount of punishment, which is a central feature of the *lex talionis*. But, because the *lex talionis* is often expressed without further justification, it lends itself easily to the claim that wrongdoers deserve to suffer is a self evident truth.

There is no question that the sentiment that the guilty deserve to suffer is widespread and extends beyond the parameters of legal punishment. If a wrongdoer suffers some accidental harm, for example, if a burglar breaks his or her leg entering a window, this is often described as 'poetic justice', or if a wicked person wins the jackpot, we tend to think of this being undeserved or unfair. We naturally feel that the good should prosper, and, perhaps even more strongly, that the bad ought to suffer.[27] It is suggested that, given that there is widespread support for the belief that wrongdoers deserve to suffer 'among the people whose moral intuitions constitute the main data we have for settling questions of value ... [it is] very likely [that the judgment is] true'.[28] Thus, retributivists assert that the strong innate cord struck by the view that wrongdoers deserve to suffer is so melodic that support from some more fundamental principle or instrumental goal is not necessary to substantiate it: the justification is self-evident. There are, however, several problems with this theory.

4.3.2 Criticisms

A whole life view of suffering

CL Ten suggests that the intrinsic retributivist faces the difficulty of explaining whether deserved suffering is influenced by past, undeserved suffering. A 'whole life view of suffering' approach requires us to determine desert, not by merely focusing on the wrongdoer's level of culpability for the particular offence, but rather by weighing all of his or her wrongs against the suffering experienced throughout his or her lifetime, which incorporates such things as undeserved suffering from social causes. On this basis, it may be that the wrongdoer, as a consequence of social deprivations, may have amassed

---

26 Packer, 1973, pp 183, 184.
27 See, also, Duff, 1986, p 198; Moore, 1998, p 150.
28 Davis, LH, 'They deserve to suffer' (1972) 32(4) Analysis 136, p 139, cited in Honderich, 1984, p 212.

credits for suffering and accordingly ought not to be punished for a particular crime.[29] However, this objection is not decisive. It looks to the quantum of punishment rather than the need for it, and in this regard it is not an objection peculiar to intrinsic retributivism. Rather, it is a matter that must be addressed by all theories of punishment. Intrinsic retributivism is a simple claim: wrongdoers deserve to be punished. It does not go on to provide how much they should be punished. Nor does it directly need to do so. This can be dealt with by invoking other principles.

The fact that other principles may be needed to supplement the primary claim of a theory is not necessarily a shortcoming. No general theory of punishment provides clear cut answers to every aspect of the punishment: this can be left to other subordinate principles. It is only where the subordinate principles which lead to the 'appropriate result' (in this case, that offenders from deprived backgrounds should be punished less severely) are not compatible with the primary claim of the theory, that one gets into strife. But, the proposition that previous hardships sustained by an offender are relevant to the amount of punishment, leaves intrinsic retributivism unscathed. First, it can simply be asserted that the whole life view of suffering is untenable. Moreover, the intrinsic retributivist could accept the whole life view of desert by extrapolating his or her primary claim to the effect that 'punishment' includes the pain naturally endured throughout life; thus, where an offender has suffered at least as much incidental hardship as is deserved by an offence, then no additional punishment is called for. There are, however, several other more telling objections against intrinsic retributivism.

Self-evident truths are generally dubious

The first relates to the reliance on self-evident or intuitive 'truths'. Reliance on such truths can only occur in the most limited of circumstances, since their persuasion is roughly commensurate with the incongruity of an assertion to the contrary. Given that there is no absurdity in the claim that wrongdoers do not deserve to suffer,[30] intrinsic retributivism is not self-verifying. While our feelings often incline us to respond favourably towards those who treat us well and wish harm towards wrongdoers, such sentiments are not universal. That a person has broken the law or, for that matter, has behaved immorally, does not compel any particular moral conclusions. We do not necessarily feel a pang of resentment towards those who drive too quickly, steal from shops or lie to others. Although we disapprove of speeding, shoplifting and lying, we recognise that it is a fact of life that such things occur and do not expect or demand that such conduct should always result in unpleasantness to the

29 Ten, 1987, p 49.
30 This point is also made by Honderich, 1984, pp 213–15.

agent. We are sometimes simply indifferent when lawbreakers go unpunished.

Intrinsic retributivism – causal not normative theory

Even if the desire to punish wrongdoers is pervasive, this does not justify punishment, since truth does not necessarily follow consensus. This is the case with empirical and supposed normative beliefs. The widely held view that the world was flat did not make it so and widespread acceptance of slavery, similarly, did not provide a justification for it. Likewise, even if we are so built that wrongdoing necessarily prompts a punitive impulse, it does not follow that intrinsic retributivism justifies punishment, any more than an innate sense of jealousy *justifies* locking up our wives. What is necessary from a normative theory is a justification of the relevant practice, not an explanation of it.

We frequently must displace our natural human responses (for example, jealousy, lust, rage and anger) by more considered and reflective dispositions, due to the harm which they cause. So, too, it could be argued with intrinsic retributivism. Of course, it could be countered that, as a psychological matter, our make up is such that it is not possible to react in a manner other than to punish wrongdoers: inferring, therefore, that it is wasteful even to consider (other) *justifications* for punishment, since there is no point in arguing against that which cannot be curtailed. This, however, is repudiated by the sheer number of counter-examples, where people bear no animosity towards those who have violated their important interests. And, indeed, as we have seen, there have been loud calls for the abolition of punishment.

Punish even when no good consequences

Even if it can be shown that punishing the guilty is an intrinsic *good*, it does not necessarily follow that punishment is justified. For, as Dolinko points out, an intrinsic good need not be a particularly important good or objective:

> I have an itch; I scratch myself; the itching ceases. The cessation of the itching sensation, I believe, is an intrinsic good. Yet it is surely a quite unimportant good, and if for some reason I could not scratch myself without creating a high risk that innocent people would die, it would be unconscionable for me to scratch anyway on the ground that doing so would bring about 'an intrinsically good state of affairs'.[31]

This emphasises the point that in evaluating the morality of any practice, consequences cannot be totally ignored. Followed to its logical conclusion, intrinsic retributivism entails that offenders should be punished even when no

---

31   Dolinko, 1997, p 521.

good comes from this. If it were positively established that overall, punishment had bad social consequences (for example, because it increased recidivism and the overall crime rate), utilitarians would abandon punishment in preference for a more effective manner of dealing with offenders. In contrast, the commitment to the type and amount of punishment by intrinsic retributivists would remain unchanged. It seems wrong to impose a harsher punishment if an offender could be reformed by a lesser sanction: 'retributive justice may be a very good thing, but the saving of souls is a much better thing'.[32] This criticism can be levelled at most retributive theories, since they do not rely on the effects of punishment to justify it, but is particularly damaging with respect to intrinsic retributivism, where there is a total absence of reasons why one should punish, beyond the mere impulse to punish.

Retributivists do not have to deny that consequences are totally irrelevant. Thus, they could attempt to invoke consequentialist considerations to veto punishment, say, where no good at all would come from it. However, as with most compromises, this risks fatally destabilising the theory. It would be unclear at what point consequences become decisive. The retributivist also would be required to give a coherent account of why consequences matter only some of the time, otherwise he or she appears to be advancing not a moral justification of punishment, but an expedient disparate set of retorts in order to justify an existing intuition.

4.3.3   Intrinsic retributivism strikes back – morality as desires

The source of the judgment that the guilty deserve to suffer is unclear. In spite of this, the most likely origin is the desire for revenge.[33] It follows that stripped bare, intrinsic retributivism amounts to the claim that offenders deserve to be punished because a wrong action naturally calls for revenge or a hostile response. This was a point acknowledged by Mackie who claimed that retributive sentiments are an ingrained part of our moral thinking. He labels as the paradox of retributivism the proposition that:

> On the one hand, a retributive principle of punishment cannot be explained or developed within a reasonable system of moral thought, while, on the other hand, such a principle cannot be eliminated from our moral thinking.[34]

In order to resolve this dilemma, he relies on the distinction between beliefs on the one hand, and desires or feelings on the other, and claims that

---

32   Ewing, 1929, p 18.
33   Eg, Ten, 1987, p 47.
34   Mackie, 1982.

retributive sentiments are desires or feelings, not beliefs,[35] and such feelings arise from the advantages to be gained through retaliatory behaviour.[36] It is natural to desire to punish wrongdoers, but our value system must look beyond such sentiments.

It can be argued that this analysis of intrinsic retributivism shows it to be the mere expression of the primitive desire to exact revenge, which emphasises reprisal above all else and that the main impact of its adoption as a rationale for punishment would be to desensitise and brutalise society. Viewed in this light, most have been prepared to dismiss intrinsic retributivism as an untenable theory of punishment.

At this point, it may seem that the above account of intrinsic retributivism is too expansive and accords more respect to it than is commensurate with its standing among contemporary theories of punishment. However, with some deft fine-tuning, a comeback may be possible. In order for this to occur, the intrinsic retributivist must embrace the concept of revenge rather than seeking to mask it, and assert that – despite the veneer of harshness of the link with vengeance – revenge is in fact not only a natural, but also an *appropriate* response to wrongdoing.

Indeed, over a century ago, Duhring claimed that the origin of the concept of justice lies in the notion of revenge: a desire which occurs naturally to retaliate against those who have done wrong, and that ultimately criminal justice is simply the public organisation of revenge.[37] He also contended that the *lex talionis* should not be dismissed because it is too barbaric, but rather because it does not go far enough; more harm than that corresponding to the crime is necessary to restore equality, since the natural desire 'for revenge does not limit itself to the magnitude of the offence: it normally goes further, and rightly so'.[38]

As to the nature of revenge, numerous explanations have been offered. Apart from Duhring's description, it has also been explained as 'an attempt to regain one's honour or social prestige';[39] and an instinct which assists in the struggle for survival, since vengeful groups are supposedly less likely to be harmed by others.[40] Nietzsche believed that an account of revenge as a biological urge for self-preservation is too limiting, since it does not explain the calculated infliction of suffering, and suggested that revenge does not stem from a single motive, but rather can arise from a variety of different

---

35 The belief/desire distinction is discussed further below.

36 Mackie, 1982, p 8.

37 Duhring, E, *Der Werth des Lebens. Eine Philosophische Betrachtung*, 1865, Breslau, cited in Small, 1997 pp 40–41.

38 *Ibid*, pp 39, 42.

39 Elster, J, 'Norms of revenge' (1990) 100 Ethics 862, as cited in Small, 1997, p 45.

40 Jacoby, S, *Wild Justice*, 1983, New York: Harper & Row, as cited in Small, 1997, p 45.

motives, including a desire for self-preservation or an attempt to restore self-esteem lost by injury.[41]

The claim that intrinsic retributivism stems from the *desire* for revenge can form the basis of an extremely coherent normative argument when coupled with the further claim that morality consists precisely of such retorts: desires; rather than *beliefs*. This puts intrinsic retributivism in its best possible light. This slight posturing has a potentially significant impact regarding the outcome of the debate on intrinsic retributivism. To see why requires a momentary excursion into the realm of metaethics. Before proceeding to this, it is important to recall that much of the above discussion is dismissive of intrinsic retributivism due to the nature of the sentiment at its core: the desire for revenge. If, however, morality is 'simply' an expression of our feelings or desires, this puts a different complexion on the matter.

The distinction between beliefs and desires

First, a little psychology. Hume's powerful theory of human motivation distinguishes between two states of mind: beliefs and desires. Beliefs are copies or replicas of the way we believe the world to be. Desires are representations of how the world is to be; they are our wants, the states that move us to act. On their own, beliefs can never provide a source of motivation; 'they are perfectly inert, and can never either prevent or produce any action'.[42] It is only our desires that can motivate us. Beliefs are mere replicas of the way we believe the world to be. We can assess beliefs for truth and falsehood – a true belief being one which is a copy of the way the world actually is. In order for an action to occur, we need a desire that prompts us to affect a certain change in the world and a belief informing us how this change can be achieved.

An important paradigm of moral judgments is that they are (apparently) used in the same manner as factual judgments: we engage in moral reflection, correction, argument and, as with other areas of human knowledge there appears to be a slow, but evident, convergence in our moral judgments. For example, it is now almost universally accepted that slavery and racism are wrong. This is called the objectivity of moral judgments and from it we can infer that moral judgments are expressions of beliefs: 'The moral truth is out there.' If beliefs are at the foundation of our moral judgments then there is little, if any, role for sentiments such as the desire for revenge in this domain. But, there is also another seemingly defining feature of moral judgments. They appear to be inherently action guiding: upon judging something right or good, we are always moved or prompted to act in accordance with that

---

41 Small, 1997, pp 46, 57.
42 Hume, 1738, p 458.

judgment; in the motivational sense, we are never totally indifferent to such judgments. This is called the practicality of moral judgments and is, purportedly, supported by the fact that it seems odd to assert that one genuinely views something to be right, but has no inkling to do it. Further, it would seem that failure to act in accordance with a moral judgment always requires some explanation, such as 'I had a stronger inconsistent need or want'. The theory which supports such a picture of morality is called internalism. Externalism is the opposite view; it claims that moral judgments are not necessarily action guiding.[43]

Morality as desires

If Hume is right, then the supposed inherent capacity of our moral judgments to guide our actions indicates that they are, or necessarily include, desires.[44] This leads to the dilemma that if moral judgments are expressions of our desires, then their objectivity is threatened. This is due to Hume's assertion that only beliefs can be true or false, and hence are subject to reason. Desires, on the other hand, are 'original facts and realities';[45] they just fall upon us. They cannot be true or false and, therefore, are not amenable to rationality. 'Tis not contrary to reason to prefer the destruction of the whole world to the scratching of my finger'.[46] A desire 'must be accompay'd with some false judgment, in order to its being unreasonable; and even then 'tis not the ... [desire] ... which is unreasonable, but the judgment'.[47] Since a desire is not subject to rational evaluation, it cannot be changed by the dictates of reason; it is only a contrary desire that can have this effect. In short, if internalism is true, the effective role of rationality in moral discourse is threatened;[48] if it is false, the problem of explaining why it is that morality moves us to the extent that it does remains.

The important point for present purposes is that if moral judgments are inherently action guiding (that is, if internalism is true), and many contemporary philosophers believe that they are, then the fact that intrinsic retributivism stems from a desire (for revenge) as opposed to a (rational) belief, is an advantage, not a drawback. The internalism/externalism debate raises for consideration one of the most fundamental and difficult problems to have bemused moral philosophers over the ages. Aside from these cursory

---

43 For a discussion of internalism/externalism debate, see Brink, 1989; Goldsworthy, 1992.

44 A claim that they were beliefs would run foul of Mackie's argument from 'Queerness': see Mackie, 1977, pp 38–42.

45 Hume, 1738, p 416.

46 *Ibid*.

47 *Ibid*.

48 For a contrary view, see Blackburn, 1981, p 181.

comments, however, it is not an issue which requires further analysis for the purposes of this book.

The nature of moral prescriptions

Even if we accept that moral judgments stem from desires, it is not the case that any desire will do. Certain desires are so repugnant that they are disqualified from forming the basis of normative prescriptions. The desire to kill or torture the innocent, no matter how pervasive, could not tenably be proffered as a normative justification for any action. To show that the desire for revenge is a candidate for moral recognition, it is first necessary to devise a test for distinguishing between desires that are morally relevant and those that are not, then it must be shown why the desire for revenge belongs to the former group. Non-cognitive theories of morality, such as emotivism and projectivism, have fared poorly in attempting to distinguish morally relevant desires from those which are irrelevant.[49] However, it is certain that one consideration relevant to determining the moral relevance of a desire must be the effect of implementing that desire. The unrestrained pursuit of revenge would result in an enormous increase in net suffering; it is likely to elicit resentment and reprisals, and would be destructive to social cohesion and individual security.

In addition to this, as a general rule, our moral standpoint looks favourably upon expressions of feelings and desires that are likely to be welcomed by the recipients of these sentiments, such as feelings of love, compassion and respect. On the other hand, desires which prompt behaviour which is generally unwelcome are morally condemned. Given the measures most people take to avoid vendettas, it is obvious that the desire for revenge belongs to the latter group.

Nietzsche also commented that revenge is always misguided because no action can reconstruct the past; no deed can be annihilated. Harming others does not eliminate one's own suffering and revenge may even be self-defeating, since, if it is satisfied, it merely 'increases the amount of suffering in the world'.[50] This view can be challenged on the basis that it wrongly assumes that revenge has a particular rationale which can be measured by the extent to which it promotes some more fundamental virtue, such as happiness, rather than being merely a fundamental desire, the aim of which is no higher than its own satisfaction. But this response runs head on into the objection, outlined earlier, that it entails that punishment is justifiable even if it results in overall bad consequences.

---

49 See, eg, Warnock, 1982, pp 24–26.
50 See Small, 1997, p 47.

Retribution not revenge

The intrinsic retributivist could try to soften his or her position by asserting that what is being appealed to is 'retribution', not revenge. It is not exactly clear in what sense retribution is being used here. However, Nozick advances five differences, and Ten another one, between revenge and retribution. Broadly, it is claimed that retribution is a manifestation of a reflective view that the guilty should be punished, as opposed to the expression of our primitive desire to punish wrongdoers. More specifically, it is claimed that:

(a) retribution is for a wrong, whereas revenge is done for a harm which need not be a wrong;[51]

(b) retribution sets an internal limit to the amount of punishment, commensurate with the seriousness of the wrong, while revenge has no such internal limits;[52]

(c) revenge is not general, since it need not commit the revenger to avenging in the future in similar circumstances;[53]

(d) retribution is inflicted only on the offender, whereas revenge may be inflicted on an innocent person who has an association with the offender, such as a relative;[54]

(e) in the case of revenge, the revenger often obtains pleasure in the suffering of another;[55] and

(f) revenge is personal, in that the revenger is typically the person wronged, but retribution generally lacks this connection.[56]

However, in relation to the first four factors, it is not clear that they represent genuine differences and, even if they do, they are irrelevant for the purpose of this discussion. The effect of the last two factors merely weakens the case for intrinsic retributivism.

In respect to point (a) it is unclear why retaliation for something which is not a wrong (such as sneezing in public) is properly defined as revenge any more than it is retribution. More properly, it would seem to simply be a case of misplaced anger. Likewise, regarding point (d), which highlights the fact that retribution is supposedly more targeted than revenge: once again, it is not clear why harm directed at a person who is not a wrongdoer is not more appropriately defined as misplaced anger, rather than revenge. In any event, the disadvantages of revenge as a foundation for intrinsic retributivism do not

---

51 Nozick, 1981, p 366.

52 *Ibid*, p 388.

53 *Ibid*, p 367

54 Ten, 1987, p 43.

55 Nozick, 1981, p 367.

56 *Ibid*.

concern the possibility of punitive measures against people other than wrongdoers.

Consideration (b) focuses on the purported distinction between retribution and proportionality, but this link is more hypothetical than real, since retribution is primarily concerned with why we should punish, not how much. Nor is point (c) significant. No sentencing system has yet been able to provide consistency in sentencing; not even those loosely based on retributive ideals. Also, consistency is not the primary objective of sentencing. As was discussed earlier, a sentencing system which consistently pursues flawed objectives simply perpetuates pre-existing injustices.

Points (e) and (f) are more significant, but only because they underline why retribution forms an even less tenable foundation for intrinsic retributivism than revenge. Point (e) charges that revenge is normally meted out by the aggrieved party, unlike retribution, which is administered by another party.[57] In this way, retribution is dispensed in a more controlled and measured fashion which eliminates some of the more unpleasant features of private revenge. But, the problem here is that however one elects to prop up intrinsic retributivism, the claim that punishment should be administered by the State does not follow from intrinsic retributivism: even if it shows that the guilty deserve to suffer, it cannot support the claim that the suffering should be deliberately inflicted on wrongdoers by the State.

Secondly, once the desire for revenge is renounced as the basis for intrinsic retributivism, its most alluring aspect (the apparent pervasiveness of the desire at its core) is lost, since it cannot be asserted as convincingly that there is a universal desire for retribution. This is the point made in (d) and is supported by the apparent disinterest of many victims of crime to the outcome of the prosecution of the offender. The statement that wrongdoers deserve retribution lacks the emotive appeal of the assertion that they deserve revenge.

The upshot of the above discussion is that retributivists are put to the task of justifying the link between punishment and wrongdoing; beyond merely asserting the appropriateness of the connection. There have been numerous attempts at establishing such a link. Three of them are considered.

---

57 In the system of punishment being considered here, this other party is always, obviously, the State.

4.4 VON HIRSCH – PUNISHMENT AS DENUNCIATION AND CENSURE

4.4.1 Outline of the theory

According to von Hirsch, the principal justification of punishment is censure: that is, to convey blame or reprobation to those who have committed a wrongful act.[58] von Hirsch thinks that censuring holds offenders responsible and accountable for their actions and that, by giving them an opportunity to respond to their misdeeds through acknowledging their wrongdoing in some form, it recognises their moral agency.

For von Hirsch, punishment actually has a dual objective. The other justification is to prevent crime. He believes that human nature is such that the normative reason for compliance must be complemented with a prudential one, otherwise 'victimising conduct would become so prevalent as to make life nasty and brutish',[59] and that 'it is the threatened penal deprivation that expresses the censure as well as serving as the prudential disincentive'.[60] Although he believes that deterrence is not a sufficient reason for punishment, he claims it is a necessary one: '... if punishment has no usefulness in preventing crime, there should ... not be a criminal sanction.'[61] Instead, there should be other means adopted to express censure.

As such, von Hirsch is clearly a consequentialist in part, since his theory of punishment is contingent upon punishment having a deterrent effect. However, he attempts to water down the consequentialist tag by asserting that although general deterrence is a necessary precondition for punishment, it is not sufficient and, indeed, only serves as a secondary justification. The overt reliance on consequentialist considerations does, nevertheless, distinguish von Hirsch's theory from traditional retributive theories, and for this reason (and the inextricable link between his theory and the principle of proportionality) his theory is most appropriately catalogued under the 'just deserts' rubric.[62]

---

58 von Hirsch, 1993. The theory is also detailed in von Hirsch, 1985; 1976; 1994, pp 115, 127.

59 von Hirsch, 1985, p 48.

60 von Hirsch, 1994, pp 115, 127.

61 von Hirsch, 1985, p 53.

62 von Hirsch argues that the blaming function is paramount: 'the preventive function operates only within a censuring framework' (1993) and that the two ideals 'cannot be collapsed into one another' (1985, p 59). Following his most recent attempt at justifying punishment (1993, above) he has been interpreted as even further shying away from what he terms a bifurcated account of punishment: see Bottoms, 1998, pp 53, 78–79.

The justification for censure

Before considering von Hirsch's theory in detail, it is worth noting that there are good consequentialist reasons in support of the basic thrust of his thesis, that censure or condemnation of the criminal is a proper response to crime. Condemning criminal activity stigmatises such conduct and serves to discourage future criminal acts:

> The disapproval expressed in punishment is assumed to influence the values and moral views of individuals. As a result of this process, the norms of criminal law and the values they reflect are internalized; people refrain from illegal behaviour, not because it is followed by unpleasant punishment, but because the behaviour itself is regarded as morally blameworthy.[63]

To make headway, von Hirsch's challenge is to provide reasons for censure which do not rely on the good consequences which follow from blaming criminals.

The most general point made by von Hirsch in defence of his theory is that responding to wrongdoing by reprobation 'is part of a morality that holds people accountable for their conduct ... It is addressed to the actor because he or she is the person responsible'.[64] While blaming people may hold them accountable for their misdeeds, this does not provide a normative justification for doing so, but rather only a factual analysis of the function of blame. Chopping off the legs of jay walkers would hold them accountable, but is nevertheless unjustifiable. The link between blame and accountability takes the matter no further than does intrinsic retributivism in search of the answer to why we *should* blame wrongdoers. To address this, von Hirsch identifies the 'positive moral functions of blaming'.[65]

4.4.2 von Hirsch's positive functions of blaming

Acknowledging the victim

He asserts that the benefits flowing from censure are threefold. First, censure addresses the victim: '... censure, by directing disapprobation at the person responsible, acknowledges that the victim's hurt occurred through another's fault.'[66] This recognition, however, need not come in the form of blame directed at the offender; a mere declaration to the victim that his or her suffering was caused by the wrongful actions of another would presumably suffice. The fact that von Hirsch requires the further step (that the offender is

---

63 Lappi-Seppala, 1998. See, also, Chapter 7.
64 von Hirsch, 1993, p 9.
65 *Ibid*, p 10.
66 *Ibid*.

told of his or her wrongdoing) indicates that there are also other goals at work here.

To this end, the satisfaction theory of punishment provides two reasons why blaming and punishing offenders is desirable. Recognising the victim's unfair fate pleases the victim and an institutional system of punishment also serves to quell the desire for socially harmful vendettas which may otherwise be unrestrained.[67]

It is essential to note that both these considerations are consequential in nature. Of course, there is normally nothing wrong with this, unless, like von Hirsch, one happens to be, at least primarily, a non-consequentialist. Another narrower problem with closely aligning the justification of punishment with the interests of the victims is the large array of victimless offences, or offences where there is no discernible victim.

Holding offenders responsible

The second positive function of blaming, according to von Hirsch, is that it addresses the criminal. The criminal is conveyed the message 'that he culpably has injured someone, and is disapproved of for having done so'.[68] This holds the offender responsible for his or her actions. However, as mentioned earlier, even if we accept this, von Hirsch is still no closer to drawing the link between punishment and crime: it is still an open question why we should blame the offender. There is no intrinsic merit in telling people that they have done the wrong thing. And even if it is felt that there is some benefit in this, it merely justifies conveying such a message, not the further step of imposing an unpleasantness.

Expectation that offenders will improve

von Hirsch, possibly in an attempt to diffuse the obvious counter that the link between punishment and crime can only be made by introducing consequentialist considerations, states that censure does not aim to change the criminal's moral attitudes or elicit any particular response: censure 'is not a technique for evoking specified sentiments'.[69] He also thinks that censure provides the criminal with an opportunity to respond (for example, by making an effort at improved self-restraint or an acknowledgment of wrongdoing) and that he or she is expected to respond: if the criminal does not respond positively to censure, this would 'itself be grounds for criticizing

---

67 Honderich, 1984, pp 43–44, concludes that retributivism comes down to claim that punishment is justified because it gives satisfaction to victims and other people, and that criminals freely and responsibly commit offences.

68 von Hirsch, 1993, p 10.

69 *Ibid*, p 10.

him'.[70] However, if the goals of punishment do not include promoting moral development, the source of such an expectation is unclear: it is as if it pops up from nowhere. Expectations, as opposed to hopes, are grounded in obligations, which in turn are derived from (voluntary or inadvertent) participation in goal-orientated practices or transactions. Obligations occur because they are necessary to facilitate the objectives of the relevant practice or transaction. There is an obligation (and hence an expectation) that each party to a contract will honour his or her promises, otherwise the purpose of the agreement will be defeated; government officials are expected to provide individuals who may be adversely affected by their decisions an opportunity to be heard on the matter, otherwise the objective of natural justice would be frustrated; and more generally we should not deliberately harm others because this violates important moral goals. von Hirsch's attempt to pluck an expectation from nowhere is an attempt to get consequentialist considerations (attitudinal reform and behavioural change) through the back door.

von Hirsch goes on to advance two other reasons in support of his claim that censure does not aim to alter the values of wrongdoers, and hence does not have a consequential foundation. First, he points out that there is no attempt to seek information about the wrongdoer's 'personality and outlook, so as to better foster the requisite attitudinal changes ... The condemnor's role is not that of mentor or priest'.[71] However, the fact that there is no positive concerted attempt to discover the particular mental processes of the criminal hardly means that there is no attempt to encourage attitudinal and behavioural reform. Advertising, political campaigns, and pressure groups bear testimony to this. The reason that we do not attempt to find out the intricate workings of each individual whose behaviour we seek to influence is that we make certain assumptions about human behaviour. One is that people respond to reason, another is that they can be moved by emotive pressure, and yet another is that they try to avoid punishment.

von Hirsch's second basis for claiming that censure does not aim to achieve moral improvement is that blame is supposedly appropriate even where it is apparent that it will have no effect on the offender's outlook: for example, where the offender is already repentant or is stubbornly defiant. However, von Hirsch provides no reason why blaming in such circumstances is appropriate, as opposed to just being a waste of time.[72] Admittedly, censure is the 'authentic expression of the condemnor's ethical judgments',[73] but, as Adams points out, if blaming is justified solely by the condemnor's desire to

---

70   von Hirsch, 1993, p 10.

71   *Ibid.*

72   It could be argued that blame is still appropriate for the (already) repentant and the defiant because it reinforces the values of the repentant and, hopefully, wears away at the defiant. However, again these considerations are both consequentialist.

73   von Hirsch, 1993, p 25.

express it, this 'still leaves one asking why the fact that visiting blame ... is something we are strongly moved to do without any further (instrumental) purpose, means that we are justified in building such responses into the institution of criminal punishment'.[74]

Addressing third parties

The third and last positive function of censure is that it supposedly addresses third parties and provides them with reasons for desistence from crime; blaming conveys the message that the relevant conduct is reprehensible, and should be eschewed. He concedes that this reason is partly consequential,[75] but attempts to steer away from it as being a purely consequentialist consideration by asserting that 'the censure embodied in the prescribed sanction serves to appeal to people's sense of the conduct's wrongfulness, as a reason for desistence',[76] as opposed to an attempt to portray that the conduct is wrong, 'for those addressed (or many of them) may well understand that already'.[77] At the bottom, though, the aim is the paradigm consequentialist goal of desistence. Tinkering with the means employed to facilitate this aim cannot alter the fundamental character of the goal: whether one trains a dog with treats or a stick, in the end the (consequential) goal is the same – to have an obedient pet.

Thus, it emerges that what von Hirsch calls the 'positive *moral functions* of blaming' are simply the 'positive consequences of blaming'.

4.4.3 Hard treatment – deterrence as a secondary rationale

von Hirsch accepts that criminal sanctions are too severe to be justified by the need for censure alone. Censure on its own only justifies the expression of blame, not the further step of imposing hard treatment. To justify the need for hard treatment, von Hirsch expressly calls into play the goal of deterrence, as a secondary purpose of punishment. He thinks that hard treatment provides prudential reasons for desistence, which supplement the normative reason supplied by censure.[78]

The critical point, here, is that the concept doing all the hard work is the utilitarian flagship of deterrence. von Hirsch attempts to distance himself from a core reliance on deterrence by stating that a primarily consequentialist account for punishment and blaming is inappropriate because this would

---

74 Adams, 1996, p 410.
75 von Hirsch, 1985, p 57.
76 von Hirsch, 1994, pp 115, 120.
77 *Ibid.*
78 *Ibid*, pp 123–24.

permit neutral sanctions which provide for hard treatment, but no censure, and, hence, fail to recognise the wrongfulness of criminal behaviour. Thus, the door would be left open for taxing offenders instead of prescribing criminal responsibility and criminal sanctions to criminal conduct.

However, this fails to recognise the good utilitarian reasons that exist for ascribing moral blame to criminal behaviour. Empirical studies have revealed that normative issues are closely linked with compliance with the law. As is discussed in Chapter 6, people do not merely obey the law because it is in their self-interest to do so, but also because they believe it is morally proper to do so.

Overview of criticisms of von Hirsch's theory

von Hirsch believes that it is 'evident enough'[79] that punishment conveys blame or reprobation, but by his own lights he accepts that the crucial issue regarding the justification of punishment is 'why should there be a reprobative response to the core conduct with which the criminal law deals?'.[80] He further accepts that punishment hurts. This being the case, to justify punishment on any grounds, one must invoke sound moral reasons. But von Hirsch, and this is the most fundamental flaw of his theory, fails to address the issue of why his censuring account of punishment is morally justifiable (apart from the utilitarian reasons that he seeks to divorce himself from). He in fact 'argues ... within, rather than for a desert based or (broadly) retributive justification of punishment'.[81] Such an approach will not sway the unconverted and so we must move on.

Thus, von Hirsch is unable to provide a rationale for censure and punishment which does not ultimately invoke consequential considerations. Despite this, it is still understandable that his theory struck a responsive chord with so many. His theory is not ostensibly consequentialist and urges the intuitively appealing principle of proportionality as the main sentencing consideration.

4.5 DUFF'S THEORY – COMMUNICATION AND RECONCILIATION

4.5.1 Outline of the theory

RA Duff advances another communicative theory of punishment. He believes that the main aim of punishment is ultimately to integrate offenders back into

79 von Hirsch, 1993, p 9.
80 *Ibid*, p 9.
81 Adams, 1996, p 408.

the community: punishment aims to induce repentance (the remorseful acceptance of guilt), self-reform, reparation (the repairing of damaged relationship with the rest of the community by genuine recognition of the wrong)[82] and, finally, reconciliation. Duff believes that criminal sanctions serve to bring 'the criminal to recognise the wrongfulness of her past conduct; to induce the kind of pain which flows from an understanding of the condemnation which they express'. The criminal is then reconciled to the good and other members of the community by expressing his or her repentant understanding through being punished.

Duff states that punishment also communicates to the rest of the community the wrongfulness of criminal conduct and to victims it represents an 'authoritative disavowal of such conduct'.[83] However, these purposes are merely subsidiary; punishment is essentially a means of engaging in a punitive dialogue with the offender 'which aims to persuade (but not to coerce or manipulate) her to recognise and repent that wrong, and thus to restore her relationship with her victim and with the community'.[84]

Thus, while Duff's theory has many similarities with von Hirsch's account of punishment, there are several points of divergence. Both theories emphasise the censuring aspect of punishment, but whereas von Hirsch claims that punishment merely aims to give offenders external (prudential) reasons for desistence, Duff is far more ambitious, claiming that through punishment we should aim to alter the moral sentiments of offenders. The other main differences between the two theories is Duff's claim that the blaming aspect of punishment itself justifies hard treatment.

The educative and cohesive function of punishment has received some judicial support. In *Williscroft*, Adam and Crockett JJ cite Sir John Barry with approval:

> The aims of punishment are often classified as retributive, preventive, deterrent, and reformative, but this classification is plainly an oversimplification. It ignores or leaves inarticulate, for example, *other purposes which the criminal law serves by its solemn procedures as a teacher of minimal standards of morality and behaviour; as an agency for the expression of public indignation and condemnation; and as a force operating to produce cohesion in society* [emphasis added].[85]

82　On Duff's account, reparation refers to moral as opposed to material reparation: Duff, 1996, pp 17, 23. His theory is also detailed in Duff, 1996, p 242. More recently, he discusses some aspects of it in Duff, 1998, p 161. I focus on his earlier work, given that this is where his views are most elaborately detailed.

83　Duff, 1986, p 236.

84　Duff, 1996, pp 17, 28.

85　[1975] VR 292, p 300.

The supposed non-coercive nature of punishment is central to Duff's theory. He contends that punishment aims to communicate to the offender the condemnation of his or her conduct and seeks for the offender to:

> ... condemn himself, and to modify his future conduct accordingly; and thus to persuade him not merely to obey the law, but to accept its justified demands and judgments. Punishment, like moral blame, respects and addresses the criminal as a rational moral agent: it seeks his understanding and his assent; it aims to bring him to repent his crime, and to reform himself, by communicating to him the reasons which justify our condemnation of his conduct.[86]

4.5.2 Criticisms

Duff's theory – retributivist?

At first glance, it may seem that Duff's account is essentially consequentialist. By aiming to reconcile criminals back into the community, he concedes that his theory has a forward looking purpose. Nevertheless, he contends that his theory is retributivist for several reasons. For Duff, the purpose of punishment is 'logically rather than contingently related to the 'means' by which it is to be achieved'.[87] And even though punishment aims at reforming and rehabilitating criminals, Duff asserts that this does not amount to a consequentialist justification since the aim lies in its internal, not instrumental, ability to promote reform and rehabilitation, which can only be achieved by bringing the criminal to 'recognise and suffer for her wrong-doing'.[88] His theory is also not consequentialist, Duff claims, because although our reasons for maintaining a system of law and punishment relate to the prevention of crime and the good of the community, we do not merely use criminals as means to achieve these ends since 'the law addresses all the citizens as rational moral agents, seeking their assent and their understanding'.[89] According to Duff, it follows that the pursuit of rehabilitation through punishment is justified even if there is no hope of reformation, since punishment in these circumstances still expresses a proper moral concern for the offender.

Duff's theory is hypothetical

A significant shortcoming of Duff's theory is that it lacks practical relevance. He admits that the sanctions which are typically imposed by our penal system are unlikely to achieve repentance, reform, reparation and reconciliation, and

---

86 Duff, 1986, p 238.
87 *Ibid*, p 234.
88 *Ibid*, p 70.
89 *Ibid*, p 238.

that the concept of punishment he propounds is only justified and appropriate in an idealistic society and legal system.

In order for punishment to be justified, he believes that the criminal must be a responsible agent and accountable to those holding him or her to account. For Duff, this requires that the law that the offender has broken embodies the 'values of a community in which she participates, and to whose values she is or should be committed. That is, she must be a citizen, of whom it can properly be said that she has an obligation to obey the law because it is *her* law'.[90] Duff goes on to claim that the law must be justified by regard to a common moral good, otherwise crimes are not destructive of morality and punishment cannot aim to restore the offender to the common good and the community. This does not require each law to be morally sound, since 'we can still owe it to our fellow-citizens to obey even an imperfect system of law, so long as it can be adequately ... justified to us in the relevant moral terms'.[91] For offenders to be properly answerable to society, it is also necessary that they have been treated as fellow citizens and accorded the concern and respect which is owed to all citizens.

Duff rightly points out that these preconditions do not exist in our social and legal system. He claims that our laws cannot be justified by reference to the common good because of our general failure to accord all citizens the concern and respect that they deserve. This, he believes, provides disadvantaged offenders the strongest moral basis for resisting punishment: 'not because their actions are justified, not because they ought to be excused, but because we lack the moral standing to condemn them'.[92] Duff appreciates that his ideal is far short of the real world and he suspects that it may be so contrary to human nature that it may not even be worth striving towards it, since this may destroy our society entirely.

The telling point to emerge here is that in our community, according to Duff, punishment is not justified. His ideal setting is so far removed from the community in which we live that his theory could be disregarded on this basis alone, especially since he is not an abolitionist and yet fails to advance an alternative account of what type of response to crime is appropriate. Nevertheless, Duff's theory raises many interesting issues concerning punishment and it would be remiss prematurely to reject all aspects of his theory: occasionally, things that are worth doing, are worth half doing.[93] Although one can hope that the criminal justice system and society in general

---

90   Duff, 1996, p 29.

91   Duff, 1986, p 292.

92   Duff, 1996, pp 17, 30, n 17.

93   Indeed, more recently, Duff has stated that sanctions, especially non custodial orders, may operate as penances: Duff, RA, 'Punishment, expression and penance', in Jung, H and Muller-Dietz, H (eds), *Recht und Moral: Beitrage zu einer Standortsbestimmung*, 1991, Baden-Baden: as cited in von Hirsch, 1993, p 75.

may eventually match Duff's ideals, even in such an environment Duff's theory is not persuasive. Duff fails to justify the purported non-coercive nature of punishment; he cannot explain the need for hard treatment and, ultimately, cannot draw the crucial normative link between crime and punishment.

Punishment: communicative (dialogue) or expressive?

A preliminary objection to Duff's theory is his characterisation of punishment as being a communicative dialogue. He claims that punishment is communicative, as opposed to expressive, since it is a means through which the community responds to criminals as rational agents through a *dialogue* in a manner which respects them as fellow members of the community. However, this ignores the fact that a dialogue requires approximately equal parties in order that there is a meaningful opportunity for a genuine exchange of views. To suggest that this occurs as part of the process of punishment totally misconceives a fundamental aspect of punishment: it is imposed, not negotiated. Once a criminal is sentenced, there is nothing which he or she can possibly advance which will alter the sentence. And, prior to sentencing, the only option for the offender is to *plead* for, rather than to request or demand, leniency. Given the weakness of the criminal's position, punishment is the antithesis of a communicative institution (at least of the kind claimed by Duff). Now, in itself, this does not totally rebut Duff's theory, however, it is a noteworthy riposte because the description of punishment as a dialogue forms a central plank of his theory of punishment which he paints as being a caring, almost altruistic, practice.

Duff's ultimate justification for punishment – respect for autonomy

Duff's justificatory account for a system of criminal law and punishment is ultimately based on the Kantian principle of respect for autonomy. Duff assumes that a fundamental tenet of morality is that all people should be treated with concern and respect. From this, it follows that we must take seriously the 'respect and autonomy of those with whom we deal'.[94]

If respect for autonomy is the guiding moral virtue, then Duff must explain how an apparently coercive institution such as punishment promotes, rather than violates, individual autonomy. Ostensibly, it is difficult to conceive of anything which is more likely to be destructive of personal autonomy than a practice which involves the deliberate and systematic *imposition* of hardship by the State. This argument is even more persuasive when we consider the type of penalties that Duff advocates. Sanctions aimed at an offender's internal moral reform are arguably akin to brain washing and

---

94 Duff, 1986, p 268.

hence pose an even more serious threat to an offender's autonomy than those which aim to provide prudential reasons for desistence. Duff is alert to these criticisms and responds by stating that punishment aimed to induce repentance and reform does not have a coercive character since offenders have a *right* to be punished, and moreover they want to be punished. These claims are now considered separately.

The right to be punished

Duff contends that an offender:

> ... has a *right to be punished*: a right to be punished rather than be subjected to some kind of manipulation or preventive treatment which would not address him as a rational agent; a right to be punished rather than be ignored or dismissed, since punishment expresses a proper response to his crime as the wrong-doing of a responsible moral agent, and a proper concern for his moral well-being as a fellow-member of the community. We owe it to him, as well as to those whom he has injured, to condemn his crime and to try to bring him to repentance and reform [emphasis added].[95]

He adds that, through punishment, we accord the criminal:

> ... the respect which is his due as a responsible moral agent – we do not simply try to manipulate or coerce him into conformity. He may therefore claim a *right* to be blamed, or even punished, for his wrongdoing; a right to be treated, respected and cared for as a moral agent.[96]

Rights and benefits

This 'rights' characterisation of punishment misconceives the nature of rights. Despite the complexities involved regarding exactly what it means to have a right, at the minimum, a right entails a plus; a benefit to the agent. To mistreat someone and to impose unpleasantness upon him or her is the direct opposite of a right.[97] As Quinton notes, 'it is an odd sort of right whose holders would strenuously resist its recognition'.[98]

Duff's response to this might be to urge us to take a broader view of the effect of punishment on the offender. According to Duff, ultimately, punishment helps offenders by improving their moral outlook and providing a means for them to be admitted once again as worthy members of the community. Thus, it could be argued that although offenders may not realise

---

95 Duff, 1986, p 263.

96 *Ibid*, p 70.

97 Duff cannot answer this criticism by falling back on his distinctive concept of punishment, since he does not push for less severe sanctions than those which are presently employed and, in fact, he does not even rule out capital punishment.

98 Quinton, 1954, pp 513–14.

the advantages which stem from punishment at the time of apprehension or sentencing, in time they will come to be grateful for the fate imposed upon them, and it is in this long term outlook where the benefit lies.

The proposition that despite the seemingly unpleasant nature of punishment, in the long run it is not something which aims to harm offenders; or something they should seek to avoid, but rather embrace, is the most pervasive, but ultimately indefensible, aspect of Duff's account of punishment. It is totally at odds with the surface nature of punishment as being an evil imposed upon wrongdoers. Duff asks of us to ignore the overt character of punishment as being a practice which harms offenders and look deeper into its purpose to picture the harmful exterior as merely being a way of imposing short term detriment for the overall *benefit of the offender*. Now, of some practices which involve short term harm, such an analysis is plausible; and is epitomised by the 'no pain, no gain' slogan. The athlete who flogs his or her body for hours on end does it with a view to attaining superior fitness, and the factory worker who slaves away tirelessly performing meaningless and degrading work does so in a bid to achieve financial security. Both endure, relatively, minor hardships in a bid to attain distant desirable objectives. Despite the harsh day to day pursuits of such people, we are willing to accept that they are nevertheless engaging in practices which are, ultimately, beneficial to them.

There appear to be two central features of activities which may be regarded as being in an agent's interest, despite their immediate harshness. Punishment does not square with either of them. The first characteristic of such practices is that they are not inherently 'seriously' harmful. A point is reached where the immediate venture is so damaging that it cannot be justified on the basis that in the big picture, it is in an agent's long term interest. Thus, we do not generally view self-mutilation or prostitution as being for the agent's benefit, no matter how much he or she wants to engage in such conduct. Criminal sanctions do not necessarily violate this requirement. For example, certain forms of gentler sanctions, such as community based orders, may be regarded as being in the long term interests of offenders. However, harsher treatments, such as imprisonment, may be so painful and oppressive as to outweigh any possible distant advantages.

A second characteristic of activities which may be justified by their positive long term effects is that they are voluntarily undertaken. We attach enormous weight to personal choice and it is for this reason that we do not generally attempt to dissuade others from engaging in practices we consider misguided or futile; such as marrying the 'wrong partner', playing computer games, reading Mills and Boon novels or studying pure mathematics. Given that offenders are forced by the machinery of the State to endure criminal sanctions, it is implausible to assert that they choose, in any sense of the word, such treatment, no matter how strongly others may think that they should for the sake of improving their moral standpoint. This is a point strongly challenged by Duff.

Offenders want to be punished

Not only does he believe that criminals have a right to be punished, but he also goes on to make the claim that they want to exercise this right: they want to be punished, no matter how determinedly wicked they appear to be. On Duff's account, the criminal really wills his or her own good, and therefore desires punishment as a means 'of restoring him to the good'.[99] Even in relation to criminals who expressly declare that they desire no moral or behavioural reformation, Duff maintains that they desire moral improvement, because they should consider it is an important goal. In this way, Duff reconstructs punishment as an exercise of an offender's autonomy, as opposed to a deprivation of it. Underlying Duff's claim that criminals want to be punished is the Kantian proposition that rational agents universalise their principles of conduct. Thus, by breaking the law, the offenders consent to being punished. However, this argument is circular: it assumes that there is a necessary link between breaking the law and being punished.

Further, given the lengthy steps that most offenders take to avoid detection and apprehension, Duff's claim is obviously counter-intuitive. He appears to be mindful of this and responds by stating that he is not making a claim about the relative strengths of the criminal's desires, but rather an assertion that the criminal should care most about his or her moral well being: 'want' in this context does not concern a 'factual or empirical claim about the relative strength of ... desires, [but] a moral claim [about what] ... [the offender] *should* desire'.[100] Duff, thereby, implies that punishment is not coercive since it aims to persuade the criminal to repent the crime and to accept and consent to the punishment as penance as a means of restoring him or her back into the community.

This account is unsatisfactory for several reasons. If we accept Duff's reasoning, there is no end to the types of interference that could be justified on the basis that 'we think it is good for them'. It would open the door for paternalist intervention, real or feigned, into every area of one's life.

Secondly, at the theoretical level, Duff misunderstands what it is to have a desire or want. Desires are the states of mind, *personal* stimuli that move us to act. As is alluded to by Duff, it may be the case that one may want something and yet make no endeavour to attain it. This is most commonly the case because our long term wants are overpowered by more pressing immediate inconsistent desires. That a person eats cake because it is a special occasion or

---

99   Duff, 1986, p 271.
100 *Ibid.*

a particularly appetising cake does not mean that he or she lacks the desire to lose weight. But, it is another thing to assert that one can desire a thing because it is felt that it would be in one's moral interest to do so. Desires do not work like this. As Hume observed several centuries ago, desires are not driven by reason.

Also, even if desires are directed by reason, Duff must still overcome the considerable obstacle of convincing criminals that they should take better care of their moral health and that punishment is a good medicine for this. Given the attempts offenders take to avoid punishment and the rate of recidivism, the overwhelming weight of empirical evidence is stacked against him. There is no evidence that offenders desire moral education or that punishment generally leads to reform or feelings of guilt:

> The idea that punishment produces a feeling of guilt in the offender is ... not confirmed by experience. Its effect is more often than not just the opposite: the offender becomes hardened in resistance to the demands of the community. Alternatively, it may have a wholly destructive effect and bring about a general demoralization.[101]

Autonomy a personal virtue

Duff's obvious counter is to emphasise that he is making a claim about what offenders *should* desire, not what they actually want. This, however, constitutes perhaps the most serious flaw in Duff's theory. At the core of his thesis is an important *personal* (as opposed to a collective principle, such as utilitarianism) moral virtue: autonomy. This involves people being able (at least to some degree) to do as *they* want. Thus, to rely on the principle of autonomy to justify punishment, Duff must present his account of punishment in a way which at least to some degree involves offenders doing as they want. This he cannot do. Instead, he invokes a collective or de-personalised notion of what others want the relevant agents (wrongdoers) to want and then attempts to portray this as respecting the autonomous wishes of wrongdoers. But this makes his account unintelligible: it is meaningless to refer to autonomy in a manner which is totally divorced from personal wants.[102] At its highest, Duff's justification for punishment is not personal autonomy, but whatever 'virtue' it is that prescribes that people ought to do what others think is in their interest. Thus, dressing autonomy up in terms of respecting the wishes that people *should* have, advances Duff's cause no further.

---

101 Small, 1997, p 57, citing Nietzsche, *The Genealogy of Morals*.

102 In circumstances where an agent does not have the capacity for rational thought and judgment we often justify things we do to them on the basis that a rational person in the agent's position would want, as opposed to what he or she actually wants, but this cannot be so in the case of punishment since, as Duff acknowledges, punishment presupposes responsibility which requires rationality and the capacity for rational thought: 1986, p 224.

Morals by force

In addition, it is extremely doubtful that punishment could serve as a vehicle for improving the moral values of offenders. Coercive measures can at best only produce prudential reasons to modify behaviour, as opposed to internal ones. This is the reason people are taught ethics, rather than having it beaten into them. In the end, the concept of forced moral development involves an internal contradiction – virtually all moral theories advocate tolerance and freedom of thought and expression as fundamental values.

Punishment and autonomy – analogy with self-defence

To buttress his view that punishment is a right reposed in offenders and a process which respects their autonomy, Duff draws an analogy with the right of self-defence. He states that:

> Just as I believe that I may properly kill an assailant to protect my or others' lives against his wrongful attack, while still respecting and responding to him as a responsible agent, I also believe that the coercive imposition of punishment on a criminal can be consistent with a respect for her autonomy.[103]

However, this analogy, rather than advancing Duff's argument, highlights its failing. Killing an assailant has nothing to do with respecting his or her autonomy. Rather, it simply demonstrates the fact that no right is absolute and, more particularly, that in certain circumstances a person may, by his or her appalling behaviour, forfeit even the most fundamental right of all. This is not to say that the assailant is normally not worthy of our concern and respect, but rather that in *these circumstances* (when attacking another) he or she abrogates his or her entitlement to be treated with such regard.[104] Likewise, where an offender seriously violates the interests of others, his or her interests can be violated to about the same extent as he or she has infringed upon the interests of others. Just as the right of self-defence is not framed in terms of the entitlements of the aggressor, neither is, nor should be, the practice of punishment.

Summary – punishment and autonomy

The reason that Duff portrays punishment as something that criminals desire is obvious: otherwise, punishment can only be a coercive institution and, hence, by punishing offenders it must follow that we are violating their

---

103 Duff, 1986, p 273.

104 This is similar to the distributive principle devised by Farrell, 1985, p 373, where he states that 'one must suffer if one's decision to do wrong makes it necessary that someone must suffer and that sufferer must either be the wrongdoer or some innocent victim'. This is discussed further, below, Chapter 6.

wishes. In a bid to circumvent this conclusion, Duff uses the term 'desire' so loosely as to deprive it of any relevant content and meaning. Thus, Duff cannot avoid the conclusion that punishment is coercive and, therefore, a violation of the offender's autonomy. At this point, his theory becomes vacuous. His fundamental moral premise concerns the inviolability of autonomy, yet in order to protect the autonomy of the rest of the community he is advocating a practice which directly impinges on the autonomy of offenders. So long as the activation of punishment depends upon a finding of criminal guilt and occurs against a background of State force, no matter how kind the stated goals of punishment may appear to be, there is little question that what is being done to the offender is ultimately for our sake, not his or hers.

Why hard treatment is necessary

Duff also has difficulty in justifying the need for hard treatment. As stated above, he believes that the essential purpose of punishment is 'to bring the criminal to recognise the wrongfulness of her past conduct; to induce the kind of pain which flows from an understanding of the condemnation which they express',[105] and ultimately restore the criminal to the community. To achieve this, Duff claims that the 'pain which expressive punishments aim to inflict or induce – the pain which wrong-doers deserve to suffer – must be mediated by the criminals' own understanding of the condemnation which they express'.[106]

However, if the aim of punishment is to reform offenders by communicating the wrongfulness of their conduct, it is difficult to understand why punishment needs to be in the form of hard treatment (such as imprisonment and fines): the verdict of the court already expresses the requisite condemnation. The process of subjecting offenders to trial, conviction and the associated moral blame would, in most cases, surely suffice to focus the attention of offenders on the wrongness of their behaviour. Even if this is inadequate, there are other (less draconian) ways to grasp their attention: 'one can shout, ring a bell or ask [them] to stand at attention'.[107] These may prove easier to ignore than the pain of hard treatment, but this does not mean that hard treatment is more effective at inducing reform.[108]

Duff's response is that mere formal condemnation does not go far enough: only hard treatment can induce repentance, reform, reparation and reconciliation. Repentance and self-reform, he asserts, are unlikely to be induced by merely formal condemnation, due to our fallible nature and

---

105 Duff, 1986, p 242.
106 *Ibid*, p 241.
107 See Ten, 1990, p 202.
108 *Ibid*.

reluctance to face up to our moral failings: '... punishment ... aims precisely to induce and strengthen ... repentance, and to make possible its expression [by accepting and undergoing punishment].'[109] It is induced by confronting the criminal with the consequences of his or her actions and strengthened by keeping his or her attention on the wrong. Undergoing hard treatment, Duff continues, also achieves moral reparation and signifies repentant recognition of wrongdoing and an assurance of the offender's respect for the victim and for the moral values by which they are bound. Reconciliation with the community, Duff claims, also requires more than simply accepting formal condemnation. Unlike purely symbolic punishment or the stigma of a conviction, hard treatment cannot be readily ignored:

> Punishment can thus be portrayed as a secular form of penance: as a way of inducing, strengthening and expressing penance ... More precisely, it must be burdensome, if it is to effectively communicate the censure which the wrongdoing deserves ... the pain involved in the repentant awareness of guilt.[110]

In summary, there seem to be three separate points that Duff makes here. First, in order to promote repentance and self-reform (compulsory) hard treatment is necessary because human nature is such that we would not willingly undergo it. Secondly, undergoing hard treatment provides a means through which repentance can be expressed: it is a way of signifying regret for previous misdeeds. Finally, the community will only accept tangible evidence of repentance before allowing the offender back into the community.

The first point, however, actually undermines Duff's theory in several ways. It emphasises the criticism made earlier that offenders do not, in any meaningful sense, desire punishment. Moreover, it entails that there are at least two sorts of offenders who should not be subjected to criminal sanctions: the already repentant and those who are beyond saving. But this is rejected by Duff. He refuses to accept that a simple apology is enough from the genuinely repentant, despite the fact that they have already undergone the necessary internal reform. And as far as the utterly defiant are concerned, he thinks that 'we owe it to every moral agent to treat him as one who can be brought to reform and redeem himself – [and] to keep trying';[111] we should not give up on them since we have a duty to treat them with concern and respect and accordingly to impose punishment aimed to restore them to the community. Even the English Court of Appeal has accepted that, in some circumstances, incorrigibility is a reason for mitigation. In *Thomas*,[112] the offenders' period of driving disqualification was reduced from two years to one year, because the

---

109 Duff, 1996, pp 17, 24.

110 *Ibid*.

111 Duff, 1986, p 266.

112 [1983] 3 All ER 756. It has been noted that the Court of Appeal would be unlikely to extend this principle beyond traffic offences: Walker and Padfield, 1996, p 55.

offender seemed to be incapable of obeying the disqualification for two years, thus increasing the likelihood of his committing further offences. Duff's determination to punish at all costs leads to the suspicion that his real justification lies elsewhere. In the absence of any other alternative justification for punishment, the only place to turn is intrinsic retributivism.

The second point made by Duff lacks empirical support. As is discussed in Chapter 6, the evidence does not support the view that offenders who undergo hard treatment are any less likely to re-offend than offenders who experience softer forms of punishment. One might even postulate that hard treatment is more likely to cause anger, frustration and a regress to one's moral health rather than repentance and reform:

> Deprivations often have the effect of focusing one's attention on one's own suffering. Being subject to hard treatment is likely to shift the agent's attention from the nature of her previous wrongdoing to the nature of her current hardships. Hard treatment might be as likely to deflect the agent's attention from her wrongdoing as focus her attention on it![113]

Inability to recognise genuinely repentant offenders

It is also questionable whether compulsorily imposed sanctions provide a suitable avenue for expressing repentance, since there is no method for distinguishing between genuine repentance and expedient compliance. Undergoing a compulsory unpleasantness under threat of force normally has nothing to do with the acceptance or expression of repentance. There is nothing inherent in the process of undergoing punishment which requires internal reform; all sentences are completed merely through some means of physical compliance; for example, by paying money or sitting in a cell for the required period. Even if sanctions were developed that required some expression of moral development, this would be superfluous. Given the strong incentive to be no longer subject to the sentencing process, one still could not distinguish between real and expedient declarations of moral well being.

Punishment and penance

Duff attempts to strengthen his claim that punishment provides a means for signifying repentance by drawing an analogy with penance. He contends that punishment is akin to compulsory penance because it expresses a concern for the offender, who through punishment is given an opportunity to atone for the injury his or her crime has caused the community. Hard treatment, he claims, makes the communicative aim more effective by forcing the criminal's

---

113 Narayan, 1993, p 177.

attention to the consequences of the crime, and it should also act as penance which the criminal wills for himself or herself.

But, this ignores the fact that penance, unlike punishment, is assumed voluntarily. As Walker points out, penance must:

> ... be preceded by confession and contrition, and must be undertaken voluntarily, or at least in obedience to the instruction of the confessor ... [In contrast] many offenders never admit their guilt, and ... many who do are unrepentant; or ... do not enter prison voluntarily or with uncoerced obedience.[114]

In relation to the third point, Duff cannot provide a coherent explanation of how hard treatment achieves reparation, why reparation is necessary for reconciliation, and further still, why it is a precondition for reconciliation. Duff believes that the criminal owes the victim a material sign of repentant recognition: 'some assurance that [the criminal] now disown[s] the hostility, indifference or contempt toward [the victim] which [the] wrong-doing displayed',[115] and that formal condemnation cannot provide this. However, the critical issue is why a sincere apology cannot provide the necessary reparation – especially since Duff concedes that the type of reparation he is concerned with is moral, not material in nature.[116] The only answer seems to be that the victim or the community demand more pain; otherwise the desire for revenge remains unsatisfied. Thus, once again Duff is cornered into intrinsic retributivism.

Utilitarianism: hard treatment and censure

Despite these criticisms of the theories by Duff and von Hirsch, there is much to be said for the central plank of their respective theories: that censure is a desirable goal of punishment. It is just that they fail to justify this goal. As noted earlier, the utilitarian has a simple answer: censuring criminal acts stigmatises criminal conduct, reinforces moral disapproval of such conduct and thereby makes it less likely that such behaviour will be engaged in. Duff and von Hirsch disagree with such an approach because they claim that it fails to explain why it is right to achieve such benefits by censuring offenders.[117] For the utilitarian, the answer is obvious: it will increase net happiness. The further step of imposing hard treatment is needed to provide an additional prudential deterrent not to engage in criminal conduct.

---

114 Walker, 1991, p 79.

115 Duff, 1996, pp 17, 23.

116 *Ibid*, p 24.

117 Duff and von Hirsch, 1997, p 112. They also assert that it relies on unproven empirical claims, but see the discussion below, Chapter 6.

4.6 UNFAIR ADVANTAGE THEORY OF PUNISHMENT

4.6.1 Outline of the theory

The unfair advantage theory of punishment is the view that offenders should be punished because they have taken unfair advantage of their victims and the community in general. The theory maintains that the criminal law confers benefits on all persons by prohibiting certain harmful acts and that these benefits can only be enjoyed if all people exercise self-restraint and do not infringe the criminal law. Lawbreakers enjoy the benefits conferred by the law, but renounce the obligations (burdens) observed by the rest of the community. They deserve to be punished because, by offending, they have taken unfair advantage of the restraints observed by the rest of the community and punishment, so the theory goes, restores the fair balance of benefits and burdens which is disturbed by crime.[118]

This theory has been subject to several damaging criticisms, some of which are so damaging that the theory has been discarded by some of its most influential proponents.[119] However, the unfair advantage theory again merits consideration due to a recent attempted resuscitation by George Sher, who attempts to meet some of the more persuasive attacks that have been levelled against the theory.[120]

One of these criticisms is that there is no workable definition of 'unfair advantage' which aptly captures the wrongfulness of crime: the exact nature of the benefit that offenders obtain from crime and the corresponding burden imposed on victims is not clear. It has been claimed that the benefit obtained by offenders is found in the renunciation of the burdens of self-restraint:

> A person who violates the rules has something others have – the benefits of the system – but by renouncing what others have assumed, the burdens of self-restraint, he has acquired an unfair advantage.[121]

This version of the unfair advantage theory has been attacked on the basis that it entails that the harshness of the sanction should be commensurate with the strength of the desire to commit the offence, thereby leading to the perverse view that tax offenders should be punished more than murderers.[122] Further,

---

118 See, eg, Morris, H, 1973; Murphy, 1979, pp 82–115.

119 Morris and Murphy have both subsequently moved away from this theory: see Morris, H, 1994; Murphy, 1985. von Hirsch also previously endorsed this theory as a partial justification for punishment, but has resiled from it because it is vulnerable to unjust society objections and fails to provide guidance on how much punishment is deserved: von Hirsch, 1993, pp 7–8.

120 For a good overview of many of the significant criticisms of this theory, see Ten, 1987, pp 52–65.

121 Morris, H, 1973, p 43.

122 Burgh, 1982, p 209.

it is apparent that the repugnance of crime, apart from some forms of property offences, rarely has anything to do with obtaining a material or tangible benefit. Sometimes, the exact opposite is true; the outcome of the offence ('the benefit') is the last thing which the offender wanted. Causing death by dangerous driving is a good example. Offenders in such circumstances do not desire to kill and would be as pleased as the rest of the community if the results of their actions could be undone. Thus, the theory has difficulty in dealing with offences where the degree of freedom obtained by the offender has no correlation with the disadvantage incurred by the victim.

4.6.2 Sher's revival and criticisms of the theory

The nature of the benefit obtained by crime

In a bid to overcome such problems, Sher suggests that the benefit derived by an offender consists of the extra freedom gained by the offender and that the benefit is measured by the strength of the constraint violated (not the strength of desire indulged).[123] For Sher, the relevant constraint is moral rather than legal. In order to correct the balance that the offender has disrupted by his or her criminal behaviour, the victim (or the community acting on the victim's behalf) must be freed from a constraint which is normally applicable and impose an unpleasantness on the wrongdoer which is about the same magnitude as the constraint violated by the offender.

Moral not legal constraints

Sher believes that the relevant constraints are moral rather than legal because our obligation to obey each law is the same and accordingly, on a law based criterion of benefits and burdens, every offender, from the shoplifter to the murderer, gains an equal amount of freedom and thus deserves the same amount of punishment. On the other hand, he contends that moral constraints are not equal, because some acts are more wrong than others, hence different wrongdoers will gain different amounts of freedoms: '... the amount of freedom gained will be proportional to the wrongness of the act performed.'[124]

However, this distinction between legal and moral norms is dubious. In relation to any norm, its degree of obligatariness depends not only upon its source, but also its content. This is especially so in relation to the duty to obey the law. The strength of the obligation depends primarily on the nature of the law and the consequence of its non-observance. The fact that the source of a

---

123 Sher, 1997, pp 166–67.
124 *Ibid.*

proscription is the law does not mean that we are equally duty bound to obey all prohibitions which share this origin. It is for this reason that most of us are normally vigilant in the observance of laws regarding not harming others, but are at times almost indifferent to abiding by regulatory laws, such as those relating to parking or registration of pets. Sher believes that the strength of moral rules varies because it is accepted that one moral obligation can override another conflicting moral obligation. But the same is also true in the case of legal obligations. Where laws appear to conflict, it is accepted that the more important law prevails (or, more accurately, obedience to the more important law will be a defence to breaching the lesser one). The legal duty to take one's very sick child to the hospital[125] will confer immunity regarding the speeding ticket received during the trip. Accordingly, it is not clear that Sher improves the theory by invoking a moral as opposed to a legal criterion of benefit.

No true fair distribution

At the core of the unfair advantage theory is the notion that benefits and burdens should be distributed equally. However, the most damaging criticism that has been levelled at the theory is that there is no true sense in which there is an equal distribution of benefits and burdens and therefore, it is argued, the theory is unable to explain coherently how offenders who have been previously wronged should be treated. If fairness requires an equal distribution of benefits and burdens, then offenders who have been previously wronged should have offence credits and be permitted enough transgressions to even the scales. Thus, the unfair advantage theory of punishment does not appear to have relevance in the real world. As Murphy has pointed out, there are enormous inequalities of income and opportunity in every society and most offenders come from the most disadvantaged sectors of the community and cannot be said to derive any meaningful benefit from the rules of society.[126] Given that the distribution of benefits and burdens is unfair in the first place, punishment will not restore any sense of fairness.

Sher attempts to circumvent this criticism by arguing that the relevant principle of fairness governs the distribution of benefits and burdens only between pairs of individuals as opposed to groups or individuals vis à vis the community. Thus, it follows that where A punches B and B punches A in return, we have a draw and punishment is not warranted. But if B punches A because C punched B or because B has previously been unfairly deprived of a benefit by the community (which is equivalent to freedom indulged in by punching another person), then B must be punished, even though from B's

---

125 The circumstances in which a legal duty is imposed are discussed in *Russell* [1933] VLR 59; *Instan* (1893) 17 Cox CC 602; *Nicholls* (1874) 13 Cox CC 75; *Gibbins and Proctor* (1918) 13 Cr App R 134. See, also, the discussion in Chapter 7 regarding the defences of necessity and duress.

126 Murphy, 1994, p 44.

perspective he or she has been subject to precisely the same amount of benefits and burdens. Sher claims that the benefit gained by B from punching A cannot be offset by the burden of being punched by another. It is on this basis that Sher approaches another interesting variant of the above situation. It has been argued that where:

> A assaults B, B assaults C, and C assaults A. In each case, an equivalent harm is inflicted on the victim. So we have three distinct acts of equal wrongdoing which proceed in a nice circle, balancing the benefits from moral restraint that each person receives. If the balancing of benefits and burdens is crucial to punishment, there should be no punishment.[127]

Sher claims that in this situation, all three deserve to be punished. Thus, focusing on the above instance of B assaulting C, the fact that B was previously assaulted by A has no bearing on the unfairness of B assaulting C because, according to Sher, the principle of fairness applies to pairs of individuals only. This unfairness will only be restored when C, or an agent acting on C's behalf, punishes B.

Sher accepts that this narrow application of the principle of fairness so far as it governs the distribution of benefits and burdens associated with compliance with the law may not be correct and that a collective principle may be more accurate, since the benefits of the legal system require the co-operation of many. Nonetheless, in the case of the distribution of benefits and burden stemming from moral compliance, Sher advances two main reasons why the principle is not collective: '... benefits of moral behavior are not mainly collective' and 'morality itself is standardly thought to be a set of rules that govern each person's treatment of each particular other person' (emphasis added).[128]

Morality – individual and group constraints

Sher's argument misrepresents a fundamental aspect of morality. Broadly, morality consists of the principles that dictate how serious conflict should be resolved. But, this is not confined to conflict between individuals. Typically, the conflict is between the interests of an individual and a large number of people and, in fact, the weightiest moral norms generally relate to conduct which affects large numbers of people. The harm caused by dumping toxic waste in the river, failing to donate money to the starving, and chopping down the rain forest is not confined to a single or particular individual, yet there is no question that such acts are morally reprehensible. Whatever else moral rules are, they are surely universalisable.[129] This means not only that

---

127 Ten, 1990, p 198.

128 Sher, 1997, p 176.

129 A judgment is universalisable if the acceptance of it in a particular situation entails that one is logically committed to accepting the same judgment in all other situations, unless there is a relevant difference: see Mackie, 1977, pp 83–102.

the same rule applies where the conduct may affect person A or B, but also where it may affect A and B.

It is also wrong to claim that the benefits of morality are not collective. To assert otherwise is to underrate the pivotal role of morality in fostering and maintaining a harmonious and secure society. Even individuals who may not have benefited directly from the observance of moral rules by others have their lives enriched by the knowledge that moral norms are generally observed. Given that moral judgments are universalisable, this gives each individual confidence about the patterns of behaviour which he or she can expect from others. This is why, in a community in which each citizen abides by the dictates of morality, each individual would feel free to walk at night, ask a stranger the time and carry money in a handbag or wallet.

Thus, there seems to be no coherent basis upon which it can be contended that the scope of the principle of fairness should be confined to pairs of individuals. A bid to do so is merely an attempt to isolate the relevant balance of benefits and burdens in a manner which preserves the credibility of the unfair advantage theory of punishment. However, fairness is not so arbitrary.

The central role of the victim

Another curious feature of Sher's theory is that he maintains that the victim is the ideal person who should inflict the punishment. Due to the risk of reprisal inherent with this, he ultimately concedes that the State should act on the victim's behalf, and while this is not perfect, he maintains 'it represents a step in the right direction ... because it symbolically lifts the moral restraints on the victim, and ... treats the wrongdoer in a normally impermissible way'.[130] This suggested role for the victim leads to suspicion that underlying the justification for punishment is the desire for personal revenge. If what is really important is that burdens and benefits are distributed equally, it should not matter how and by whom this distribution is achieved. Sher concedes that his account '*does* legitimate a form of retaliation' and regards this 'not as criticism of [his] account but rather as evidence that retaliation has received bad press'.[131] This merely fuels the suspicion that the unfair advantage theory is merely being used to cloak the desire for revenge in the language of fairness; in which case the balancing of benefits and burdens is irrelevant to Sher's theory.

Fair distribution weighed against other virtues

Further, while it may be fair to ensure that distribution of benefits and burdens is not violated by immoral behaviour, this does not necessarily justify

---

130 Sher, 1997, p 168.
131 *Ibid*, p 179.

punishment. For it is also desirable that people should not be subject to the type of unpleasantness which is constituted by punishment. When these two virtues clash, Sher weighs the former more heavily, but no reason is given for this. If it transpired that punishment increased the crime rate, this would further upset the fair distribution, yet Sher would still be compelled to punish,[132] making his theory self-defeating.

Accordingly, Sher's attempt to revive the unfair advantage theory should be rejected on the basis that the theory still succumbs to the decisive objections which have been levelled at it.

4.7 CONCLUSION

Retributivism has been the dominant theory of punishment for the past two or three decades. This is despite considerable definitional problems associated with the concept and a lack of convergence towards any particular retributive theory. The enormous array of contemporary retributive theories makes it impossible to examine exhaustively each theory. This chapter has focused on what I consider to be the four most influential retributive theories.

Examined closely, each of the theories failed to justify the link between crime and punishment. von Hirsch's theory is incoherent because ultimately, he relies on consequential considerations to do all of the heavy work. This being so, he offers no reason why we should not adopt a purely consequentialist theory. Duff's theory mischaracterises the nature of punishment, while Sher's attempted revival of the unfair advantage theory is ultimately unable to circumvent the deep problems which have previously beset the theory. Intrinsic retributivism is the most coherent retributive theory, which is somewhat ironic given that it is the least popular theory amongst contemporary adherents. Ultimately, it too is unconvincing because the desire for revenge is an inappropriate moral ideal. However, intrinsic retributivism, owing to its internal coherence, provides the firmest platform of all retributive theories from which to launch a counter-attack. Its future prosperity is likely to turn on future developments in the metaethical domain.

The sheer number and breadth of retributive theories means that it is premature to assert positively that no retributive theory of punishment can possibly justify punishment. However, given the breadth and popularity of the retributive theories which have been examined in this chapter, enough has been said in order to redirect the search for a coherent justification for punishment. The most promising path is the one leading towards utilitarianism. Without adverting to consequentialist considerations, it is impossible to justify the link between crime and punishment:

---

132 See Ten, 1991a, pp 366, 369.

We can justify rules and institutions only by showing that they yield advantages. Consequently, retributivist answers to the problem can be shown, on analysis, to be either mere affirmations of the desirability of punishment or utilitarian reasons in disguise ... To say, with Kant, that punishment is a good in itself, is to deny the necessity for justification; for to justify is to provide reasons in terms of something else accepted as valuable.[133]

A convincing utilitarian justification of punishment will obviously need finally to meet the traditional attacks which resulted in its demise. In particular, a counter must be developed to the argument that a utilitarian system of punishment permits all types of reprehensible practices, such as punishing the innocent. There matters are now considered.

133 Benn and Peters, 1959, pp 175–76.

CHAPTER 5

IN DEFENCE OF A UTILITARIAN THEORY OF PUNISHMENT: PUNISHING THE INNOCENT AND THE COMPATIBILITY OF UTILITARIANISM AND RIGHTS

5.1 INTRODUCTION

As was discussed in Chapter 3, the reasons that utilitarianism has lost favour as a justificatory theory of punishment are not primarily concerned with whether it can adequately justify punishment. Even most retributivists agree that the simple appeal to overall good consequences serves as a sound justification for punishment. The main criticisms of the utilitarian theory are directed at the perceived inability of utilitarianism to confine punishment and other forms of harsh treatment to wrongdoers.

This chapter focuses on the theoretical attacks that have proved most damaging in diminishing the appeal of utilitarianism as a justification for punishment. As we saw earlier, these attacks come broadly in two forms: that utilitarianism commits us to punishing the innocent and that it is inconsistent with the concept of individual rights. It is argued that neither of these criticisms is insurmountable. Punishing the innocent is no worse than other acts or practices which we condone in extreme situations, hence, it does not follow that any theory which approves of such an outcome must necessarily be flawed. Further, while rights are now the conventional moral currency, on critical evaluation, non-consequentialist moral theories (which underpin most retributive theories) are unable to justify the foundation and existence of rights. In fact, utilitarianism is the only moral theory which can provide a firm basis for rights, including the right of innocent people not to be punished.

5.2 PUNISHING THE INNOCENT AND UTILITARIANISM

5.2.1 Outline of the objection

A famous illustration of the objection concerning punishing the innocent is McCloskey's famous small town sheriff example:

> Suppose a sheriff were faced with the choice of either framing a negro for a rape which had aroused white hostility to negroes (this negro believed to be guilty) and thus preventing serious anti-negro riots which would probably lead to loss of life, or of allowing the riots to occur. If he were ... [a] utilitarian he would be committed to framing the negro.[1]

---

1   McCloskey, 1969, pp 180–81.

5.2.2 Utilitarian responses

Punishing the innocent only a theoretical problem

There have been several attempts to counter this objection. First, it has been suggested that examples which supposedly commit a utilitarian to punishing the innocent are impossible in the real world and, hence, need not be addressed.[2] Punishing the innocent may at times provide short term benefits, such as securing social stability, but these are always more than offset by the likelihood of greater long term harm due to the loss of confidence in the legal system and the associated loss of security to all members of the community who will fear that they may be the next person framed, once the inevitable occurs and it is disclosed that an innocent person has been punished. However, with only a little imagination, the above example can be tightened up, by introducing considerations that significantly reduce or totally obviate the possibility of disclosure, so that the only logical utilitarian conclusion is to punish the innocent. For example, McCloskey's hypothetical example could be altered by providing that the town was an isolated one, hence there is no opportunity for help to arrive before the riots occurred. Also, the crime should be murder, not a rape, in which case there is one less person who could reveal the miscarriage of justice that has occurred, and thus the risk of a possible loss of respect and confidence in the law is not as significant. Even if the process of modifying such examples appears to far remove them from the real world, it is still a situation which the utilitarian must deal with. As Ten notes, 'fantastic examples', as he labels them, which raise for consideration fundamental issues, such as whether it is proper to punish the innocent, play an important role in the evaluation of moral theories since they sharpen the contrasts between them and illuminate the logical conclusions of the respective theories. In this way, they test the true strength of our commitment to the theories.[3] Thus, fantastic examples cannot be dismissed summarily on the basis that they are 'simply' hypothetical.

Definitional arguments

An argument which has been used to buttress the punishing the innocent attack on utilitarianism is that such an outcome is inconsistent with the definition of punishment: 'punishment must not only be *of* an offender; it must also be for *her* offence';[4] 'even if the world gathered all its strength, there is one thing it is not able to do, it can no more punish an innocent [person] than it can put a dead person to death'.[5]

2   See, eg, Sprigge, 1965, p 272.
3   Ten, 1987, pp 18–25.
4   Duff, 1986, p 152.
5   Kierkegaard, S, *Purity of the Heart is to Will One Thing*, 1961, Collins, Fontana, p 85, as cited in *ibid*, Duff, p 152.

However, this approach cuts both ways. If by definition, punishment can only be imposed on the guilty, it follows that the issue of punishing the innocent is one which the utilitarian need not even begin to tackle. The definition of punishment which is adopted applies independently to the justificatory theory of it. Accordingly, it is open for the utilitarian to adopt the above definition and rest his or her case on the basis that one cannot be committed to that which is logically impossible.[6]

Ultimately, however, as Armstrong points out, definitional disputes are not likely to resolve normative issues. Irrespective of how punishment is defined, the utilitarian cannot sidestep the problem of punishing the innocent, since the objection loses none of its force if the question is framed in terms of 'why shouldn't we do to the innocent that which, when it's done to the guilty, is known as punishment?'.[7] This requires a substantive, not a formal response.

Before turning to this, in a bid to highlight the futility of definitional arguments in this area, it is illuminating to note the caginess with which they may be, and have been, used. The fact that it makes sense to assert that 'he was punished for something he did not do'[8] has been used to take a cheap shot at retributivism, since it supposedly shows that punishment of the innocent is possible and thereby retributivism, which links punishment to a past crime, must be wrong.

Substantive response – hard cases lead to hard decisions

The more promising utilitarian response is not to attempt to deflect or avoid the conclusion that there may be some extreme situations where utilitarianism commits us to punishing the innocent. Rather, it is to accept this outcome and to contend that, as horrible as this may seem on a pre-reflective level, it is not a matter which, on closer consideration, *really* insurmountably troubles our sensibilities to the extent that it entails that any theory which approves of such an outcome must necessarily be flawed.[9] By drawing comparisons with other situations in which we take the utilitarian option, it is contended that punishing the innocent is not a practice which is necessarily unacceptable.

The view that punishing the innocent is the morally correct action in some circumstances is consistent with, and accords with, the decisions we as individuals and societies as a whole readily have made and continue to make when faced with extreme and desperate circumstances. Once we come to grips with the fact that our decisions in extreme situations will be

---

6   See Quinton, 1954, p 533.
7   Armstrong, 1971, pp 19, 34.
8   *Ibid*, pp 19, 20 – Armstrong, sensibly, rejects this criticism.
9   The distinction I am making between intuitive moral judgments and those formed after due reflection is similar to that made by Hare between intuitive and critical levels of moral thinking: see Hare, 1981.

compartmentalised to desperate predicaments and will not have a snowball effect, and serve to diminish henceforth the high regard we normally have for important individual concerns and interests, we find that when placed between a rock and a hard place we do and should – though perhaps somewhat begrudgingly – take the utilitarian option. In the face of extreme situations, we are quite ready to accept that one should, or even must, sacrifice oneself or *others* for the good of the whole.

For example, in times of war, we not only request our strongest and healthiest to fight to the death for the good of the community, but we often demand that they do so, under threat of imprisonment or even death. Quite often, they *must* battle against hopeless odds, in circumstances where we are aware that in all probability they will not return. And what is more, they must do so. Give their lives. Not because they want to, not because they are bad, but merely because it would be good for the rest of us – classical utilitarian reasoning. Faced with the reality of the decisions we *do* make in such horrible situations, the examples proffered against utilitarianism about the terrible things it entails, such as punishing the innocent, lose their bite. Horrible situations make for appalling decisions whichever way we turn, but at the death knell we do make the utilitarian choice because of our lack of true commitment to any higher moral virtue. By opting for the utilitarian line, we are soothed by the one saving grace: at least the level of harm has been minimised. When the good of many or the whole is a significant threat, we have no difficulty selecting certain classes of innocent individuals, whose only 'flaw' is their sex, state of health, and date of birth to go in to bat for the rest of us. Their protests that they should not be compelled to go because it impinges on their civil, legal or human rights to such matters as life and liberty, or their desperate appeals to other virtues such as justice or integrity, fall on deaf ears. For this is serious stuff now – our lives (or other important interests) are at stake. Such appeals should be saved for rosier times.

The decisions we actually make in a real life crisis are the best evidence of the way we actually prioritise important competing principles and interests. Matters such as rights and justice are important, but in the end are subservient to, and make way for, the ultimate matter of significance: general happiness. Bad as it seems, imprisoning the innocent is certainly no more horrendous than the decisions history has shown we have made in circumstances of monumental crisis.

A pointed example is the decision by the English Prime Minister of the day, Winston Churchill, to sacrifice the lives of the residents of Coventry in order not to alert the Germans that the English had deciphered German radio messages. On 14 November 1940, the English decoded plans that the Germans were about to air bomb Coventry. If Coventry were evacuated or its inhabitants advised to take special precautions against the raid, the Germans would know that their code had been cracked, and the English would be unable to obtain future information about the intentions of its enemy. Churchill elected not to warn the citizens of Coventry, and many hundreds were killed in the raid which followed. The lives were sacrificed in order not to reveal the secret that would hopefully save many more lives in the future.[10]

A famous modern day example which comes closest to the dilemma of choosing whether to frame the innocent or tolerate massive abuses of rights followed the Rodney King beating in Los Angeles in March 1991. The four police officers who beat King were acquitted under State law of any offence regarding the incident. Riots ensued, resulting in widespread looting, damage to property, and dozens of deaths. Shortly afterwards, the federal Government announced the almost unprecedented step that the police officers, who, one must remember, were found not guilty of any offence, would be tried on federal civil rights charges relating to the incident. Two of the police officers were duly found guilty for violating King's civil rights, despite the apparent double jeopardy involved, and were sentenced to 30 months' imprisonment. Whatever one's view of the government's motivation for committing the police officers on federal charges, it seems that justice took a back seat – for a while.[11]

This is not to suggest that the officers were, in fact, innocent – in fact, the video evidence of the beating seemed to provide almost irresistible evidence to the contrary. It is also not to suggest that the double jeopardy rule is sacrosanct. As was noted in the Macpherson Report,[12] which examined the police incompetence and deliberate obstruction that enabled the killers of the black student Stephen Lawrence, in 1993, to walk free, it may be desirable to amend the rule. However, it is widely accepted that the double jeopardy principle is an important safeguard in our criminal justice system. Hence, such considerations do not significantly undermine the fact that the King case shows that when the community is desperate, it is willing to violate commonly accepted individual rights and protections.

Significantly, such decisions have subsequently been immune from widespread or persuasive criticism. This shows not only that when pressed, we *do* take the utilitarian option, but also that it is felt that this is the option we *should* take.

---

10 See 'Utilitarian ethics', in Velasquez and Rostankowski, 1985, Chapter 4.

11 For an account of these events, see Gibbs, 1996; Cole, 1999.

12 Macpherson, W (Sir), *The Stephen Lawrence Inquiry*, Cm 4262–1, February 1999, Chapter 47, recommendation 38: The report noted that 'perhaps in modern conditions such absolute protection [in the form of the *autrefois acquit* rule] may sometimes lead to injustice. Full and appropriate safeguards would be essential. Fresh trials after acquittal would be exceptional. But we indicate that at least the issue deserves debate and reconsideration, perhaps by the Law Commission, or by Parliament' (para 7.46). See, also, Law Reform Commission, *Double Jeopardy*, Consultation Paper No 156, 1999.

What we actually do does not necessarily justify what ought to be done. Morality is normative, not descriptive in nature: an 'ought' cannot be derived from an 'is'.[13] Nevertheless, the above account is telling because the force of the punishing the innocent objection lies in the fact that it supposedly so troubles our moral consciousness that utilitarianism can thereby be dismissed on the basis that the outcome is so horrible that 'there must be a mistake somewhere'. However, the objection loses its force when it is shown that punishing the innocent is, in fact, no worse than other activities we condone.

5.3 PUNISHING THE INNOCENT AND RETRIBUTIVISM

5.3.1 Outline of the objection

It has been pointed out that it is not only a utilitarian system of punishment that may permit punishment of the innocent:

> Retributivists who advocate punishment are relevantly like utilitarians who will sacrifice the welfare of innocents for the greater good, since retributivists are willing to trade the welfare of the innocent who are punished by mistake for the greater good of the punishment of the guilty. While never intending to punish the innocent, they nevertheless do not choose to withdraw their support for arrangements that have this result.[14]

5.3.2 Retributive responses

Increase of safeguards against wrongful convictions

It is inevitable, given the fallibility of any institution, that any criminal justice system will at times inflict punishment on the innocent. A good example is the recent scandal centred upon a corrupt Los Angeles police officer, Rafael Perez. As part of a plea bargain with prosecution authorities after Perez was caught stealing cocaine from a police evidence room, Perez admitted that he 'perjured himself at least 100 times in court, wrote more than 100 false reports and stole as much as $80,000 from the people he arrested'.[15] According to Perez, during the mid to late 1990s, he and his partner Nino Durden regularly planted drugs

---

13 This has been used as an argument against a naturalistic view of morality. However, see Pigden, 1991, pp 421, 422–26, where he points that this phenomenon simply reflects the conservative nature of logic – you cannot get out of it, what you do not put in.

14 Schedler, 1980, p 189. For this reason, he concluded that retributivists simply cannot support the institution of punishment.

15 'Exonerated officers say Perez squealed on them for plea bargain': 13 May 2000: http://www.channel2000.com/news/stories/news-20000513-184114.html. See, also, Andrews, M, 'One hundred frame-ups admitted in widening Los Angeles police scandal', 28 January 2000: http://www.wsws.org/articles/2000/jan2000/lapd-j28_prn.shtml.

and weapons on innocent people and then lied on their reports and in court to secure convictions. As a result of Perez's admissions, about 100 convictions were set aside.[16]

The problem of punishing the innocent could be largely circumvented by increasing the amount and level of safeguards in the criminal justice process. For example, the standard of proof could be raised from beyond reasonable doubt (or being 'sure of guilt', as is the case in England and Wales) to, say, beyond any possible doubt; admissible evidence could be limited to direct observations of the relevant act; and a confession could be made a mandatory precondition to a finding of guilt. However, such a response is not open to retributivists. It would be self-defeating, since it would result in more innocent people being harmed than is presently the case as a result of our imperfect criminal justice system. Any retributive theory must have at its foundation some theory of morality, given that the prohibition against punishing the innocent is not a free standing principle. The broader principle which logically flows from this prohibition is that people who are not blameworthy in any way should not be harmed. The effect of radically increasing the amount of legal safeguards in criminal cases would result in very few guilty people being punished and thereby an increase in the amount of crime and innocent people being harmed.

The doctrine of double effect

A common retributive response to the problem of punishing the innocent is that offered by Duff, who denies that punishing the innocent is a concern for the retributivist, since, unlike the utilitarian situation, punishment of the innocent is *not intended* and occurs despite the aims of a retributive system of punishment.[17] The credibility of this response turns on the persuasiveness of the distinction between consequences which are intended and those that are merely foreseen.

Outline of the doctrine of double effect

Underpinning Duff's argument is the doctrine of double effect, which provides that it is morally permissible to perform an act having two effects, one good and one evil, where the following elements are satisfied: the good consequence is intended and the bad merely foreseen, there is proportionality between the good and bad consequences, and those consequences occur almost simultaneously.

---

16 By 4 August 2000, there had been in fact 98 convictions that had been set aside due to the police corruption scandal that stemmed from Perez's admissions: 'Another conviction overturned in LAPD scandal', 4 August 2000:
http://www.cnn.com/2000/LAW/08/04/lapd.conviction.

17 The same point is made by Moore, 1993, p 20.

The doctrine has a rich history and is frequently appealed to as a purported justification for acts or practices which produce foreseen undesirable consequences. For example, this is the reason why it is, supposedly, permissible to bomb an enemy's ammunition factory in wartime, even though it will result in the certain death of civilians, and why it is justifiable to kill an unborn baby where this is necessary to save the mother, and why self-defence is legitimate.[18] In the case of euthanasia, it is employed as a justification for alleviating pain by increasing doses of pain killers even when it is known that this will result in death – the intention is to reduce pain, not to kill.

The legal status of the doctrine is unclear. In *Nedrick*,[19] the House of Lords held that foresight, even of near certainty, was not the same as intention, whereas in *Hyam*[20] Lord Hailsham was of the view that one who blows up an aircraft in order to obtain money intends to kill.[21] However, the courts have endorsed the doctrine in relation to euthanasia. In *Adams*, it was held that it is permissible to relieve suffering even if the measure incidentally shortens life.[22] This has, at least implicitly, been endorsed in subsequent cases.[23]

Is there a distinction between intended consequences and foreseen consequences?

However, the moral significance of the doctrine is much in dispute. Glover gives the example of a terrorist who, for the purpose of making a (legitimate) political protest, throws a bomb into a crowd, killing several people.[24] He correctly points to the difficulty in ascertaining whether the deaths are intentional or merely foreseen. The above examples illustrate that inevitability of the deaths cannot be used to impute intention, for the doctrine provides that foreseen consequences which are certain need not be counted as intentional. Thus, the fact that the terrorist is possibly more certain to kill

---

18 Although there are also other justifications for self-defence.

19 [1986] 1 WLR 1025, p 1028.

20 [1975] AC 55, p 75.

21 To explain this incongruity, it has been suggested that where the motive is honourable, there is room to distinguish between foresight and intention: Lanham, D, 'Euthanasia, pain killing, murder and manslaughter', in McKie, 1994, pp 67, 73. However, this cannot be used to give a general account of the difference between that which is intended and foreseen, since this distinction is itself meant to be a test by which the moral status of an act can be evaluated. The doctrine would be redundant if the moral status of the act was clear from the outset.

22 [1957] Crim LR 365, p 375.

23 See *Cox* (1992) 12 BMLR 38, p 39; *Airedale NHS Trust v Bland* [1993] AC 789, p 867; *Auckland Area Health Board v AG* [1993] 1 NZLR 235, p 248; *Re J (Wardship: Medical Treatment)* [1991] Fam 33, p 46.

24 Glover, 1977, p 88.

innocent people than the institution of punishment is to punish innocent people is irrelevant.

It is also beside the point that the institution of punishment does not aim to punish specific innocent individuals. For not only would the terrorist be pleased if no person was killed, but as far as he or she is concerned, the crowd consists of random unidentified individuals. Thus, there appears no principled reason to maintain that the terrorist intends to kill, whereas the institution of punishment does not intend to punish the innocent: in both instances, if the respective objectives could be achieved without the harmful by-products, the agents would be pleased. This alludes to the central flaw in the doctrine of double effect, which is that it is not possible to provide a general account of the distinction between what is intended and what is merely foreseen which applies in all circumstances. It is illusory to claim that intentions are divisible, along the lines of good and bad consequences of an act.

The preferable view is that there is no inherent distinction between consequences that are intended and those that are foreseen. We are responsible for all the consequences that we foresee, but nevertheless elect to bring about. Whether or not we also 'intend' them is irrelevant. Underlying the doctrine of double effect, and the only coherent basis for the distinction adverted to by the doctrine, is nothing more than the consequentialist view that it is permissible to do that which is 'merely foreseen' if the adverse consequences of the act are outweighed by the good consequences that are 'intended'. Utilitarianism deals with the difficulties that are sought to be overcome by the doctrine in a far more comprehensible and straightforward manner. The reason that neither the doctor who administers a lethal dose of pain killers, nor the legal system which punishes the innocent (believed guilty) is blameworthy has nothing to do with the fuzziness relating to what is intended as opposed to foreseen. It simply follows because, in all the circumstances, the good consequences outweigh the bad. Further, from the perspective of the innocent person who is punished, it certainly does not matter whether his or her punishment was intentional or merely foreseen: it hurts just the same. Notwithstanding this, an institution which causes such hurt is still morally justifiable, because it leads to a happier situation overall, than the alternative – abolishing punishment.

In the end, the motivation for the doctrine of double effect seems to be to provide a means for deontological theories which employ notions of absolute (or near absolute) rights to deal with the difficult, but inevitable, situations where there are conflicts between different rules or rights, or even different applications of the same rule or right. The doctrine maintains absolutism by utilising the fiction of merely foreseen consequences and absolving liability for them.

The innocent not used as a means

However, there may yet be another way in which the retributivist may attempt to defend a system of punishment which, unfortunately but invariably, will result in the punishment of some innocent people. This adverts less crudely to the distinction discussed earlier regarding the identity of victims who are incidentally harmed as a byproduct of what is thought to be a generally desirable act, and invokes the Kantian concept of means and ends.

The nature of this distinction is illustrated by the following example. It is necessary to build a bridge between two suburbs. Two different types of bridges are possible. If proposed bridge A is built, actuarial studies show that it is certain that two people will die during the construction. If bridge B is constructed, it is known in advance that a particular workman will die. It is contended that the utilitarian, on this information alone, would elect route B.[25]

On the other hand, a powerful deontological argument can be made in favour of bridge A, because unlike in case B, no individual is being used simply as a means for a particular end. This follows from the fact that each person who is involved in the project or is in some way affected by it *may also ultimately benefit* from the project. For example, he or she may use the bridge or be paid a salary for working on its construction. It may be argued that the terrorist example is analogous to situation B and the retributive system of punishment to situation A. Although the terrorist kills victims who are unknown to him or her, they are nevertheless specific people whose identity is ascertainable at the time of the act and they have no prospect of benefiting from the legitimate protest. Not so in the case of a retributive system of punishment, which unintentionally punishes an innocent person. The identity of the 'offender' is not known at the time of conviction and sentence, and may never be known. Even though the innocent who are punished ultimately do suffer, they are part of a general practice through which they, too, may have prospered. In this sense, so the argument runs, they are not sacrificed for the good of the whole.

---

25 I thank Chin Liew Ten for this point and example. It should be noted, however, that this conclusion is by no means certain. A utilitarian could argue that earmarked deaths are worse than statistical ones because of the desensitisation that would follow if defined individuals were allowed to die. As an empirical fact, we seem to be built in such a way that when an identifiable individual is experiencing pain and suffering (or is in need of help), this impacts on us far more heavily than when it is experienced by faceless strangers. Thus, in 1995, the Australian Government spent $5.8 m rescuing French sailor Isabelle Autissier who was stranded while on a solo frolic around the world, when the same money could have saved thousands of starving people around the world. Thus, unless the number of statistical deaths is significantly more than earmarked ones, a utilitarian may prefer to opt for bridge A. Nevertheless, I assume that the utilitarian has a preference for route B.

However, even putting to one side the difficulties associated with the means and ends distinction, this retributive approach to the dilemma is unsatisfactory. At the time an innocent person is punished, there is always at least one person who is aware of the injustice: the 'offender'. It is not to the point that the system is oblivious to the innocence of the 'offender' at the point of conviction and sentence. If the system was really concerned with the unfairness, it would have taken measures to avoid the predicament eventuating; by implementing safeguards, of the type mentioned earlier, to prevent wrongful conviction. By persisting with such a defence of their theory, retributivists are expressing either feigned concern or blissful ignorance. Even more generally, it is immaterial that the 'offender' could have potentially benefited from the institution of punishment. He or she did not, and is a victim of it, and it is unrealistic to expect meaningful solace to be attained through such unrealised *potential:* in any meaningful sense of the word, he or she is being sacrificed for the good of the whole.

The moral relevance of intentions

A related problem for the retributivist, especially in respect to the doctrine of double effect, is the absolute faith and reliance placed on the concept of intentions. Non-consequentialist moral theories of morality invariably assert that intentions have intrinsic moral relevance: the intention to help others is worthy of moral praise, while the intention to harm justifies moral condemnation. On its face, this may seem incontrovertible. However, the picture becomes less clear if one considers the case of 'Jack'.

Jack is generally a good person; more often than not he intends to assist others that he believes are not as fortunate as him. However, he is not very bright. His parents who, unknown to Jack, are very wealthy, have always been extremely paranoid and untrusting of others, believing that others wish to exploit their wealth. Accordingly, they have been extremely vigilant to ensure that Jack is sheltered from the outside world, to the extent that Jack, despite being an adult, has never attended school (or received any other form of meaningful education) and, accordingly, has a very poor understanding of the empirical cause and effects systems which operate in the world: so poor that he never manages to succeed in implementing his intentions so far as they affect his relationships with others, and, in fact, he always produces the morally opposite result. Thus, when he wants to harm people, instead of robbing them, he gives them money (because he believes that money is a cause of unhappiness) and when he wants to help, he punches them (believing this to be a form of affection). Given that Jack's beliefs are so entrenched that they are beyond revision, even the most ardent non-consequentialist would prefer the 'nasty' Jack and would agree that it would be far better to live in a world of 'nasty' rather than 'nice' Jacks.

The only reason that we generally view intentions as being inherently worthy of praise or blame is that most us have sufficient factual knowledge about the empirical processes in the world to set in train the appropriate causal processes to achieve our intentions. Hence, there is a *very close connection* between intentions and consequences. If it transpired that intentions generally had no connection with consequences, they would promptly become morally irrelevant. The above account of Jack may seem far fetched, but the point that the example seeks to drive home is already entrenched in the context of other mental states we experience. We are not responsible or culpable for other mental states we experience which do not produce harmful consequences. We are not condemned for the aspirations or intentions we experience while dreaming or for our private wishes which we do not act upon. To the extent that we may be criticised when our dark private wishes became public, this is merely because it is assumed that they reflect upon sinister personal traits which may in the future guide our conduct and lead to undesirable consequences. But, absent the possible connection between our private wishes and ultimate consequences, they are not objects of praise or blame. Thus, the only basis for ascribing moral relevance to intentions is because of their close link with consequences. When this link is severed, it becomes apparent that at the bottom, the only things which really matter are consequences, and the appeal of distinctions or doctrines which bank on the purported significance of intentions readily dissipates.

The point being made here is not as revisionary as might first appear. It is not contended that intentions and other types of mental state, such as recklessness and negligence, are irrelevant and that accordingly, we ought to abandon the heavy reliance generally placed on them, and thereby, for example, implement a strict liability system of law.[26] As an empirical fact, as has been stated, there is a close connection between our intentions and actions and therefore, the person who intentionally brings about a harmful act is more blameworthy than one who does so due to, say, indifference or mistake. Even though the immediate and direct consequences are identical, the person who deliberately sets in train a causal process which results in harm to another deserves greater blame and punishment because such behaviour in general is likely to lead to more suffering long term, and thus stern measures must be implemented to deter similar behaviour in the future.

The law and intentions

Mental states do have a role; however, they are not the ultimate considerations which are relevant to moral responsibility. And despite the

---

26 Especially of the type proposed by Wootton, 1981, where she contends that the function of the criminal law is to prevent socially harmful acts, and that therefore, *mens rea* is not relevant to criminal liability; although it does have a role in sentencing.

general significance attached to mental states by our legal system, whereby substantial emphasis is attached to precise mental states (such as recklessness, negligence and carelessness), ultimately the law recognises that mental states *per se* are irrelevant. No matter how pervasively wicked a person may be, or how resolutely they may intend that a certain harmful state of affairs should eventuate, no legal responsibility is ascribed until and unless such mental states are accompanied by actions. The only possible exception to this is the law relating to attempted criminal offences. However, even here the degree of intrusion into the principle that intentions are *per se* irrelevant is only marginal, if at all. For liability to occur, it is necessary for the offender, as well as possessing the requisite mental state, to perform *actions* which are very close to committing the substantive offence: the actions must be immediately, and not merely remotely, connected with the completed offence.[27]

Deliberately punishing and inadvertently punishing the innocent

The retributivist could yet contend that a system which deliberately punishes the innocent is nevertheless worse than one where this occurs inadvertently, because it is surely likely to lead to more innocent people being punished, and to the corruption of a greater number of officials involved in the practice.

However, the first point overstates the likelihood of the utilitarian calculus actually coming down in favour of punishing the innocent, while the second alludes to some of the reasons why it is extremely rare, if ever, that utilitarianism will condone such an outcome.

While punishing the innocent may, in rare circumstances, promote the utilitarian aims of punishment, practical realities militate heavily against such a course being pursued, due to the significant danger that it will ultimately result in widespread community unrest and turmoil. A recent example is the large scale civil unrest in Malaysia in October and November 1998 following the arrest, beating, and detention of the opposition leader, Anwar Ibrahim, for what were widely assumed to be fabricated criminal charges of sexual misconduct (homosexuality) and related corruption offences. The first anniversary of this arrest (in which time Ibrahim had been sentenced to six years' imprisonment for corruption offences – the sodomy trial was still continuing)[28] was marked by a protest involving about 10,000 people.[29] While it is impossible to articulate exhaustively in advance the circumstances in which the utilitarian is committed to punishing the innocent, it is evident that one precondition to this is certainty, or near certainty, that the innocence of the

---

27 See, eg, *Mohan* [1976] QB 1; *Smith* [1975] AC 476.

28 However, on 8 August 2000, Mr Ibrahim was found guilty of sodomy and sentenced to nine years in jail: see Baranee Krishnaan, K, 'Protests as Anwar convicted of sodomy' (2000) *The Age*, 9 August, p 1.

29 'Protests mark Anwar anniversary' (1999) *The Age*, 21 September, p 16.

'offender' will never be disclosed. Realistically, given the large number of officials involved in bringing a person to 'justice' (due to the separation of administrative and judicial power in most jurisdictions) it is extremely rare that this requirement will be satisfied.[30]

If, following a proper setting of the utilitarian scales, where *all* of the above variables are included (including the corrupting affect that punishing the innocent would have on the officials involved), it transpires that punishing the innocent will maximise happiness, then it is open for the utilitarian to assert that this does not reveal a shortcoming in the theory, since such an outcome is appropriate after all. To attack this response in a manner which does not beg the question, the retributivist must provide as a reason for the supposed wrongness of punishing the innocent, something beyond the mere assumption that it is abhorrent. This is best done by invoking the concept of rights.

5.4 UTILITARIANISM AND RIGHTS

It has been asserted that utilitarian responses to the charge that utilitarianism permits punishing the innocent all fail because, no matter how they are framed, they miss the full force of what is wrong with punishing the innocent. The wrongness of punishing the innocent is not a question of weighing up the contingent consequences, but is evident from the act itself.[31]

There are two ways this argument can be developed. First, that it is necessarily always the case that punishing the innocent is wrong and that this is apparent from our intuitions. At the pre-philosophical level, this argument is appealing; however, as we saw earlier, intuitions are incapable of conclusively settling moral issues.

To this end, the better argument is that punishing the innocent is wrong because it violates some fundamental virtue: namely, the right not to be punished without having committed an offence. Such a right is recognised in some form or another in numerous international covenants and charters.[32] This direct and somewhat narrow attack on the utilitarian theory of punishment is only one of three ways in which the concept of rights may be used to attack the utilitarian theory.

---

30 See, also, Rosen, 1997, who argues that the reason that utilitarianism *supposedly* permits punishing the innocent stems from the flawed assumption that utilitarianism justifies punishment on the basis of deterrence alone, whereas deterrence is only one of several relevant factors in the utilitarian theory of punishment. Whether there are, in fact, other considerations that the utilitarian can invoke to justify punishment is discussed in the next chapter.

31 Ten, 1987, pp 35–36. See, also, Duff, 1986, pp 160–61.

32 See, eg, the Universal Declaration of Human Rights 1948, Art 9; International Covenant of Civil and Political Rights 1967, Art 9(1).

The second manner is by resorting to the concept of rights to underpin a retributive theory of punishment. Many retributive theories, to varying degrees, have attempted to seize on the notion of rights. The retributive theory which relies most heavily on the notion of rights is rights retributivism, which provides that punishment is justified because, where an offender violates the rights of his or her victim, the offender thereby forfeits some of his or her rights. The theory also contends that punishment must be proportionate to the offence and provides a formula for achieving this: the offender should be deprived of the same or equivalent rights to those that have been violated by the crime. Rights are equivalent when people would be indifferent to preferring the rights violated to those lost through punishment. In terms of drawing the justificatory link between crime and punishment, this is said to be found in the fact that the offender has violated the rights of another.[33]

There are, however, several problems with this theory. For example, Honderich points out that rights retributivism does not advance the justificatory link between crime and punishment any further than intrinsic retributivism.[34] The claim that one has violated the rights of another provides no further reason beyond the simple assertion that one has acted wrongly to justify punishment. It is not as if certain wrongs, those that involve infraction of rights, are any more or less deserving of punishment. Certainly, rights retributivism adverts expressly to a particular moral theory; however, there is nothing inherent in the concept of rights which mandates or permits a punitive response for violation of them.

These cursory observations aside, the discussion does not focus directly on either of the above two rights based arguments. Rather, it will address the third and broadest, and most persuasive, argument that has been utilised by rights proponents against utilitarianism. Put simply, it is the claim that rights based theories are the soundest moral theories and, accordingly, all other moral theories, particularly utilitarianism, must be rejected. If rights based moral theories are correct, it follows that utilitarianism, in all of its applications, including the practice of punishment, must be rejected. In order for the utilitarian theory of punishment to regain some ground, it is necessary to discredit the plausibility of rights based moral theories. If this can be done, the other more specific rights based objections discussed above will also be debunked.

First, the nature of rights based theories is outlined.

---

33   Goldman, 1979, p 51.
34   Honderich, 1984, pp 217–18.

5.4.1 The nature of rights based theories

Numerous rights based theories have been advanced and, as a result of the colossal, and apparently ever increasing, amount of ethical language which is expressed in the form of rights, such theories present the greatest challenge to utilitarianism. Rights talk transcends all areas of moral discourse. As was indicated in Chapter 3, rights are now the conventional moral currency. There is no shortage of rights based theories; the main differences between them typically being the precise rights which are acclaimed, the basis of the rights, and the absolutism with which they apply. The main role of rights in deontological theories is to protect people from being compelled to do something against their wishes for the good of another or the general good. The foregoing discussion looks at arguably the two most influential contemporary rights theories, those of Ronald Dworkin and Robert Nozick. However, many of the observations I make in relation to these theories are applicable to most other rights based theories.

Dworkin – concern and respect

For Dworkin, rights are 'political trumps held by individuals',[35] which protect them from the pursuit of common goods: 'the prospect of utilitarian gains cannot justify preventing a man from doing what he has a right to do',[36] and the general good is never an adequate basis for limiting rights. He asserts that people have rights when there are good reasons for conferring upon them benefits or opportunities despite a community interest to the contrary.

According to Dworkin, in order to take rights seriously, one:

> ... must accept one or both of two important ideas. The first is the vague but powerful idea of human dignity. This idea, associated with Kant ... supposes that there are ways of treating a man that are inconsistent with recognising him as a full member of the community, and holds that such treatment is profoundly unjust. The second is the more familiar idea of political equality.[37]

Observance of these ideals leads to the fundamental right of equal concern and respect, which is the foundation of Dworkin's rights thesis. It makes sense to say a person has a right if that right is necessary to protect the person's dignity or his or her standing as being equally entitled to concern and respect. To treat one with concern is to treat one as a human being, capable of suffering and frustration, and to accord respect is to recognise one as a human being capable of forming and acting on intelligent conceptions of how life should be lived.[38]

---

35 Dworkin, 1977, p xi.

36 *Ibid*, p 193.

37 *Ibid*, p 198.

38 *Ibid*.

Nozick – rights which exist in a state of nature

Robert Nozick's rights theory stems from his analysis of the legitimate role of the State.[39] I am not so much concerned here with the end product of this State, but rather with his picture of morality which underpins it. Nozick believes that morality is founded on rights. For him, the rights we have are those which supposedly exist in a state of nature and derive from our natural liberty. This gives rise to several distinct rights: the right to absolute control over ourselves; the right to be free from all forms of physical violations; and the right to acquire property and other resources as a result of the proper exercise of our personal rights. These rights are contingent upon not violating the same rights of others. We also have the right to exact retribution against, and compensation from, those who violate our rights. Moral rights are said to act as side constraints on the actions of others and cannot be violated even to achieve greater goods. Thus, on Nozick's account, moral rights are negative rights; there are no positive rights such as the right to welfare or health care.

The rights explosion gives a running start to rights based moral theories or claims or protections couched in such language. An ethical theory or moral principle which is clearly rights based is ostensibly at an enormous advantage over other theories, such as utilitarianism, which give no natural weight to individual rights.

5.4.2 The case against rights based theories

One of the main problems with rights is that there appears to be no basis to stop their expansion. It seems the number of alleged rights has blossomed exponentially since the basically protective rights of life, liberty and property were advocated in the 17th century. Nowadays, all sorts of dubious claims have been advanced by reference to them. For example, 'the right to a tobacco-free job', the 'right to sunshine', the 'right of a father to be present in the delivery room', the 'right to a sex break',[40] and even 'the right to drink myself to death without interference'.[41] The 'right to die'[42] is also, arguably, a member of such an incredible group. Owing to the great expansion in rights talk, rights are now in danger of being labelled as mere rhetoric and losing their cogent moral force: '... an argumentative device capable of justifying anything is capable of justifying nothing.'[43]

---

39 Nozick, 1974.

40 These examples are cited by Kleinig, 1978, pp 36, 40.

41 Benn, 1967, p 196.

42 This supposed right has gained widespread support in the context of the euthanasia debate. See, eg, *Rodriguez v AG British Columbia* [1994] 85 CCC (3d) 185, *per* Cory J.

43 Sumner, 1987, pp 8–9.

In order for rights proponents to capitalise on the wave of support currently enjoyed by rights based theories, and for such theories to be capable of having a persuasive and meaningful role in post-philosophical moral discourse, it is necessary to provide rights a foundation which can be used to solve several key problems concerning them, otherwise 'to settle controversial matters by appeal to moral rights, human or otherwise, may be to do no more than pit one set of prejudices against others'.[44] The problems which need to be addressed include, what is a right? where do rights come from? what is their justification? how can we distinguish real from fanciful rights? when, if ever, can rights be overridden? and which right takes priority in the event of clashing rights? Overall, rights based theories fare poorly in meeting the challenges posed by such questions.

The definition of a right

A difficulty which has persistently plagued rights based theories is that of defining exactly what is meant by the concept of a right. Following the work of Hohfeld,[45] there is no shortage of definitions which have been advanced. McCloskey believes rights to be simply entitlements,[46] while in Sprigge's view, 'the best way of understanding ... that someone has a right to something seems to be to take it as the claim that there are grounds for complaint on their behalf if they do not have it'.[47] Still further, rights have been defined as: claims and entitlements to benefit from the performance of obligations;[48] 'those minimum conditions under which human beings can flourish [as moral agents] and which ought to be secured for them, if necessary by force';[49] and the liberties each man hath, to use his own power, as he will himself, for the preservation of his own nature'.[50] Galligan defines a right as a 'justified claim that an interest should be protected by the imposition of correlative duties';[51] while Campbell notes that 'the standard view is that rights are *moral* entitlements and human rights are those moral entitlements which are the possession of *all persons everywhere*'.[52]

---

44 Campbell, T, 1988, p 44.
45 Hohfeld defined four categories of rights: claim-rights, privileges, powers and immunities. He qualifies this by stating that only a claim-right accords with the proper meaning of the term: Hohfeld, 1964.
46 McCloskey, 1976, p 115.
47 Sprigge, 1987, pp 216–17.
48 Marshall, 1973, pp 228, 241.
49 Kleinig, 1978, pp 44–45.
50 Hobbes, 1968, pp 84–85.
51 Galligan, 1988, p 88.
52 Campbell, T, 1996a, p 164.

For all that, I shall not get weighed down on the issue of what is a right. Having acknowledged at the outset the important role rights have in morality, such an inquiry could only be of minor significance to the discussion at hand. Whatever the outcome of the exercise, it is highly improbable that it would have an impact upon the role and proliferation of rights in moral discourse. Even if it was concluded that it is not possible to provide a coherent definition of rights, but rather that rights were, say, some multiformal types of claims with no common feature, it is still necessary to adequately fit the concept into an account of morality. Rights have become such an entrenched feature of the moral (and legal)[53] landscape that it is now too late to simply dismiss them on the basis that they are merely the product of faulty analysis or logic or 'nonsense on stilts'.[54] Even if such claims may have been tenable at some earlier point, rights now have such an inextricable connection with morality that they have possibly reshaped its meaning. Any moral theory which failed to account for such a notion is likely to be readily dismissed as being irrelevant. Thus, it is accepted that a right is a coherent concept.

However, for the sake of completeness I believe the following to be the correct definition of a right. A right is a presumptive benefit or protection one can assert against others.[55] Presumptive, because it is never indefeasible or absolute. A benefit means a positive entitlement such as the right to welfare. A protection is a negative entitlement, such as the right to be free from a particular violation. Hart's view that a right necessarily requires that the holder must be in a position to elect whether or not to exercise it,[56] does not appear to be correct. It does not seem to be overly straining the language to assert that children, the mentally handicapped or even animals have rights.[57] For example, it is appropriate to speak of the mentally disabled as having the right to have children, or children as having the right not to be physically abused, and such issues are normally discussed in terms of rights without even the hint of incoherency.

---

53 See Bagaric, 1997b, p 374, where I argue that the High Court of Australia has been heavily influenced by the rights movement.

54 Bentham, 1962, p 489; see, also, pp 523–24.

55 A similar definition is advanced by Campbell, T, 1996a, pp 166–67: '... rights simply are rule-protected interests.'

56 Hart, 1955.

57 See, also, Campbell, T, 1996c, p 123; Marshall, 1973, pp 228, 235.

The justification for rights and situations involving clashing rights

The basis of rights – concern and respect?

A much more serious problem which plagues rights theories is that of justifying the existence of rights. While, on its face, Dworkin's theory sounds tenable, if we look just below the surface, we find a conspicuous lack of substance. Sure, it is comforting and agreeable to claim that we are all entitled to concern (since we can all suffer) and respect (since we have the capacity to make intelligent decisions about how to live our lives) and even more comforting that this should be in equal amounts. But ignoring pleasantries for a moment, the question is why, beyond perhaps wishful thinking, are we so entitled? Furthermore, why does this form the core of morality?

Concern and respect are no doubt desirable virtues, and ideally, the more the better, but they would not appear to be any more important and desirable than, say, sympathy, compassion, courtesy, love and honesty. Dworkin contends that the right to equal concern and respect is a fundamental right because it does not conflict with another person having the same right. However, numerous other vague ideals, if attributed to all, such as the 'right to be treated with compassion and honesty', would also not cause conflict, but no reason is given why they are not selected as the basis for all other rights.

More generally, Dworkin provides that 'a man has a moral right ... if for some reason the State would do *wrong* to treat him in a certain way, even though it would be in the general interest to do so' (emphasis added).[58] However, this is merely to swap one piece of rhetoric for another. Wrong: by what standard? Dworkin would do well to attempt to justify the right to equal concern and respect by developing the notions of dignity and equality which supposedly underpin this fundamental right. However, he refuses to take up this challenge. Even though he frankly concedes that dignity is a 'vague'[59] ideal, he provides that he 'does want to defend or elaborate these ideas [the notions of equality and dignity], but only to insist that anyone who claims that citizens have rights must accept ideas *very close* to these' (emphasis added).[60]

Accordingly, when it comes down to establishing the foundation of rights, Dworkin's theory is seriously deficient. He frankly concedes that the existence of rights cannot be demonstrated, and attempts to mitigate the harm from this by merely stating that because a statement cannot be demonstrated to be true does not mean that it is not true.[61] However, while this may be so, the same

---

58 Dworkin, 1977, p 139.

59 *Ibid*, p 198.

60 *Ibid*, p 199. In Dworkin, 1979, pp 113, 127, 136, he outlines what he believes is entailed by the notion of equality, but still does not articulate how and why this could form the basis of morality.

61 Dworkin, 1977, p 81.

reasoning could be used to defend claims about unicorns and witches.[62] 'Philosophers frequently introduce ideas of dignity, respect, and worth at the point at which reasons appear to be lacking, but this is hardly good enough. Fine phrases are the last resort of those who have run out of arguments';[63] which Dworkin (nearly) has.

Dworkin has one more attempt to explain where rights come from and why they exit:

> So if rights make sense at all, then the invasion of a relatively important right must be a very serious matter. It means treating a man as less than a man, or as less worthy of concern than other men. The institution of rights rests on the conviction that this is a grave *injustice*, and that it is *worth paying the incremental cost* in social policy or efficiency to prevent it [emphasis added].[64]

The first point to note is that it is not open for Dworkin simply to assume that it makes sense to speak of (non-consequentialist) rights. Secondly, it is also not playing by the rules for him to resort to the nebulous notion of justice to justify (or buttress) his theory of rights without a meaningful elaboration of this concept. Finally, he gives no indication about the currency he is employing when he asserts that it is worth paying 'the cost' to acknowledge rights. This last point is also fatal to his suggestion regarding when it is permissible to limit rights.

Dworkin and clashing rights

Dworkin states that there are three situations where a right may be limited:

> First, the Government must show that the values protected by the original right are not really at stake in the marginal case, or are at stake in some attenuated form. Second, it might be shown that if the right is defined to include the marginal case, then some competing right, in the strong sense defined earlier, would be abridged. Third, it might be shown that if they were so defined, then the cost to society would not be simply incremental, but would be of a degree far beyond the cost paid to grant the original right, a degree great enough to justify whatever assault on dignity or equality might be involved.[65]

The first of these suggestions is of little guidance, since it effectively deals with situations where rights are, on second glance, not applicable. The second suggestion refers to Dworkin's supposed distinction between rights in a strong sense and in a weak sense. Strong rights are those which are wrong to interfere with and weak rights refer to activities which are not wrong to

---

62   See MacIntyre, 1995, pp 715, 717.
63   Singer, 1986, pp 215, 228.
64   Dworkin, 1977, p 199.
65   *Ibid*, p 200.

pursue.[66] However, even if one ignores the questionable nature of such a distinction,[67] it hardly addresses the issue here, since even on Dworkin's account, rights in the sense of entitlements which place limits on actions of others are all strong rights. The final stipulation is the most far reaching and thus promising, but in the end is devoid of content, since it prescribes a balancing process; however, it does not assign a unit of measurement by which the 'cost' can be measured.

Nozick – the basis for rights and clashing rights

In regard to identifying the content of rights, Nozick's theory is far more precise. As was detailed above, Nozick particularises the rights which he claims we possess. He also has a straightforward answer regarding the problem of conflicting rights. He asserts that, given that rights are negative in character, serving merely as side constraints, requiring others to refrain from certain types of actions, as opposed to requiring agents to perform certain acts, they are absolute and never clash.

However, Nozick suggests nothing which overcomes arguments which have been persuasively advanced against the notion of absolute rights. The absurdity of absolute rights is supported by the extreme lengths some have gone to in order to attempt to justify such a notion. For example, in search of an absolute right it has been stated that 'the right of a mother not to be tortured to death by her son is absolute'.[68] However, even such extreme examples fail. One could hardly begrudge a son torturing his mother to death if this is only way to save the lives of all his other relatives whom the mother was about to kill unjustifiably.

Further, Nozick's theory falls at the first hurdle. It fails to provide any justification for his set of fundamental rights. He asserts that his list of rights permits a person the capacity to shape his or her life in order to have a meaningful life. This, however, ignores the fact that to have anything approaching a meaningful life requires the provision of certain necessities, such as shelter, food and health care; which Nozick denies the right to. The claim that certain rights are supposedly to be found in a state of nature is also dubious. The same could be claimed of any other so called right, such as the right to a sex break. And just because something is natural is not itself morally significant. It is also natural to display jealously and anger, but this hardly

---

66 The example Dworkin gives of a weak right is the right of a captured enemy soldier to attempt to escape, even though we are not wrong to attempt to foil the escape attempt.

67 Weak rights are not accompanied by duties, and it is arguable whether such interests are rights in the conventional sense (see discussion, above, regarding the definition of a right) as opposed to merely being privileges.

68 Gewirth, 1982, p 232.

makes it justifiable to act upon or encourage such impulses. To call a right a natural right is no more compelling than to label it a human right.[69] In this respect, the term 'human' right suggests that species membership alone is adequate to create and safeguard a right. As Benn points out, 'if such rights are human rights, [why] should someone's, [say], being guilty of a crime deny him enjoyment of them? Do people enjoy such rights as men and women, or only as well behaved men and women – *quamdiu se bene gesserint*? Ultimately, rights appear to lack a foundation and an origin. Not surprisingly, even some rights proponents have conceded that rights are 'inherently controversial'.[70]

The other significant defect of Nozick's account is that it is too revisionary. Acceptance of it would require the abandonment of too many established moral principles and duties. The maxim of positive duty (which provides that we must assist others in serious trouble, when assistance would immensely help them at no or little inconvenience to ourselves)[71] would obviously be the first to go. On Nozick's view, morality does not require us to save the baby in the puddle. While the maxim is not set in concrete, we would need far more persuasive reasons than Nozick's theory to retract our commitment to it.

Marmor and clashing rights

Other attempts to deal with the problem of clashing rights fare no better than the above accounts. For example, it has been suggested that rights can be limited or overridden only in order to secure some other more important or pressing right. This has been dubbed the Newtonian conception of the limit of rights, because it operates in a similar way to the Newtonian law of inertia: 'a right will continue to be in force so long as it does not collide with another right which conflicts with it.'[72] Thus, clashes of rights are resolved by securing 'the set of rights that would maximally satisfy the most extensive set of rights for each person, which is compatible with the similar rights of others'.[73] However, the problem with such an approach is that, again, there is no barometer which can be used to measure the respective importance of rights. In discussing the paradox of the right to do something which a person ought not to, Marmor gives the example of the right to get married even where it seems that it is a 'wrong' decision because it will ruin both lives. The Newtonian conception of rights explains this on the basis that the right of personal choice is so paramount that we think that it is more *important* for a person to chose her spouse for herself than to choose correctly. But the question remains: important by what standards? It could be equally argued

---

69 Benn, 1978, pp 59, 62–63.
70 Marmor, 1997, p 17.
71 See Bagaric, 1997c, p 143.
72 Marmor, 1997, pp 1–2, 11.
73 *Ibid*, p 9.

that one has the 'right' to prevent a foredoomed marriage, where the marriage would ruin the lives of the prospective husband and wife, because it is more important that people have, overall, fulfilling and enjoyable lives than be permitted to select their partner.

The Newtonian conception is ultimately rejected by Marmor, on the basis that rights are not limited only when they clash with other rights, but have internal limits imposed well before this on account of the fact that rights impose duties on others and these burdens must be taken into account at the outset when the interests of the potential right holder and others are compared. This consideration not only determines the limits of a right, but also whether it exists at all:

> A's right to x can only be justified, initially, if we think that A's interest in x is important enough to warrant imposing a duty on others, and *only to that extent*. Namely to the extent that the burden involved in the imposition of the duties does not out-weigh the importance of the interest in question.[74]

However, there are two problems with this analysis. First, there is again no standard by which importance is to be evaluated. The tenable argument that the importance of a right is commensurate with its value to the right holder is rejected by Marmor on the grounds that rights benefit not only the right holder, but promote the common or general good. This highlights the second difficulty, which is that in weighing the interests and impositions that Marmor claims are integral to the determination of a right, a utilitarian calculus must be engaged. He denies this on the basis that the 'cost-benefit analysis is not necessarily a quantitative matter; the intrinsic values and relative importance of the interests in question matter too'.[75] However, by failing to elaborate on the nature of these 'intrinsic' values, the theory becomes vacuous.

Illustration of inability of rights theories to resolve
conflicting rights – Siamese twins case

It is not difficult to cite examples which demonstrate the total impotence of rights based theories to resolve moral dilemmas. A recent example is the outcome and reasoning in the case of *A (Children)*[76] – the Jodie and Mary Siamese twins case.[77]

---

74 Marmor, 1997, p 10.

75 *Ibid*, p 13.

76 B1/2000/2969, 22 September 2000: http://www.courtservice.gov.uk/judgments/judg-home.htm (henceforth *A (Children)*). All page numbers refer to the page number of the document printed from this site.

77 Now, what we do actually do, does not justify what ought to be done. Morality is normative, not descriptive in nature: an 'ought' cannot be derived from an 'is'. Still, the above account is telling because the force of the punishing the innocent objection lies in the fact that it supposedly so troubles our moral consciousness that utilitarianism can thereby be dismissed on the basis that the outcome is so horrible that 'there must be a mistake somewhere'. But this loses its force when it is shown that punishing the innocent is in fact no worse than other activities we condone.

In *A (Children)*, the English Court of Appeal was confronted with what it understandably termed the truly agonising dilemma of what ought to be done in the case of conjoined twins: Marie and Jodie.[78] They each had their own brain, heart and lungs and other vital organs and they each had arms and legs. They were joined at the lower abdomen, and could be separated. But the operation would kill the weaker twin, Mary. Her lungs and heart were too deficient to oxygenate and pump blood through her body. Had she been born a singleton, she would not have been viable and resuscitation would have been abandoned. She would have died shortly after her birth. She was alive only because a common artery enabled her sister, who was stronger, to circulate life sustaining oxygenated blood for both of them. Separation would have required the clamping and then the severing of that common artery. Within minutes of doing so Mary would die (and ultimately – following the operation – did so). Yet, if the operation did not take place, both would have died within three to six months, or perhaps a little longer.

The parents refused to consent to the operation. The twins were equal in their eyes and they could not agree to kill one even to save the other. As devout Roman Catholics, they sincerely believed that it is God's will that their children were afflicted as they are and they must be left in God's hands. The doctors believed that they could carry out the operation so as to give Jodie a life which would be in most respects relatively normal.

In the circumstances, the hospital sought a declaration that the operation may be lawfully carried out. Johnson J, in exercise of the inherent jurisdiction of the High Court, granted it on 25 August 2000. The parents applied to the Court of Appeal for leave to appeal against his order. The court, while granting permission to appeal, unanimously dismissed the appeal.

The judgment in *A (Children)* is over 100 pages in length. The justificatory rationale adopted by two of the Lord Justices, Ward and Brooke LJJ, is found in about a dozen words. After considering a plethora of 'relevant' rights claims, including the right to life and the parents right to choose and getting no closer to a solution, the answer was only forthcoming when the Lord Justices eventually got around to looking at the situation from a utilitarian perspective. In the end, they resolved the matter 'by choosing the lesser of the two evils and so finding the least detrimental alternative'.[79]

Of course, it is theoretically possible to try to resolve such dilemmas on the basis of rights theory alone, but this can lead to somewhat curious results. In an attempt to buttress his view that surgery would be in Mary's best interests, Walker LJ stated:

---

78 The following facts are taken from the judgment of Ward LJ, pp 7–8.
79 See Ward LJ, p 42.

That surgery would also be in [the] 'best interests of Mary, since for the twins to remain alive and conjoined in the way they are would be to deprive them of the bodily integrity and human dignity which is the right of each or them'.[80]

To this end, he cited Thomas J in *Auckland Area Health Board v AG*:[81] '... human dignity and personal privacy belong to every person, whether living or dying.'[82]

The conclusion reached by Walker LJ is quite remarkable when one remembers that he is taking about the interests of Mary, whom the operation will kill. Bodily integrity and human dignity sound like fine ideals, and undoubtedly the more the better, but they would not seem to be of much value in the grave. Surely a precondition to the splendour of such virtues is one's existence. The failure to grasp this rather basic point is the sort of perverse logic that stems from reliance on a normative system which is devoid of a logical foundation.

What rights do we have?

Another difficulty with rights based theories is that we are typically left with no guidance concerning the specific rights we have. Dworkin acknowledges the obvious – that 'it is much in dispute ... what particular rights citizens have'[83] – however, he offers surprisingly little to deal with this. For Dworkin, the rights that we have are those which ensure the principle of equal concern and respect is upheld. He states that the central issue is what inequalities are justified, and goes on to state that two rights flow from the abstract right to equal concern and respect. The first is the right to equal treatment; defined as the right to the same distribution of goods or opportunities as anyone else. The second, which he claims is more fundamental then the first, is the right to treatment as an equal, that is, the right to equal concern and respect in how these goods and opportunities are distributed.

However, this fails to advance his position any further. The two more specific rights Dworkin expounds are just as vague as his general principle. Both employ the notion of concern and respect and the formula is even more generalised by resort to the ill defined notion of equality. Such vague aspirations 'dissolve into generalised moral values which cannot function as rights by giving us a relatively objective and politically uncontroversial way of determining entitlements by reference to an authoritative system of norms'.[84]

---

80 Ward LJ, p 98.
81 [1993] 1 NZLR 235, p 245.
82 Ward LJ, p 98.
83 Dworkin, 1977, p 184.
84 Campbell, T, 1988, p 54. Campbell's critique of Dworkin's theory is on pp 45–65.

The vacuousness of rights based theories and their propensity to confuse is no more apparent than in the punishment debate where a 'right to be punished' has been suggested. Morris (in a similar vein to Duff) declares that the right to be punished stems from 'a right to be treated as a person which is a fundamental human right belonging to all human beings by virtue of their being human. It is also a natural, inalienable, and absolute right'.[85] The right to punishment was discussed at length in the previous chapter; however, it is worth mentioning at this point to highlight and reinforce the fuzzy reasoning and fantastic claims that can be made due to the lack of coherency and precision of rights based theories, which simply offer no workable mechanism to distinguish between real and illusory rights.

5.4.3 The instability of the rights thesis – consequences the ultimate consideration

A further flaw in the theories of both Dworkin and Nozick is that by conceding that, in some situations, consequences prevail, their respective theories become unstable. Despite his absolutist tones, Dworkin accepts that it is correct for a government to infringe on a right when it is necessary to protect a more important right, or to ward off 'some great threat to society'.[86] In a like manner, Nozick states that teleological considerations would take over to 'avert moral catastrophe'.[87] But, both fail to state, even loosely, at what point we reach a great threat to society or a moral catastrophe and consequentialist considerations legitimately 'kick in' to guide conduct.

By making this concession, which is necessary to avoid the even less plausible position that rights are absolute, the theories become irrelevant. When consequential considerations are admitted as being relevant, the theories become hybrid and the main theoretical advantage of a deontological theory, the absolute protection given to people against certain intrusions, is forsaken. The problem is heightened because, in both cases, we are given no guidance as to when consequentialist considerations become overriding. Owing to the lack of specificity in this regard, it could be argued that even Dworkin and Nozick accept that punishing the innocent is permissible where the lives of many are at stake. At this point, rights theories collapse: they can neither rely fully on the theoretical justifications of deontological or consequentialist theories.

In summary, the present state of affairs regarding rights based moral theories is still best summarised by Hart:

---

85 Morris, 1971, pp 76, 92.
86 Dworkin, 1977, pp 199–202.
87 Nozick, 1981, p 95.

It cannot be said that we have had ... a sufficiently detailed or adequately articulated theory showing the foundation for such rights and how they are related to other values. Indeed the revived doctrines of basic rights are ... in spite of much brilliance still unconvincing.[88]

The paradox of rights is also noted by Campbell: '... the idea of human rights is at this time so well accepted and internationally utilised that it is difficult to acknowledge just how flimsy are its political foundations.'[89]

5.5 UTILITARIAN JUSTIFICATION FOR RIGHTS

As stated earlier, the core of perhaps the most damaging criticisms of utilitarianism is that it is antagonistic to the concept of rights. It is claimed that utilitarianism does not take seriously the distinction between human beings, because it prioritises net happiness over individual sacrifices, and hence fails to protect certain rights and interests that are so paramount that they are beyond the demands of net happiness.[90] It is not difficult to see the basis for this criticism. Utilitarianism is a maximising principle, the aim being to maximise the net happiness. On the other hand, the notion of rights is individualising, the purpose being to accord each individual certain interests.

Rights do, however, have a place in a utilitarian ethic, and what is more, it is only against this background that rights can be explained and their source justified. Utilitarianism provides a sounder foundation for rights than any other competing theory. For the utilitarian, the answer to why rights exist is simple: recognition of them best promotes general utility.[91] Their origin accordingly lies in the pursuit of happiness. Their content is discovered through empirical observations regarding the patterns of behaviour which best advance the utilitarian cause. The long association of utilitarianism and rights appears to have been forgotten by most. However, over a century ago it was Mill who proclaimed the right of free speech, on the basis that truth is important to the attainment of general happiness and this is best discovered by its competition with falsehood.[92]

Difficulties in performing the utilitarian calculus regarding each decision make it desirable that we ascribe certain rights and interests to people, which evidence shows tend to maximise happiness – even more happiness than if we

---

88 Hart, 1983, p 195.

89 Campbell, T, 1996a, p 164.

90 Rawls, 1971.

91 According to Mill, 'to have a right is ... to have something which society ought to defend ... [if asked why] ... I can give no other reason than general utility': Mill, 1986, pp 251, 309.

92 *Ibid*, pp 141–83.

made all of our decisions without such guidelines.[93] Rights save time and energy by serving as shortcuts to assist us in attaining desirable consequences. By labelling certain interests as rights, we are spared the tedious task of establishing the importance of a particular interest as a first premise in practical arguments.[94] There are also other reasons why performing the utilitarian calculus on each occasion may be counter-productive to the ultimate aim. Our capacity to gather and process information and our foresight are restricted by a large number of factors, including lack of time, indifference to the matter at hand, defects in reasoning, and so on. We are quite often not in a good position to assess all the possible alternatives and to determine the likely impact upon general happiness stemming from each alternative. Our ability to make the correct decision will be greatly assisted if we can narrow down the range of relevant factors in light of predetermined guidelines. This is precisely the practice which is employed by our legal system.

The aim of the system is to attain justice. In order to achieve this, judges do not pursue this result by whatever means they believe appropriate to the case at hand. They are bound by procedural guidelines, such as the adversarial system and rules of evidence, and substantive principles, such as the presumption of innocence and the equitable notion of unconscionability, which represent processes that experience has shown, if followed, will generally produce the just result at the end of the day.[95] Similarly, in the case of utilitarianism. History has shown that certain patterns of conduct and norms of behaviour, if observed, are most conducive to promoting happiness. These observations are given expression in the form of rights which can be asserted in the absence of evidence why adherence to them in the particular case would not maximise net happiness.

Thus, utilitarianism is well able to explain the existence and importance of rights. It is just that rights do not have a life of their own (they are derivative, not foundational), as is the case with deontological theories. Owing to the derivative character of utilitarian rights, they do not carry the same degree of absolutism, or 'must be doneness', as those based on deontological theories. However, this is no criticism of utilitarianism, rather it is a strength since, as was discussed earlier, it is farcical to claim that rights are absolute.

Another advantage of utilitarianism is that only it provides a mechanism for ranking rights and other interests. In event of clash, the victor is the right which will generate the most happiness. The interests which are normally targeted by criminal sanctions, such as freedom, reputation and property

---

93 However, rights are never decisive and must be disregarded where they would not cause net happiness (otherwise this would be to go down the rule utilitarianism track).

94 See, also, Raz, 1986, p 191.

95 This is not dissimilar to Rawls' concept of pure procedural justice: Rawls, 1971, pp 83–92.

ownership, are generally very high on most people's scale of things that make them happy, thus there are strong utilitarian reasons for not encroaching on them. Significant counter-benefits (such as deterrence and incapacitation, and so on) must be produced to justify the violation of such interests. This is almost infinitely more so where a person is not guilty of an offence, given the potential violation of other interests which weigh heavily on the happiness register of most, such as the need for transparency and accountability in the legal system. Thus, there is not only a place, but a high ranking for the right not to be punished without a prior determination of guilt in the utilitarian calculus. It is rare that happiness will be maximised by violating this right. This underpinning and approach to the problem of punishing the innocent provides the greatest degree of protection against such a practice.

5.6 UTILITARIANISM AND THE SEPARATENESS OF PERSONS

This type of reasoning extends to fend off not only problems associated with rights, but also to counter more generally attacks which are based on the claim that utilitarianism does not accommodate the separateness of persons. Take, for instance, Williams' classic Jim and Pedro example, which aims to show that utilitarianism fails to accord sufficient weight to our integrity. Jim is a botanist on an expedition in a small South American town where the ruthless government regards him as an honoured visitor from another land. He goes into town and sees 20 Indians tied up. Pedro, the captain in charge, explains that the Indians are a random group of inhabitants who, after recent protests against the government, are about to be executed to deter others from protesting. Since Jim is an honoured guest, Pedro offers him the 'privilege' of killing one of the Indians himself. If he accepts, as a special mark of the occasion, the other Indians will be spared. If he refuses, they will all be killed. Jim realises it is impossible to take the guns and kill Pedro and the large number of other soldiers. The Indians and other soldiers understand the situation, and the Indians are begging for him to take up the offer.[96]

Williams argues that if Jim was a utilitarian, he would be required to kill the Indian. Williams' quarrel is not necessarily with the result that utilitarianism commits one to (in fact he has subsequently stated that he, too, would shoot the Indian), but with the reasoning process employed by the utilitarian to resolve the dilemma, and consequently the fact that one can be certain that killing the Indian is indeed the right choice. Williams contends that utilitarianism cuts out considerations which most would think integral to such cases, such as the idea that each of us is specially responsible for what he

---

96   Williams, B, 1973, p 99.

or she does, rather than what others do. This makes integrity unintelligible, because it fails to appreciate the relationship between a man and his projects. Utilitarianism fails to accept that 'among the things that make people happy is not only making other people happy, but being taken up or involved in a vast range of projects ... [such as being] committed to a person, a cause, an institution, a career, one's own genius, or the pursuit of danger'.[97]

However, this fails to recognise the important role that the pursuit of projects and commitments and their accomplishment have in promoting happiness. True it is that, like rights, in the utilitarian scheme of things projects have no intrinsic or absolute value. But, surely this must be correct. An aim or pursuit is not justified simply because one describes it as a project. Hitler had a project; but so what.

Williams accepts that the general aim of maximising happiness does not require the direct pursuit of this goal at every point along the way and that people with projects are perhaps happier than those without, and accordingly that utilitarianism can ascribe some weight to projects. However, he argues that this is not an adequate response, because ultimately our ability to pursue our projects is subject to the innumerable projects of others which our actions may affect:

> The utilitarian response is to neglect the extent to which [one's] actions and his [or her] decisions have to be seen as the actions and decisions which flow from the projects and attitudes with which he [or she] is most closely identified. It is thus, in the most literal sense, an attack on his integrity.[98]

Thus, the heart of Williams' objection is that generally, we should only be responsible for the consequences we have orchestrated, and that we cannot be expected to drop or comprise projects which may be so strongly held to be defining of our lives simply because the utilitarian sum may happen to come down against us.

But, utilitarianism does give considerable weight to such considerations, even more than Williams is prepared to accept. The pursuit of projects is integral to the attainment of personal happiness.[99] And, we cannot at every single point be expected to save the world: we simply do not know how; and an attempt to do so would be self-defeating. But one thing we do know is what works for each of us and, accordingly, the collective pursuit of our individualist aims is at most points likely to be the best method of maximising happiness. This is one reason that utilitarianism attaches an enormous amount of weight to personal liberty. As was declared by Mill:

> The sole end for which mankind are warranted, individually or collectively, in interfering with the liberty of action of any of their number, is self-protection.

---

97 Williams, B, 1973, p 112.
98 *Ibid*, pp 116–17.
99 See Chapter 7, regarding the results of the 'happiness' study by Professor Argyle.

The only purpose for which power can be rightfully exercised over any member of a civilised community, against his will, is to prevent harm to others. His own good, either physical or moral, is not a sufficient warrant.[100]

Liberty, like all other virtues, is not absolute and must be forsaken on rare occasions: one being where the maxim of positive duty applies. And it is for this reason that Jim ought to shoot. He can demonstrably assist a large number of others by positively interjecting.

Another supposed utilitarian failing that Williams claims is exposed by the Jim and Pedro example is the assuredness and conclusivity that it deals with complex moral dilemmas. Williams claims that resolution of the Jim and Pedro dilemma requires consideration of several difficult issues, including the distinction between 'my killing someone, and its coming about because of what I do that someone else kills them' and how much it matters that the people at risk are actual as opposed to future or elsewhere. On the contrary, the fact that utilitarianism provides definite answers to difficult moral situations is an enormous advantage of the theory; not a weakness. It is not to the point that utilitarianism 'cuts out a kind of consideration which for some others makes a difference to what they feel about such [a case]'.[101] Rather, utilitarianism is the only theory which cuts through the verbiage and distractions to provide a coherent answer to complex moral dilemmas.

5.7 THE DECISIVENESS OF CONSEQUENCES

As we have seen, ultimately all moral theories at some point bow to the weight of consequences. Logically, it must follow that, at the bottom, this is what matters most. This being the case, it is nonsensical to allow other considerations to have a primary role in our moral reasoning.

Soccer, rights and consequences

In this respect, an analogy may again be drawn with soccer. In evaluating how well a soccer team plays, many different considerations are relevant: how much speed and endurance the players have; their skill in passing the ball; their ability to cross the ball; their caginess in playing the offside rule; their natural brilliance and flair; their ability to withstand pressure (including penalty shoot outs); their defensive, offensive and midfield proficiency; the tactical prowess of the coach; and so on. While all of these considerations are

---

100 Mill, 1986, p 135. The courts, too, have heavily endorsed the central role of personal liberty; see, eg, Lord Mustill in his dissenting judgment in *Brown* [1993] 2 WLR 556, p 600.

101 Williams, B, 1973, p 112.

important in determining how good any team is, in the end, in respect to any particular match, the only thing that matters is the scoreboard. Maximum points can be gained in relation to all the relevant indicia that go to making a team a good one and indeed to that team playing a good game, but ultimately, if the side fails to put the ball in the net more times than its opponent, this comes to naught. All that really matters is the scoreboard outcome at the end of the game. Every player and passionate fan would gladly prefer to win a game despite faring poorly on the indicia that are generally used to evaluate a team, rather than playing a 'perfect' match and having an unlucky loss. For example, in the 1990 World Cup, Brazil (who were rated clearly as the best side in the world) totally dominated Argentina in general play, with almost the total game being played in its attacking half. Brazil played superbly, and as a result had countless scoring opportunities, and on several occasions hit the cross bar. Argentina were totally outplayed, however, they managed to convert their single counter-attack into an unlikely goal to win the match. Despite Brazil's on field dominance, virtually the whole nation went into mourning after the match, while the Argentines celebrated long and hard.

Everyone knew that Brazil was the better side; they should have won and thoroughly deserved to do so. But, in the end, all that mattered was the outcome. So, too, with morality: interests such as rights and integrity are all important barometers regarding the appropriateness of our moral judgments, but ultimately, they must make way for the ultimate gauge – the consequences of our actions.

While on soccer, it also emphasises why utilitarianism does not require that at every point, we should seek to maximise happiness. A team, no matter how talented, would be unlikely to win a single match if each player shot at goal on every occasion he or she had control of the ball.

Strangely, nearly all moral theories which ostensibly place a premium on virtues other than consequences accept that at some point, these other virtues must be subordinated to consequential considerations; however, they persist in denying that consequences are ultimately the dominant moral consideration. This is probably because of a belief that consequences are somewhat fluky and have little connection with processes and principles observed along the way. However, this ignores that nearly always the side with the best defence, midfield, attack, and with the most skilful players, and so on will score more goals. Thus, we are still justified in attaching considerable weight to matters such as skill, speed and technical proficiency. And, most importantly, the basis for according weight to such matters is evident. So, too, a utilitarian theory of morality provides a secure foundation for interests such as integrity and rights, including, of course, the right not to be punished unless one is guilty of an offence.

5.8 CONCLUSION

The main theoretical criticisms of a utilitarian theory of punishment are unconvincing. Sure, the utilitarian is committed to punishing the innocent in rare circumstances. However, on a post-philosophical consideration of this, one's conscience is not so unduly disturbed that it must follow that the underlying theory must be erroneous. We are prepared in other contexts to make decisions which even more seriously violate the interests of individuals for the good of the whole. Further, retributivists, too, must accept that any system of punishment will invariably result in some innocent people being punished. The response that this is permissible because it is unintended, though foreseen, is wanting because there is no principled basis for a morally relevant distinction between acts which are intended and those which are foreseen.

The criticism which underlies most attacks on utilitarianism is that it fails to pay sufficient weight to individual rights and interests, and thereby permits all types of offensive practices. This has led to a proliferation in, and widespread support for, rights based moral theories. Despite their promise, such theories lack substance. Ironically, only utilitarianism adequately justifies the notion of rights and provides coherent answers to difficulties confronted by rights based theories.

Accordingly, the main theoretical attacks on a utilitarian system of punishment are surmountable. The time is now right to reassess the empirical data regarding the efficacy of punishment to attain the utilitarian based sentencing objectives, such as deterrence and rehabilitation. If this is promising, utilitarianism will form the basis of a coherent and persuasive theory of punishment which could be used to pave the way for future sentencing practices and guidelines.

CHAPTER 6

INCAPACITATION, DETERRENCE AND REHABILITATION: FLAWED IDEALS OR APPROPRIATE SENTENCING GOALS?

6.1 INTRODUCTION

This chapter focuses on the damaging pragmatic criticisms of the utilitarian theory of punishment. The broadest criticism is that the utilitarian objectives of punishment are not achievable, hence the utilitarian theory should be rejected.

Utilitarian objectives of punishment: incapacitation, rehabilitation and deterrence – pillars of sentencing systems

As was alluded to in Chapter 5, there are several good consequences that utilitarians traditionally claim stem from punishment. In short, they are incapacitation, deterrence, and rehabilitation. This chapter considers whether a system of criminal punishment can achieve these ideals. This will primarily involve a consideration of the relevant empirical evidence, although some of the more damaging theoretical criticisms that have been made against general deterrence and rehabilitation are also discussed.

In terms of the scope and relevance of this chapter, it should be noted that although incapacitation, deterrence and rehabilitation have a utilitarian foundation, they are still pivotal considerations in sentencing law and practice. Hence, the matters raised in this discussion extend beyond the philosophical domain to the more concrete issue of whether the sentencing system should continue to pursue the objectives of incapacitation, deterrence and rehabilitation – irrespective of which theory of punishment is adopted.

Summary

This chapter involves a consideration of a large amount of empirical data so, at this point, a summary of the findings may be helpful. It is suggested that incapacitation should be discarded as a sentencing objective owing to our inability to distinguish with any degree of confidence offenders who will re-offend from those who will not. Rehabilitation, too, is a misguided sentencing objective. There is no firm evidence that it works. Even more fundamentally, it is an inappropriate sentencing objective due to the inherent contradiction between punishing a person while simultaneously attempting to promote his or her internal reform. The only demonstrable benefit of punishment is that it deters a great many people from committing offences. This single verifiable good is sufficient to provide a utilitarian justification for the practice.

Although there does not seem to be a direct correlation between heavier penalties and crime, it is certain that there is a connection between some penalty and the crime rate. The most notable practical implication from this analysis is that prison should be used far more sparingly; and when it is, the length of sentences should generally be reduced. In this chapter, the utilitarian theory of punishment which I advance diverges significantly from traditional utilitarian thinking in the area. Most of the traditional utilitarian objectives of punishment are discarded, leaving (absolute) general deterrence as the sole good consequence of punishment.

6.2 INCAPACITATION

6.2.1 Definition and overview

The goal of incapacitation shall be considered first, since it appears to be the most readily attainable. Incapacitation involves rendering an offender incapable of committing further offences. Apart from capital punishment, no sanction can ever hope to prevent offenders from re-offending totally. All sanctions involving some degree of supervision or interference with the freedom of the offender, such as probation, licence cancellation orders and community work orders limit, to at least some extent (if merely by reducing the hours left in the day), the opportunity for further offending. Prison is the sentencing option that most effectively prevents re-offending, and this discussion focuses on imprisonment as the paradigm incapacitative sanction. However, even imprisonment does not guarantee success. While in prison, offenders have the opportunity to damage property and assault other inmates and guards, and so on. The offending behaviour is at least restricted (geographically) to the confines of the prison and the likelihood of offences being committed is significantly reduced by the high level of scrutiny. Thus, while we can never be sure that punishment will totally prevent criminal behaviour, it is clear that the goal of rendering offenders incapable of re-offending is largely achievable.

The relevance of incapacitation to sentencing law and practice

Most sentencing statutes in Australia refer to incapacitation as an objective of sentencing.[1] Incapacitation is particularly relevant to sentencing where there

---

1   Eg, Sentencing Act 1991 (Vic), s 5(1)(e); Penalties and Sentences Act 1992 (Qld), s 9(1)(e); Criminal Law (Sentencing) Act (SA) 1988, s 10(i); Sentencing Act 1995 (NT), s 5(1)(e); Sentencing Act 1997 (Tas), s 3(b), (which stipulates community protection as the main purpose of sentencing). The term normally used is protection of the community, rather than incapacitation, but since the other goals of sentencing, such as denunciation, deterrence, rehabilitation and just punishment (which it is often said are merely means to achieve community protection) are normally also expressly mentioned, in this context community protection must mean incapacitation.

is a significant (real or perceived) risk of recidivism.[2] In the US, while incapacitation is generally not expressly invoked as a discrete sentencing objective, it is the cornerstone and primary rationale underlying the widespread mandatory sentencing regimes that have produced an explosion in the prison population.[3] For the first three-quarters of this century, the US imprisoned about 110 persons per 100,000 of population; now the rate is approximately 600 per 100,000.[4] This represents an increase of over 500% over the past two decades, and in raw figures there are now approximately two million people in US prisons. In Australia, during the 10 year period from 1988 to 1998, the number of prisoners grew from about 12,000 to 20,000 – a somewhat more 'modest' increase of 80%. In terms of prisoners per 100,000 of population, in March 1999, the Australia-wide figure was 142, although there were significant disparities across the country. For example, the rate in Victoria was 79 per 100,000, while the Northern Territory was reaching figures akin to the US with a rate of 476 per 100,000.[5]

A similar, though less drastic trend is emerging in the UK. Incapacitation is the rationale most evident on the face of the Criminal Justice Act 1991 (UK).[6] This was complemented by a 'Prison Works' policy in the mid-1990s, which was introduced by the former Home Secretary, Michael Howard.[7] In the 15 year period from 1980 to 1995, the increase in the prison population was about 20% – from 42,000 to just over 50,000.[8] This figure rose sharply in the mid 1990s. By April 1997, the prison population in England and Wales passed 60,000, equating to a detention rate of 116 per 100,000.[9]

At the outset it should be noted that utilitarians can place only limited reliance on incapacitation in order to justify punishment. Incapacitation cannot serve as a general justifying aim of punishment or sentencing, given the small number of sanctions which effectively render offenders incapable of committing offences. However, it may yet be possible for utilitarians to rely on incapacitation to support a system of punishment.

---

2   *Brewster* (1980) 2 Cr App R(S) 191, p 192.

3   Zimring and Hawkins, 1995, p 3, go further and claim that incapacitation is the 'principal justification for imprisonment in American criminal justice'.

4   Blumstein, 1998, p 129.

5   All the figures relating to the prison population rate in Australia are at: Australian Bureau of Statistics, *Australia Now: Crime and Justice – Prisoners in Australia* http://www.abs.gov.au.

6   Criminal Justice Act 1991 (UK), ss 1 and 2. This has now been consolidated as the Powers of Criminal Courts (Sentencing) Act 2000 (UK), ss 79 and 80.

7   The prison works theme underpinned some aspects of the White Paper, *Protecting the Public*, Cm 3190, 1996. The figures used by Michael Howard in an attempt to justify his policy have been heavily criticised: see, eg, Association of Chief Officers of Probation, *Probation Works Better than Prison*: http://www.penlex.org.uk/pages/pbworks.html.

8   Ashworth, 1995, p 216.

9   http://www.penlex.org.uk/pages/prteurop.html.

6.2.2 Community protection

Given that confining offenders prevents them from causing further harm in the community, it may seem that enough has already been said to invoke incapacitation as a means of increasing happiness. As Bentham noted, *'for a body to act in a place* it must be there'. When imprisoned 'for a given time: he will neither pick a pocket, nor break into a house, nor present a pistol to a passenger ... within that time'. While this may be so, the efficacy of incapacitation is not directly related to the height of the prison wall. It is necessary to look at not only the immediate consequences, but also the indirect and distant consequences of a practice when assessing its impact on overall happiness.

From this perspective, the picture is more complex and less promising. It may well be that incapacitation is pointless because the offenders who are being imprisoned would not have re-offended in any event. There is also the danger that incapacitation may lead to more crime due to the possible brutalising experience of jail; making it more likely for offenders to commit serious offences when they are released. Such an attitude is epitomised by the sentiments expressed in the White Paper which formed the basis of the Criminal Justice Act 1991 (UK): '... imprisonment provides many opportunities to learn criminal skills from other inmates.'[10]

This draws to the surface the real appeal of incapacitation as a sentencing goal: its capacity to protect the community. That community protection is the ideal underpinning the objective of incapacitation is also evident from the fact that when the link between incapacitation and community protection is questioned, the impulse to incarcerate offenders begins to wane. Whether incapacitation is a higher or lower order utilitarian goal of punishment is more than simply a matter of semantics. It has important practical considerations when assessing the efficacy of punishment to attain utilitarian ideals. Viewing incapacitation as a means of protecting the community makes clear the underlying assumptions regarding the goal of incapacitation and thwarts the argument that simply because certain sentences render offenders incapable of committing crime, this increases community safety and thereby happiness.

The primacy of community protection as a goal of sentencing was noted by Brennan J in *Channon*:

> The *necessary and ultimate justification for criminal sanctions is the protection of society* from conduct which the law proscribes. ... Criminal sanctions are purposive, and they are not inflicted judicially *except for the purpose of protecting society*; nor to an extent beyond what is necessary to achieve that purpose.[11]

---

10 Great Britain, 1990, para 3.2.
11 (1978) 20 ALR 1, p 5.

It follows that in assessing the efficacy of incapacitation as an objective of sentencing, the ability of sanctions to render offenders incapable of re-offending is a necessary, but not sufficient requirement. Whether the ultimate objective of community protection can be achieved through incapacitation, as has been alluded to, depends on two main variables. The first is the likelihood that an offender would have offended during the term of imprisonment if he or she was in the community. Then there is the possible corrupting effect of prison, to the extent that it increases the propensity of prisoners to commit offences when released. If offenders are more prone to commit offences when they come out of prison than before they went in, this could offset any good arising from the prevention of offences during the term of imprisonment.

The corrupting effect of prison

The evidence concerning the possible corrupting effect of prison is, perhaps somewhat surprisingly, encouraging. Although, anecdotally, it seems plausible to suggest that imprisonment provides an opportunity to learn more criminal skills, there is no evidence that offenders who have been incarcerated have a higher rate of recidivism. About 20 years ago, the Report of the US Panel of National Research Council concluded that 'there are no statistically significant differences between the subsequent recidivism of offenders, regardless of the form of "treatment"'.[12] Today, there is still no firmer data on whether prison increases the crime rate by 'facilitating the spread of criminal know-how'.[13]

Identification of offenders likely to re-offend

Before considering the ability of authorities to identify likely recidivists, it should be noted that broadly two different types of people can (and have been) the target of incapacitative sanctions. The most common are offenders in the proper sense: those who have already been convicted of offences and who, it is suspected, may re-offend. In this context, the effect of endorsing incapacitation as a sentencing rationale is normally to extend the length of the prison sentence for a longer period than is commensurate with the seriousness of the immediate offence. The other group are those who have not committed an offence (or who have committed an offence, but have served their period of punishment), but are nevertheless suspected of being 'dangerous'. Dangerous offenders raise peculiar moral problems, which are discussed in Chapter 8. The present focus is on 'offenders' in the proper sense.

12 Blumstein *et al*, 1978, p 66.
13 Ashworth, 1995, p 224.

False positives

As is discussed in Chapter 8, the evidence suggests that we cannot distinguish with any meaningful degree of confidence those offenders that will re-offend from those that will not. This is so, irrespective of whether we use psychological predictive techniques or those which draw on more supposed concrete risk factors such as employment history and the age at which a person first started offending.[14]

That a person has previously committed a serious offence is a particularly poor guide to identifying future serious offenders. A recent study tracked the offending behaviour of 613 offenders released from prison in New Zealand for a two and a half year period. The study revealed that those who would be classified as serious offenders[15] were no more likely to receive a further conviction within two and a half years after release than ordinary offenders and were, in fact, less likely to be imprisoned within that time.[16] It was also found that of all serious offences committed by the entire sample group, the vast majority were committed by offenders who were imprisoned for non-serious (or ordinary) offences. In total, only 30 of the sample of 613 offenders committed a serious offence within the follow up period. And, it was noted that there is very little hope of achieving crime control through altering the definition of a serious offence.

The most recent extensive review of incapacitation research notes that current predictive techniques 'tend to invite overestimation of the amount of incapacitation to be expected from marginal increments of imprisonment'.[17] The ability to predict which offenders are likely to re-offend is so poor that it has been estimated that the increase in crime rate if prison use was reduced or abolished could be as low as 5%.[18]

General incapacitation

So much, then, for predictive techniques and the goal of special or selective incapacitation. Incapacitation can also be pursued in a far cruder fashion. This involves imprisoning large numbers of offenders simply on the basis that they have committed a criminal offence, which need not be particularly serious; irrespective of their perceived likelihood of re-offending. This is termed

---

14 Greenwood, 1982, claimed that it was possible to identify high risk robbers and burglars by identifying several supposed risk factors. However, it seems that the technique used was flawed: see Blumstein, Cohen and Visher, 1986.

15 On the basis of the definition in the Criminal Justice Act 1985 (NZ), s 2. This essentially relates to crimes of serious violence, such as manslaughter, wounding and robbery.

16 See Brown, M, 1998, p 713.

17 Zimring and Hawkins, 1995, p 86.

18 Cohen, 1978, p 209.

general (or collective) incapacitation. Little or no effort is made to predict future offending patterns, whether on the basis of previous criminal history or other considerations. The most obvious justification for this type of approach is the belief that we ought to get tougher on crime and punish criminals more severely. This backward looking rationale obviously has retributive overtones. However, if one adopts the theory that if you fire off enough shots, you are bound to make at least a few hits, then general incapacitation may also have a plausible utilitarian foundation.

A recent natural experiment in California provides us with the best evidence regarding the efficacy of general incapacitation. Following the introduction of tougher sentencing laws, the prison population in California in the 10 year period from 1980 to 1990 quadrupled, representing an increase of 120,000 prisoners; such an increase being 'without precedent in the statistical record of imprisonment in the Western World'.[19] Zimring and Hawkins compared California's movements in crime rates (which were downward) and incarceration levels between 1980 and 1990 with those of 16 other American States that contain metropolitan areas with populations in excess of 350,000. This was done in order to control temporal trends in California that are not connected to changes in incarceration policy. The data failed to show a general causal connection between an increased use of incarceration and a reduction in crime, and in particular, there was no such connection in California. The 'correlation between variations in incarceration and in aggregate crime is −0.09, a minute (and statistically insignificant) negative correlation'.[20]

Three strikes laws and crime rate

This result did not, however, dampen the pursuit of the incapacitative ideal. In the mid-1990s, California embarked on a three strikes sentencing policy (which has now swept much of the US),[21] which imposes mandatory long jail terms on repeat offenders and has now resulted in the incarceration of even greater numbers of offenders. In the most extensive research to date on the effects of such laws, Stolzenberg and d'Alessio analysed the impact of California's three strike laws in the 10 largest cities in the State. California was chosen as an ideal location because it was one of the first places to implement mandatory three strike laws (in March 1994); a large number of people have

---

19 Zimring and Hawkins, 1995, p 104.

20 *Ibid*, p 107.

21 Three strikes laws are now in more than 20 different States – they were first introduced in Washington in 1993. For a discussion of these laws see Austin *et al*, 2000, pp 134–42. The Californian laws are discussed in greater detail in Chapter 10. The UK has also recently introduced mandatory penalties; see Crime (Sentences) Act 1997, ss 2–4 (now consolidated as the Powers of Criminal Courts (Sentencing) Act 2000, ss 109–11). This is discussed in greater detail in Chapter 10.

been charged under the law (over 3,000); and it has one of the toughest laws in the US. In California, an accused with one prior serious or violent felony conviction[22] must be sentenced to double the term they would have received for the instant offence. Offenders with two or more such convictions must be sentenced to life imprisonment, with the minimum term being the greater of: 25 years; three times the term otherwise provided for the instant offence; or the term applicable for the instant offence plus appropriate enhancements. The current offence does not have to be for a serious and violent felony – any felony will do. It was anticipated that these laws, by effectively removing career criminals from society, would result in a significant reduction in crime. For example, the 1994 RAND study predicted that serious crime in California would be reduced by 28%, reaching a peak reduction of 400,000 crimes in 2000.[23] However, the results of the study showed that California's three strikes law had no observable influence on the serious crime rate and 'did not achieve its objective of reducing crime, through either deterrence or incapacitation'.[24] Only once city (Anaheim) experienced a substantial reduction in the rate of serious crime. This was regarded as possibly being an aberrant finding.

Other factors relating to incapacitation

In terms of the general effectiveness of incapacitation, the Report of the Victorian Sentencing Committee noted that there are two competing views. Proponents of incapacitation argue that there are a finite number of potential criminals and that the level of crime can simply be reduced by lowering the number of criminals in circulation at any given time. Critics argue that there is a natural equilibrium in the rate of crime: there are more potential criminals at any point in time than there are opportunities to act; thus, if one criminal is removed from circulation, another simply bobs up to take his or her place.[25] The evidence favours the natural equilibrium view. As the Victorian Sentencing Committee noted, in countries which incarcerate a high rate of offenders, there is no decline in criminality. This is precisely what occurred following the enactment of harsh mandatory sentencing laws aimed at drug crimes in the US:

> There is no evidence that harsh drug law enforcement policies have been at all successful. Anyone who is removed from the street is likely to be replaced by

---

22 There are 28 different 'serious' felonies (including burglary) and 17 'violent' felonies (including robbery in an inhabited house). For further discussion, see Owens, 1995, p 891.

23 It was estimated that most of the drops would be in burglary and assault: Greenwood *et al*, 1994.

24 Stolzenberg and d'Alessio, 1997, p 467.

25 Victorian Sentencing Committee, 1988, p 99.

someone drawn from the inevitable queue of replacement dealers ready to join the industry. It may take some time for recruitment and training, but experience shows that replacement is easy and rapid.[26]

6.2.3 The problem of persistent minor offenders

If one focuses solely on the number (as opposed to the type) of previous convictions, there is a far greater ability to identify future offenders. Studies in the UK have shown that offenders with five or more previous convictions have an 87% chance of being convicted of another offence within six years.[27] However, high rates of recidivism relate mainly to minor offenders.[28] Similar findings have been reported in Australia. According to the Australian Institute of Criminology, approximately two-thirds of sentenced offenders received into prison have already served a sentence in prison.[29] The results confirmed that previous detention is not a strong indicator regarding future propensity to commit serious offences. About half of those convicted of serious offences had not previously served a prison term. However, about 90% of those sent to prison for 'other good order' offences and almost 80% of those sent to prison for 'justice/security offences' (mainly breaches of court orders) were serving a repeat term.

The problem then remains as to what ought to be done with the large number of persistent minor offenders whom we are relatively confident will re-offend. One approach is to impose increasingly longer periods of imprisonment for each offence.[30] In the 1975 case of *Clarke*, Lawton LJ strongly disapproved of the notion of progressively more severe sanctions, and in the course of varying an 18 month prison sentence to a two pound fine for damaging a flower pot, stated that the criminal justice system should not be used as 'dustbins for the difficult'.[31] The Australian courts, however, have not always adopted such an approach.

Slicar J in *Bernes*, quoting Fox and Freiberg, noted that:

> In the absence of statutory directions to the contrary, there is no principle of sentencing that demands that increasingly more severe sanctions be administered to persons who persist in their criminality. A person who serves a sentence for a crime is regarded as having paid the penalty in full and as one

---

26 Blumstein, A, 'Prisons', in Wilson JQ and Petersilia, J (eds), *Crime*, 1994, San Francisco: ICS, cited in Tonry, 1996, p 141.

27 Philpotts and Lancucki, 1979, p 16.

28 See Ashworth, 1995, pp 154, 166.

29 'Prison sentences in Australia' (September 1989) 20 Trends and Issues in Crime and Criminal Justice, Australian Institute of Criminology, Canberra, 1989, p 5.

30 See Ashworth, 1995, pp 153–54, and the discussion in Chapter 10 below.

31 (1975) 61 Cr App R 320, p 323.

who ought not suffer again for the offence by having a sentence for a later crime increased because of the earlier offending.[32]

However, the court stated that this proposition:

... might be unexceptional but its implications should not be simplistically extended. The character, response to previous sanction and general attitude towards compliance with the law of a recidivist preclude lenient sentences, since those factors act as predicators of future conduct and reaction.[33]

The court then approved of a the passage in *Hindle* that stated 'a court can do little more than treat a person of this nature as a public nuisance and remove him from circulation so that he ceases to prey upon his fellow citizens as long as is reasonably possible'.[34] After reviewing data from the Australian Institute of Criminology,[35] it observed that 'there does seem to be in Australia a tendency to increase the sentences of recidivists and major offenders accompanied by less frequent use of short sentences';[36] and went on to endorse incapacitation as a rationale for sentencing.

Prioritising the goal of incapacitation for minor persistent offenders, however, seems misguided. Certainly, we can predict with a high degree of confidence that such offenders will continue to cause a nuisance to the community. Detaining them for a period significantly longer than is commensurate with the seriousness of the offence violates the principle of proportionality. This is not an insurmountable obstacle for the utilitarian, since (like all principles) proportionality is not sacrosanct, but what is telling from the utilitarian perspective is that the practice of imprisoning offenders for minor offences for significant periods is self-defeating. The cost of imposing progressively more severe penalties for minor serious offenders is likely to outweigh the security benefit to the community – it is illogical for society to spend $1,000 to punish a wrong which it believes is worth $500.[37] However, this is the path which the unrestrained pursuit of incapacitation leads to. The RAND Organisation in the US estimated that the cost of enforcing the Californian three strikes laws will be $5.5 bn annually, and by 2002, the corrections budget will double from 9% to 18% of the overall State budget. In order to fund this (assuming no increase in tax) it is estimated that

---

32 (1998) unreported, Tasmanian Court of Criminal Appeal, 2 April, p 3. The passage stems from *O'Donnell v Perkins* [1908] VLR 537.

33 *Ibid.*

34 *Hindle* (1981) unreported, Victorian Supreme Court, 3 April, referred to by Fox and Freiberg, 1999, p 271.

35 Which showed that on average, offenders who have previously served a term in prison under sentence will serve an average of two weeks longer than those who have not previously served a sentence in prison, despite the fact that first timers are just as likely to be imprisoned for serious offences.

36 *Bernes* (1998) unreported, Tasmanian Court of Criminal Appeal, 2 April.

37 See Bagaric, 1998, p 270.

spending in areas such as higher education, workplace safety and pollution control will need to drop by over 40%.[38] Even if one ignores the economic cost, in light of the limited protective measures that prison seems to provide, the unhappiness caused to the offender may of its own outweigh the security benefits to the community.

6.2.4 Incapacitation and sense of safety

There is, however, yet another good consequence of incapacitation: the feel safe factor. It would seem that rendering known offenders incapable of re-offending increases the community's sense of safety and security. There is obviously no empirical data on exactly how much easier people sleep due to the knowledge that another offender has been locked away, but even if this sense of relief is exaggerated, it cannot be ignored. Despite this, very little weight should be attributed to this perception of security. Speculative and remote consequences always carry less weight on the utilitarian scales and this is even more so where they stem from false information. If imprisoning fewer offenders leads to a significant reduction in the sense of community safety, the best solution would be to increase community awareness about the real risks associated with convicted serious offenders re-offending. The risk of being a victim of crime is greatly exaggerated in the minds of most people: '... crime is not random. It is patterned. The way that people become offenders is patterned, and the way that people become victims is patterned.'[39] Accordingly, there would seem to be much merit in the view that the best way to deal with the perception of rising crime may be to simply advise the community to turn off the television.[40]

6.2.5 Summary

Incapacitation aims to protect the community. While confining individuals prevents them from committing further offences in the community during the period of detention, on the whole it is an inappropriate sentencing objective owing to our inability to distinguish offenders who are likely to commit further serious offences from those who will not. The benefits, in the form of preventing crime, derived from incapacitating large numbers of possible offenders are likely to be more than offset by the harm in imprisoning offenders who in fact would not have offended.

---

38 Greenwood *et al*, 1994.
39 Schwartz, MD, 'Why are we so afraid?' (1999) *The Age*, 14 October, p 17.
40 *Ibid*.

This does not mean that incapacitation should never have a role in sentencing. Although there are no reliable techniques for identifying people who may, in the future, commit serious offences, unfortunately there are some individuals who appear so determinedly evil, such as serial killers and rapists,[41] that it would be remiss to allow them to remain in the community. However, given the fortunate scarcity of such people, it is inappropriate to extrapolate any sentencing objectives directed towards them to the general community. To do so would be to allow hard cases to make bad law.

6.3 DETERRENCE

6.3.1 Definition and overview

Broadly, there are two aspects of deterrence. Specific deterrence aims to discourage crime, by punishing offenders for their transgressions and thereby convincing them that crime does not pay. General deterrence seeks to dissuade potential offenders, by the threat of anticipated punishment, from engaging in unlawful conduct by illustrating the unsavoury consequences of offending. Deterrence is clearly a forward looking sentencing objective; focusing solely on preventing harm, by either punishing the offender or dissuading others who come to know of the punishment. For Bentham, general deterrence was the primary good consequence of punishment:

> General prevention ought to be the chief end of punishment, as it is its real justification ... [W]hen we consider that an unpunished crime leaves the path of crime open, not only to the same delinquent, but also to all those who may have the same motives and opportunities for entering upon it, we perceive that the punishment inflicted on the individual becomes a source of security to all. That punishment which, considered in itself, appeared base and repugnant to all generous sentiments, *is elevated to the first rank of benefits, when it is regarded not as an act of wrath or of vengeance against a guilty or unfortunate individual who has given way to mischievous inclinations, but as an indispensable sacrifice to the common safety* [emphasis added].[42]

The relevance of deterrence to sentencing law and practice

Deterrence has a central role in sentencing law and practice. It has even been endorsed as the paramount objective of sentencing. Nearly half a century ago the New Zealand Supreme Court in *Radich* stated that 'in all civilised countries,

---

41 As to the type of people that fit into this category, see the 'vivid danger' test proposed in Bottoms and Brownsword, 1982, p 240.

42 Bentham, J, 'The principles of penal law' in Bowring, J (ed), The Works of Jeremy Bentham, 1838–43, p 396. For Bentham, specific deterrence and rehabilitation were second order objectives after general deterrence.

in all ages, [deterrence] has been the main purpose of punishment and still continues so'.[43]

This passage has been cited with approval in numerous cases[44] and deterrence remains a key sentencing objective in most Australian jurisdictions.[45] General deterrence has been held to be particularly important where the offence is prevalent;[46] public safety is at issue;[47] the offence is hard to detect;[48] or involves a breach of trust;[49] and where vulnerable groups need protection.[50] Specific deterrence is a weighty consideration for offenders with significant prior convictions, since it is assumed previous sanctions have failed to stop their offending behaviour. On the other hand, offenders who are genuinely remorseful about their conduct or co-operate with authorities in an attempt to redeem themselves are regarded as less likely to re-offend, hence the need for specific deterrence is lessened.[51]

The importance placed by the courts on general deterrence

The allegiance by the courts to general deterrence theory is so steadfast that they have refused to relinquish it even in the face of apparent legislative rejection of it as a goal of sentencing. General deterrence is not specifically mentioned as one of the relevant sentencing factors stated in the Crimes Act 1914 (Cth).[52] This was apparently in response to a recommendation by the Australian Law Reform Commission that it not be adopted as an objective of sentencing on the basis that sentences should be commensurate with the seriousness of the offence committed. It was considered unfair to pass heavier sanctions on a particular accused because of what others might do.[53] Despite this, the court in El Karhani, in the course of noting that general deterrence is

---

43 *Radich* [1954] NZLR 86, p 87.

44 Eg, see *Walden v Hensler* (1987) 163 CLR 561, p 569; *Williscroft* [1975] VR 292, pp 298–99; *Cooke* (1955) 72 WN (NSW) 132, p 136.

45 Sentencing Act 1991 (Vic), s 5(1)(b); Criminal Law (Sentencing) Act 1988 (SA), s 10(j); Sentencing Act 1995 (NT), s 5(1)(c); Penalties and Sentences Act 1992 (Qld), s 9(1)(c).

46 *Williscroft* [1975] VR 292, p 299; *Taylor* (1985) 18 A Crim R 14.

47 *Dixon-Jenkins* (1985) 14 A Crim R 372, p 376.

48 *Jamieson* [1988] VR 879; *Pantano* (1990) 49 A Crim R 328, p 338.

49 *Hawkins* (1989) 45 A Crim R 430. In *Barrick* (1985) 7 Cr App R(S) 142, the English Court of Appeal issued a guideline judgment stating that breach of trust by professional workers was a significant aggravating factor and urged more severe penalties for such offences.

50 *Kumantjara v Harris* (1992) 109 FLR 400; *Kane* (1987) 29 A Crim R 326.

51 As to the statutory basis of the relevance of remorse, see, eg, Sentencing Act 1991 (Vic), s 5(2)(e) (a plea of guilty is evidence of remorse), and Crimes Act 1914 (Cth), ss 16A(2)(f) and (h).

52 See s 16A(1) and (2); however, specific deterrence is s 16A(2)(j).

53 Australian Law Reform Commission, 1988, p 18.

one of 'the fundamental principles of sentencing, inherited from the ages',[54] put down the legislative omission of general deterrence to a 'legislative slip'.[55] It stated that it is still an important sentencing consideration and no less important than the other factors expressly mentioned, although it is absent from the detailed list of relevant sentencing criteria.

The courts in the UK have been equally unprepared to let go of deterrence. Although, on its face, the Criminal Justice Act 1991 (UK) makes no mention of deterrence, and s 2(2)(a) (now consolidated as s 80(2)(a)) of the Powers of Criminal Courts (Sentencing) Act 2000 (UK), declares that the sentence shall be that which is commensurate with the seriousness of the offence, it has been held that:

> The purposes of a custodial sentence must primarily be to punish and to deter. Accordingly, the phrase 'commensurate with the seriousness of the offence' must mean commensurate with the punishment and deterrence which the seriousness of the offence requires.[56]

Despite the enthusiasm expressed by courts, and to a lesser extent the legislatures, towards deterrence it has been subject to two substantial criticisms. First, that it does not work, and secondly (in relation to general deterrence), it has been contended that it is repugnant that a person should be sacrificed for the benefit of others.[57] These criticisms are considered in that order.

Legal approach to claim that deterrence does not work

The most damaging criticism of deterrence theory is that it does not work. Punishment involves inflicting pain on offenders and thus it has been claimed that it cannot be justified by deterrence theory unless there is an *ascertainable* benefit to the community.[58] The most ready response to this is that even if there is no evidence to support deterrence theory, not to worry, we should merely assume that it does.

In *Yardley v Betts*, the court stated: '... the courts must assume, although evidence is wanting, that the sentences which they impose have the effect of deterring at least some people from committing crime' (emphasis added).[59] Similarly, in *Fern*, King CJ held that 'courts are *obliged to assume* that the punishments which Parliament authorises will have a tendency to deter people from committing crimes. The administration of criminal justice is

---

54   (1990) 21 NSWLR 370, p 378.

55   *Ibid.*

56   *Cunningham* (1993) 14 Cr App R(S) 444, p 447.

57   *Peterson* [1984] WAR 329, p 344.

58   See, eg, Zimring and Hawkins, 1973, pp 43–44.

59   *Yardley v Betts* (1979) 1 A Crim R 329, p 333.

based upon that assumption'.[60] This peculiar fondness of deterrence as a rationale for sentencing is not confined to Australian courts. Commenting on the general approach by the Canadian Courts to the issue, Ruby states:

> One does not know what secret information trial judges may possess unknown to social scientists and lay men alike, but there is a distinct shortage of statistical analysis upon which to base [the view that individuals may be deterred by severe sentences] ... It seems almost to be the case that there exists a fear on the part of the judges that if they let loose of the straw of general deterrence, the waters will take them and all will be lost.[61]

The source of this imperative to rely on deterrence as a sentencing goal is unclear. It is not as if there is a shortage of other sentencing objectives which are open to the courts to justify punishing wrongdoers: denunciation, rehabilitation, reparation, just to name a few. Even if there were not, it would seem far more appropriate to abandon punishment altogether than to punish criminals on the basis of a flawed rationale.

Thus, a precondition for deterrence to serve as a rationale for punishment is that it does work. Common sense indicates that we normally act in a prudential manner and seek to avoid undesirable consequences. This lies at the core of the economic theory of deterrence which contends that people will commit crime if the expected benefit of the crime exceeds the expected cost.[62] However, common sense also indicates that we do not always act prudentially. If deterrence is to form the basis of such a hurtful practice as punishment, some hard evidence is needed.

6.3.2 The effectiveness of special deterrence

It is inordinately difficult to obtain information regarding the effectiveness of sanctions in deterring offenders from committing offences at the expiry of a sanction. Offenders may not re-offend for numerous reasons, apart from the fear of being subject to more punishment. The offending may have been a one off in any event; a suitable opportunity may not again present itself; rehabilitation may have occurred; or the offender may get a job. It is also possible that an offender may simply 'grow up'. Empirical evidence strongly supports the view that criminal behaviour is a young man's endeavour. Studies in the US have shown that the peak age for violent offences is 18, the

---

60 *Fern* (1989) 51 SASR 273, p 274.

61 Ruby, 1994, p 7.

62 See Posner, 1997, Chapter 7. The benefits of crime include not only financial gain but also non-economic gain, such as satisfaction obtained in extracting revenge. The costs of crime include expected punishment as well as opportunity costs, such as the offender's time.

peak age for property offences is 16, and the rate of offending then typically declines at the age of 30.[63]

However, the evidence that is available supports the view that severe punishment (namely imprisonment) does not deter offenders: the recidivism rate of offenders does not vary significantly regardless of the form of punishment or treatment that they are subjected to.[64] As we have seen, despite the widely held belief that prisons are more likely to further corrupt offenders than they are to rehabilitate or deter, there is no demonstrable evidence of this either.[65]

Nigel Walker, on the other hand, uses the results of the findings of a six year follow up study of a large sample of offenders sentenced in Wales and England in January 1972 to support the view that there is evidence that imprisonment does serve to deter some offenders.[66] The study revealed that reconviction rates for imprisonment were lower than for suspended sentences. This hypothesis, though, is far from strong. As Walker notes:

> Strictly speaking, all that this tells us is that the suspended sentence is less effective than an actual prison sentence. It is theoretically possible that the absolute efficacy of an actual prison sentence is nil (or even a minus quality) and that the absolute efficacy of a suspended sentence is even less: that is, that it increases the likelihood of reconviction.[67]

While Walker ultimately thinks that this explanation is unlikely, it is unsound to rely on comparisons involving the use of suspended sentences. The sting in the suspended sentence supposedly lies in the risk that the offender may be sent to jail if he or she transgresses during the term of the sentence. However, as is discussed in Chapter 8, it is erroneous to describe such a risk as being capable of comprising a punitive measure. Every person in the community faces the risk of imprisonment if he or she commits an offence punishable by imprisonment.[68] In this way, the natural and pervasive operation of the criminal law casts a permanent sword of Damocles over all our heads: each action we perform is potentially subject to the criminal law. Despite this, it has never been seriously asserted that we are all undergoing some type of criminal punishment. Accordingly, the suspended sentence is not, in fact, a

---

63 See Farrington, 1986, Vol 7, p 189; Nagin, Farrington and Moffitt, 1995, p 111.

64 The Panel on Research on Deterrent and Incapacitative Effects, 'Incapacitation', in Blumstein *et al*, 1978, p 66. More recent evidence confirms this: see Tonry, 1996, p 102.

65 There is, however, evidence that the more prison sentences a person serves, the more likely he or she is to re-offend: Walker, 1985, pp 166–69.

66 See Walker, 1991, p 44.

67 *Ibid*.

68 Which are the only types of offence for which a suspended sentence may be restored. See, eg, Sentencing Act 1991 (Vic), s 31(1); Powers of Criminal Courts Act 1973 (UK), s 23(1).

sanction in the proper sense. Walker further notes that the results of the same survey indicated that reconviction rates for offenders dealt with by way of fine were about the same as that expected for the whole sample; 'neither markedly better nor markedly worse than those for imprisonment'.[69] Thus, when a hard form of treatment (imprisonment) is compared with the fine, which is a much softer sanction, there is no variation in the reconviction rate. However, if specific deterrence did work, one would expect the pain of imprisonment to be a far more powerful regulator of future behaviour than a fine.

Accordingly, there is insufficient evidence, one way or another, to form a considered view on whether subjecting offenders to punishment is more likely to make them law abiding citizens in the future.

6.3.3 The effectiveness of general deterrence

In terms of analysing the evidence concerning the efficacy of general deterrence, there are broadly two different levels of inquiry. Marginal deterrence concerns whether there is a direct correlation between the severity of the sanction and the prevalence of an offence. Absolute deterrence relates to the threshold question of whether there is any connection between criminal sanctions and criminal conduct.

The failure of marginal deterrence

There have been numerous attempts to ascertain if there is a connection between penalty levels and crime rate. However, it has proven very difficult to convincingly prove or disprove such a link. This is principally due to the large amount of other variables which contribute to the overall crime rate, such as the social and economic conditions in the community and community attitude towards crime. In order confidently to ascertain the link between crime and penalty level, it would be necessary to freeze all of the other variables which may affect crime rate while increasing the penalty level. Even if this can be done, it is difficult, except perhaps in relation to homicide offences, to get accurate information regarding actual crime rates due to the large number of offences which are unreported. The complexity of the inquiry is highlighted by the Report of the Panel of the National Research Council in the US which, after noting that there was some evidence of a link between lower sanctions and higher crime rates, reported that this may be the effect, rather than the cause, of higher crime rates. The strain on the criminal justice system from increasing levels of crime may make it more likely for increasingly busy judges and prosecutors to reduce or dismiss charges and

---

69   Walker, 1991, p 45.

impose less severe sentences.[70] Overall, the Panel concluded that the research evidence that does exist regarding marginal deterrence is, overall, inconclusive:

> We cannot yet assert that the evidence warrants an affirmative conclusion regarding deterrence. We believe scientific caution must be exercised in interpreting the limited validity of the available evidence and a number of competing explanations for the results. Our reluctance to draw stronger conclusions does not imply support for the position that deterrence does not exist, since the evidence certainly favors a proposition supporting deterrence more than it favors one asserting that deterrence is absent.[71]

In a similar vein, after a comprehensive review of the evidence regarding marginal deterrence, Zimring and Hawkins stated that:

> Studies of different areas with different penalties, and studies focusing on the same jurisdiction before and after a change in punishment level takes place, show rather clearly that the level of punishment is not the major reason why crime rates vary. In regard to particular penalties, such as capital punishment as a marginal deterrent to homicide, the studies go further and suggest no discernible relationship between the presence of the death penalty and homicide rates.[72]

The failure of even the death penalty to act as a marginal deterrence is exemplified by the experience in New Zealand. During the period of 1924 to 1962 there were periods when the death penalty (for murder) was in force, then abolished, then revived, and abolished again. The changes generally followed some level of public debate and were well publicised. Although there were fluctuations in the murder rate during this period, they bore no connection to the death penalty.[73]

In a more recent study, it has been postulated that an escalation in penalty level resulted in an *increase* in offending behaviour. Following the introduction of the well publicised Crime (Serious and Repeat Offenders) Act 1992 (WA), which was targeted at reducing the number of high speed pursuits involving stolen vehicles and which significantly increased the penalties for such offences, there was a substantial increase in the rate of offences (motor vehicle thefts and associated arrests) which were a trigger for high speed pursuits.[74]

---

70 The Report of the Panel of the National Research Council, in Blumstein *et al*, 1978, p 39.
. 71 *Ibid*, p 7.
72 Zimring and Hawkins, 1973, p 29.
73 See Walker, 1969, pp 60–61, 191. For more recent analysis, with essentially the same result, regarding the efficacy of the death penalty as a deterrent, see Hood, 1996, Chapter 6, esp pp 211–12.
74 Broadhurst and Loh, 1995, p 55. The number of actual police pursuits was not an accurate indicator, because following the Act, police pursuit practices had changed, which resulted in many pursuits being called off or not commencing in the first place.

In many parts of the US, however, there has been a drop in the serious crime rate over the past decade or so. Superficially, one might think that this provides strong evidence of the deterrent effects of severe mandatory sentencing regimes. However, as we have seen, there is no verifiable link between such measures and the drop in crime. It may well be that the drop in crime stems from more distant and subtle factors. It has been recently claimed that 50% of the fall in the US crime rate is a result of an increased number of women from disadvantaged groups (teenagers, the poor and minority groups), whose children would have been most likely to commit crimes as adults, choosing abortion after it was legalised in the 1970s. This ostensibly incredible finding is supported by the fact that States with high abortion rates in the 1970s had bigger drops in crime in the 1990s; with each 10% rise in abortions corresponding to a 1% drop in crime two decades later.[75]

Thus, there is no persuasive evidence to support marginal deterrence. In a very insightful passage in *Pavlic*, Green CJ and Wright J noted that:

> General deterrence is only one of the factors which are relevant to sentence and must not be permitted to dominate the exercise of the sentencing discretion to the exclusion of all other factors ... although a court is entitled to proceed on the basis that there is a general relationship between the incidence of crime and the severity of sentences, *there is no justification for the view that there exists a direct linear relationship* between the incidence of a particular crime and the severity of the sentences which are imposed in respect of it such that the imposition of heavier sentences in respect of a particular crime will automatically result in a decrease in the incidence of that crime [emphasis added].[76]

The one area in which there is some promising data regarding marginal deterrence is in relation to planned offences. Harding found that robbers less frequently resorted to guns if carrying a firearm carried a significant extra penalty.[77] This is precisely as common sense would indicate. Deterrence assumes that people behave rationally and weigh up the advantages and disadvantages of a proposed course of conduct. Where an offence is committed 'in the heat of passion' or otherwise on the spur of the moment, it is difficult to see how deterrence could have any role. Given that deterrence is directed at those capable of making rational and prudent assessments about the advantages and disadvantage of criminal conduct, it has been accepted

---

75 Ellison, M, 'US study ties crime fall to abortions' (1999) *The Age*, 11 August, p 13.

76 (1995) 5 Tas R 186, p 190.

77 Harding, 1990. Harding, however, suggests that sentences can only serve as effective deterrents when combined with publicity and education. Other recent studies have also concluded that the most effective deterrent measures are altering community attitudes, publicity and a general crime prevention strategy: see, eg, Riley, 1991.

that it is not an appropriate consideration in respect to offenders who are mentally ill,[78] young[79] or who committed the offence while provoked.[80]

The success of absolute general deterrence

The news on absolute deterrence, however, is much more positive. There have been several natural social experiments where there has been a drastic reduction in the likelihood (perceived or real) that people would be punished for criminal behaviour. The key aspect about these events is that the change occurred abruptly and the decreased likelihood of the imposition of criminal sanctions was apparently the only changed social condition.

Perhaps the clearest instance of this is the police strike in Melbourne in 1923, which led to over one-third of the entire Victorian police force being sacked.[81] Once news of strike spread, mobs of thousands of people poured into the city centre and engaged in widespread property damage, looting of shops, and other acts of civil obedience including assaulting government officials and torching a tram. The civil disobedience lasted for two days, and was only quelled when the government enlisted thousands of citizens, including many ex-servicemen, to act as 'special' law enforcement officers. This behaviour was in complete contrast to the normally law abiding conduct of the citizens of Melbourne. Similar civil disobedience followed the police strike in Liverpool in 1919 and the internment of the Danish police force in 1944.

The results of these social experiments also counter the argument that deterrence does not work, because it only addresses those who do not need it: that is, law abiding citizens.[82] It would seem that there are many citizens who would readily break the law if they thought they could do so with impunity.

The Canadian Sentencing Commission, after reviewing the available literature, also took the view that absolute deterrence works:

> Even if there seems to be little empirical foundation to the deterrent efficacy of legal sanctions, the assertion that the presence of some level of legal sanctions has no deterrent effects whatsoever, has no justification. The weight of the evidence and the exercise of common sense favour the assertion that, taken together, legal sanctions have an overall deterrent effect which is difficult to evaluate precisely.[83]

---

78   *Champion* (1992) 64 A Crim R 244, pp 254–55; *Anderson* [1981] VR 155, pp 159–61, 163–64.
79   *George* [1986] Tas R 49; *GDP* (1991) 53 A Crim R 112, pp 115–16.
80   *Okutgen* (1982) 8 A Crim R 262, pp 264, 266.
81   The discussion regarding the events of the strike comes from Milte and Weber, 1977, pp 287–92.
82   See Mathiesen, 1994, pp 221, 231.
83   Canadian Sentencing Commission, 1987, p 136.

The view that there is a general link between punishment and crime rate is in accordance with econometric research that shows an inverse relationship between the incidence of violent offending and the use of imprisonment, but that the length of imprisonment is irrelevant.[84] As Walker points out, this suggests that if people think about consequences before acting violently, it is about whether they are likely to go to prison, but not how long.[85] Similar results have been observed in relation to the robbery rate: the higher the probability of being imprisoned, the fewer robberies there are. The length of the prison term is far less significant.[86] It is noteworthy that this link goes beyond merely supporting absolute deterrence theory and goes a small way to establishing the plausibility of some degree of marginal deterrence.

This was a matter noted by the Supreme Court of South Australia in *Johnston*:

> The typical dangerous driver is not a hardened criminal. The thought of prison is as frightening to him as it is to almost all citizens who are not hardened offenders. The deterrent to such a person is the *threat of imprisonment rather than the duration of the threatened imprisonment*. If a driver is not deterred from a dangerous course of driving by the threat of imprisonment for 18 months or two years, is it realistic to suppose that he will be deterred by the prospect of two and a half or three and a half years' imprisonment? [emphasis added].[87]

6.3.4 Other factors relevant to deterrence

The risk of detection and deterrence

It has been contended that the most important consideration regarding deterrence is not the penalty, but rather the perceived likelihood of apprehension. The Canadian Sentencing Commission noted that 'the old principle that it is more the certainty than the severity of punishment which is likely to produce a deterrent effect has not been invalidated by empirical research'.[88] The connection between the certainty of punishment and crime rate has been reproduced by numerous studies.[89] This point, too, has not been missed by the courts:

> The deterrent to an increased volume of serious crimes is not so much heavier sentences as much as the impression on the minds of those who are persisting in a course of crime that *detection is likely* and punishment is certain. The first of

---

84 Wolpin, 1978.
85 Walker, 1991, p 17.
86 See Ehrlich, 1973. The data was based on the robbery rate in the US in 1940, 1950 and 1960.
87 (1985) 38 SASR 582, p 586.
88 Canadian Sentencing Commission, 1987, pp 136–37.
89 Some of these studies are reported in Wilson, 1994, p 176.

these factors is not within the control of the courts, the second is. Consistency and certainty of sentence must be the aim ... Certainty of punishment is more important than increasingly heavy punishment [emphasis added].[90]

The apparent success of recent zero tolerance policing, which involves a greater police presence strictly enforcing minor offences, appears to confirm this.[91] In New York City, where zero tolerance policing has received most publicity, the rates of violent and property crime have fallen annually since 1992, with a reduction in the overall crime rate of 35%.[92]

Nonetheless, the link between the likelihood of punishment and crime does not militate against the claim that absolute deterrence works. It must be the case that the reason why the likelihood of being detected acts as a retardant to crime is the underlying assumption that *if* caught, some evil awaits. If rather than punishing offenders, police handed out lollies or movie tickets, one suspects that more police would result in more crime.

Moral values underlying law

It has also been postulated that another important consideration regarding deterrence is the values underpinning the law. Following a 1984 study of about 1,500 people who lived in Chicago regarding their contact with legal authorities, it was noted that normative issues are closely linked with compliance with the law.[93] People do not merely obey the law because it is in their self-interest to do so, but also because they believe it is proper to do so. The judgment that it is appropriate to obey the law, not only is affected by the internal content of the law, but by the attitude of the community towards those who enforce the law. Thus, the perception of a legitimate police force makes it more likely that laws will be observed. The concept of tying criminal sanctions with the community's moral disapproval of the act is strongly embodied in the Scandinavian sentencing systems, where it is assumed that:

> The disapproval expressed in punishment is assumed to influence the values and moral views of individuals. As a result of this process, the norms of criminal law and the values they reflect are internalized; people refrain from illegal behaviour, not because it is followed by unpleasant punishment, but because the behaviour itself is regarded as morally blameworthy ... The

90 *Griffiths* (1977) 137 CLR 293, p 327.
91 Zero tolerance policing is founded on the 'broken windows' theory, which provides that strict enforcement of minor crime and restoring physical damage and decay, such as broken windows and graffiti, would prevent the fostering of an environment which was conducive to more serious offences being committed: see Wilson and Kelling, 1982.
92 Grabosky, 1999, p 2. Grabosky notes that zero tolerance policing is not solely responsible for the drop in crime. He suggests that there are numerous contributing factors, such as sustained economic growth.
93 Tyler, 1990, pp 107, 175–76. See, also, von Hirsch *et al*, 1999, Chapter 8.

effective functioning of criminal law is not based on fear, but on legitimacy and acceptance.[94]

The normative aspect of lawful compliance, however, does not detract from the effectiveness of punishment to operate as a general deterrent, rather, it supports the view that the most effective laws are those that have widespread acceptance.

6.3.5 Theoretical objections – scapegoats

Exemplary punishment – scapegoats

The main theoretical criticism of deterrence is that it opens the way for the imposition of harsher, exemplary, sentences in order to deter others from committing similar offences. It was the possibility of exemplary punishment that led the Australian Law Reform Commission to reject general deterrence as an appropriate rationale for sentencing: 'to impose a punishment on one person by reference to a hypothetical crime of another runs completely counter to the overriding principle that a punishment imposed on a person must be linked to the crime that he or she has committed'.[95] At the core of this objection is the Kantian maxim that a person should always be treated as an end, and never as a means.

Despite the weight that the courts customarily ascribe to deterrence, like all other sentencing rationales it has been recognised that it should, at times, make way for other considerations, such as rehabilitation, and that it is subject to the constraints of proportionality. The courts, therefore, normally avoid using people as scapegoats. This is not always the case, however:

> There are offences where the deterrent principle must take priority and where sentences of imprisonment may properly be imposed, even on first offenders of good character, to mark the disapproval by the law of the conduct in question and in the hope that other people will be deterred from like behaviour.[96]

In view of the above analysis of the empirical information relating to marginal deterrence, this objection is not relevant. There is no evidence to support any good coming from the imposition of unduly heavy penalties. However, if evidence does eventually establish the efficacy of marginal deterrence, then the utilitarian is committed to disproportionate sentences and thereby must address the scapegoats issue.

---

94 Lappi-Seppala, 1998.
95 Australian Law Reform Commission, 1988, p 18. See, also, *Cunningham* (1993) 14 Cr App R(S) 444.
96 *Thompson* (1975) 11 SASR 217, p 222.

The objections to exemplary punishment are of the same nature, but not as powerful as those concerning punishing the innocent. As we saw in Chapter 4, at the post-philosophical level, punishing the innocent does not insurmountably trouble our sensibilities and is no worse than other practices which we as a society condone. This being the case, the less unpalatable practice of exemplary punishment presents even less of a problem for the utilitarian. Exemplary punishment is far less repugnant than punishment of the innocent because we are dealing with actual wrongdoers who have, at least to some extent, contributed to their plight. If marginal deterrence is shown to work, then by not increasing the level of punishment for offenders beyond that which is otherwise justified, we are choosing not to implement a practice that will decrease the chance that innocent people will be harmed by other wrongdoers. Thus, we would effectively be placing the interests of wrongdoers above those of innocent members of the community. This violates the principle that 'one must suffer if one's decision to do wrong makes it necessary that someone must suffer and that sufferer must either be the wrongdoer or some innocent victim'.[97] Where wrongdoers force such a choice on us, it is difficult to argue that they are not the ones who must wear the loss.

It is also important to note that there is a limit to the level of disproportionality that will be tolerated by a utilitarian. It seems safe to assume that extremely disproportionate penalties, especially if coupled with a high rate of enforcement, would be effective in reducing crime. A mandatory death penalty without trial administered by robot parking meters,[98] one would think, would result in far more diligent observance of parking restrictions. It has been argued that utilitarians who believe that the justification for punishment stems from its deterrent effects are committed to this type of penalty.[99] This, however, evinces a misunderstanding of the utilitarian thesis. In such a case, the amount of suffering inflicted by the punishment exceeds the harm that would have occurred if there was no punishment.[100] Such examples merely underscore the fact that, like all utilitarian ideals, deterrence policy cannot be pursued unabated, and there must be some (albeit loose) correlation between the crime and punishment.

Deterrence cannot set penalties

Ashworth argues that another problem with deterrence is that we lack sufficient empirical knowledge on which to base the calculation of penalties.[101] This is true, but the utilitarian is not committed to deterrence as

---

97   Farrell, 1985, p 373.
98   This example is used by Beyleveld, 1979.
99   See Armstrong, 1971, p 19.
100 See, also, Ten, 1987, pp 141–43.
101 Ashworth, 1998a, pp 44, 51.

the only principle that is relevant to punishment. As we shall see in the next chapter, in order to determine the amount of punishment, the utilitarian may well be able to invoke other standards, such as the principle of proportionality.

6.3.6 Conclusion

Ultimately, deterrence does work, at least to the extent that if there was not a real threat of punishment for engaging in unlawful conduct, the crime rate would soar. It follows that the threat of punishment discourages potential offenders from committing crime. This justifies the punishment of wrongdoers. The evidence does not support the view however, that this relationship operates in a linear fashion: that is, the deterrent effect of sanctions does not increase in direct proportion to the severity of sanctions. Thus, while the objective of deterrence justifies imposing punishment, it is only a remote consideration when it comes down to the question of how much punishment should be imposed. However, it does seem that certain penalties (on their own, regardless of their duration or precise gravity) such as prison may deter more than others. Imprisonment should, therefore, be imposed for the most serious offences, but deterrence theory does not justify exceedingly long periods of detention. The precise duration of penalties must be determined by other sentencing considerations, such as proportionality.

6.4 REHABILITATION

6.4.1 Definition and overview

Rehabilitation, like specific deterrence, aims to discourage the commission of future offences by the offender. The difference between the two lies in the means used to encourage desistence from crime. Rehabilitation seeks to alter the values of the offender so that he or she no longer desires to commit criminal acts: it involves the renunciation of wrongdoing by the offender and the re-establishment of the offender as an honourable law abiding citizen, and is achieved by 'reducing or eliminating the factors which contributed to the conduct for which [the offender] is sentenced'.[102] Accordingly, it works through a process of internal attitudinal reform, whereas specific deterrence seeks to dissuade crime simply by making the offender afraid of again being apprehended and punished. There are numerous types of treatment that have been used in a bid to reform offenders. Some attempt to deal with the perceived underlying cause of criminality by providing drug and alcohol

---

102 *Channon* (1978) 33 FLR 433, p 438.

programmes, or anger management courses. Newly developed cognitive-behavioral programmes encourage offenders to think before acting and consider the consequences of their actions. Other methods attempt to equip offenders better for life in the community, via educational or skills courses.

The utilitarian foundation for rehabilitation is clear. Rehabilitation assists the offender by encouraging him or her to become a law abiding member of the community. It is also of benefit to the community: '... where there is sufficient probability that [the offender] will become a useful ... member of society the public interest may be better served by not sending the offender to gaol.'[103]

The relevance of rehabilitation to sentencing law and practice

Despite the progressive and superficially appealing nature of rehabilitation as a sentencing objective, its reception by the courts and legislators can at best be described as lukewarm. Most sentencing statutes in Australia accord some weight to rehabilitation,[104] but the courts generally view it as a lower order sentencing objective.[105] It is generally pursued not for its own ends, but because it may fulfil some other sentencing objective, such as community protection. In respect of very grave offences, rehabilitation is sometimes regarded as irrelevant.[106] Where it is pursued, it is subject to the constraint of proportionality; therefore, the court cannot punish an offender more severely in a bid to cure him or her.[107]

Rehabilitation also has a minor role in sentencing in the UK. It is one of the purposes of a probation order and a combination order,[108] and the suitability of the offender is a key consideration in determining the restrictions that form part of all community orders.[109] Judges are also given wide discretionary power to mitigate a sentence by taking into account 'any such matters as, in the opinion of the court, are relevant in mitigation of sentence'.[110] Ashworth suggests that this permits the courts to have regard to rehabilitation in a far wider range of circumstances.[111] It could be argued that all community orders (not merely probation and combination orders) have a rehabilitative

---

103 *Hogon* (1987) 30 A Crim R 399, p 403.

104 Sentencing Act 1991 (Vic) s 5(1)(c), Crimes Act 1914 (Cth) s 16A(2)(n); Penalties and Sentences Act (Qld) 1992, s 9(1)(b); Criminal Law (Sentencing) Act 1988 (SA), s 10(m).

105 See, eg, *Ioannou* (1985) 16 A Crim R 63, p 70; *Davey* (1980) 50 FLR 57, pp 65–67; *Hogon* (1987) 30 A Crim R 399, p 404.

106 See *Kane* [1974] VR 759, pp 766–67; *Williscroft* [1975] 292, pp 300, 302.

107 *Freeman v Harris* [1980] VR 267, p 281.

108 Powers of Criminal Courts (Sentencing Act) 2000 (UK), ss 41 and 51.

109 *Ibid*, s 35(5)(b).

110 Criminal Justice Act 1991, s 28.

111 Ashworth, 1995, p 82.

component, since they are certainly softer than imprisonment. For adult offenders, the community orders that are available are: curfew orders,[112] community service orders,[113] drug treatment and testing orders,[114] in addition to probation and combined orders. However, this is clearly not the intention of the legislature. Section 35(3)(b) of the Powers of Criminal Courts (Sentencing) Act 2000 provides that a community order 'shall be such as in the opinion of the court [is] commensurate with the seriousness of the offence ...'; thereby ensuring that any rehabilitative ideology associated with community orders is trumped by the principle of proportionality.

In the US, rehabilitation was arguably the primary goal of sentencing until the 1970s. This goal was pursued so vigorously that sentences were often in the form of indeterminate terms of imprisonment, on the rationale that an offender should not be released until he or she was rehabilitated. However, the rehabilitative ideal is now totally swamped by considerations of just deserts and the objective of incapacitation.

6.4.2 Empirical evidence

Initial scepticism

The most damaging objection against rehabilitation as a suitable goal of sentencing has been that it does not work. Following extensive research conducted between 1960 and 1974, Martinson, in a very influential paper, concluded that empirical studies had not established that any rehabilitative programmes had worked in reducing recidivism.[115] The Panel of the National Research Council noted that there were no significant differences between the subsequent recidivism rates of offenders regardless of the form of punishment. 'This suggests that neither rehabilitative nor criminogenic effects [that is, the possible corrupting effects of punishment] operate very strongly.'[116]

More promising evidence

However, several years later, Martinson softened his position, stating that some types of rehabilitation programmes, particularly probation parole, may be effective and that generally 'no treatment ... is inherently either substantially helpful or harmful. The critical factor seems to be the *conditions*

---

112 Powers of Criminal Courts (Sentencing Act) 2000 (UK), s 37.
113 *Ibid*, s 46.
114 *Ibid*, s 52.
115 Martinson, 1974, p 25.
116 Blumstein *et al*, 1978, p 66.

under which the program is delivered'.[117] And, indeed, there is now mounting evidence that rehabilitation works for some in some circumstances:

> Research so far has on the whole confirmed what one would expect: that individual success may sometimes be claimed by routine psychotherapy or counselling with intelligent, articulate neurotic offenders; by guidance in personal, social, and domestic matters among those hampered by incompetence in these spheres; by sympathy and encouragement for those unsure of their limits and capabilities; and by direct assistance and support for those weighed down by practical difficulties. But none of these approaches is appropriate for other than a minority of the offender population, whose misdemeanours reflect some real psychological maladjustment and not just their social 'deviance'.[118]

That there is some level of success with rehabilitative techniques in relation to the least dysfunctional offenders, is not so much evidence of a victory for the rehabilitative ideal, as it is for the fact that some people are likely to only occasionally dabble in crime.

Brody, however, gives two reasons why it would be premature to dismiss the rehabilitative ideal. Generally, 'only a limited range of sentencing alternatives have been studied and consequently only a relatively small portion of the offender population has ever been considered';[119] and the 'reason why treatment has so often been shown to have no effect ... is simply that none has been given'.[120] Brody suggests that there is typically little tangible difference (in terms of such things as the services that are available and staff-inmate ratio) between punitive and treatment institutions.

Overall, the jury is still out on the ability of criminal sanctions to reform offenders: '... our understanding ... of what works, with which offenders and under what conditions, in reducing offending ... [is] still embryonic.'[121] Moreover, we are likely to be waiting some time before firm evidence is forthcoming regarding the effectiveness of sanctions to rehabilitate, due to the large number of possible causes for desistence from crime. Where an offender does not re-offend, there are always at least two possible causes of this: genuine moral reform or the fear of again being subject to punishment. In most cases, there are also numerous other considerations that may be relevant, such as employment, education and family situation.[122] This makes it very difficult to conduct or observe controlled experiments which provide pointed information regarding the effectiveness of rehabilitative sanctions.

---

117 Martinson, 1979, p 254.

118 Brody, 1998, pp 9, 11.

119 *Ibid*, p 10.

120 *Ibid*.

121 McIvor, 1992, p 13.

122 See, also, Report of the Victorian Sentencing Committee, 1988, p 83; Walker, 1991, p 43.

The most that can be confidently said at this point regarding the capacity of criminal punishment to reform is that there is some evidence that it will work for a small portion of offenders and that there is no firm evidence showing that it cannot work for the majority of offenders. However:

> ... treatments do not ... exist ... that can be relied upon to decide sentences routinely – that can inform the judge, when confronted with the run-of-the-mill robbery, burglary, or drug offence, what the appropriate sanction should be, and provide even a modicum of assurance that the sanction will contribute to the offender's desistence from crime.[123]

6.4.3 Theoretical problems

Rehabilitation not for the offender

Given that rehabilitation aims to assist the offender to overcome the difficulties that have resulted in the offending behaviour and the offender is likely to be more fulfilled by adopting a law abiding lifestyle, on its face rehabilitation is the most humane justification for punishment. This overt concern for the welfare of the offender, however, is not indicative of the underlying aim of rehabilitation: it is not so much a case of what can be done *for* the offender; as what can be done *to* him or her (for the sake of the rest of us). Opponents of rehabilitative sentencing have criticised it precisely on this basis: despite the humane exterior of rehabilitative techniques, they are anything but caring, since they are concerned not with the offender's needs, but are simply a means of improving our lot by reducing recidivism.[124]

In this regard, the critics are right. Punishment by its very nature is the antithesis of a caring institution; it is an unpleasantness designed to harm offenders. Any good which may come from it for the offender, is incidental to the broader objectives of punishment; and the only broader aim which rehabilitation can promote within the confines of penal practices is community protection by making it less likely that offenders will re-offend.

From the offender's perspective, rehabilitative measures (being softer in nature) are nevertheless still generally preferable to purely penal ones. The fact that these responses are pursued because his or her interests are tied to those of the community does not diminish the nature of the personal benefits that flow to the offender – in the same way that we do not find it perturbing that we only have a job because it benefits our employer. This criticism only has some force if one adopts the Kantian notion that people should never be

---

123 von Hirsch and Maher, 1998a, pp 26, 27.
124 *Ibid*, pp 28–29.

used simply as a means; however, this is clearly not a principle which utilitarians regard as being absolute.

Disproportionate punishment

Rehabilitation has also been criticised because it purportedly permits grossly disproportionate punishments. It has been suggested that the rehabilitative ideal justifies punishing a person for the rest of his or her life if that is how long it takes to reform the offender successfully.[125] However, it is a fallacy to assert that a proper application of the utilitarian theory of punishment justifies such extreme and prolonged forms of rehabilitation. As Ten points out, 'if the only way to reform an offender who steals a loaf of bread is to subject him to a prolonged period of treatment, then it is obvious that the "cure" is worse than the "illness", and would for that reason alone be rejected'.[126]

Rehabilitation and punishment not compatible

A more fundamental problem with rehabilitation is that it may not be compatible with the notion of punishment. There are two underlying assumptions concerning rehabilitation. The first is that people's values can be changed: more specifically, that their judgments concerning the appropriateness of breaking the criminal law to fulfil their desires can be altered. This seems valid. The reason that we engage in moral discourse is that we assume that values and beliefs are not set in stone. This seems to be supported by some degree of empirical evidence. As we have seen, over the past half-century there has been a discernable worldwide trend towards the greater recognition of moral interests; typically labelled 'human rights'. Thus, there is a strong basis for confidence that educative techniques can be devised to teach offenders to accord greater respect to the interests of others. Indeed, recent evidence suggests that cognitive-behavioural rehabilitation programmes, which focus on the links between beliefs, attitudes and behaviour, are extremely promising. Following a recent wide ranging review of the published studies in rehabilitation (which compared the recidivism rate of offenders who were subject to rehabilitative treatment to those who were not), Howells and Day suggest that these are most successful types of programme. Cognitive-behavioural programmes target factors that are (presumably) changeable and are directed at the 'criminogenic needs' of offenders, that is, factors which are directly related to the offending, such as anti-social attitudes; self-control; and problem solving skills.[127] Promising programmes have been developed in the areas of anger management, sexual

---

125 Armstrong, 1971, pp 19, 27–33.
126 Ten, 1987, p 142.
127 Howells and Day, 1999.

offending and drug and alcohol use. These appear to be more successful than programmes based on such things as confrontation or direct deterrence, physical challenge, or vocational training. Three judges in Missouri have even taken to imposing transcendental meditation programmes as part of the probation conditions of minor offenders; apparently with great success.[128]

The more questionable assumption is that the values of offender can be altered in the context of *punishing* an offender. Punishment, by its very nature, must hurt. Whether it is possible to rehabilitate people in an environment which is punitive is unclear. There seems to be an inherent contradiction between deliberately subjecting one to pain and at the same time trying to get him or her to see things your way. The more tolerant, understanding and educative we are in trying to facilitate attitudinal change in others, the closer we come to providing them with a social service.[129] For example, cognitive-behavioural programmes focus on the *needs* of offenders and attempt to meet these needs by education and counselling with the aim of reshaping their beliefs, attitudes, and values and improving their problem solving capacity, in order that they no longer engage in criminal behaviour. Such programmes seem to work best in community settings rather being delivered in institutions.[130] There is very little difference between such programmes and educational courses within the community (which are enthusiastically undertaken by many law abiding members of the community). This is all the more so, given that it is a feature of many rehabilitative 'sanctions' that they cannot be 'imposed' unless the offender consents to them.[131] By making the interests of the offender paramount, the modern rehabilitative programmes are more akin to welfare services than punitive sanctions. In order for the goal of rehabilitation to justify punishment, at the minimum, it must be shown that reform is attainable in a setting that is primarily directed to imposing unpleasantness on the offender, otherwise the sentencing system would in fact provide an incentive to commit crime. People with social or psychological problems, such as a depressive condition, poor employment skills, a lack of an education, or those who simply want to update their computer skills would view criminal conduct as a way to gain assistance in these areas. There is no evidence in support of rehabilitation in an environment which is primarily

---

128 Farrant, D, 'Meditation: a serene but effective path to criminal enlightenment' (1999) *The Age*, 16 November, p 6.
129 The distinction between punishment and a social service is employed by von Hirsch and Maher, 1998b, pp 26, 30.
130 Howells and Day, 1999, pp 4, 5.
131 Eg, in Victoria, community based orders or intensive corrections orders (which both have a counselling/rehabilitative component) cannot be imposed without the consent of the offender: Sentencing Act 1991 (Vic), ss 20, 36. In the UK, however, consent as a requirement for a community order has been removed in the majority of cases. However, it is still a necessary precondition for drug treatment and testing orders (Powers of Criminal Courts (Sentencing) Act 2000 (UK), s 52).

punitive. Whether this tension is irreconcilable remains to be seen, but one suspects that it will be: the more 'punishment' begins to look to like treatment, the less likely it is that people will seek to avoid it.

6.5 CONCLUSION

On the basis of current empirical evidence, the objectives of incapacitation, specific deterrence and rehabilitation cannot be invoked by the utilitarian to justify punishment. Incapacitation is flawed since we are very poor at predicting which offenders are likely to commit serious offences in the future. There is nothing to suggest that offenders who have previously been punished are less likely to re-offend, thus there is no basis for pursuing the goal of specific deterrence. Also, there are no far reaching rehabilitative techniques which have proven to be successful. Even more telling is the fact that the goals of punishment and rehabilitation may be internally inconsistent. It follows that specific deterrence and rehabilitation should be abolished as objectives of sentencing (as should any policies or principles based on them), unless and until there is firm evidence that they work.

However, experience shows that, absent the threat of punishment for criminal conduct, the social fabric of society would readily dissipate. Crime would escalate and overwhelmingly frustrate the capacity of people to lead happy and fulfilled lives. Thus, while there is only one objective of punishment which the utilitarian can invoke, this is more than sufficient to justify the practice of State imposed unpleasantness on those who violate the criminal law.

Despite this, there is insufficient evidence to support a direct correlation between higher penalties and a reduction in the crime rate. This means that while deterrence justifies punishing offenders, it is of little relevance in fixing the amount of punishment. This must be done by reference to other utilitarian ideals, and, as is discussed in the following chapter, to this end the principle of proportionality ought to be the guiding determinant.

The main rationales underlying the move towards harsher penalties are incapacitation and (marginal) general deterrence. Given that these objectives are flawed, it follows that the trend in most Western countries towards harsher penalties should be stopped. Any intuitive unease that this would inevitably lead to increased crime rates is, to a large extent, allayed by a comparison of sentencing practice in jurisdictions such as Finland and Sweden. In both these countries, sentencing premiums are not attached to pursue the aims of incapacitation or deterrence and the main determinant in setting criminal sanctions is the principle of proportionality.[132] The prison rate in these countries is about half of that in Australia,[133] and when offenders are sent to prison they do not stay very long – prison sentences exceeding five years are rare.[134] Moreover, the crime rate in both these countries compares favourably with that in Australia. The rate in Finland is about 35% lower than that in Australia,[135] while in Sweden it is about 25% higher.[136] England and Wales fare only slightly better than Australia. As we saw earlier, the imprisonment rate in England and Wales is approximately 116 per 100,000 people, which is about 20% less than Australia. However, in the financial year 1999/2000 there were 5.3 million offences recorded by police in England and Wales (an increase of 3.8% over the previous 12 months),[137] which equates to about a rate of 10,100 offences per 100,000[138] – which is about 10% higher than in Australia.

The overall number of offences reported to police is obviously a very rough measure of crime rate and is a very crude basis for an international comparison. The comparison can be affected by a range of factors, including differences in the list of offences which are included in overall crime figures and differences in the rules in which multiple offences are counted.[139] However, the above results are in keeping with international victimisation surveys. The most recent International Crime Victimisation Survey (in 1995)[140] shows that England and Wales had higher levels of victimisation risk (31) than Sweden (24) or Finland (19), although the difference in the victimisation rate for contact crime (robbery, assault and sexual assault) was not as marked: England and Wales (3.6); Sweden (3.4); Finland (2.9).

---

132 For an account of Swedish sentencing and practice, see Jareborg, 1995, p 95; for a comparison of Swedish and Victorian incarceration rates (in 1991) see Tonry, 1995, pp 267, 279–81. For an excellent overview of the Finnish system, see Lappi-Seppala, 1998.

133 In 1997, the imprisonment rate in Finland was 58 per 100,000 people. In Sweden (in 1995) the rate was 66 per 100,000: *ibid*, Lappi-Seppala, Table C 12. As we saw earlier, the figure in Australia is about 140 per 100,000 population.

134 von Hirsch, 1993, p 43.

135 In Finland, the crime rate in 1997 was 6,795 reported crimes (against property and persons) per 100,000 population: Lappi-Seppala, 1998, Table F. In Australia, in 1998, the rate was about 9,285 (the figures for causing death while driving were not available): Australian Bureau of Statistics, *Australia Now: Crime Recorded by Police* (2000) Table 11.13.

136 The rate in Sweden in 1995 (later figures were not available) was 11,536 per 100,000 population: Lappi-Seppala, 1998, Table F.

137 Home Office, *Criminal Statistics: England and Wales 1999* (December 2000) 15.

138 *Ibid*, 26.

139 See Barclay and Travis, 1998.

140 The results of the survey are reprinted in *ibid*.

PART C

CHAPTER 7

PROPORTIONALITY IN SENTENCING: ITS JUSTIFICATION, MEANING AND ROLE

7.1 INTRODUCTION

The final part of this book (Chapters 7 to 11) examines more closely the practical implications that a utilitarian theory of punishment has for sentencing law and practice. In the previous chapter it was suggested that, in determining how much to punish, the principal consideration should be the seriousness of the offence. The focus of this chapter is to examine the justification for the principle of proportionality. Chapters 8 and 9 discuss the form that punishment should take. The factors that are relevant to determining how much to punish are analysed in Chapter 10 and, to a lesser extent, in Chapter 11. The main focus of Chapter 11 is the means by which sentences should be determined.

The principle of proportionality in sentencing is a splendidly simple and appealing notion. In its crudest, and most persuasive, form it is the view that the punishment should equal the crime. The proportionality principle strikes a strong intuitive cord, and probably for this reason is embodied not only in sentencing law, but transcends many other areas of the law. As Fox notes, the notion that the response must be commensurate to the harm caused, or sought to be prevented, is at the core of the criminal defences of self-defence and provocation. It is also at the foundation of civil law damages for injury or death, which aim to compensate for the actual loss suffered, and equitable remedies, which are proportional to the detriment sought to be avoided.[1]

Recently, the High Court of Australia has also seized on the concept of proportionality as a limiting factor regarding the exercise of the implied incidental power and purposive powers under the Australian Constitution. In exercising these powers, the validity of a statute depends on whether it is appropriate or adopted to its legislative purpose: '... a reasonable proportionality must exist between the designated object or purpose and the means selected by the law for achieving that object or purpose.'[2] The proportionality criterion has also been used to determine whether a law infringes a constitutional limitation, express or implied, which restricts a head of power.

The importance of proportionality in sentencing is underlined by the fact that it is one of the few principles of sentencing where there appears to be

---

1 Fox, 1994, p 491. See, also, Fox, 1988.

2 *Nationwide News Pty Ltd v Wills* (1992) 177 CLR 1, p 29; *Cunliffe v Commonwealth* (1994) 182 CLR 272, p 297.

some degree of consensus among lawyers and philosophers regarding its relevance and significance, notwithstanding the gulf that normally exists between sentencing and theories of punishment. As is discussed below, the High Court of Australia has declared that it is the primary objective of sentencing and many philosophers have expressed similar sentiments concerning its importance in a system of punishment.

The proportionality principle has proved so alluring that, in many parts of the Western world, it is one of the main goals of sentencing. Despite this, sentences vary markedly not only across, but also within jurisdictions: '... the same offender can be sentenced to 200 years in one country, whereas he would be sentenced to 15 years in another.'[3] The main reason that adoption of the proportionality principle has not facilitated uniform sanctions for like offences is because the principle is poorly defined and understood. There is consensus only in abstract. The principle is so nebulous that it would be misleading to assert that it provides a meaningful guide to sentencers. In order to get to the bottom of proportionality, it is necessary to determine the factors that are relevant to the seriousness of the offence and how offence severity should be gauged. This can only be done in light of an understanding of the justification for the principle. However, this, too, is the subject of intense debate. The primary focus of this chapter is to determine the rationale, if any, for the principle of proportionality. Once the justification for proportionality is ascertained, the narrower, and more pragmatic issues concerning it, such as when, if ever, proportionality may be violated, the factors that are relevant to the seriousness of an offence and the severity of punishment fall into place.

The first section of this chapter outlines the nature of the proportionality principle and its present role in sentencing law and practice. After considering some definitional matters, the factors that are relevant to the seriousness of an offence are then analysed. This is followed by a discussion of the justification for proportionality. Although it is traditionally believed that the utilitarian theory of punishment is antagonistic to the principle of proportionality, it is argued that, in fact, the utilitarian theory best underpins the proportionality principle. A utilitarian justification for the principle also serves to provide coherent and definitive answers to problems concerning the gravity of an offence and the severity of punishment. The same broad common denominator (happiness) resolves both matters.

---

3   Kuhn, A, 'Public opinion and sentencing', paper delivered at the Sentencing and Society Conference, 24–26 June 1999, Scotland.

7.2 THE ROLE OF PROPORTIONALITY IN SENTENCING

7.2.1 Statement of the principle

In short, the principle of proportionality is that the punishment should fit the crime. It operates to 'restrain excessive, arbitrary and capricious punishment'[4] by requiring that punishment must not exceed the gravity of the offence, even where it seems certain that the offender will immediately re-offend. For example, in *Jenner*, a term of imprisonment was reduced despite the fact that the court believed that 'it appeared likely that [the offender] would commit a crime as soon as he was released from prison'.[5]

The principle was more fully explained by the High Court in *Hoare*:

> A basic principle of sentencing law is that a sentence of imprisonment imposed by a court should never exceed that which can be justified as appropriate or proportionate to the gravity of the crime considered in light of its objective circumstances.[6]

Similarly, the Canadian Supreme Court has provided that:

> It is basic to any theory of punishment that the sentence imposed must bear some relationship to the offence, it must be a 'fit' sentence proportionate to the seriousness of the offence. Only if this is so can the public be satisfied that the offender 'deserved' the punishment he received and feel a confidence in the fairness and rationality of the system.[7]

7.2.2 The primacy of proportionality

Proportionality and the common law

Proportionality is one of the main objectives of sentencing and the Australian High Court decisions of *Veen (No 1)*[8] and *Veen (No 2)*[9] even went as far as pronouncing it as the primary aim of sentencing in Australia. It is considered so important that it cannot be trumped even by the goal of community protection, which at various times has also been declared as the most important aim of sentencing.[10] Thus, in the case of dangerous offenders, while community protection remains an important objective, at common law it cannot override the principle of proportionality. It is for this reason that preventive detention is not sanctioned by the common law.

---

4   Fox, 1994, p 492.
5   [1956] Crim LR 495.
6   (1989) 167 CLR 348, p 354.
7   *Reference re s 94(2) Motor Vehicle Act* (1985) 23 CCC (3d), 289, p 325.
8   (1979) 143 CLR 458, p 467.
9   (1988) 164 CLR 465, p 472.
10 See, eg, *Channon* (1978) 20 ALR 1; *Valenti* (1980) 48 FLR 416, p 420.

In many other jurisdictions, the principle of proportionality is also rated highly. For example, in relation to the Canadian sentencing system it has been noted that: '... the paramount principle governing the determination of a sentence is that the sentence be proportionate to the gravity of the offence and the degree of responsibility of the offender for the offence.'[11] Similar views are expressed in the White Paper underpinning the Criminal Justice Act 1991 (UK), which declares that the aim of the reforms is to introduce a 'legislative framework for sentencing, based on the seriousness of the offence and just deserts'.[12]

Statutory recognition of the proportionality principle

Proportionality has also been given statutory recognition in most Australian jurisdictions. For example, in Victoria, the Sentencing Act 1991 (Vic) provides that one of the purposes of sentencing is to impose just punishment,[13] and that in sentencing an offender, the court must have regard to the gravity of the offence[14] and the offender's culpability and degree of responsibility.[15] The Sentencing Act 1995 (WA) states that the sentence must be 'commensurate with the seriousness of the offence',[16] and the Crimes Act 1900 (ACT) provides that the sentences must be 'just and appropriate'.[17] In the UK, the just deserts sentencing rationale endorsed in the White Paper was not ultimately expressly adopted as the main sentencing objective of the Criminal Justice Act 1991 (UK). However, significantly, the message was received in relation to the length of custodial sentences.[18] The principle of proportionality has been endorsed in some parts of the US where presumptive sentencing guidelines have, since the late 1970s, represented the main approach to sentencing reform (see Chapters 10 and 11). The main variables relevant to the determination of such sentences are the objective seriousness of the offence and the offender's previous criminal history.[19]

---

11 Canadian Sentencing Commission, 1987, p 154.

12 Great Britain, 1990, para 2.3. For judicial endorsement of the principle in the UK, see *Skidmore* (1983) 5 Cr App R(S) 17, p 19; *Moylan* [1970] 1 QB 143, p 147.

13 Section 5(1)(a).

14 Section 5(2)(c).

15 Section 5(2)(d).

16 Section 6(1)(a).

17 Section 429(1). The Sentencing Act 1997 (Tas), which is one of the most recent significant sentencing reforms in Australia, does not, however, refer to the principle of proportionality.

18 Section 2(2)(a) (now consolidated as Powers of Criminal Courts (Sentencing) Act 2000, s 80(2)(a)). It is also relevant regarding the imposition of community sentences: Powers of Criminal Courts (Sentencing Act) 2000, s 35.

19 However, as is discussed below, prior criminality is not necessarily relevant to proportionality, despite the views of some leading retributivists.

7.2.3   The rise of proportionality

The primacy now enjoyed by the proportionality principle in the sentencing domain has been relatively short lived. Its rise has resulted from a move away from utilitarian objectives of punishment, and its close association with a retributive theory of punishment, which, as we saw earlier, is now the most influential theory of punishment.

Traditionally, proportionality is thought to sit most comfortably with a retributive theory of punishment, because for the retributivist, the criterion for determining the amount of punishment is retrospective, namely, the seriousness of the offence. Indeed, as was alluded to in Chapter 4, Andrew von Hirsch argues that proportionality should be the main goal of sentencing. Future orientated goals do not cloud the prime objective of retributive punishment, which is to punish offenders for the harm they have done. Accordingly, proportionality is the cornerstone of many retributive theories.

In contrast, the principle of proportionality does not appear to be of direct relevance to the utilitarian sentencing calculus. For the utilitarian, prospective considerations such as the need for deterrence would appear to be the guiding considerations in determining how much punishment is warranted.

Given the relatively short period of dominance by retributive theories, it is perhaps not surprising that legislatures in many jurisdictions have already made significant incursions into the principle.

7.2.4   Statutory incursions into the proportionality principle

In Victoria, serious sexual, drug, arson or violent offenders[20] may receive sentences in excess of that which is proportionate to the offence. Indefinite gaol terms may also be imposed for offenders convicted of 'serious offences',[21] where the court is satisfied 'to a high degree of probability' that the offender is a serious danger to the community.[22] As was outlined in Chapter 2, the Northern Territory and Western Australia have introduced mandatory jail terms for certain property offences.

Similar measures to those implemented in Victoria have been introduced in the UK. Section 1(2)(b) of the Criminal Justice Act 1991 (now consolidated as s 80(2)(b) of the Powers of Criminal Courts (Sentencing) Act 2000) cuts across the just deserts background of the Act by providing that where an offence is a violent or sexual offence, a custodial sentence shall not be imposed unless only such a sentence is adequate to protect the public. In determining

---

20 Sentencing Act 1991 (Vic), Part 2A.

21 *Ibid*, ss 18A–18P. Serious offences include certain homicide offenders, rape, serious assault, kidnapping and armed robbery (s 3).

22 *Ibid*, s 18B(1).

the length of the sentence, the court is not to focus primarily on the seriousness of the offence, but the need to 'protect the public from serious harm from the offender'.[23] As is discussed in Chapters 10 and 11, in the US, three strikes laws, operating federally and in a number of States, require courts, when imposing penalties for certain types of repeat offenders, to look beyond the circumstances of the immediate offence, and impose harsh mandatory sentences, thus trumping the principle of proportionality.

The desirability of such exceptions to the proportionality principle can only be determined in light of an understanding of the rationale for the principle. This is considered below, but first some housekeeping in the form of attending to some definitional issues.

7.3 DEFINITIONAL MATTERS

7.3.1 Proportionality – limiting or determining?

Broadly, there are two ways that the proportionality principle can operate. In most jurisdictions, the principle of proportionality is used to provide a ceiling on the level of punishment; thus, it operates as a limiting consideration. This leaves a considerable amount of room for judicial discretion in sentencing; proportionality sets the outer limits of the sentence, however, this can be reduced by the operation of other relevant sentencing factors, such as rehabilitation and an offender's personal circumstances.

The second way in which proportionality can supposedly operate is as a determining principle, whereby other possible goals of punishment, such as deterrence and rehabilitation, are taken out of the sentencing inquiry, and the amount of punishment is a function solely of the seriousness of the crime. Here, there is obviously far less room for other factors to reduce the sentence. It is suggested that proportionality only in this sense ensures that the punishment fits the crime.[24] This is the notion of proportionality endorsed by its most influential advocate, Andrew von Hirsch, and which purportedly underpins sentencing grids in numerous States in the US that set presumptive sentences for a wide range of criminal offences. However, even in this sense, proportionality is still not truly determining. As is discussed in Chapter 10, many retributivists concede that there is still some room for considerations personal to the offender to have a role in calculating the amount of punishment. For example, von Hirsch contends that offenders with prior

---

23 Criminal Justice Act 1991 (UK) s 2(2)(b) (now consolidated as Powers of Criminal Courts (Sentencing) Act 2000, s 80(2)(b)). For a discussion of the manner in which these sections have been interpreted and their background, see Henham, 1997b, pp 494–98.

24 Fox, 1994, p 495.

convictions should be punished more severely than first time offenders and infers that deprived social background[25] may also have a role within a sentencing practice that adopts a 'determining' account of proportionality.

The decisiveness of proportionality in setting the amount of punishment depends upon the range of other principles and objectives that are properly relevant to sentencing. We saw in the previous chapter that considerations such as the offender's prospects of rehabilitation and need for specific deterrence are inappropriate sentencing goals. However, there is a plethora of other factors (especially those personal to the offender) which are customarily regarded as being highly relevant to the severity of the penalty. The weightiest of these is normally prior convictions. If the relevance of such considerations can be impugned, the principle of proportionality will take on a more determining character. The relevance of prior convictions and (some) other sentencing considerations is discussed further in Chapters 10 and 11. Apart from denying the relevance of sentencing variables, another way in which proportionality could assume a more authoritative role in fixing the quantum of punishment is if other considerations which are thought relevant to the sentencing inquiry are, in fact, embodied within the proportionality principle. The feasibility of this is discussed below. For present purposes, it is sufficient to note that in most jurisdictions, proportionality is applied in a limiting fashion, whereby it sets the upper ceiling of the penalty.

7.3.2 Ordinal and cardinal proportionality

It has been suggested that there are yet another two senses of proportionality. The first is ordinal proportionality, which concerns how offenders are punished relative to each other. It focuses on the relative seriousness of offences and comes down to the view that offenders who commit graver offences should receive sterner penalties. More fully, von Hirsch states that it has three features.[26] Parity, which requires that similar crimes deserve similar penalties. Ranking order, which means that more severe crimes are accorded more severe sanctions. The last requirement concerns spacing of penalties, and provides that the space between the seriousness of penalties should be commensurate with the difference in the seriousness of the offence.

In order for the scaling to commence, a starting point is needed. This is determined by selecting a particular crime or crimes (benchmark crimes) and

---

25 Although he is very cryptic on this point: see von Hirsch, 1993, pp 98–99, 106–08; 'Proportionate sentences: a desert perspective', in von Hirsch and Ashworth (eds), 1998, pp 168, 176–67. Ashworth, 1995, pp 122–24, more pointedly states that deprived social background is a factor which reduces culpability.

26 See von Hirsch, 1993, Chapter 7.

setting an appropriate sanction. Sanctions are then selected for all other crimes by comparing their seriousness with the benchmark crime and adjusting the penalty up or down accordingly. This process of anchoring the penalty scale is termed cardinal proportionality. Obviously, much depends on the benchmark, and in this regard it seems any penalty will do, so long as it does not violate the wide and loosely defined boundaries of cardinal proportionality.

von Hirsch believes that cardinal proportionality is not absolute, it is a convention. It is essentially a relative concept, however, at the extremes, there is a limit to the level of punishment which can be imposed. 'If suitable reasons can be established for objecting to ... [a] convention (for example, on grounds that it depreciates the importance of the rights of those convicted of ... low-ranking crimes) ... a non relative constraint is reached.'[27] This serves to anchor the penalty scale. In earlier writings, von Hirsch states that cardinal proportionality may be breached where the sanction 'fails to accord respect to the person punished' (emphasis added),[28] or where it 'denigrates the defendant's *right to liberty*' (emphasis added).[29] This anchoring point is, however, not absolute in the true sense. It is only absolute within the legal system under consideration, since different jurisdictions have different starting points which are generally determined without considered reflection, but are merely accepted as being intuitively correct.

The distinction between ordinal and cardinal proportionality must be treated with some caution. While it is not illusory, it does not provide a meaningful distinction in terms of giving substance to the proportionality principle. All the hard work still remains to be done. Getting back to basics for a moment, the starting point is that the gravity of an offence depends on its seriousness, where seriousness is gauged on the basis of certain (albeit, yet to be determined) criteria. Application of this standard to each offence will determine the seriousness of the offence. Logically, this task can be undertaken without one eye being kept on how other offences have been graded; in the same way that one grades mathematics papers: two times two is four, irrespective of what the other papers say. Ordinal proportionality is no more than an appeal to consistency; which requires that more grave offences are not treated less seriously than comparatively more minor offences. Thus, for example, murder must be treated more harshly than robbery, which in turn must be punished more severely than theft. However, this appeal to consistency is not a defining characteristic of proportionality. It is merely an incidental feature that will follow if the seriousness of each offence is ranked properly according to the same indicia. Beyond this, ordinal proportionality may be used to act as a check on the outcome of applying the relevant indicia

---

27 von Hirsch, 1994, pp 115, 129.
28 von Hirsch, 1985, p 44.
29 *Ibid*.

to each offence. If the result of such an analysis reveals disturbing rankings, for example, if it transpired that theft was more serious than murder, this breach of ordinal proportionality would suggest that the factors supposedly governing cardinal proportionality are incorrect or wrongly applied. However, this is not to set ordinal proportionality as a discrete defining requirement of proportionality. It is merely to recognise it is a by-product of a correct application of the appropriate variables relevant to cardinal proportionality and a tool that may be used to loosely check estimates of cardinal proportionality.

The most controversial aspect of von Hirsch's analysis of cardinal proportionality is his claim that it is a relative concept. This is right only to a point. Although the importance of certain interests varies across (and sometimes within) cultures, it may yet be possible to identify a sufficiently pervasive human concern or interest which is sensitive to such variations and, in this way, an objective formula for offence seriousness may be determined. This idea is developed below.

These preliminary matters aside, I will now focus on the first substantive issue at hand. As was adverted to earlier, the enthusiasm for the principle of proportionality is not matched by its clarity. The key concept regarding proportionality is the objective seriousness of the offence; however, this concept is so vague that it does not take the issue any further. In order for proportionality to be of practical guidance, it is necessary to give some content to the factors that are relevant to the gravity of the offence. After this, the commensurability between the offence and sanction must be determined.

7.4 FACTORS RELEVANT TO THE SERIOUSNESS OF AN OFFENCE

7.4.1 The approach by the courts

The courts have not attempted to define exhaustively the factors that are relevant to proportionality. The broad approach taken to this problem is to adopt the principle that the upper limit for an offence depends on its objective circumstances. Rather than positively defining these objective circumstances, it has proved easier to dismiss some considerations as being irrelevant. 'Good character ... repentance, restitution, possible rehabilitation and intransigence'[30] have been excluded.[31] However, some factors have been positively identified as relevant to offence seriousness. These include: the consequences of the offence, including the level of harm; the victim's

---

30 *Veen (No 2)* (1988) 164 CLR 465, p 491.
31 See, also, *Hoare* (1989) 167 CLR 348, p 363.

vulnerability and the method of the offence;[32] the offender's culpability, which turns on such factors as the offender's mental state[33] and his or her level of intelligence; the level of sophistication involved;[34] the protection of society;[35] and even the offender's previous criminal history.[36]

The problem, though, with such a list is that despite its non-exhaustive character, it is too particular, and no more than a Who's Who list of aggravating factors. Once considerations such as the method of the offence and a victim's vulnerability are included, there appears to be no logical basis for not including other considerations that are typically thought to increase the severity of an offence, such as breach of trust, the prevalence of the offence, profits derived from the offence, and an offender's degree of participation. Such an approach would merely turn the inquiry full circle to about the point it is currently at: a system where certain considerations are commonly believed to be relevant to the seriousness of the offence, but absent a fundamental principle against which these largely intuitive variables can be assessed and weighed. A more reasoned approach is required.

7.4.2 Living standard approach

Outline of the living standard approach to offence seriousness

von Hirsch and Jareborg have gone some way down this path, in what has been described by one pre-eminent commentator as the 'foremost modern attempt to establish some parameters for ordinal proportionality'.[37] They start with the assumption that the:

> ... seriousness of a crime has two dimensions: harm and culpability. Harm refers to the injury done or risked by the act; culpability to the factors of intent, motive and circumstances that determine the extent to which the offender should be held accountable for the act.[38]

In relation to the culpability component, they are content to import substantive criminal law doctrines of culpability – such as intention, recklessness and negligence – and excuses – such as provocation – into the sentencing stage. But they contend that such an approach is not possible with respect to harm, where they claim that 'virtually no legal doctrines have been

---

32 This includes the matters such as use of weapons, whether there was a breach of trust: see Fox, 1994, pp 499–500.

33 Eg, whether it was intentional, reckless or negligent.

34 See Fox, 1994, pp 498–501; New South Wales Law Reform Commission, 1996a, pp 62–64.

35 *Veen (No 2)* (1988) 164 CLR 465, p 474.

36 *Mulholland* (1991) 1 NTLR 1.

37 Ashworth, 1995, p 93.

38 von Hirsch and Jareborg, 1991, p 1.

developed on how the gravity of harms can be compared'.[39] Thus, the focus of their inquiry is to give content to the harm component.

They approach this task by considering the seriousness of an offence against a background of important human concerns and confine their analysis to conduct that is (already) criminal and injures or threatens identifiable victims. Aggravating or mitigating considerations are not addressed due to the complexity that this would import. In a bid to gauge the level of harm caused by an offence, the starting point for von Hirsch and Jareborg is to use a broad based 'living standard' criterion where the gravity of criminal harm is determined 'by the importance that the relevant interests have for a person's standard of living'.[40] The living standard focuses on the means or capabilities for achieving a certain quality of life, rather than actual life quality or goal achievement.

They formulate four living standard levels, which are used to determine the degree to which a particular crime affects a person's living standard. The most important is subsistence, which equates to survival with no more than basic capacities to function. Then follows minimal well being and adequate well being, which mean maintenance of a minimum and adequate level of comfort and dignity, respectively. Finally, there is enhanced well being, which is defined as significant enhancement in quality of life. The most grievous harms are those which most drastically diminish one's standard of well being. Thus, a crime which violates the first level (subsistence) is the most serious, whereas one which infringes only enhanced well being is the least serious.

Next, they determine the types of interest which are violated or threatened by the paradigm instances of particular offences. They identify four basic types of interest. In descending order, they are: physical integrity; material support and amenity (ranging from nutrition and shelter to various luxuries); freedom from humiliating or degrading treatment; and privacy and autonomy. Some interest dimensions, such as physical integrity, are applicable to all of the grades on the living standard scale, depending on the level of intrusion, whereas other interests such as privacy and autonomy are confined to levels including and below minimum well being.

After the interest (or interests) violated by the typical instance of a particular offence is ascertained, the effect on the living standard is then determined. For example, in the case of a stock in trade burglary, physical integrity is not affected and, assuming the item stolen is inexpensive and easily replaceable, material amenity is also scarcely affected. Privacy is more significantly affected, hence on the living standard it ranks at level 4 (as affecting enhanced well being).

---

39   von Hirsch and Jareborg, 1991, p 3.
40   *Ibid*, p 12.

A crime may violate more than one type of interest and, therefore, result in multiple living standard ratings in different dimensions. For example, an assault which causes only minor injury would rank low on the physical integrity dimension (thus, possibly, at level 4 on the living standard – as violating enhanced well being), but high in the freedom from humiliation component. This gives it an overall 3 rating on the living standard, since it is contended that a certain level of self-respect is part of minimal well being. To account for such 'combinations' (and discounts), the effect on the living standard is mapped onto a harm scale, which has five graduations, ranging from grave to lesser. As an example, living standard 1 (subsistence) maps onto the grave level and level 4 (enhanced well being) equates to the second lowest level of harm: lower intermediate.

After the harm scale score is determined, discounts are accorded where crimes create only a risk or threat to a particular interest: the remoter the risk or less likely the threat, the greater the discount. As such, attempted offences are regarded as being less serious than completed ones. von Hirsch and Jareborg do not address at length the issue of culpability, but imply that discounts should also be given for less blameworthy states of mind. Thus, harm caused, say, negligently does not rate as high as when it is caused intentionally.

Criticisms of the living standard approach to offence seriousness

There appears to be considerable merit in the above type of approach to determining the factors that are relevant to the level of harm caused by an offence. In a nutshell, the argument is that the seriousness of an offence is gauged by the impact that the crime has on the living standard of the typical victim. To determine the seriousness of a crime, a logical starting point appears to be to assess the level of detriment that it inflicts, where the level of detriment is viewed from the perspective of important human concerns. von Hirsch and Jareborg identify what they feel are important human concerns and also go about ranking them – as they must do, to give some content to their formulation. However, the problem with their ranking system is that despite the fact that they concede that their analysis is normative, since it is a theory on how harms ought to be rated, it is devoid of an underlying rationale. Intuition aside, we are not told why privacy and autonomy are any less important than, say, freedom from humiliation. In order to determine issues such as this, an underlying moral theory is needed. von Hirsch and Jareborg accept this; however, they are content to rest their case on the basis that an 'articulated moral theory' underpinning the living standard is beyond the scope of their discussion.[41] They go on to state that they are 'not trying to develop an invariant harm analysis, but instead to derive ratings applicable

---

41   von Hirsch and Jareborg, 1991, p 15.

here, given certain prevailing social practices and also certain *ethical traditions'* (emphasis added).[42] Some of the social practices they assume are spelt out, such as that, as a result of social convention, the home is important for a comfortable existence. However, the detail we are not told is what 'ethical traditions' have been assumed.

We are informed that the living standard for gauging harm is used because 'it appears to fit the way one ordinarily judges harms'.[43] Further, the 'living standard provides, not a generalised ethical norm, but a *useful* standard which the law can use in gauging the harmfulness of criminal acts' (emphasis added).[44] This, however, misses the point: useful in what sense? Any standard is useful, because for one it will assist in achieving uniformity in sentencing, but so what; a standard based on spiritual, or purely economic well being will also achieve this. von Hirsch and Jareborg attempt to turn the criticism that their theory lacks a justification on its head: '... the living standard approach also has the advantage of a certain modesty; no "deep" theory or preferred life-aims or appropriate social roles is presupposed.'[45] This provides no reason why their theory should not be overlooked in preference of a theory that has a 'deep' underlying rationale. They make the further point that the State should protect victimising harm, because people require certain 'resources to live decent lives'.[46] However, without an underlying theory, no justification is offered why the institution of punishment should be targeted at intrusions which frustrate the leading of 'decent' lives any more than those which interfere with the leading of rewarding, epicurean, or for that matter downright scurrilous lives.

A utilitarian theory of offence seriousness

The selection and adoption of certain harms in preference to others can only be justified by reference to an underlying moral theory. To this end, an obvious candidate is utilitarianism, which offers a simple method for determining the types of interest that are relevant to harm seriousness: the reason that some interests are important and worthy of protection by the criminal law is because they are integral to the attainment of happiness. In fact, the approach adopted (and conclusions reached) by von Hirsch and Jareborg has uncanny similarities with a transparently utilitarian evaluation of harm analysis. The considerations they identify are no more than a rough armchair utilitarian scale of the primacy of interests relevant to happiness. For example, it seems evident that the most essential requirement to the

---

42 von Hirsch and Jareborg, 1991, p 15.

43 *Ibid*, p 11.

44 *Ibid*, pp 11–12.

45 *Ibid*, p 12.

46 *Ibid*, p 12.

attainment of any degree of meaningful happiness is physical integrity and subsistence, followed by material support and minimal well being and so on. The type of infringement which most seriously interferes with our capacity to attain happiness is to our physical integrity. The next thing many seem to value most is material support. Freedom from humiliation and privacy and autonomy, though not necessarily in that order, are also important interests towards the road to happiness.

A far more persuasive manner to gauge the seriousness of harm is to adopt a utilitarian primary rationale and then to prescribe weight to defined interests in accordance with empirical observations about the interests that are valued most highly. This may seem imprecise, given the immense diversity in human aims and interests; however, such diversity does not present an insurmountable obstacle.

Promising research suggests that we are not all that different after all in respect to the things that make us happy. The results of a recent study, following 11 years of research based on thousands of questionnaires, have revealed a general convergence in the things that make us happy. For example, the study has shown that money does not guarantee happiness. People on middle incomes are just as happy as the rich, and only the very poor are less happy (happiness only increases with income, where people believe they are being paid more than they expect). In keeping with this, it was revealed that the purchase of luxury items, such as expensive clothes and oil paintings, makes us no happier. One of the main guarantees of happiness (especially for men) is marriage, largely due to the companionship and emotional support which it provides. The corollary of this is also true: divorced and separated people are the least happy (even more so than people who have been widowed). Also, the more challenged a person is, whether by a job, hobby or sport, the happier he or she is likely to be.[47]

von Hirsch and Jareborg, perhaps anticipating that they may be accused of merely reverting to a utilitarian doctrine of punishment and human interests, expressly reject this on the basis that a utilitarian theory of punishment is concerned only with future orientated goals, such as estimating how future harm may be reduced through certain penal strategies, unlike a retributive account which focuses only on the amount of harm which has been caused: '... we are assuming a past-oriented and retributive account for how much to punish ... not a future-oriented and preventive one.'[48]

---

47 The study was conducted by Professor M Argyle, and is due to be published shortly. One quirky result was that people who watch television soaps were happier than those who did not, but watching lots of soaps was counter-productive to happiness. See Reid, T, 'Some research that may bring you a degree of happiness' (1998) *The Age*, 6 October, p 10. See, also, Argyle, 1987.

48 von Hirsch and Jareborg, 1991, p 16.

This is a puzzling argument. It comes down to the view that because the seriousness of an offence is not exhaustive of the type of considerations that are relevant to the utilitarian sentencing calculus, therefore, the underlying standards being used to gauge crime seriousness cannot be utilitarian. All theories of punishment accept that the harm caused by crime is at least one of the reasons why a punitive response is called for. Thus, the determination of the amount of harm is central to all theories of punishment. The fact that an answer to this inquiry does not settle the issue of how much to punish is irrelevant – one step at a time. Moreover, where a solution to a complex problem requires consideration of several distinct matters, surely the soundest approach is to determine each matter in accordance with an overarching theory or principle. This is precisely the view propounded by Ashworth, another leading retributivist, who asserts that considerations which are relevant to proportionality should 'flow from the same source as the rationale(s) of sentencing'.[49] This being so, it is clear why von Hirsch and Jareborg are keen to distance their analysis from any utilitarian overtones: if a utilitarian theory of harm is adopted, why not then adopt a utilitarian theory of punishment?

7.4.3 The law of criminal defences and proportionality

von Hirsch and Jareborg are also not correct in stating that 'virtually no legal doctrines have been developed on how the gravity of harms can be compared'.[50] The courts, unwittingly, have gone some way towards weighing the relative importance of human concerns. However, this has not occurred in the field of sentencing law and practice. Sentencing principles which have evolved over the years are a poor guide to the relative seriousness of conduct because, as Ashworth notes,[51] disproportionate weight is often given to aggravating or mitigating factors in respect of particular offences. Additionally, penalties are often imposed without regard to standard types of penalty for other types of offence. To the extent that courts, in sentencing, do make across the board comparisons with other types of offence, the ranking is not authoritative because it is hypothetical; there is no conflict between one type of interest which has been violated and another. A further problem is that many offences capture a wide range of conduct. For example, the offence of theft encompasses both a spur of the moment taking of a chocolate bar and a meticulously planned dishonest appropriation of millions of dollars from a charity. Accordingly, it is difficult to make meaningful comparisons of offence seriousness based on the range of penalties imposed.

---

49 Ashworth, 1995, p 147.

50 *Ibid*, p 3.

51 *Ibid*, p 126.

The key to the present inquiry is to broaden the horizons a little beyond sentencing and focus on the law of criminal defences. This is the area of law which most directly involves the clashing of competing interests and where the courts have been forced to consider in a real sense the relative importance of these interests and thereby, albeit inadvertently, provide a ranking of them. Admittedly, this exercise, too, has been performed without an underlying rationale. Criminal defences have not been developed with an eye to any overarching principle. Yet, this process has one distinct and enormous advantage over other approaches: it is practical; at the end of each decision were real rights and interests. And nothing is more likely to sharpen and focus the intellect more than the realisation that at stake are important concrete interests.

Necessity and duress

The most significant defences (in terms of the breadth of conduct they apply to) are necessity and duress. Necessity has three elements:

> [First], the criminal act or acts must have been done only in order to avoid certain *consequences* which would have inflicted irreparable evil upon the accused or upon others whom he was bound to protect ... [Secondly], the accused must honestly believe on reasonable grounds that he [or she] was placed in a situation of imminent peril ... [Finally], the acts done to avoid the imminent peril must not be out of proportion to the peril to be avoided [emphasis added].[52]

In short, the defence will apply to excuse otherwise harmful criminal conduct where the reason for the conduct is to avoid greater harm occurring: '... it is justifiable in an emergency to break the letter of the law if breaking the law will avoid a greater harm than obeying it.'[53] Necessity is a defence to all conduct except murder.[54] This is due to the fear that were necessity to excuse murder it 'might be made the legal cloak for unbridled passion and atrocious crime'.[55] Although such sentiment is probably more emotive than real, this is the legal position which has prevailed for well over a century, and confirms that the interest rated most highly by the courts is human life. Physical integrity and property interests are also rated highly. The risk to life or property justifies breaches of laws aimed to regulate and co-ordinate human

---

52 *Loughnan* [1981] VR 443, p 448. See, also, *Dawson* [1978] VR 536, p 543.

53 O'Connor and Fairfall, 1996, p 103.

54 *Dudley and Stephens* (1884) 14 QBD 273. However, see *A (Children)* B1/2000/2969, 22 September 2000: http://www.courtservice.gov.uk/judgments/judg-home.htm, where two of the Lord Justices (Ward and Brooke LJJ) were prepared to extend the defence of necessity to the truly unique facts of the case (see Chapter 4).

55 Lord Coleridge in *Dudley and Stephens* (1884) 14 QBD 273, p 288.

affairs;[56] and it is permissible to violate laws protecting physical integrity or property in order to prevent greater interferences with these interests. Thus, for example, it is permissible to sterilise a person who is incapable of consenting in order to save his or her life or prevent deterioration in the person's mental or physical health.[57]

The defence of duress exculpates otherwise criminal behaviour which is committed in response to threats of immediate death or serious personal violence, to the accused or another, that are so great to overbear the will of the ordinary person.[58] As with necessity, it does not excuse murder:

> Though a man be violently assaulted, and hath no other possible means of escaping death, but by killing an innocent person; this fear and force shall not acquit him of murder; for he ought rather to die himself, than escape by murder of an innocent.[59]

This again underlines the primacy of human life. Duress is, however, a defence to all other offences, including the serious offences of escape from custody,[60] drug importation,[61] and fraud.[62]

There are several illuminating matters to emerge from a consideration of the above two defences. First, an approximate hierarchy of important human concerns has been developed. At the top is human life, then physical integrity, followed by property rights, and then comes mental integrity. Thus, for example, in order to protect one's physical safety, it is permissible to destroy or damage the property of others or threaten to do so.

Secondly, the law of criminal defences has essentially a consequentialist foundation. With only some minor glitches it seems that the basic pattern to emerge is that all behaviour which would otherwise be criminal is justified if it is committed in order to avoid a less harmful outcome. When the law is required to determine in a concrete manner important competing interests, intellectual niceties such as (absolute) rights and other deontological considerations are swept aside; consequences being the only relevant currency.

Thus far, a consideration of criminal defences has shown that as far as the courts are concerned, the most important consideration to the availability and

---

56   *Johnson v Phillips* [1976] 1 WLR 65, Wien J. It is also a defence to gaol-break where the prisoner believes it is necessary to avoid death or serious injury: *Loughnan* [1981] VR 443, pp 457–58.

57   *In Re F (Mental Patient: Sterilisation)* [1990] 2 AC 1.

58   *AG v Whelan* [1934] IR 518, p 526; *Lawrence* (1980) 32 ALR 72, pp 91–104, 135–45. Other aspects of the defence are discussed in *Dawson* [1978] VR 536, pp 537–38, 541.

59   Blackstone, *Commentaries on the Laws of England*, Book 4, 1769 (1966 edn), Oxford: Clarendon, p 30. See, also, *Abbot* [1977] AC 755, pp 764–65; *Howe* [1987] AC 417, p 429.

60   *Dawson* [1978] VR 536.

61   *Lawrence* (1980) 32 ALR 72.

62   *Osborne v Goddard* (1978) 21 ALR 189.

scope of a defence is the consequences flowing from the otherwise criminal act compared to the likely consequences which would have resulted if the act was not committed. From this it follows that in defining the seriousness of an offence, a central consideration is the level of harm caused by the offence. This analysis sits most comfortably with a utilitarian rationale of punishment, although, as we have seen, retributivists are also not slow to invoke such considerations.

7.4.4 Criminal defences and culpability

The law of criminal defences reveals that mental states are also relevant to the determination of criminal liability and offence severity. This is evident from defences such as insanity, provocation, mistake and intoxication. Generally, where a person engages in conduct which is otherwise criminal, and harms another, however, does so without being aware of the wrongness of his or her actions, the person is not criminally liable. Similar considerations apply in relation to the substantive criminal law, where reckless and negligent offences are (typically) not regarded as being as grave as intentional ones. Thus, it is apparent that according to established legal doctrine, culpability is also relevant to the seriousness of the offence.

Recapping the points that have emerged from a consideration of the law of criminal defences: both consequences and culpability may serve to either totally or at least partially (in the case of provocation) excuse otherwise criminal conduct and are the only factors which can obviate the criminality of conduct. The corollary of this is that when one is attempting to determine the factors that are relevant to the seriousness of an offence, these factors, in the end, appear to be the only ones that are relevant.

7.4.5 Proportionality and aggravating and mitigating circumstances

As we saw earlier, the courts, in gauging the seriousness of an offence, have permitted a wide range of variables other than the harm caused and the offender's culpability to come into play. However, there are several problems with allowing factors not directly related to the offence to have a role in evaluating offence seriousness.

First, as has been discussed, many of the sentencing variables which are currently regarded as key considerations in the sentencing calculus, such as the offender's prospects of rehabilitation and the need for specific deterrence, are in fact misguided.

Secondly, it is contradictory to claim that the principle of proportionality means the punishment should be commensurate with the seriousness of the offence, and then to allow considerations external to the offence to have a role in determining how much punishment is appropriate. Once the inquiry extends to matters not even remotely connected with the crime, such as the offender's upbringing or previous convictions, the parameters of *the offence* have been clearly exhausted (see, further, Chapter 10).

Finally, by allowing such considerations a look in, much of the splendour of the principle of proportionality dissipates. The principle then cannot be claimed as being indicative of anything: to ascertain how much to punish, the simplistically appealing idea of looking only at the objective seriousness of the offence is abandoned and the inquiry must move elsewhere – and indeed everywhere. Giving content to the principle of proportionality would become unworkable. In each particular sentencing inquiry, the principle would need to be flexible enough to accommodate not only the objective circumstances of the offence, but also the mitigating circumstances. Given the uniqueness of each offender's personal circumstances and the vast number of variables which are supposedly relevant to such an inquiry,[63] and the fact that mitigating factors often pull in a diametrically opposite direction to the objective factors relevant to the offence, any attempt to provide a workable principle of proportionality must fail. It was for this reason that von Hirsch and Jareborg, when elaborating on the matters that are relevant to gauging the seriousness of the offence, declined to consider aggravating and mitigating circumstances. A non-tautologous definition of proportionality would be impossible if the proportionality principle must accommodate the full range of supposed sentencing considerations.

There may still be a role for circumstances which are not relevant to the objective seriousness of the offence in the determination of the appropriate penalty. However, the basis for their relevance must stem from other considerations which are thought to be integral to the sentencing calculus – for example, it could be argued that remorse is relevant because it reflects on the character of the accused.[64]

The picture regarding the offence seriousness limb of proportionality is now clear. The gravity of the offence is determined by a consideration of two factors: the harm caused and the culpability of the offender. Although the courts have yet to acknowledge this, the harm/intention approach to proportionality has been adopted in some jurisdictions. In Finland, Art 6 of the Penal Code provides that punishment shall be proportionate to the damage and danger caused by the offence and to the guilt of the offender manifested in the offence. In Sweden, Chapter 29 of the Penal Code provides that sentences shall be based on the penal value of the offence which is

---

63 The principle would need to be so extensive to include all of the 300 or so factors that the courts have recognised as being relevant sentencing considerations: see Chapter 2.

64 Although, as is discussed in Chapter 10, character is not a consideration which is properly relevant to the determination of how much to punish.

determined with special regard to 'the damage, wrong or danger occasioned by the criminal act, to what the accused realised or should have realised about this, and to the intentions or motive he may have had'.

As is noted above, there are many circumstances in which the proportionality principle is violated. In order to ascertain the desirability of incursions into the principle, it is necessary to determine its ranking and priority relative to other sentencing goals. This can only be ascertained by considering its underlying rationale. An inquiry into the justification of proportionality will also assist in checking the conclusions reached above. To establish properly the considerations that are relevant to the seriousness of an offence, it is necessary to determine the justification for the principle of proportionality.

7.5 THE JUSTIFICATION OF PROPORTIONALITY

7.5.1 Retributivism and proportionality

Proportionality is most naturally associated with a retributive account of punishment. I shall consider whether the link between these two ideals is as firm as is generally believed. Given the vast array of retributive theories, it is not possible to consider every retributive argument in favour of proportionality. The focus is on the most influential accounts that have been advanced.

Censure and proportionality

von Hirsch believes that the following three steps justify the proportionality principle:

(1) The State's sanctions against proscribed conduct should take a punitive form; that is, visit deprivations in a manner that expresses censure or blame.

(2) The severity of a sanction expresses the stringency of the blame.

(3) Hence, punitive sanctions should be arrayed according to the degree of blameworthiness (that is seriousness) of the conduct.[65]

The major problem with this argument is the second part of the first premise. The claim that a sanction should express blame stems from von Hirsch's underlying theory of punishment; however, by his own lights, this tells only part of the story. von Hirsch's theory of punishment focuses heavily on the claim that the aim of punishment is to express censure; that is, to convey

---

65   von Hirsch, 1993, p 15.

condemnation or blame directed at a responsible wrongdoer. However, more fully, for von Hirsch the purpose and function of punishment is actually twofold: '(1) to *discourage* [criminal] conduct, and (2) to express disapproval of [criminal] conduct and its perpetrators' (emphasis added).[66]

And, he attempts to gain much mileage from the deterrent justification. As we saw in Chapter 4, he invokes the deterrence rationale in an attempt to justify the need for hard treatment (given that he concedes that censure alone cannot justify such treatment).

Given that punishment, according to von Hirsch, has two purposes, it is untenable to then claim that the amount of punishment which is deserved is determined solely by its censuring goal. This, in turn, undermines the credibility of the second premise, since logically, both rationales for punishment must affect the inquiry of how much to punish. This being the case, it may be necessary to impose sanctions that are significantly more severe than is required to match the blameworthiness of criminal conduct.

von Hirsch is alert to this criticism, and responds by stating that despite his bifurcated account of punishment, prevention cannot be invoked in deciding how much to punish, because proportionality would then be undermined.[67] But, this misses the point that proportionality is not a justification for punishment, merely a restraint on it; derived from the rationale for punishment. Further, if one wishes to remain true to one's theory, as Hirsch clearly does, dissatisfaction with an outcome of it calls for a re-appraisal of the appropriateness of the outcome; it does not justify expedient application of the theory. In a second counter, von Hirsch provides that sterner sanctions in order to satisfy the deterrent role of punishment are unjustified because this amounts to 'tiger control',[68] which fails to address the offender as a moral agent. This fails to circumvent my initial criticism, and only confirms that von Hirsch believes that a consequence of his theory is unpalatable; and yet he still wishes to embrace his theory.

Lex talionis

The principle of proportionality perhaps sits most comfortably with the *lex talionis* approach to punishment – an eye for an eye, a tooth for a tooth. However, there are numerous shortcomings of the theory. The *lex talionis* has no clear application in relation to many offences: '... what penalty would you inflict on a rapist, a blackmailer, a forger, a dope peddler, a multiple murderer, a smuggler, or a toothless fiend who has knocked somebody else's teeth out?'[69]

---

66 von Hirsch, 1985, p 52.
67 *Ibid*, p 16.
68 *Ibid*, p 17.
69 Kleinig, 1973, p 120.

It has been suggested that a more plausible interpretation of the *lex talionis* is that the punishment and the crime should be equal or equivalent.[70] However, this fails to provide even a vague formula by which the different currencies of crime and punishment can be equated and does not address the issue of why we ought to punish.

Intuitive appeal of proportionality

Retributivists may seek to capitalise on the self-evident appeal of the proportionality principle. However, on a post-philosophical level, this charm readily dissipates. Followed to its logical conclusion, the proportionality principle requires punishment even when no good would stem from it.

The intuitive appeal of the proportionality principle is also challenged by claims that it is too soft. As we saw in Chapter 4, Duhring criticised the proportionality principle (in the form of the *lex talionis*) not because it is too barbaric, but rather because it does not go far enough.

With its emphasis on revenge, this argument may appear to represent an overly emotive response to punishment and criminality. However, it highlights the fact that intuition often cuts both ways and is nearly always a poor substitute for reason. I now turn to what I consider to be the most convincing rationale for the principle of proportionality.

7.5.2 Utilitarianism and proportionality

Proportionality has traditionally been thought to have no role in a utilitarian theory of punishment. However, Bentham outlined a general argument which provides a utilitarian justification for proportionality: 'the greater the mischief of the offence, the greater is the expense, which it may be worthwhile to be at, in the way of punishment'.[71] Thus, the greater the harm caused by an offence, the more severe the punishment may be before it outweighs the suffering caused by the offence. Rather than focusing squarely on retrospective considerations to do with the nature of an offence to determine how much to punish, utilitarians place greater emphasis on prospective matters, such as the need for deterrence, rehabilitation and so on. Given this, it is understandable that criticisms of utilitarianism have been made to the effect that it justifies substantial punishment for minor offences, where this is necessary to reform the offender.[72] Such objections, though, are misguided, since they overemphasise one utilitarian purpose of punishment. It cannot be forgotten that the utilitarian regards punishment as inherently bad, and thus it is

---

70 Ten, 1987, p 153.

71 Bentham, 1970, p 168. This is also discussed by *ibid*, Ten, pp 143–44.

72 See Armstrong, 1971, p 19.

unsupportable where the overall bad consequences outweigh its good effects. And, it is hardly contentious that the harm caused by, say, the theft of a loaf of bread is less than the pain of gaoling the offender for many years in order to stop similar behaviour.[73]

Bentham also argued in favour of the proportionality principle on the basis that if crimes are to be committed, it is preferable that offenders commit less serious rather than more serious ones. He believed that sanctions should be graduated commensurate to the seriousness of the offence so that those disposed to crime will opt for less serious offences. In the absence of proportionality, potential offenders would not be deterred from committing serious offences any more than minor ones, and hence would just as readily commit them. This argument, however, has been persuasively criticised by von Hirsch, who points out that there is no evidence that offenders make comparisons regarding the level of punishment for various offences.[74]

However, there is yet another basis upon which proportionality may have a role in utilitarian punishment. Disproportionate sentences risk placing the entire criminal justice system into disrepute because such sentences would offend the principle that privileges and obligations ought to be distributed roughly in accordance with the degree of merit or blame attributable to each individual.[75] Clear violations of this principle lead to antipathy towards institutions or practices which condone such outcomes:

> Proportion in punishment is a widely found and deeply rooted principle in many penal contexts. It is ... integral to many conceptions of justice and as such the principle of proportion in punishment seen generally acts to annul, rather than to exacerbate, social dysfunction.[76]

Indeed, it is felt that one of the main reasons for the success of the Finnish criminal justice system is the emphasis placed on the principle of proportionality: '... principles of proportionality and perceived procedural fairness are key factors that influence the willingness of the people to conform to the law.'[77] The kind of mindset which may emerge if proportionality is ignored is demonstrated by reaction following the revelation that Kerry

---

73 See, also, Ten, 1987, pp 141–42.

74 von Hirsch, 1985, p 32.

75 In essence here I am employing a concept of desert, however, unlike retributivist it is justified on the basis of forward looking considerations. A similar concept is employed by Duncan Jones, AE, in *Butler's Moral Philosophy*, 1952, Harmondsworth: Penguin. But see Kleinig, 1973, pp 56–57, who criticises this notion of desert as being confused with usefulness. It could be argued that the principle I am invoking at this point is similar to the argument (which I rejected in Chapter 4) in support of intrinsic retributivism, that there is a pervasive desire to punish the guilty. However, unlike in the case of intrinsic retributivism, the principle of proportionality is not being advanced as a self-evident truth, but (as I discuss below) rather because it is claimed that if it is observed, it will instrumentally lead to good consequences.

76 Harding and Ireland, 1989, p 205.

77 Lappi-Seppala, 1998, Part II, para 3.

Packer, Australia's wealthiest individual, whose personal wealth exceeds five billion dollars, paid no tax over the period 1989–1993.[78] After a protracted investigation by the Australian Taxation Office into his financial affairs, the Federal Court ruled that according to the law which existed at the time, the zero tax paid by Packer correctly represented the full extent of his tax liability.[79] This led to howls of community resentment and enmity, most notably in the form of countless calls to talk-back radio and letters to newspapers, towards the taxation system in Australia. The credibility and legitimacy of the entire system was questioned because it failed to ensure that the level of tax paid by Packer was in proportion to his ability to pay. The same principle underlies the general community attitude towards punishing criminals. A legal system that repeatedly condoned excessively harsh, or for that matter lenient, sentences would eventually lose the support of many members of the community. This may result in less co-operation with organisations involved in the detection and processing of criminals and thereby lead to fewer crimes being reported and solved and ultimately a diminution in community safety; thereby undermining the important role of the criminal law in promoting general happiness.[80]

Culpability in a utilitarian theory of punishment

In order to press home the utilitarian case for proportionality, there remains the obstacle of justifying the role of culpability in the determination of offence seriousness. Ultimately, utilitarianism defers to the weight of consequences, and allocating a pivotal role to other considerations seems to sit uncomfortably with this. This is in contrast to the relative ease with which retributivists enlist considerations relating to an offender's degree of wrongdoing. Non-consequentialist moral theories of morality, which typically underpin retributive theories of punishment, assert that intentions have intrinsic moral relevance: the intention to help others is worthy of moral praise, while the intention to harm justifies moral condemnation.

However, the utilitarian can also justify the relevance of culpability to offence seriousness. As far as the utilitarian is concerned, culpability is an important consideration regarding offence seriousness. It is just that it has a secondary role in the utilitarian calculus, which must always yield to consequences as the ultimate determinant. The reason that culpability is

---

78　See (1998) *The Age*, Melbourne, 15 October, p 3.

79　Packer rejected an offer to settle the matter with the Taxation Office out of court on the basis that he pay $30.55 for the three year period. Packer managed to minimise his tax essentially through the use of foreign tax shelters.

80　Although criminals are not renowned for engendering community support or sympathy, see Chapter 11 below regarding the recent demonstrations in Melbourne against mandatory sentences. Further, as is also discussed in Chapter 11, harsh sentencing laws often result in criminal justice officials resorting to surreptitious tactics to avoid the operation of such laws.

important is that offenders who intend the harm caused by their crimes are a greater threat than those who merely harm others through, say, accident, or even negligence or recklessness. But, it is important to emphasise that intention[81] has no intrinsic relevance. This, however, is not a weakness of the theory, and accords with the actual significance normally attributed to intentions. This was highlighted by example of Jack in Chapter 5. As was stated earlier, this does not mean that intentions and other types of mental states are irrelevant and that a strict liability system of law should be adopted. There is a close connection between our intentions and actions and therefore the person who intentionally brings about a harmful act is more blameworthy than one who does so due to, say, indifference or mistake. Even though the immediate and direct consequences are identical, the person who deliberately sets in train a causal process which results in harm to another deserves greater punishment because such behaviour carries a greater certainty of suffering, and needs to be more strongly deterred.

Although the bottom line regarding a utilitarian ranking of seriousness can be reduced to one variable – the consequences of the offence (essentially the harm done or risked) – one need not be short-sighted and, accordingly, there is room for intention to play an important role regarding offence seriousness. Thus, even where an offender attempts to commit an offence, but fails to cause any harm, the utilitarian is still justified in punishing the offender, since he or she has demonstrated a predisposition which may lead to undesirable consequences if not retrained or discouraged.

Proportionality not absolute

A further objection is that the proportionality principle is not an absolute prescription in a utilitarian theory of punishment. This is correct. Yet, this is not criticism, since no principle or virtue is absolute, and on rare occasions the proportionality principle may need to make way for more pressing objectives. However, what utilitarianism does do is make proportionality the strongest virtue it can be, since it is only here that it has a secure foundation. Further, proportionality can be violated only where this will maximise happiness; however, given that there is a lack of convincing evidence supporting the efficacy of punishment to attain the traditional utilitarian objectives of punishment that could theoretically call for harsher sentences (incapacitation, specific deterrence, marginal general deterrence and rehabilitation), there is no basis for imposing penalties which exceed the severity of the offence.

---

81 It should be noted that I do not equate culpability only with intention. It can also be manifested in terms of recklessness, negligence, and careless. Intention is merely the most serious form of culpability.

Slightly more punishment?

Even if one ignores the possible application of other sentencing objectives to the determination of penalty severity, an argument could be made out on prudential grounds that the harshness of the penalty should exceed the seriousness of the offence. If disproportionate penalties were not imposed, it could be contended that self-interested, rational people would have no reason to not commit crimes where the advantage to them is about the same as the detriment caused by the offence. This is because the chances of apprehension and conviction are always less than certain, and accordingly, the probability of this multiplied by the amount of unpleasantness caused by a proportionate sanction is less than the initial gain to the offender. Taking the simple case of shoplifting as an example, if the proportionate penalty for stealing a $500 item is equal to this sum, that is a $500 fine (or an equivalent unpleasantness, say, five days' imprisonment), it could be argued that all self-interested prudent people should shoplift. A rational offender would only entertain second thoughts about this if the threatened penalty equalled the harm caused by the offence divided by the probability of being caught and convicted. For example, if half of all shoplifters are apprehended and successfully prosecuted, the penalty for stealing a $500 item, it could be reasoned, should be $1,000. Theoretically, this argument is valid, but there is no evidence that potential offenders engage in such mental arithmetic, and the fact that there is no verifiable link between penalty severity and crime rate militates strongly against such evidence emerging.

7.6 COMMENSURABILITY BETWEEN THE OFFENCE AND THE SANCTION

Finally, it is time to consider (briefly) the other key problem regarding proportionality: how to weigh the severity of the punishment with the seriousness of the offence. The relative brevity of this discussion is not a reflection of the importance or the level of controversy in this area. Rather, given the discussion above, the answer to this problem is straightforward.

To the problem of ordering the severity of penalties, the utilitarian has a relatively simple response. The type and degree of punishment imposed on the offender should cause him or her to experience a degree of unhappiness about equal to the amount of unhappiness caused by the offence. The harm caused by crime and the benefits of punishments are calculated by reference to the same variable, happiness.

Even some retributivists come close to such a formula. von Hirsch asserts that an interests analysis, similar to the living standard analysis he adopts for gauging crime seriousness, should be used to estimate the severity of penalties.[82] Ashworth states that proportionality at the outer limits 'excludes punishments which impose far greater *hardships* on the offender than does the crime on victims and society in general' (emphasis added).[83]

Although there are practical empirical difficulties associated with applying the utilitarian calculus, at least it lays down a workable formula. Retributivists, on the other hand, attempt to weigh the severity of the punishment against the seriousness of the crime; however, they have no obvious variable to start with. Ultimately, they are forced to rely expediently on consequential considerations.

It has been suggested that one cannot grade the severity of penalties because painfulness is a subjective concept.[84] A taxi driver who is deprived of his or her licence feels the pain far more severely than a person who works from home. This is no doubt true, but the same applies regarding the harm caused by criminal offences. Pickpocketing $5 from Bill Gates is hardly likely to cause him even the slightest angst, whereas stealing the last $5 from a hungry, homeless person may have a devastating impact upon him or her. Despite the enormous difference in the impact of these offences, the law has no difficulty in making theft an offence; and, secondly, it has not resiled from evaluating the general seriousness of such conduct. This is because, in relation to any body of law, generalisations must be made about the things that people value and the typical effect of certain behaviour on these interests.

The way to minimise the subjectivity problem regarding the severity of sanctions is to ensure that criminal sanctions target interests which are widely coveted, such as liberty, the ownership of property and other social privileges which are typically incidental to leading a happy life. One illuminating point to emerge from this, which is elaborated in Chapter 9, is that it implies that the range of criminal sanctions should be extended and the fixation on imprisonment should be reduced. The types of interest that are normally targeted by criminal sanctions hardly exhausts the list of interests that are generally an incident of happiness.

7.7 CONCLUSION

The principle of proportionality prescribes that the severity of the sanction should be equal to the seriousness of the offence. This concept has proved difficult to implement. There have been two main reasons for this. First, there is no true appreciation of what factors are relevant to the seriousness of an offence. It has been suggested that this is gauged solely by reference to the

---

82 von Hirsch and Jareborg, 1991, pp 34–35.

83 Ashworth, 1995, p 97.

84 Walker, 1991, p 99.

amount of unhappiness caused by the offence. Secondly, there is no principled method for ascertaining the severity of punishment. This, too, has been addressed, by employing the same common denominator: happiness. These conclusions flow from the fact that a utilitarian theory of punishment best underpins the principle of proportionality. A consideration of the law of criminal defences has shown that the courts, over the ages, have employed essentially consequential considerations in evaluating the seriousness of 'criminal' behaviour. This adds weight to the theory that, at the bottom, offence seriousness is solely a variable of the amount of harm caused by the offence. Harm includes culpability; not because culpability is intrinsically relevant, but because of the close connection between intentions, actions and consequences.

A utilitarian approach to the proportionality principle entails that proportionality is the principal consideration in fixing penalty levels. Departures from proportionate penalties are permissible only in order to pursue more pressing utilitarian objectives of punishment. However, given the serious questions raised by recent empirical evidence regarding the efficacy of punishment to attain the objectives of incapacitation, rehabilitation, specific deterrence and marginal general deterrence, the principle of proportionality will generally be decisive in setting the penalty level. The imposition of penalty levels that are proportionate to the severity of the offence (which are not corrupted by considerations related to other (misguided) penal objectives) would lead to significant improvements in the consistency and fairness of the sentencing process.

CHAPTER 8

SUSPENDED SENTENCES AND PREVENTIVE SENTENCES: ILLUSORY EVILS AND DISPROPORTIONATE PUNISHMENTS

8.1 INTRODUCTION

The next two chapters consider the type of sanctions that ought to be imposed if a utilitarian theory of punishment is adopted. The discussion commences by considering the appropriateness of some existing sanctions and, in this respect, the focus is primarily on suspended sentences and preventive sentences. It is suggested that the type of analysis and methodology adopted in this chapter can be used to assess the appropriateness of many other types of criminal sanction.

A suspended sentence threatens future harm for criminal conduct that has already occurred. It is a term of imprisonment, the execution of which is wholly or partly suspended. Ostensibly, it is a heavy sanction. The suspended sentence is frequently employed to punish serious breaches of the criminal law. For example, in 1996, there were over 5,000 suspended sentences imposed in Victoria alone.[1] During this period, in the county and Supreme Courts of Victoria (which have jurisdiction over the most serious criminal offences), the suspended sentence was the second most commonly imposed sanction, comprising about 30% of all sanctions.[2] On the face of it, such figures are unremarkable and are unlikely to prompt consternation, since the popularity of the suspended sentence among sentencers is matched by the enthusiasm for them among recipients. It has been noted that a 'defendant who has committed an offence so serious as to merit imprisonment but who has had that sentence wrongly suspended is obviously more likely to be out celebrating than dashing to the Court of Appeal'.[3] It is argued that there is good reason for offenders' enthusiasm towards suspended sentences; they do not constitute a recognisable form of punishment at all, and should therefore be abolished as a sentencing option.

The suspended sentence will then be compared with the preventive (or protective) sentence.[4] Ostensibly, suspended sentences and preventive

---

1   There were 360 suspended sentences imposed in the county and Supreme Courts and 4,760 in the magistrates' courts: Caseflow Analysis Section, Courts and Tribunal Services Division, Department of Justice, Victoria, *Sentencing Statistics: Higher Criminal Courts Victoria*, 1996, p 137; Caseflow Analysis Section, Courts and Tribunal Services Division, Department of Justice, Victoria, *Sentencing Statistics: Magistrates' Court Victoria*, 1996, p 242.

2   More precisely, the figure is 29.8% (360 of a total of 1,205 penalties that were imposed): *ibid, Sentencing Statistics: Higher Criminal Courts Victoria*, p 137.

3   Campbell, JQ, 1995, p 294.

4   The terms preventive sentence and protective sentence are used interchangeably.

sentences may appear to have little in common and it might, therefore, seem discordant to discuss them together. However, a comparison of the two sentences reveals two 'unifying' points. First, the preventive sentence is the logical converse of the suspended sentence. A preventive sentence inflicts immediate harm on an 'offender', normally in the form of imprisonment, on account of threatened future criminal conduct; while the suspended sentence threatens a future evil (in the form of restoration of the term of imprisonment which has been suspended) for criminal conduct that has already occurred. Suspended and preventive sentences are also alike in that both violate the principle of proportionality, which forms another basis on which suspended sentences should be abolished. Despite this symmetry, suspended sentences are generally widely accepted, while preventive sentences are almost universally condemned. A discussion of suspended sentences and preventive sentences will serve as a practical illustration of the constraints that the proportionality principle imposes on criminal sanctions.

In the last part of this chapter, I consider sanctions which are even softer than suspended sentences. These are orders in the form of unconditional release of the offender or orders requiring that the offender be of good behaviour (these are often referred to as bonds). Even though, on their face, such sanctions are less punitive than suspended sentences, they are less objectionable because, generally, they do not purport to impose pain on offenders and, indeed, are meant to apply only where there is no need for punishment.

8.2 BACKGROUND AND OVERVIEW OF SUSPENDED SENTENCES

Sanctions in the form of suspended sentences have a long history; their first use can be traced back to the ecclesiastical courts in the 14th century.[5] Today, the suspended sentence is available as a sentencing option in the UK and all Australian jurisdictions – although they were only recently re-introduced in New South Wales following an absence of about 15 years.[6] Suspended sentences have been subject to the greatest amount of empirical analysis in Victoria and the UK, and hence this discussion will focus largely on their availability and use in these jurisdictions. They were introduced in Victoria in 1915, but were not available in England until 1967.

In these jurisdictions, suspended sentences are regarded as heavy sanctions. For example, in Victoria they rank fourth in the hierarchy of gravity

---

5   For a history of suspended sentences, see Ancel, 1971.
6   They were re-introduced pursuant to the Crimes (Sentencing Procedure) Act 1999 (NSW), s 12.

of sanctions behind immediate terms of imprisonment, combined custody and treatment orders, and intensive correction orders. They are commonly described as a threat perched like the sword of Damocles over the head of offenders during the period of operation.[7] All terms of imprisonment of not more than three years may be wholly or partly suspended in Victoria,[8] and the maximum operational period of a suspended sentence, the period during which the offender must not commit another offence, is three years.[9] The position is similar in England, where any sentence of imprisonment of two years or less may be wholly or partly suspended for a period of between one and two years.[10] The reason that suspension is allowed only in relation to relatively short sentences of imprisonment is because it is felt that any sentence beyond this would be for an offence that is so serious that it would be inappropriate to suspend punishment.

Where a suspended sentence is breached, there is a presumption favouring its restoration.[11] In the UK and Victoria, if the offender commits an imprisonable offence during the period of the suspended sentence, the court must activate the suspended sentence and commit the offender to prison, unless it would be unjust to do so.[12] In Victoria, the presumption is even stronger because in determining if it would be unjust to activate the term of imprisonment, only exceptional circumstances may be considered.[13]

On balance, suspended sentences are viewed favourably by courts and commentators. However, they have come under criticism in two respects. First, on the basis that the reasoning process leading to their imposition is logically unsound. Secondly, that they have been unsuccessful in achieving their (perceived) aim of reducing prison numbers. Although both these criticisms are of some merit, it is argued that neither constitutes a decisive attack on suspended sentences as a sentencing option. This is followed by a discussion of a far more persuasive objection to suspended sentences.

---

7   See, eg, *Locke and Paterson* (1973) 6 SASR 298, pp 301–02; *Edwards* (1993) 67 A Crim R 486.

8   Sentencing Act 1991 (Vic), s 27(2A).

9   *Ibid*.

10 Powers of Criminal Courts (Sentencing) Act 2000 (UK), s 118.

11 Where, however, a suspended sentence is not activated, other options include: extending the term of the suspended sentence; activating only part of the term; and taking no action at all (Sentencing Act 1991 (Vic), s 31(5); Powers of Criminal Courts (Sentencing) Act 2000 (UK), s 119).

12 Sentencing Act 1991 (Vic), s 31(5A); Powers of Criminal Courts (Sentencing) Act 2000 (UK), s 119(2).

13 This is in contrast to the position in the UK, where the court may consider all the circumstances. For interpretation of this, see *Stacey* [1994] Crim LR 303; *Moylan* [1970] 1 QB 143; *Saunders* (1970) 54 Cr App R 247.

8.3 CRITICISMS OF SUSPENDED SENTENCES

8.3.1 The reasoning process underlying imposition of suspended sentences

Conceptual incongruity underlying the imposition of suspended sentences

A paradoxical aspect of suspended sentences is that, strictly, they may be imposed only where it is felt that an immediate custodial sanction is appropriate.[14] The court must first reach the conclusion that an immediate term of imprisonment is warranted, fix the sentence and only then consider whether to suspend the sentence.[15] The absurdity in such an approach stems from the fact that an immediate term of imprisonment is a sanction of last resort; it can only be imposed if the sentencer is satisfied that the purpose or purposes for which the sentence is imposed cannot be achieved by a sentence that does not involve the confinement of the offender.[16] If all the factors in mitigation have been considered at the outset and an immediate custodial sentence is imposed, there is nothing left which can reduce the severity of the penalty.[17] Once sentences higher up in the sentencing hierarchy than a suspended sentence have been dismissed as too mild, it is farcical to claim that a suspended sentence is appropriate, particularly when there are no new variables to tip the scales further in favour of a more lenient disposition. It is an affront to both the laws of physics and logic to propose that vacuity can produce change.

The main purpose in suspending a sentence is to encourage reform of the offender,[18] and thus the main consideration in determining whether or not to suspend a sentence is the prospect of rehabilitation.[19] This accords with the historical aim of the suspended sentence, which is to prevent criminal behaviour, rather than to match a penalty with the gravity of the offence.[20] In view of this, the reasoning process behind suspended sentences can be defended by arguing that while such sentences are only imposed where it is determined that an immediate sentence is appropriate, a softening in the sanction can occur where the offender has particularly good prospects for rehabilitation. However, this is unsound. Prospects of rehabilitation are, and should be, factored into the initial sentencing determination, rather than counted twice.

---

14 Sentencing Act 1991 (Vic), s 27(3); Powers of Criminal Courts Act 1973 (UK), s 22(2)(a).

15 See *Trowbridge* [1975] Crim LR 295.

16 Sentencing Act 1991 (Vic), s 5(3), (4); Criminal Justice Act 1991 (UK), s 1(2)(a), (b) (now consolidated as Powers of Criminal Courts (Sentencing) Act 2000 (UK), s 79(2)(a), (b)).

17 See, also, Thomas, 1979, p 244.

18 See, eg, *Robinson* [1975] VR 816, p 828; *Davey* (1980) 50 FLR 57.

19 See, eg, *Gillan* (1991) 54 A Crim R 475; *Malvaso* (1989) 168 CLR 227.

20 See Ancel, 1971, p 12.

The confusion that the above approach encourages is illustrated by the comments of an English magistrate, JQ Campbell, who, in opposition to the changes placing stricter limits on the availability of suspended sentences in the UK since October 1992, stated that 'if I am dealing with a case where I would have suspended a custodial sentence prior to October 1992 but now feel prevented from doing so it would be fundamentally unjust to impose an immediate custodial sentence'.[21] This sentiment is clearly erroneous. A suspended sentence should not have been imposed in the first place if it was unjust to impose an immediate term.

Practical problems stemming from the reasoning process underlying suspended sentences

In light of the incongruity of the logical reasoning underlying the imposition of suspended sentences, it is hardly surprising that certain anomalies or unanticipated consequences have emerged regarding their use. Empirical studies reveal that only about half of suspended sentences imposed appear to represent a diversion from immediate custodial sentences, while the other half reflect net widening, that is, imposing a suspended sentence in circumstances where a less severe penalty would otherwise have been imposed.[22] Suspended sentences have also resulted in a trend towards sentence inflation, whereby offenders are given extra time in light of the term being suspended. A survey by Tait regarding the use of suspended sentences in Victoria during the period 1985–91 showed that, for Victorian magistrates, the inflation rate was about 50%.[23]

In terms of the main recipients of suspended sentences, evidence seems to support the view that they are used largely as a means of appearing tough on those who are normally treated leniently anyway: middle class offenders and those with a settled life style.[24] A survey by Moxon in 1988 of Crown Courts disclosed that suspended sentences were common in breach of trust of cases, typically involving white collar workers.[25] Where they were imposed on those with a criminal record, this was generally in relation to those who appeared to have a more settled future.[26]

The absurdity associated with the reasoning process behind suspended sentences is not, however, a persuasive reason for their abolition. For this is

---

21 Campbell, JQ, 1995, pp 294–95.

22 Tait, 1995, p 149.

23 Eg, a six month suspended term was seen as equivalent to an immediate term of about four months: *ibid*, pp 153–54.

24 See Moxon, 1988, p 35.

25 *Ibid*, pp 34–36: it was noted that 29% of sentences for theft in breach of trust were suspended, despite the principle that suspended sentences are rarely appropriate in such cases.

26 *Ibid*, pp 35–36.

merely a contingent matter which has no bearing on the intrinsic character of the suspended sentence as a criminal sanction. For example, a necessary and sufficient precondition to a suspended sentence could just as easily be that it is the most appropriate sanction in light of its ranking in the sentencing hierarchy, whatever this might be. However, if suspended sentences are to remain a viable sentencing option, the need for transparency and intellectual honesty requires revision regarding the circumstances in which they may be imposed.

8.3.2   The 'success' of suspended sentences

The position in England

In England, the suspended sentence was introduced, without detailed consideration of its use in other countries,[27] as part of an effort to reduce prison numbers.[28] To this end, it appears to have failed:

> The accumulated evidence is not encouraging. If the main object of the suspended sentence was to reduce the prison population, there are considerable doubts as to whether it has achieved this effect. It may have even increased the size of the prison population.[29]

It is suggested that there were three reasons for this failure. First, on many occasions, accused received suspended sentences where previously they would have received a non-custodial order such as a fine. Secondly, the term of a suspended sentence was generally longer than an immediate custodial sentence and upon breach, the term was often implemented in full and consecutively. Finally, for the next offence committed after a suspended sentence, the natural penalty was a period of imprisonment.[30] Other reasons advanced for the failure of the suspended sentence are that:

> [It was seen as a] convenient *via medium*, midway between the custodial and non-custodial penalties, so that courts previously hesitating between the two and coming down on the side of non-custodial penalties would now choose the suspended sentence as an obvious alternative; and secondly, that many [sentencers] did not share the official Government thinking behind the introduction of the suspended sentence, and saw it not as an alternative to prison but as an especially effective Sword of Damocles which would deter individual offenders much more surely than probation or the fine.[31]

---

27 Bottoms, 1979a.
28 Advisory Council on the Penal System, 1978, para 263.
29 Jenkins, R, Home Secretary, in HC Committee Debates, Standing Committee A (session 1966–67) Vol II Cols 544–45, as cited in Bottoms, 1979a, p 438.
30 *Ibid*, Bottoms, pp 438–39.
31 *Ibid*, p 444.

Despite the apparent failure of suspended sentences to live up to expectations, the Advisory Council on the Penal System on Sentences of Imprisonment, in its report in 1978, proposed no change in relation to suspended sentences.[32] It stated that one of the benefits of the suspended sentence was that it provided courts with a sanction allowing offenders to avoid actual imprisonment; 'roughly three-quarters of offenders given suspended sentences are not imprisoned for the offence for which the suspended sentences were given'.[33] However, as Bottoms has pointed out, 'it is the ultimate impact on the prison population of the whole effect of a suspended sentence, not just the apparent immediate impact, which really matters for penal analysis'.[34]

The ineffectiveness of the suspended sentence in reducing the prison population is demonstrated by the fact that since it was abolished in England in 1982 for offenders under the age of 21, there is no evidence that this resulted in an increase in the number of immediate custodial sentences regarding such offenders.[35]

The dissatisfaction with the suspended sentence as a punitive measure in England culminated with measures being taken to reduce its use. As a result of changes introduced by the Criminal Justice Act 1991 (UK), which came into effect in October 1992, the use of suspended sentences, in terms of the overall number of penalties imposed, fell from 10% to 1% for males and from 8% to 2% for females.[36] This change occurred primarily because it became a requirement that custodial sentences were to be suspended only in exceptional circumstances.[37] Obviously, the message that the suspended sentence 'should be used far more sparingly than it has been in the past'[38] was clearly received by the courts.

The experience in Victoria

The English experience of suspended sentences is in contrast to that in Victoria, where the overall impact of suspended sentences has resulted in a reduction in the prison population.[39] As was adverted to earlier, the suspended sentence is a widely utilised sanction in Victoria. For example, in 1991, it accounted for 5% of all sanctions imposed in the magistrates' court

---

32 Advisory Council on the Penal System, 1978, para 263.

33 *Ibid*, para 266.

34 Bottoms, 1979a, p 439.

35 Ashworth, 1995, p 286.

36 *Ibid*, pp 10 and 287.

37 Powers of Criminal Courts Act 1973 (UK), s 22(2)(b), as amended by the Criminal Justice Act 1991 (UK), s 5(1) (now consolidated as Powers of Criminal Courts (Sentencing) Act 2000 (UK), s 118(4)). This has been interpreted very strictly: *Okinikan* (1992) 14 Cr App R(S) 453; but see *Cameron* [1993] Crim LR 721.

38 *Lowery* (1993) Cr App R(S) 485.

39 Tait, 1995, pp 157–59.

and 20% of sanctions imposed by the county and Supreme Courts (the Higher Courts).[40] By 1996, this had grown to about 6% and 30% respectively.[41]

In Victoria, the breach rate for suspended sentences in 1990 was 18%, which was less than half the rate in England. The activation rate for those breaching suspended sentences was also significantly less in Victoria than in England: 54%, compared to about 80%.[42] The difference in the breach rates can be explained on the basis that the length of the operational period of suspended sentences in England was up to three years, as opposed to one year in Victoria.[43]

Accordingly, to the extent that their objective is to reduce prison numbers, suspended sentences have succeeded in Victoria. In light of this, Tait concludes that:

> [Suspended sentences] are still something of a mystery. They threaten future pain to ensure present compliance. They depend for their success on the avoidance of certain behaviours rather than the performance of activities. They appear to be inconsistent with other forms of penalty which extract money, work, reporting behaviour or loss of liberty. In a system which prides itself on proportionality and consistency, it is hard to make a case for an invisible, intangible, but frequently irresistible sanction. Except that it works.[44]

Evaluating suspended sentences by reference to reduction in prison numbers

However, Tait's argument is flawed. Sentencing options cannot be evaluated on the basis of their impact on the frequency with which other sentencing options are used. Otherwise, it could be argued that mandatory prison sentences for road traffic offences are desirable because they would reduce the amount of fines issued. More particularly, the effect on the prison population is not a weighty, far less the sole, consideration by which the success of a criminal sanction may be assessed. If keeping people out of gaol is the measure of success, absolute victory could be achieved by merely opening the prison gates. Less drastically, prisons would be almost totally emptied by converting every prison term of less than 12 months automatically into another sanction, such as probation or a fine. But, as should be apparent by now, such suggestions totally miss the point. Indeed, in many circumstances, it may be that keeping people out of prison is undesirable.

---

40 Tait, 1995, p 149. The significantly greater portion of suspended sentences imposed by the higher courts follows from the fact that about 70% of all sentences passed in these courts involve a gaol term, compared to approximately 10% of the sentences passed in the magistrates' court.

41 *Op cit*, fns 1 and 2.

42 See Tait, 1995, p 155.

43 This was extended to two years in April 1991 and three years in September 1997 (Sentencing Act 1991 (Vic), s 27(2)).

44 Tait, 1995, p 159.

The crucial, and indeed only, question in relation to the effectiveness of sentencing options is whether they fulfil the objectives of a properly considered and coherent system of punishment. Imprisonment is not an objective, but rather a means, of punishment. As was noted earlier, general deterrence is the main objective of suspended sentences. On this rationale, suspended sentences rate fairly poorly, because, as is discussed in the next section, they fail at the first hurdle: they do not constitute a form of punishment. It should be noted that if this is correct, then suspended sentences should be abolished irrespective of which theory of punishment one adopts. All theories of punishment agree that wrongdoers should be punished – the point of divergence being why they should be punished.

8.3.3   Whether suspended sentences constitute punishment

Despite the ostensible severity of suspended sentences, there have been some reservations expressed about their punitive impact. In *King*, Lord Parker stated that 'in many cases [where a suspended sentence is imposed] it is quite a good thing to impose a fine, which adds a sting to what might otherwise be thought by the prisoner to be a let-off'.[45] Even reports generally supportive of suspended sentences as a sentencing option have acknowledged that 'excessive mitigation [is] inherent'[46] in them. The 1990 Home Office White Paper noted that:

> Many offenders see a suspended sentence as being a 'let off' since it places no restrictions other than the obligation not to offend again. If they complete the sentence satisfactorily, all they have felt is the denunciation of the conviction and sentence, any subsequent publicity and, of course, the impact of acquiring a criminal record.[47]

Against this, the suspended sentence has been described as a significant punishment,[48] which carries a serious stigma.[49] Further, suspended sentences have been defended on the basis that the most effective way to prevent criminal behaviour is by internal restraints stemming from education and socialisation and that a threat of punishment is 'just as "real" as any of the other fears, expectations, obligations, and duties which populate the social world ... and this threat is more individualised and immediate when a court imposes such a sentence'.[50] It has also been suggested that the suspended

---

45   [1970] 1 WLR 1016.

46   Advisory Council on the Penal System, *Sentences of Imprisonment: A Review of Maximum Penalties*, 1978, HMSO, para 268.

47   White Paper: *Crime, Justice and Protecting the Public* (HMSO, 1990), para 3.20.

48   See, eg, *H* (1993) 66 A Crim R 505, p 510; *Elliott v Harris (No 2)* (1976) 13 SASR 516, p 527.

49   *Gillan* (1991) 54 A Crim R 475, p 480.

50   Tait, 1995, p 146. See, also, Bottoms, 1981.

sentence may be conceived as punishment since it 'is not something which the offender welcomes in itself'.[51]

To get to the bottom of whether a suspended sentence constitutes a form of punishment it is necessary first to investigate the essential nature of punishment and then to break down the suspended sentence into its constituent parts to ascertain how it squares with the concept of punishment.

The nature of punishment

In Chapter 3, it was noted that an enormous number of definitions of punishment had been advanced over the ages. However, upon cutting through much of the emotive language employed in many of the definitions and noting that there are still many unresolved issues about the nature of punishment, one settled feature which emerged was that punishment involves an unpleasantness imposed on the offender. This incontrovertible and seemingly innocuous truth is fatal to the continuation of the suspended sentence as a sentencing option.

The components of the suspended sentence

The suspended sentence has two components. The first is the term of imprisonment which is imposed. Clearly, it cannot be argued that this constitutes a form of unpleasantness, since by the very nature of the sanction it is suspended precisely in order to avoid its effective operation. The other aspect of the suspended sentence is the possibility that the period of imprisonment may be activated if a condition related to the sentence, namely that the offender not re-offend, is breached during its operation.[52] And, it is this feature of the suspended sentence which supposedly carries the sting. Accordingly, although the suspended sentence contains no tangible inherent unpleasantness, a real unpleasantness is imposed, since the people undergoing it face the risk of activation in the event of a breach.

However, it is erroneous to describe such a risk as being capable of comprising a punitive measure. Every person in the community faces the risk of imprisonment if they commit an offence which is punishable by imprisonment.[53] In this way, the natural and pervasive operation of the criminal law casts a permanent sword of Damocles over all our heads: each action we perform is subject to the criminal law. Despite this, it has never been

---

51 Ten, 1987, p 2.

52 The fact that a conviction also must normally be recorded when a suspended sentence is imposed is not an integral part of the suspended sentence. This association is merely contingent: there is nothing to prevent a system making a conviction optional where a suspended sentence is imposed.

53 Which are the only type of offences for which a suspended sentence may be restored: Sentencing Act 1991 (Vic), s 31(1); Powers of Criminal Courts Act 1973 (UK), s 23(1).

seriously asserted that we are all undergoing some type of criminal punishment. It follows logically that the risk of imprisonment in the event of a future commission of a criminal offence is not a criminal sanction; it is a nullity in terms of punitive effect. The situation is obviously somewhat more precarious for those undergoing suspended sentences: in addition to the risk faced by all of us of imprisonment if we commit a criminal offence, they have the more specific risk that commission of an offence may also result in them being imprisoned by virtue of restoration of the sentence which is suspended. But this additional risk is of precisely the same *nature* (the possibility of imprisonment in the event of committing an offence) as that borne by all members of the community. It is irrelevant that for those undergoing suspended sentences, the likely level of unpleasantness is greater should the risk eventuate; the difference is one of degree, not nature. It is important to note that this conclusion follows not from a 'mere' value judgment, but is rather an irresistible mathematical truth: two times zero is still zero.

The illusory punitive nature of the suspended sentence is emphasised by the fact that it is not only offenders who breach suspended sentences who receive a greater penalty than is warranted by the immediate offence. Offenders with prior convictions are also typically dealt with more harshly than those without a criminal record. Though offenders are, ostensibly at least, not punished again for their previous crimes, the earlier offending may disentitle them from leniency by not allowing a reduction in sentence for good character. Despite this, it cannot be contended that offenders who have 'served their time' are still undergoing punishment.

Thus, the true picture seems to be that the suspended sentence suffers from the fundamental flaw that it does not constitute a discernible unpleasantness. Rather, it merely signifies a possible future unpleasantness: if there is no breach, there is no evil. Moreover, given that avoidance of the unpleasantness for those undergoing suspended sentences is totally within their control, during the period of 'sentence' they are in the identical position as the rest of the community, in so far as being subject to criminal sanctions is concerned. The equation is the same: offend and risk jail; abide by the law and suffer no unpleasantness.

Community attitudes regarding suspended sentences

Surveys regarding community attitudes about the ranking of penalties have shown that few are deceived by the superficial punitive veneer of the suspended sentence. A survey conducted in Philadelphia and Pennsylvania asked respondents (consisting of a group of police officers, a group of inmates, a group of probation officers and an undergraduate criminology class) to rank 36 different penalties, ranging from death to a $10 fine, in order of severity.[54]

---

54   See Sebba and Nathan, 1984, p 228. The most severe sanction was rated one.

These penalties included suspended sentences of three years, 12 months and six months. The mean rank orders for these from the four groups[55] were 27, 30 and 32 respectively. All the suspended sentences ranked in order of severity below a fine of $500[56] and above a fine of $250.[57] It was concluded that 'a suspended sentence involving the prospect of a possible prison sentence for a specified term is less burdensome than the immediate inconvenience of probation supervision or a financial penalty'.[58]

In England, a survey revealed that members of the public viewed the suspended sentence as the least punitive sanction of seven common penalties. The suspended sentence was considered more lenient than probation and even softer than a small fine.[59] Such a view appears to be widespread. A survey of lay justices found that suspended sentences of six months were regarded as more lenient than probation of two years and both of these sanctions were below a £100 fine.[60] The conclusion to be drawn is that suspended sentences are regarded as more lenient than almost any sentence of peremptory punishment, and 'although apparently second only to immediate imprisonment on the sentencing hierarchy, [the suspended sentence] is treated in practice as an option much lower down the ladder'.[61]

The inadequacy of suspended sentences as a punitive measure is further illustrated by comparing them with their converse: protective (or preventive) sentences.

8.4 BACKGROUND AND OVERVIEW OF PREVENTIVE SENTENCES

8.4.1 The nature of preventive sentences

A preventive sentence is a sanction that is imposed in response to some future harm that it is anticipated the 'offender' may commit. Morris neatly encapsulates the essence of preventive sentences by comparing them to pre-

---

55 There was a strong correlation from the results of each group, hence it was legitimate to average the scores of the four groups.

56 Which was ranked 26th: Sebba and Nathan, 1984, p 228.

57 Which was ranked 33rd: *ibid*.

58 *Ibid*, p 231. An earlier survey conducted by Sebba revealed that a $250 fine was regarded as more severe than a six month suspended sentence: Sebba, 1978.

59 Walker and Marsh, 1984, p 31. A suspended sentence was regarded as the least punitive of the penalties which respondents were requested to place in order of most to least punitive. The rankings which occurred were: 12 months' imprisonment, one month's imprisonment, $100 fine, $40 fine, community service, probation and, finally, the suspended sentence.

60 Kapardis and Farrington, 1981.

61 Freiberg and Fox, 1986, p 228.

emptive strikes: '... in the criminal law, if not in international relations, the pre-emptive strike has great attraction; to capture the criminal before the crime is committed is surely an alluring idea.'[62]

Thus, the protective sentence imposes a present evil, normally in the form of imprisonment, for criminal behaviour which has not as yet occurred and may in fact never occur. It is aimed at people whose perceived propensity for engaging in violent[63] behaviour is so high that they are an unacceptable risk to the community.

Two other types of sentence have also loosely been referred to as protective sentences: indefinite sentences and additional fixed sentences. Indefinite sentences are penalties imposed without a termination date. They can be imposed at the outset or as an extension of a normal sentence. Indefinite sentences are typically reviewable at defined intervals by a court and are now available in many Australian jurisdictions. Additional sentences are sanctions that are imposed beyond that which is appropriate for the particular offence, normally due to previous offences which have been committed by the offender.[64] The main difference between preventive sentences on the one hand and indefinite and additional sentences on the other is that preventive sentences relate solely to anticipated future harm, rather than, at least partly, to conduct which has already occurred. It is for this reason that only protective sentences are properly the inverse of suspended sentences. Accordingly, the focus in this chapter is only on protective sentences.

8.4.2 Preventive sentence legislation

In Australia, there have been two separate pieces of legislation which have provided for protective sentences: the Community Protection Act 1990 (Vic) and the Community Protection Act 1994 (NSW). Both were *ad hominem* in nature: each was directed at a particular 'dangerous' individual. The Victorian Act targeted Garry Webb (also known as Garry David) and the New South Wales legislation applied only to Gregory Kable.

The Victorian Act allowed for the preventive detention of Garry David for up to 12 months if the Supreme Court was satisfied that he presented a risk to the safety of any member of the public and that it was likely that he would commit any act of personal violence to any other person. The NSW legislation

---

62 Morris, N, 1994, pp 238, 241.

63 The economy of dangerousness was not always the risk to physical integrity. In the early part of this century, it was the risk to one's property: Pratt, 1997, pp 8–70.

64 Sentencing Act 1991 (Vic), Pt 2A; Criminal Justice Act 1991, ss 1(2)(b), 2(2)(b) (now consolidated as Powers of Criminal Courts (Sentencing) Act 2000, ss 79(2)(b) and 80(2)(b)).

provided that a court could order the preventive detention of Gregory Kable for up to six months where it was satisfied on the balance of probabilities that Kable was more likely than not to commit a serious act of violence. This legislation was enacted in response to concerns that Kable, who was due for release after serving a sentence for the manslaughter of his wife, would harm relatives of the deceased whom he had sent threatening letters from jail. Multiple applications could be made for the detention of Kable; thus, effectively, he could be detained indefinitely.

The Victorian Act was repealed in 1993 following the suicide death of Garry David. In *Kable*,[65] the New South Wales Act was ruled invalid by the High Court. By a four to two majority,[66] it was held that the Act violated the separation of powers doctrine embodied in Chapter III of the Commonwealth Constitution, because it conferred a non-judicial function on the Supreme Court by requiring the court to participate in a process which was 'far removed from the judicial process that is ordinarily invoked when a court is asked to imprison a person',[67] and was so repugnant that it exceeded the outer limits of judicial power.

Each member of the majority had different reasons for striking down the Act. However, there were several features of the Act which the court found particularly offensive. For one, it removed the ordinary protections inherent in the judicial process by permitting the deprivation of liberty without a finding of guilt for an offence.[68] The Act also enabled an opinion to be formed on the basis of material that may not be admissible in legal proceedings.[69] Also, the outcome of any application appeared to be predetermined by the legislature, since it clearly was not envisaged that an order to detain Kable would be refused, and thereby the Act seemed to make the court an instrument of the legislature.[70] Finally, there was the *ad hominem* nature of the legislation.[71]

Thus, the legislation in *Kable* was struck down by the High Court due to unique features of the Act which the court believed infringed the separation of powers doctrine embodied in the Constitution.[72] However, there is a more general objection to protective sentences, which stems from their incompatibility with the principle of proportionality. Before discussing the application of the principle of proportionality to protective (and suspended)

---

65 *Kable* (1996) 189 CLR 51.

66 Toohey, Gaudron, McHugh and Gummow JJ; Brennan CJ and Dawson J dissenting.

67 *Kable*, (1996) 189 CLR 51, p 122, *per* McHugh J.

68 See *ibid*, pp 106–07, *per* Gaudron J; p 98, *per* Toohey J; p 122, *per* McHugh J; pp 132–34, *per* Gummow J.

69 See, eg, *ibid*, pp 106–07, *per* Gaudron J; p 122, *per* McHugh J.

70 *Ibid*, p 122, *per* McHugh J.

71 *Ibid*, p 134, *per* Gummow J; p 98, *per* Toohey J.

72 For an analysis of *Kable*, see Miller, J, 'Criminal cases in the High Court of Australia' (1997) 21 Crim LJ 92; Bagaric and Lakic, 1999.

sentences, the arguments which are normally levelled against protective sentences are first considered.

8.5   OBJECTIONS TO PREVENTIVE SENTENCES

8.5.1   Punishment for crimes not yet committed

The most common objection to protective sentences relates to the notion of punishing people for crimes that have not been committed. This line of reasoning has been developed in several ways. It has been claimed that it is simply inherently unfair to punish in such circumstances.[73] And, it has been argued that protective sentences are intuitively antagonistic to the notion of punishment: 'one may promise punishment (or reward) for a future action, but to award it in advance would somehow seem to make it something else; a deterrent or incentive.'[74] The persuasiveness of such arguments is now examined in light of the different theories of punishment.

The first point to note is that a sound argument can be mounted that protective sentences are not intrinsically wrong, and that any intuitive unease towards them stems not from their perceived unfairness, but from an underlying acknowledgment that human conduct can never be accurately determined in advance. If human conduct could be accurately predicted, the intuitive disquiet about preventive sentences would, in many instances, readily dissipate. For example, if a person who was aware of the tragic events in Port Arthur, Tasmania, on 28 April 1996, when Martin Bryant killed 35 people,[75] went back in time to a moment shortly before the incident and had the opportunity to impose a protective sentence upon Bryant, it is doubtful whether many informed people would raise the slightest protest at the decision to imprison Bryant. Predictions about human behaviour will, of course, never become so accurate that such tragedies could be precisely forecast. However, as was alluded to in Chapter 4, fantastic examples such as this are helpful since they sharpen and illuminate the real premises and assumptions underlying our sentiments and conclusions.

Utilitarian and retributive approaches to protective sentences

The suggestion that the above example shows that protective sentences are not inherently wrong is perhaps somewhat premature, since it may depend

---

73   See Victoria Law Reform Commission Report 31, *The Concept of Mental Illness in the Mental Health Act 1986*, 1990, where it is argued that preventive sentences are an affront to civil liberties.

74   Walker, 1991, p 69.

75   See '32 slain in our worst massacre' (1996) *The Australian*, 29 April, p 1 (it subsequently emerged that another three people were also killed by Bryant).

on which theory of punishment is being invoked. Clearly, from a utilitarian perspective, there is no absolute obstacle to protective sentences; they are justified where this will increase net happiness. Thus, if we could be certain that a person would in the future commit an act resulting in immense suffering, then net happiness would be advanced by imprisoning the potential offender.

However, this conclusion does not follow as surely from a retributive theory of punishment. It has been noted that retributivists are committed to the position that preventive sentences are necessarily wrong:

> Once an offender has undergone his 'just deserts' sentence, he has 'paid his debt to society' and is fully entitled to be released. To subject him to a further period of imprisonment is to punish him not for past offences, but for possible (and only possible) future offences.[76]

Morris claims that preventive sentences are wrong even if we could be certain that the offender will offend in the future. He contends that people should be punished for what they have done, not for what they will or might do. People should be treated as responsible moral agents who can choose whether or not to commit future crimes, rather than treating them as 'unexploded bombs'.[77]

Wood rejects the proposition that the retributivist is necessarily committed to the inherent wrongness of preventive sentences, on the basis that retributivism only offers a theory of punishment, not a complete account of circumstances in which people can be forcibly detained. Wood argues that while protective sentences are unjustified, civil detention of dangerous offenders may be permissible on retributivist grounds as this has nothing to do with questions of desert, but rather with social protection.[78] However, the distinction between a protective sentence and civil detention appears illusory. Civil detention still amounts to deprivation of liberty against one's will. This constitutes a form of punishment on the basis of the definition adopted earlier: an unpleasantness imposed on a person. A feathered bird with a bill that quacks is a duck irrespective of what one chooses to call it. Lewis makes the point somewhat more eloquently:

> To be taken without consent from my home and friends; to lose my liberty; to undergo all those assaults on my personality which modern psychotherapy knows how to deliver ... to know that this process will never end until either my captors have succeeded or I have grown wise enough to cheat them with apparent success – who cares whether this is called Punishment or not?[79]

Thus, given that it cannot be tenably asserted that forcible detention is not punishment, it may seem that the retributivist may be committed to

---

76 Wood, 1989.
77 Morris, N, 1994, p 238.
78 Wood, 1988, pp 425–26.
79 Lewis, 1971, pp 301, 304.

denouncing protective sentences *per se*. This is all the more so given that most retributive theories, at least on their face, confine punishment to cases of deliberate wrongdoing.

This latter point may appear to constitute a decisive argument against protective sentences in a retributive system of punishment. However, this is not necessarily the case if the concept of criminality is expanded slightly. While dangerousness in itself does not amount to a criminal offence, it does imperil the security of the community and, because of this threat, it could be argued that punishment is warranted. Viewed in this light, the dangerous person is not innocent: through his or her behaviour, he or she has caused social evil. Such an approach is supported by the fact that retributivists have no difficulty with punishing people who engage in other types of conduct where the harm consists solely of threatening to violate the security of others. In this way, exhibiting tendencies, by words or conduct, which are viewed as potentially likely to lead to aggressive or harmful behaviour towards others could be classified as criminal behaviour and would be akin to offences such as stalking, threats to kill, and conduct endangering life or persons. It follows that even the retributivist is not necessarily logically committed to denouncing protective sentences and may, therefore, be willing to punish people purely on account of their dangerousness.

It should be noted that the above analysis applies irrespective of whether or not the person has committed previous acts of violence. To the contrary, Gross contends that protective sentences are only justified for those who have already committed offences, because by doing so they have breached their supposed social contract with the rest of society which provides that once a person commits an offence, they forfeit certain rights and society can deal with them as it sees fit.[80] Not only is the existence of such a contract highly dubious, but it is unclear why the focus of the inquiry should be solely on past conduct, when the aim of protective sentences is to prevent future harm and/or to curtail existing community unease about the prospect of such harm. Previous conduct is only one of many factors that may lead to a diagnosis of dangerousness – if one was aware in advance of the events of the Port Arthur massacre, whether or not Bryant had prior convictions would be totally irrelevant to a decision regarding the appropriateness of a protective sentence.

8.5.2 Inability to predict dangerousness

Thus, it would appear that whichever theory of punishment one adopts, there is no fundamental objection to punishing people for crimes that they have not committed. Despite this, protective sentences are unjustified. The real

---

80 Gross, 1981, p 272.

objection to protective sentences lies not in their premature character (this is merely a matter of timing), but in our inability confidently to predict future human conduct. Given the complexity and unpredictability of human nature, it is impossible to forecast future behaviour with any degree of certainty. Future promises, undertakings and declared intentions are one guide, but are far from conclusive. People change for the worse, but for the better as well. Behaviour is not only contingent upon fundamental values and beliefs, but also on the circumstances in which we find ourselves.

Although past conduct may be regarded as a powerful indicator of future propensities,[81] and arguably basic values and predispositions are pervasive,[82] current empirical evidence reveals that there is no reliable method for predicting dangerousness. Parke and Mason have noted that:

> There is a wealth of material on the assessment of risk and the prediction of dangerous behaviour. But despite these vast outpourings, there are no reliable actuarial and statistical devices as yet that can predict with any degree of certainty the likelihood of dangerous behaviour.[83]

The empirical evidence which does exist reveals a tendency to exaggerate greatly the probability of future dangerous behaviour.[84] Few serious offenders commit other serious offences[85] and studies have shown that in predicting dangerousness, psychiatrists are wrong about 70% of the time.[86] In *Kable*, Gaudron J described the prediction of dangerousness as 'the making of a guess – perhaps an educated guess, but nonetheless a guess'[87] and McHugh J stated that it is 'a prediction which can at best be but an informed guess'.[88] Curiously, while the psychiatric profession has repeatedly stressed the unreliability of psychiatric predictions of dangerous behaviour, the courts appear to be increasingly relying on them.[89]

Thus, it is impossible to be confident that a court which undertakes an inquiry into the dangerousness of an individual, using the best possible resources available, is likely to come to the correct decision.

---

81 See comments in *Kennan v David (No 2)* (1991) unreported, Supreme Court of Victoria, Hedigan J, 15 November, p 33.

82 See Williams, 1990, pp 181–82, where he argues that in relation to people convicted of serious violent offences, reliable predictions can be made regarding their future conduct. However, as was pointed out by Fairall, 1993, p 51, Williams offers no empirical evidence in support of such an assertion.

83 Parke and Mason, 1995, p 322.

84 See Morris, N, 1994, and Wood, 1988 and 1989; Floud, 1982; Brody and Tarling, 1981.

85 Floud, 1982, p 217.

86 Monahan, 1984. Another study revealed a false positive rate of about 65%: see Kozol, 1982, p 267.

87 (1997) 189 CLR 51, p 106.

88 *Ibid*, p 123. See, also, *Veen (No 1)* (1979) 143 CLR 458, pp 462–67, 494.

89 Morris, N, 1994, p 244.

Given this, the unease towards protective sentences stems not necessarily from the conviction that people should not be punished for crimes that they have not committed, but from the fact that we cannot predict with any degree of confidence that left to their own devices, they would in fact commit serious offences in the future. This objection to protective sentences has a strong foundation in sentencing law: the principle of proportionality.

8.5.3   Violation of the principle of proportionality

As we saw in the previous chapter, the principle of proportionality provides that the punishment should fit the crime. It operates to restrain excessive punishment by requiring that punishment must not exceed the gravity of the offence, even where it seems certain that the offender will immediately re-offend. This is also the case for dangerous offenders where, at common law, the objective of community protection is secondary to the principle of proportionality. A sentence cannot be increased beyond that which is commensurate with the gravity of the offence in order to increase the period for which the community is protected: '... an extension [in sentence] by way of preventive detention ... is impermissible, [however] an exercise of the sentencing discretion having regard to the protection of society among other factors ... is permissible.'[90] Even more pointedly, in *Chester*, the High Court of Australia held that 'the fundamental principle of proportionality does not permit the increase of a sentence of imprisonment beyond what is proportional to the crime merely for the purpose of extending the protection of society from the recidivism of the offender'.[91] And, it is for this reason that it is 'firmly established that our common law does not sanction preventive detention'.[92]

As was argued in the previous chapter, the principle of proportionality is justifiable on the basis of a utilitarian theory of punishment, because disproportionate sentences risk bringing the entire criminal justice system into disrepute. A significant difference between a utilitarian and retributive justification for proportionality is that in the case of the former, proportionality is not absolute; it can be violated where this will maximise happiness. However, for the purposes of this discussion, this distinction is not significant. While the retributivist may have a more absolute argument for rejecting protective sentences, the utilitarian need only seriously consider protective sentences if the accuracy of predictions of dangerousness improved such that liberty (which has enormous weight in the utilitarian calculus) is outweighed by the amount of harm a person may cause and the likelihood of

---

90   *Veen (No 2)* (1988) 164 CLR 465, p 473.
91   *Chester* (1988) 165 CLR 611, p 618.
92   *Ibid*.

the harm eventuating. It is unclear whether violence prediction will ever reach a sufficiently advanced state that the utilitarian need even contemplate such a balancing task.

While the incompatibility of the proportionality principle with protective sentences is clear, it should also be noted that this incompatibility extends to suspended sentences. This follows from an aspect of proportionality which is often overlooked: that it is a double edged sword. A sentence which does not give sufficient weight to the seriousness of the offence violates the proportionality principle in the same way as a sentence overstating the gravity of the offence. 'Logically, proportionality operates to define the lower, as well as the upper reaches of punishment, thus containing excessively lenient as well as overly severe responses to crime.'[93] Although, pragmatically, it is rare for the principle of proportionality to be invoked as a basis for increasing a sanction, if the principle is to be treated seriously, there is no basis for selective application. A sanction which is a nullity in terms of the amount of unpleasantness it imposes clearly infringes this other limb of the proportionality principle.

8.6 MORE ILLUSORY SANCTIONS – DISCHARGES AND BONDS

The conclusions reached in relation to the lack of bite of the suspended sentence apply even more so in relation to several other types of sentencing dispositions. The softest sentencing option available in Victoria is unconditional release, by way of dismissal or discharge.[94] Similar sentencing options are available in all other Australian jurisdictions. Only slightly more exacting is what is traditionally known as the common law bond. Despite differences in nomenclature, all Australian jurisdictions continue to provide for sanctions, the essence of which is release of the offender on the condition that he or she undertake to be of good behaviour for the duration of the order and appear for sentence when, and if, required to do so. If the conditions of the order are complied with, the offender is discharged at the date on which the matter has been adjourned to. Where the offender fails to comply with the conditions of the undertaking, he or she may be re-sentenced for the original offence. In Victoria, this sentencing option is termed release on conditional adjournment.[95] Both of these sentencing options are available in the UK, where sentencers have the power to discharge an offender absolutely or on

---

93 Fox, 1994, p 495.

94 Sentencing Act 1991 (Vic), ss 73, 76.

95 *Ibid*, ss 72, 75.

the condition that he or she does not commit an offence during a specified period, not exceeding three years.[96]

It is clear that dismissals or discharges do not constitute a type of pain. Apart from losing the time to attend court, the offender is no worse off after being sentenced: such sentences 'require nothing from the offender, and impose no restrictions on future conduct'.[97] Conditional adjournments operate in a similar way to suspended sentences, in that if the offender does not break the law, no unpleasantness will follow. However, they are even softer than suspended sentences because, while breach of a conditional adjournment subjects the offender to re-sentencing for the original offence, there is no presumption that a harsh punishment, such as imprisonment, will be imposed.

Thus, both of these sanctions can be criticised on the same basis as the suspended sentence: they do not constitute a recognisable form of pain. However, discharges and conditional adjournments have a far sounder footing than suspended sentences. Although they do not hurt, unlike suspended sentences, they are not meant to. For example, in the UK they can be imposed when the court is of the view, 'having regard to the circumstances including the nature of the offence and the character of the offender, that *it is inexpedient to inflict punishment* and that a probation order is not appropriate' (emphasis added).[98] In Victoria, the circumstances in which a dismissal, discharge or adjournment can be ordered include where 'it is inappropriate to inflict punishment other than nominal punishment';[99] the offence is 'trivial, technical or minor';[100] or extenuating or exceptional circumstances exist that justify mercy being accorded to the offender.[101]

Thus, such sanctions do not purport to be something that they are not. However, there seems to be a need for some re-assessment of the circumstances in which they are imposed. In Victoria, for example, in slightly more than 19% of all cases decided in the magistrates' court in 1996, the penalty imposed for the principal offence was a dismissal, discharge or a conditional adjournment.[102] In the UK, there is also a widespread use of such dispositions, increasing from 9% in 1983 to 18% in 1993 for males aged 21 and over.[103]

---

96 Powers of Criminal Courts (Sentencing) Act 2000 (UK), s 12.

97 Ashworth, 1995, p 254.

98 *Ibid.*

99 Sentencing Act 1991 (Vic), s 70(1)(d).

100 *Ibid*, s 70(1)(b).

101 *Ibid*, s 70(1)(e).

102 Victoria, Caseflow Analysis Section, Courts and Tribunals Services Division, Department of Justice, Magistrates' Court Sentencing Statistics 1996, p 146.

103 Ashworth, 1995, p 256.

Such dispositions may be appropriate where there is no good to be derived from harming the offender, because the objective of general deterrence is not applicable on the facts of the case. This might be the case where the offence is a very minor one of its type. However, it is hard to conceive that this might be so in relation to almost one-fifth of matters coming before the courts.

It is appropriate to preserve sanctions such as discharges and conditional adjournments;[104] however, sentencers need to be astute to the fact that discharges and conditional adjournments do not amount to punishment and thus, these sanctions should be reserved for the rare cases where extreme leniency is appropriate. This would require strict legislative guidelines restricting the use of such sentences.[105]

8.7 CONCLUSION

Suspended sentences should be abolished as a sentencing option. This is primarily because they do not constitute a recognisable form of punishment. They also violate the important sentencing objective of proportionality. This is apparent from the symmetry between suspended sentences and preventive sentences. Whereas preventive sentences inflict immediate harm on an 'offender', normally in the form of imprisonment, on account of threatened future criminal conduct, suspended sentences threaten future evil (restoration of the term of imprisonment) for criminal conduct that has already occurred. This symmetry may be questioned on the basis that while preventive sentences generally prompt intuitive unease, suspended sentences are widely accepted. However, this divergence of sentiment is explicable on the basis of the victims of the unfairness in the respective cases. In the case of the protective sentence, the aggrieved party is the accused, whereas with suspended sentences the aggrieved party is the entire community, which foregoes its entitlement to punish an offender appropriately. Thus, the reason that intuitively we find suspended sentences far less repugnant than protective sentences is the same reason we assume that it is worse to punish the innocent than to acquit the guilty: with the former, the apparent harshness is directed at a particular identifiable individual who must bear the entire brunt of the injustice, real or perceived, whereas in the case of the suspended sentence, the unfairness is diluted by being spread amongst each member of the community.

In principle, this distinction is irrelevant and cannot be permitted to subvert the conclusion that suspended sentences infringe the principle of

---

104 Although to have two different types of non-punitive penalty is an overkill. One of them ought to be abolished.

105 In Chapter 11, I discuss situations where punishment may be of no benefit.

proportionality in the same manner as protective sentences. Both are inappropriate sentencing options. Moreover, this conclusion follows irrespective of which theory of punishment one adopts.

Sentences in the form of discharges and conditional undertakings also do not inflict any meaningful degree of pain on offenders; however, sentencing dispositions of this type are appropriate so long as they are reserved for (the rare) cases where there is no benefit to be derived from punishing the offender.

CHAPTER 9

NEW CRIMINAL SANCTIONS –
INFLICTING PAIN THROUGH THE DENIAL
OF EMPLOYMENT AND EDUCATION

9.1 INTRODUCTION

Whereas in the previous chapter it was argued that certain existing sanctions should be discarded, in this chapter it is contended that there are several new types of sanction that ought to be employed. In meting out punishment, freedom and material wealth are the primary interests targeted by the criminal justice system of most Western countries. There is good reason for this: most people covet these interests and hence, one can be relatively sure that such deprivations will work – they will hurt.

But in some cases, neither imprisonment nor a fine is an appropriate sentencing disposition. The offence may not be serious enough to warrant a prison term, and may be too serious for a fine, or the offender may not have the resources to pay a fine. To fill this void, most jurisdictions have a range of 'intermediate sanctions'. The exact make up of intermediate sanctions varies across jurisdictions.[1] And, indeed, the term 'intermediate sanctions' does not have a set meaning. Tonry uses it to mean punishments lying between 'ordinary' probation[2] and imprisonment, including fines and community service orders.[3] In this book, the definition is used to refer to sanctions between fines and imprisonment. Again, there is no convergence in the form of such sanctions or their specific nomenclature.[4] Such sanctions are sometimes referred to as probation, community orders, intensive supervision probation or intensive corrections orders. But, the core feature of such sanctions is that they involve some degree of supervision and hence some encroachment on the offender's liberty, but to a significantly lesser degree than imprisonment.

Intermediate sanctions, however, have failed to fill the gap between incarceration and fines. Sentencers often view them as being soft, owing to the relatively modest constraints they entail, and hence imprisonment is still generally regarded as being the only appropriate sanction for 'serious' offences. The absence of other sentencing options which are perceived as

---

1   For an overview of the characteristic features of many types of intermediate sanctions, see Clear and Hardyman, 1990; Morris and Tonry, 1990.

2   In some jurisdictions, this is more commonly known as a bond (see Chapter 8).

3   See Tonry, 1998, p 291.

4   They are sometimes referred to as community sentences or punishments. See, eg, Ashworth, 1995, p 269.

being heavily punitive is one reason for the explosion in the prison rate in many Western countries.

Indeed, rather than providing a serious alternative to imprisonment, there is often a net widening effect associated with intermediate sanctions. Further problems with these sanctions are that, because of their supervisory nature, they involve a drain on community resources, and there is no firm evidence suggesting that, despite their rehabilitative overtones, they are successful in reducing recidivism.

The criminal justice system has been too slow and uncreative in developing efficient and effective ways of punishing offenders. There are numerous other ways we can be sure of hurting people apart from interfering with their freedom or taking away some of their wealth. It is suggested that new sentencing options should include the annulment or suspension of an offender's academic qualifications and the disqualification of an offender from working or being enrolled in an educational course. These sanctions should be used as alternatives to incarceration.

These new sanctions are likely to be far more effective and efficient in punishing offenders than the range of indeterminate sanctions that are presently available.

The following section considers the principles that should underpin the practice of criminal punishment. Part 9.3 briefly examines the sanctions that are presently employed and the need for new criminal sanctions. The last substantive part of this chapter outlines the essential features of the proposed sanctions.

9.2 PRINCIPLES GOVERNING CRIMINAL SANCTIONS

9.2.1 The nature of criminal punishment

To determine the form that punishment ought to take, the most fundamental starting point is the definition of punishment. As we saw in Chapter 3, the minimum requirement of any criminal sanction is that it should be unpleasant; it must involve hardship or pain. This might seem so obvious to be almost tautologous, but as was discussed earlier, it a point that has been apparently missed in relation to some 'sanctions', such as suspended sentences and some forms of cognitive-behavioural programmes.

The need for punishment to actually hurt also stems from the theoretical justification of punishment. The primary utilitarian goal of general deterrence is likely to be frustrated if potential offenders do not fear the punishment that may be meted out to them if they violate the criminal law. If one adopts a utilitarian theory of punishment, the same common denominator which justifies punishment (happiness) can also be invoked in determining the form that punishment should take: whatever it is that makes offenders unhappy. The desirability of the reforms discussed in this chapter, however, is not contingent upon the acceptance of utilitarian theory of punishment. As we have seen, most contemporary retributivists also accept the need for hard treatment.

9.2.2 Effectiveness

In order for criminal sanctions to hurt in each particular case, they ought to target the most strongly and widely coveted human interests. Owing to the diversity of human nature, there is no guarantee that any type of criminal sanction will bite in every case. Even prison does not harm everyone.[5] To those who place a premium on liberty, even a short prison term may deprive them of much that is meaningful in life; to others it is merely a hiccup in a generally blasé and aimless life. However, such anomalies do not prevent there being better and worse approximations concerning the pervasiveness and depth of common human interests.

9.2.3 Efficiency

Apart from being effective in delivering pain, there are two other important guiding principles which are relevant in formulating criminal sanctions. First, criminal sanctions should be as economical as possible to administer and enforce. Sanctions which involve a high degree of supervision or are programme based create a strain on scarce community resources and aggravate the pain that the community has already suffered as a result of the commission of the offence. If sanctions are too expensive to apply or enforce, the whole exercise threatens to become self-defeating. The interests of the community may be better served by not punishing at all, rather than utilising public resources to punish minor and middle range offenders.

9.2.4 Important moral proscriptions

The final principle is that criminal sanctions should not violate important moral proscriptions. Despite much uncertainty regarding the form and content of moral judgments, as was pointed out in Chapter 4, one important issue upon which there is general convergence is that moral judgments are

---

5   Eg, a career criminal, Eric Cahill, on being released from jail after serving more than 13 years for a series of rapes, embarked on a flagrant offending spree to get back in jail. On one occasion he received a one month term of imprisonment, and appealed, claiming that it was too lenient: Paxinos, S, 'Bizarre rapist returns to jail' (1999) *The Age*, 16 October, p 8.

universalisable. A judgment is universalisable if the acceptance of it in a particular situation entails that one is logically committed to accepting the same judgment in all other situations, unless there is a relevant difference. Due to the vagaries involved with identifying 'relevant differences', practices and principles that are condoned in one context risk being perpetuated to other (similar, but in fact relevantly different) situations. This argument is normally termed the slippery slope or dangerous precedent argument, and has proved to be particularly persuasive in the context of the euthanasia debate. Five inquiries which have been conducted to inquire into the desirability of decriminalising euthanasia have all advised against it, largely due to the perceived slippery slope dangers of such a reform.[6] Thus, in punishing offenders, treatment that is clearly inhumane or violates other important moral norms is undesirable.[7] The manner in which society treats offenders says as much about the standards of the community as it does about the criminals it is punishing: '... a society that fails to deal with cruelty will probably also need to develop mechanisms to desensitize itself to suffering. In so doing, it will diminish itself.'[8]

Accordingly, two potentially effective and efficient forms of punishment are excluded. Corporal punishment is inappropriate because it sends a signal, however subtle, that there are circumstances in which it is permissible to violate the physical autonomy of others in order to get one's way.[9] Quite rightly, the human body is no longer regarded as an appropriate object of punishment and over the past century or so, there has been a pronounced movement from corporal punishment to the greater use of imprisonment. This has been instrumental to the supposed 'civilisation' of punishment:

> Physical pain, the pain of the body itself is no longer the constituent element of the penalty. From being an art of unbearable sensations punishment has become an economy of suspended rights.[10]

---

6   Law Reform Commission of Canada, *Euthanasia, Assisting Suicide and the Cessation of Treatment* (1982); Social Development Committee of the Parliament of Victoria, *Inquiry Into Options for Dying With Dignity* (April 1987); Great Britain, *House of Lords Select Committee on Medical Ethics* (1994); New York State Task Force on Life and the Law, *When Death is Sought: Assisted Suicide and Euthanasia in the Medical Context* (1994); and Canada Special Senate Committee on Euthanasia and Assisted Suicide, *Of Life and Death* (1995).

7   See Kleinig, 1998, p 273, who argues that even imprisonment compromises the human regard to which offenders are entitled.

8   *Ibid*, p 283. This comment is made in the context of imprisonment, but applies even more so in the context of corporal punishment. Cruelty has been defined as 'the wilful inflicting of physical pain on a weaker being in order to cause anguish and fear': Shklar, 1984, p 8.

9   For an overview of the advantages of corporal punishment, see Harding and Ireland, 1989, pp 187, 193. See, also, Newman, 1983, who argues that corporal punishment is not necessarily less parsimonious than imprisonment and makes out a case for punishment by electric shock:.

10 Focault, 1977, p 11. See, also, Kleinig, 1998, pp 273, 278.

Inflicting physical violence on an offender's family would also be an efficient and potentially effective means of punishment; however, owing to the proscription against punishing the innocent,[11] it, too, is disqualified as a means of inflicting pain on offenders.

In some jurisdictions, moral constraints regarding the nature of punishment are given legislative force. For example, s 3 of the Human Rights Act 1998 (UK) provides that 'no one shall be subjected to torture or to inhuman or degrading treatment or punishment'.[12] Although the protections set out in s 3 are somewhat nebulous, and therefore potentially wide ranging, this is most unlikely to present an obstacle to the sanctions proposed in this chapter. It is not envisaged that even more intrusive sanctions, such as imprisonment, violate the constraints on inhuman or degrading treatment.

Application of the principles

On the basis of the above principles, the threshold issue in devising a system of criminal punishment is to identify the interests that people value. Once this is done, the severity of the penalty can be determined quite readily: '... severity is ... a matter of how much a sanction intrudes upon the interests a person typically needs to live a [happy] life.'[13] It seems safe to suggest that the interests we tend to hold most strongly are (a) physical integrity[14] and (b) liberty (in terms of freedom from interference) – certainly, we scream loudest when these interests are violated. In order to determine which other interests are most strongly and widely held, we need to consider the ends to which people put most of their time and energy. On this basis, it would seem that other important interests are (not necessarily in this order) (c) family, (d) material wealth, (e) occupation, and (f) education.[15]

Once one disregards physical integrity and family, this leaves four other interests as potential targets of criminal sanctions. Liberty and material wealth are already the subject of criminal sanctions. However, despite the theoretical basis for making educational and work interests the subject of criminal sanctions, they are untouched by the process of criminal punishment. Reputation is also an interest which many covet, but it is not an interest which criminal sanctions should directly target. For those who care about it, it is

---

11 As we saw in Chapter 5, this principle, like all principles, in a utilitarian ethic is not, however, absolute.

12 The purpose of the Act is to give effect to the rights and freedoms guaranteed under the European Convention on Human Rights. For an overview of the Act, see Ovey, 1998.

13 von Hirsch, 1993, p 60. The phrase von Hirsch actually uses is a good life (instead of a happy life), but in my view there is no meaningful distinction.

14 The importance of physical integrity is discussed in Bagaric, 1997c.

15 The main objects of punishment identified by Harding and Ireland include considerations (a), (b) and (d), but in place of the other three are reputation, social relations and spiritual well being: see Harding and Ireland, 1989, p 186.

already stripped by the process of trial and conviction. For those that are more thick skinned, no amount of adverse publicity will increase the level of harm. In the next section, it is argued that the failure of existing sanctions to punish a large number of offenders effectively and efficiently also provides strong pragmatic grounds for expanding the range of interests which are the subject of criminal sanctions.

9.3 PROBLEMS WITH EXISTING SANCTIONS

Prison is too costly

Imprisonment is the cornerstone of the system of punishment and the harshest criminal sanction in most Western countries.[16] It is the only effective means of depriving an offender of his or her liberty. While in prison, not only are offenders prevented from mixing with the rest of the community, but their conduct within the confines of the prison is also normally closely scrutinised. The main advantage of imprisonment as a sentencing option is that we can be almost certain that it will inflict pain:

> The loss of freedom imposed upon a prisoner deprives him or her of a finite resource, namely time ... Death is a certainty for everyone, and it can therefore be argued that all prisoners must inevitably experience an irreplaceable loss of time.[17]

However, prison has at least one serious shortcoming: it costs too much. Every public dollar spent in housing prisoners is one less dollar that is available for other public goods, such as health and education. As we saw in Chapter 6, in some jurisdictions, the growing use of imprisonment threatens to affect significantly the quality of other public amenities.

Fines are often unpaid

Fines are the other major weapon used against offenders.[18] The fine is a particularly effective sanction. Most people work hard to attain material wealth, and hence feel a considerable sting when some of it is taken from them. Further, for better or worse, modern civilisation has constructed a system whereby virtually everything can be measured in monetary terms. There is a common currency not only for commodities, but also for far more intangible concepts, such as reputation and physical injury.

---

16 With the glaring exception of the death penalty, which still exists in many parts of the US.

17 Ashworth and Player, 1998, pp 251, 259–60.

18 Although compared to their use in the UK (and many other parts of Europe) and Australia, they are infrequently used in the US: see Tonry, 1996, pp 124–26.

Given the pervasiveness of the interest in material wealth and the efficient manner in which monetary deprivations can be exacted, the fine should be the sanction of choice in most cases. However, a problem with fines is that some people have too much money and many do not have enough for a fine to be effective. Depending on the peculiar circumstances of the offender, a fine may be too easily paid or not at all. Even where a poor offender can afford to pay the fine, an equity issue often occurs: a fine which devastates a poor person may have no impact on a rich person. This problem has been addressed in some European countries by the concept of unit fines,[19] whereby the amount of the fine is determined by reference to the offender's daily income. Theoretically, this is a sensible idea, but it has proven to be practically unworkable in some jurisdictions due to the difficulty and time spent in actually determining an offender's 'income'. Such practical problems ultimately led to the unit fine scheme being rejected in France and England.[20]

Even if practical problems concerning the concept of a unit fine can be overcome, the impact of a fine, of whatever magnitude, can only bite so much, thus there is a need for sanctions of greater severity. While a fine is efficient and can be 'cleanly applied ... [it can also be] relatively easily forgotten'.[21] Thus, we have this void where offences are not serious enough to deserve a custodial sentence, yet are too serious to be dealt with by way of fine.

Intermediate sanctions

This gap between a fine and imprisonment is presently (ostensibly) filled by a range of intermediate sanctions. As was alluded to earlier, the essential feature of these sanctions is that they encroach on the offender's freedom to some extent. This intrusion can be as slight as simply requiring the offender to notify authorities of a change of address and receive visits from a designated officer;[22] to more onerous requirements, such as curfews[23] or home detention or arrest.[24] The requirement that offenders undergo drug and alcohol testing

---

19 Eg, Sweden, Germany and Finland. For further discussion, see New South Wales Law Reform Commission, 1996a, p 377; Grebing, 1982.

20 For a discussion of the difficulties which resulted in the abolition of the unit fine system which operated in the UK between 1991 and 1993, see Greene, 1998, p 270.

21 Harding and Ireland, 1989, p 195; Tonry, 1996, pp 124–27.

22 Eg, this is a standard requirement of a probation order in the UK: Powers of Criminal Courts (Sentencing) Act 2000, s 41. In Victoria, this is a core condition of 'community based orders' and 'intensive corrections orders': Sentencing Act 1991 (Vic), ss 20, 37.

23 See, eg, Powers of Criminal Courts (Sentencing) Act 2000, ss 37 and 38 (which provide for the electronic monitoring of curfew orders).

24 For a discussion regarding the merits of house arrest, see Ball et al, 1988, p 134; Aungles, 1994; Tonry, 1996, pp 117–20.

is a common feature of many intermediate sanctions,[25] as is a community work component.[26]

Most of us tend to place a high value on our liberty, and hence feel some sting when it is eroded to any degree. But just how much pain is exacted by only relatively slight intrusions on our liberty is unclear. For those with a lot of leisure time, the answer is probably not much, for others it may simply mean that they have to learn to become a bit more efficient in their daily activities. In any event, intermediate sanctions have failed to make a positive mark on the sentencing landscape.

They have failed to reduce the reliance on imprisonment:[27] '... the goals of diverting offenders from prison and providing tough, rigorously enforced sanctions in the community have proven largely incompatible.'[28] Further, the 'soft' overtones of intermediate sanctions have done little to change the widely held view that only 'imprisonment counts'[29] and, in many instances, have led to net-widening; that is, they tend to draw more from the pool of offenders who would otherwise be treated less harshly than those who would have been dealt with more severely.[30] As a result, the void between fines and imprisonment is normally filled by simply imprisoning offenders who commit middle-range offences. A further problem with intermediate sanctions is that close supervision of offenders reveals higher levels of breaches and violations than are found in less intensive sanctions.[31] Finally, there is the cost of enforcement; while intermediate sanctions are significantly cheaper than imprisonment, they are nevertheless expensive in absolute terms.[32]

9.4 NEW SANCTIONS

Many people spend an enormous amount of time, energy and resources obtaining an education and working. The widespread nature and intensity of

---

25 See, eg, Sentencing Act 1991 (Vic), 38(1)(d).

26 See, eg, Powers of Criminal Courts Act 1973 (UK), s 14; the maximum amount of hours of work that can be ordered is 240. In Victoria, a work component is a core component of an intensive corrections order and an optional component of a community based order. In either case, the maximum work hours that can be ordered is 500: Sentencing Act 1991 (Vic), s 109.

27 See, eg, Austin and Krisberg, 1982.

28 Tonry, 1996, p 101.

29 *Ibid*, p 128.

30 See, eg, *ibid*, Chapter 4.

31 *Ibid*, p 101.

32 *Ibid*, p 107. It is not even clear that the total cost related to intermediate sanctions is cheaper than imprisonment: see Morris and Tonry, 1990, pp 157–59.

the desires to obtain an education and work makes these interests prime targets for inflicting unhappiness. The essential features of how the proposed sanctions could operate is now outlined.

9.4.1 The employment sanction

Outline of the sanction

The 'employment sanction' would consist of an order prohibiting the offender from engaging in employment (paid or unpaid)[33] for a defined period. For most people, the pain of this sanction would go beyond the consequential loss of income, hence this punishment is likely to bite far more than a fine. Many people view their job as a defining aspect of their personhood. Even more than this, the employment sanction will block participation in one of the most commonly pursued human endeavours and projects. For many, this is likely to produce a significant level of unhappiness:

> Humans realize themselves through activity, and though that activity need not be work, productive work activity represents one of major ways in which we break the bonds of solipsistic subjectivity and are able to influence the world beyond us.[34]

This view is reinforced by the results of a recent study (see Chapter 7), which revealed that the more challenged a person is, whether by a job, hobby or sport, the happier he or she is likely to be.

Costs associated with the employment sanction

Not only is the employment sanction likely to cause considerable pain to most offenders, but compliance and enforcement costs associated with it are likely to be minimal. Most developed countries already have records, normally through the department of taxation, which one assumes could be cross-matched by the relevant enforcement authority to ensure compliance.

Offenders who are subject to the employment sanction will obviously need to survive somehow, and thus it may be feared that this sanction may lead to a net increase in government expenditure on the criminal justice system. This problem, however, can be circumvented by limiting the use of the employment sanction to circumstances in which a prison sentence would have otherwise been imposed – the cost of housing a person in prison being far less than sustaining him or her on welfare in the community.

---

33 The order should extend to unpaid work to minimise the opportunity for offenders circumventing the order by deferring payment until after the expiration of the order.

34 Kleinig, 1998, p 293.

9.4.2 The education sanction

Outline of the sanction

There are two broad ways in which the 'education sanction' could operate. The milder form of the sanction would simply disqualify a person from undertaking any educational course for a set period. This is particularly suitable for those already enrolled in such courses, since existing participation in a course is strong evidence of a desire to attain formal qualifications.

The sterner form of this sanction would either annihilate a person's *past* educational achievements totally or suspend them for a defined period. The sanction would be imposed by an order declaring that, say, a university degree or trade qualification is null and void or suspended for a defined period (as the case may be), thereby preventing the offender from using this qualification where it is a prerequisite to further studies or practising in relevant professions or vocations. Of course, it would not always stop the offender working altogether. The knowledge gained in acquiring an educational qualification cannot be obliterated, but in an age where formal qualifications count for much, it would significantly reduce the employment options available to many offenders. Where the offence is especially serious, the education sanction could be combined with the employment sanction, thereby preventing the offender from working or studying (and, where appropriate, also taking away previous educational qualifications).

Costs associated with the education sanction

The cost involved in ensuring compliance with the education sanction is also likely to be modest. To this end, an 'Education Deletion and Suspension' registry should be established. This would keep records of all people disqualified from study and of any suspensions or disqualification of qualifications. The information should be available to the public, in order that it could be accessed by educational institutes and potential employers.

Some aspects of the education (and employment) sanction are already effectively imposed in some jurisdictions. Many professional bodies have a process whereby members who are convicted of criminal offences risk losing their licence to practice. The advantage of the education sanction, however, is that it makes this process more certain and integrated.

9.4.3 The circumstances in which the sanctions are appropriate

The circumstances in which the new sanctions should be imposed can be summarised in three short propositions:

(a) the new sanctions should be imposed in all cases where a term of imprisonment would otherwise be imposed; except where

(b) the offence is so serious that only a jail term is commensurate with the gravity of the offence; or

(c) the personal circumstances of the offender are such that it appears that the offender will not be inconvenienced by either of the sanctions.

These principles are now discussed more fully.

Alternative to imprisonment

Given the energy devoted to educational and vocational pursuits and the happiness derived from them, it is apparent that they are interests rated highly by many. The corollary of this is that the deprivation of or interference with these interests constitutes a significant unpleasantness. For many, the pain of losing one's hard-earned degree would be on a par to a term of imprisonment of about the same length that it took to acquire the degree. Thus, the extinguishment of a four year law degree would correlate closely to a four year jail term. This is especially so, given that the sanction not only makes the toil of the past years of study largely superfluous, but also deprives the offender of the future benefit of the qualification. Accordingly, it seems logical that the education sanction should be confined to circumstances where only a term of imprisonment would otherwise be imposed. For example, an accountant who is convicted of causing death by dangerous driving[35] or serious fraud, could have his or her qualification annulled rather than receiving the normal jail term.

Although the employment sanction is not as stern as the education sanction (since it only affects an offender's future aspirations), nevertheless, it would also cause significant pain to most people. Given that most who have the opportunity to work spend about half of their productive time doing so, it seems reasonable that the employment sanction is approximately half as severe as imprisonment. In light of this, albeit loose parity, the employment sanction should also be restricted to circumstances where gaol is appropriate Thus, a two year prison term for burglary, for example, would equate to a work sanction of about four years.

When is the offence too serious?

There is no clear point at which an offence becomes too serious to be dealt with by way of the proposed sanctions. The principle of proportionality is the guiding determinant regarding the severity of criminal punishment. The main considerations relevant to offence severity are the harm caused by the offence and the offender's culpability. Physical integrity is the interest coveted most

---

35 In Victoria, causing a death by dangerous driving is termed 'culpable driving' and is normally dealt with by way of a gaol term of about three years; see Fox and Freiberg, 1999, p 898.

highly, thus it seems tenable to assert that the harshest sanction available in our criminal justice system (imprisonment) should be confined to serious violations of this interest.

This is similar to Andrew von Hirsch's suggestion that incarceration should be limited to violent crimes and serious white collar crimes, and that the duration of confinement for these offences should not be longer than three years, except for homicide, where duration should be up to five years.[36] This approach may seem untenable, in light of the move towards tougher (often mandatory) sentences in many Western countries over the past decade. However, as has been discussed, empirical evidence has failed to establish any good consequences stemming from such an approach.

The new sanctions are appropriate for all offences except those involving serious violence to the person, such as homicide and rape. In particular, there is no reason in principle why all property offences cannot be dealt with by way of the proposed sanctions, subject to the foregoing consideration.

Type of offenders who are suitable for the new sanctions

At first glance, it may appear that the proportion of offenders who are suitable candidates for the employment and education sanctions is very limited, given that many people appearing before the courts have no formal education and are unemployed (the over-representation of the underprivileged in prison is discussed in Chapter 10). However, the new sanctions, in particular the employment sanction, have the capacity to inflict significant harm to offenders who possess neither of these characteristics.

People become disappointed and displeased by not only the deprivation of a quantifiable good, but also by the denial of the *opportunity* to attain such a good. It is largely for this reason that we find the existence of formal barriers to access by certain groups of social goods and services so repugnant. Although, in many nations, there are vast disparities along racial, ethnic and gender lines in terms of enrolment in educational courses and employment in elite professions, most communities are willing to tolerate those disparities provided that there are no *formal* barriers to minority groups participating in such practices. Opportunity or potential – though it may never be realised – is in itself a highly desirable virtue. The criminal justice systems of many jurisdictions already endorse this principle, at least implicitly. For example, *unlicensed* traffic offenders are punished by disqualifying them from obtaining a licence for a certain period.

There are few offenders who have no desire to work. Even unemployed offenders are likely to feel the pain of the imposition of a formal obstacle on the search for work. The employment sanction is, therefore, suitable even for

---

36 von Hirsch, 1976, Chapter 16.

the unemployed. However, offenders who are already actively employed at the time of the imposition of the sanction will no doubt feel a greater discomfort. The added punishment of the loss of an existing job could be accommodated by a deduction, of 20% for example, from the length of the employment sanction.

Thus, where the personal circumstances of the offender are such that it seems likely that he or she will feel the pain of either of the proposed sanctions, the court should then be required to convert the prison term into one, or where appropriate a combination of both, of the proposed sanctions unless the offence involves serious violence to the person.

An offender's previous behaviour is obviously the best evidence regarding whether or not the offender is likely to be inconvenienced by either of the proposed sanctions. It would seem safe to assume that a middle aged offender who has not enrolled in a course of education for over 20 years has no genuine interest in ever doing so. On the other hand, an offender who has been employed for two of the past three years would presumably feel the pain of an order preventing him or her from being employed for a defined period.

In light of the above discussion, it is evident that relatively clear parameters can be set regarding the circumstances in which the proposed sanctions should be imposed. Although issue may be taken with some of the above suggestions, this is not a basis for rejecting the employment and education sanction – only a reason for further discussion and refinement. The same problems apply no less acutely in relation to existing sanctions. For example, there is no clear basis for determining the parity and interchangeability of existing sanctions which are seemingly disparate, yet this has not proven to be insurmountable. In Victoria, for example, a fine can be discharged by imprisonment or community work in default of payment at the rate of $100 per day or $20 per hour, respectively.[37]

Rehabilitation

One likely objection to the employment and education sanctions is that they undercut the objective of rehabilitation. However, as was discussed in Chapter 6, the empirical evidence that is available suggests that rehabilitation is a misguided sentencing objective. In particular, there is nothing to suggest that imprisonment (the sanction which the proposed sanctions are designed to replace) has any rehabilitative effect whatsoever.

---

37 See Fox and Freiberg, 1999, pp 414–15. For a discussion regarding the concept of sanction (or punishment) units see Tonry, 1996, p 131; and 1998, p 291.

9.5 CONCLUSION

The range of human interests that are the subject of criminal punishment are too narrow. Freedom and financial wealth do not exhaust the sphere of human concerns. Most people have a strong desire to attain educational qualifications and to work. There are two chief pragmatic advantages which would flow from targeting these interests by criminal sanctions.

First, the compliance and enforcement costs to the community related to the education sanction and the employment sanction are minimal. Secondly, because these sanctions are capable of biting so hard, in most cases, they offer an effective alternative to imprisonment.

It could be argued that the education sanction and the employment sanction are, in fact, too harsh: '... it is inhumane to deny people adequate opportunities to exercise their bodies, it is degrading to deny them mental stimuli.'[38]

Such criticisms, however, merely reinforce the likelihood that the proposed sanctions will be effective in reducing the increasing reliance on imprisonment, and will not simply result in the net-widening phenomenon that has beset other forms of intermediate sanctions.

---

38 Kleinig, 1998, p 293. This comment was made in the context of conditions in prison, but could be equally directed to the proposed sanctions.

CHAPTER 10

DOUBLE PUNISHMENT AND PUNISHING CHARACTER – THE UNFAIRNESS OF PRIOR CONVICTIONS

10.1 INTRODUCTION

This chapter continues looking at the practical implications of adopting a utilitarian theory of punishment. The discussion moves from focusing on the type of sanctions which ought to be imposed to a consideration of the reasons and factors that are properly relevant to the determination of how much to punish. This chapter focuses on the sentencing consideration which traditionally weighs heaviest on the minds of sentencers: previous convictions.

Much of what is wrong with sentencing law and practice relates to the use that is made of prior convictions. They are the primary cause of disproportionate sentences; in fact, rarely does so much turn on so little. In some jurisdictions they can be the sole difference between a small fine and life imprisonment. The impact can be so great that the price paid for stealing a pizza can be as great as that for rape or child molestation.[1] Prior convictions also perpetuate existing social injustices by leading to harsher penalties for offenders from deprived social backgrounds. Not surprisingly, they are the feature of sentencing practice which offenders resent most.[2]

Broadly, there are three approaches that can be used to deal with prior convictions. First, they can simply be ignored.[3] Secondly, at the other end of the spectrum, they can be used as a basis for imposing progressively more severe sanctions for each new offence. This is called the cumulative principle,[4] and was the dominant approach to sentencing recidivists during the second half of the 19th century.[5] Thirdly, and in the middle, there is what is termed the progressive loss of mitigation theory, which is the view that a degree of mitigation should be accorded to first time offenders or those with a minor criminal record. This mitigation is used up by offenders who repeatedly come before the courts, thereby resulting in increased penalties for recidivists. However, unlike with the cumulative principle, there is a limit, set by the principle of proportionality, to how much more harshly recidivists can be punished.

---

1   See Stolzenberg and d'Alessio, 1997.
2   See Walker, 1985, p 127.
3   This is termed 'flat-rate sentencing': see Ashworth, 1995, p 152.
4   *Ibid*, p 153.
5   Henham, 1997, p 266.

This chapter examines the use that ought to be made of prior convictions in sentencing. First, the current legal position is examined. The legal and philosophical arguments regarding the relevance of prior convictions are then evaluated. It is contended that imposing harsher penalties on offenders for what they have done in the past not only violates the proscription against punishing people twice for the one offence, but also amounts to the unacceptable notion that people should be punished for their character, as opposed to what they have done. A solution is offered regarding the relevance that prior convictions should have: their significance should be nought. This may at first seem too revisionary, but a closer look at the workings of the criminal justice system reveals that the bulk of prior convictions are already dealt with in this way. Finally, it is argued that ignoring prior convictions will significantly reduce the inherent bias of the current sentencing practice against people from deprived social backgrounds.

10.2 THE RELEVANCE OF PRIOR CONVICTIONS TO THE SENTENCING PROCESS

10.2.1 Australia

Common law

In Australia, at common law, there is 'no principle of sentencing that demands increasingly more severe sanctions be administered to persons who persist in their criminality'.[6] However, recidivists are treated more harshly because their prior convictions are said to disentitle them from leniency, which is normally accorded to a first offender.[7]

In *Veen (No 2)*, the High Court set out three other grounds for imposing harsher penalties on recidivists:

> The antecedent criminal history is relevant ... to show whether the instant offence is an uncharacteristic aberration or whether the offender has manifested in his commission of the instant offence a continuing attitude of disobedience of the law. In the latter case, retribution, deterrence and protection of the society may all indicate that a more severe penalty is warranted. It is legitimate to take account of the antecedent criminal history when it *illuminates the moral culpability* of the offender in the instant case, or *shows his dangerous propensity* or shows a need to impose condign punishment to *deter the offender and other offenders* from committing further offences of a like kind [emphasis added].[8]

---

6   Fox and Freiberg, 1999, p 269.
7   See, eg, *Baumer* (1988) 166 CLR 51, p 58.
8   *Veen (No 2)* (1988) 164 CLR 465, p 477.

It has also been held that a prior criminal history is relevant by showing that the offender's prospects of rehabilitation are poor.[9] However, irrespective of the reason that prior convictions are said to be relevant, at common law they cannot be used as a basis for imposing a sentence that is disproportionate to the gravity of the immediate offence. Accordingly, the progressive loss of mitigation theory is effectively the guiding principle regarding the relevance of prior convictions at common law in Australia.

Statutory incursions into the principle of proportionality

Despite the position at common law, as we saw in Chapter 7, most States in Australia now have statutory provisions that substantially increase the importance of prior convictions and cut across the principle of proportionality. In Victoria, for example, protection of the community is the principal purpose of sentencing in relation to offenders who commit certain types of sexual, violent, drug, or arson offences (serious offenders) *and* have one or (in the case of certain sexual offences) two previous convictions for similar offences. In order to achieve this purpose, the Sentencing Act 1991 (Vic) expressly provides that a sentence longer than one which is proportionate to the gravity of the instant offence may be imposed.[10] Offenders who commit serious property offences ('continuing criminal enterprise offences') are liable to a maximum term of imprisonment of two times the length of the maximum term prescribed for the instant offence or 25 years (whichever is the lower) for a third similar offence.[11] Additionally, offenders who commit a 'serious offence'[12] may be sentenced to an indefinite term of imprisonment.[13] Theoretically, this applies to even first offenders, but prior history and character are key considerations in deciding if such a sentence is appropriate.[14] Similar indefinite sentencing provisions are also found in other Australian States.

The indefinite sentencing provisions in South Australia are the most sweeping. Offenders who are convicted of certain offences after having two, or in some cases three,[15] prior convictions for offences of the same class are liable to be detained indefinitely. Unlike the indefinite sentencing provisions in the other States, the South Australian model is not targeted at offenders who commit particularly serious crimes. Qualifying offences include larceny, false pretences, forgery and burglary.

---

9 See *O'Brien* [1997] 2 VR 714.

10 Sentencing Act (1991) Vic, ss 6A–6F, esp s 6D(6).

11 *Ibid*, ss 6H, 6I.

12 As defined in *ibid*, s 3.

13 *Ibid*, s 18A.

14 *Ibid*, ss 18B(1)(a), 6.

15 Namely for class 5, 6, 7 or 8 offences: see Criminal Law (Sentencing) Act 1988 (SA), s 22(1).

While the Northern Territory three strikes laws mandate harsh sentences even on first timers, there is a significant emphasis on prior convictions. As we saw in Chapter 2, for adults, the penalty for a first relevant property offence is 14 days' imprisonment; 90 days for a second offence; and 12 months where the offender has convictions for two or more prior property offences.

10.2.2 United Kingdom

Common law

The common law position concerning the relevance of prior convictions in the UK closely resembles the position in Australia. Although, formally, offenders with a criminal history are not said to be punished any more severely (because of their record), they lose good character as a source of mitigation and hence, effectively, are dealt with more harshly. A limit to just how much more harshly they can be punished is set by the principle of proportionality, which fixes the upper ceiling for the offence. In *Queen*, the Court of Appeal stated that:

> The proper way to look at the matter is to decide a sentence which is appropriate for the [instant] offence ... Then in deciding whether that sentence should be imposed or whether the court can extend properly some leniency to the prisoner, the court must have regard to those matters which tell in his favour; and equally to those matters which tell against him, *in particular his record of previous convictions* [emphasis added].[16]

However, as Ashworth points out, the failure by the courts to set any precise ceilings or give an indication regarding the extent of deductions that should be made for previous good record, means that in practice prior convictions have a far more important bearing on sentence: '... the plasticity of "ceilings" enables the courts handing down sentences to declare that progressive loss of mitigation is the principle, while handing down sentences on recidivists which veer towards the cumulative principle.'[17]

Statute

Section 151(1) of the Powers of Criminal Courts (Sentencing) Act 2000 (UK) expressly provides that in considering the seriousness of an offence, the court may take into account previous convictions or any failure of the offender to respond to previous sentences. This effectively endorses the progressive loss of mitigation approach as being the way in which the courts must, at least formally, treat prior convictions.[18]

---

16 (1981) 3 Cr App R(S) 245, p 246.
17 Ashworth, 1995, p 159.
18 See Wasik and von Hirsch, 1994.

Sentencing statistics confirm that in the UK, offenders with prior convictions are treated significantly harsher than first time offenders. Thirty-three per cent of male offenders aged 21 and over with 10 or more previous court appearances were sentenced to immediate custody in 1998 (later figures are not available) compared with 12% of first time offenders and 22% of offenders with three to nine previous appearances.[19] The disparity for male offenders aged 18 to 20 was even more marked. For offenders in this age group, over half convicted on 10 or more previous occasions were sent to a young offender institution compared to 8% for first offenders.[20]

The recent introduction of mandatory and minimum custodial terms has made matters significantly tougher for many offenders with prior convictions. Pursuant to the Powers of Criminal Courts (Sentencing) Act 2000 (UK), a court must impose an automatic life sentence on any offender who is convicted of a 'serious offence'[21] where the offender has a previous conviction for such an offence, except where there are exceptional circumstances.[22] The Act also imposes a mandatory seven year jail term for a third class A drug trafficking offence.[23] Section 111 of the Act imposes a mandatory sentence of three years' imprisonment for offenders convicted of a third domestic burglary (committed after 30 November 1999), unless it 'would be unjust to do so in all the circumstances'. Prior to these provisions, mandatory sentences were absent from the UK since 1891.[24]

---

19 Home Office, *Criminal Statistics: England and Wales 1999*, Cm 4649, London: HMSO, p 206, fig 9.3.

20 *Ibid*, fig 9.2.

21 This essentially relates to crimes of violence such as murder, manslaughter, rape and armed robbery.

22 See s 109. In *Buckland* [2000] 1 WLR 1262, the rationale of the serious offender provision was described as follows: '... the section is founded on an assumption that those who have been convicted of two qualifying serious offences present such a serious and continuing danger to the safety of the public that they should be liable to indefinite incarceration and, if released, should be liable indefinitely to recall to prison.' The court declined to impose a life sentence after finding that the accused did not present a serious and continuing danger to the public. This more flexible approach was affirmed in *Offen* (2001) *The Times*, 9 February, where the Lord Chief Justice, Lord Woolf, said that in line with the Human Rights Act 1998 (UK), automatic life sentences should only be imposed if the offender poses a significant risk to the public. Accordingly, if an offender does not constitute a significant risk to the public, that was an exceptional circumstance which would justify a court in not imposing an automatic life sentence. In assessing the degree of risk that the offender posed to the public, relevant factors included the period of time between the offences and the similarity between the offences. It was further observed that the exceptional circumstances clause should be interpreted in a just, arbitrary and proportionate manner.

23 Section 110. The mandatory can be avoided where there are 'specific circumstances' that would make it 'unjust in all the circumstances'. For a discussion of these provisions and the arguments raised for and against, see Henham, 1997a.

24 For an overview of these provisions see Henham, 1998; Thomas, 1998.

10.2.3 United States

The US is the least pleasant place for an offender with prior convictions to be. The combination of presumptive guidelines and mandatory sentencing laws represent the dominant approach to sentencing reform in the US since the 1970s.[25] Both are extremely severe on recidivists.

The most widely publicised presumptive sentencing system is the grid system in Minnesota.[26] This utilises two core variables in arriving at a sentence. The vertical axis of the grid lists the severity levels of offences in descending order of severity (there are 10 different levels). The horizontal axis provides a (seven level) criminal history score, which reflects the offender's criminal record. The presumptive sentence is the sentence which appears in the cell of the grid at the intersection of the offence score and offender score. Where the sentence is one of imprisonment, the sentence is not expressed precisely, but rather within a small range. The range allows for the operation of aggravating and mitigating circumstances, other than those relating to an offender's prior criminal history. Sentences may only be imposed outside the range where substantial and compelling circumstances exist.[27] Thus, prior criminal history ranks alongside the seriousness of the instant offence as the most important sentencing consideration. In Minnesota,[28] prior convictions can mean a vast difference in ultimate disposition. For example, for a first offender convicted of theft (over $2,500) or non-residential burglary, there is a non-custodial presumptive sentence, whereas for an offender with a 'criminal history score'[29] of six or more, the presumptive sentence is a 23 month jail term.

Mandatory sentences have been adopted in every State in the US. These laws generally apply in relation to serious offences, such as murder and rape, but may also apply to less serious felonies where the accused has previous felony convictions.[30] The harshest type of mandatory sentencing laws are the three strikes laws, which have been adopted in over 20 States.[31] For example, as was outlined in Chapter 6, in California, accused with one prior serious or violent felony conviction must be sentenced to double the term they would have otherwise received for the instance offence. Offenders with two or more

---

25 See, further, Tonry, 1996, p 146.

26 In the US, over a dozen other States also utilise sentencing grids: see Frase, 1995, pp 169, 171.

27 For a more detailed explanation of the Minnesota grid system, see von Hirsch, 1995, p 149.

28 By comparison to other jurisdictions, the Minnesota grid is relatively soft on prior convictions; although the Oregon grid is less severe on prior history: see von Hirsch, *ibid*.

29 Each offence is given a score; the more serious the offence, the higher the score.

30 Tonry, 1996, p 146.

31 See Austin *et al*, 2000.

such convictions must be sentenced to a term of life imprisonment with the minimum term being the greater of: (a) 25 years; (b) three times the term otherwise provided for the instance offence; or (c) the term applicable for the instance offence plus appropriate enhancements. The importance attributed to convictions is exemplified by the fact that the current offence does not have to be for a serious and violent felony: any felony is sufficient.

10.2.4 Overview of relevance of prior convictions

Offenders with prior convictions are dealt with more severely than first timers. At common law in Australia and the UK, the amount of extra punishment is kept in check by the principle of proportionality. This principle, however, is so nebulous that recidivists are often punished *significantly* more severely than first timers who commit otherwise identical offences.

Legislation in many jurisdictions places far more emphasis on previous convictions by providing for, and in some cases mandating, grossly disproportionate sentences for repeat offenders. The difference in the way recidivists are treated compared to ordinary offenders is so pronounced that we now effectively have a bifurcated or twin track sentencing system: one track provides harsh penalties for offenders with prior convictions and the other treats first timers leniently.[32]

10.3 THE DOCTRINAL BASIS FOR PRIOR CONVICTIONS

Ostensibly, the debate regarding the relevance of prior convictions involves the clash of two important principles. According to the first, it is unjust to punish a person twice for the same offence. To do so not only violates the rule of law virtues of certainty and finality, but also prevents offenders from moving on with their lives. The second, counter-principle is the intuitively appealing ideal that people who break the law for the first time should be treated less severely than repeat offenders.[33]

As we have observed, the tension between these two principles has been resolved firmly in favour of the latter. There are two broad reasons that have been advanced for this, depending on which theory of punishment one endorses. Retributivists rely on the progressive loss of mitigation theory, while those who adopt a utilitarian theory of punishment rely on the

---

32   The bifurcation phrase is normally used in relation to offenders with priors for serious offences. See, eg, Bottoms, 1977, pp 88–90, but as we have seen often, even prior convictions for not so serious offences are sufficient to invoke vastly different treatment.

33   See, eg, Henham, 1997, p 266.

supposed instrumental good effects (such as incapacitation and deterrence) of punishing recidivists more sternly. Although, in my view, the utilitarian theory of punishment should be adopted, the progressive loss of mitigation theory is examined because of its widespread appeal. After an examination of this theory, the utilitarian reasons in favour of giving weight to previous convictions in the sentencing calculus are discussed.

10.3.1 Progressive loss of mitigation theory

Outline of the argument

The progressive loss of mitigation theory, endorsed by the courts in Australia and the UK, provides that a degree of mitigation should be extended to first offenders or those with only minor criminal records. The theory claims that we do and should punish recidivists more harshly, but denies that this is *because of* their prior convictions; rather it is because they are disentitled from leniency that is accorded to first time offenders or offenders with minor records. The theory extends limited patience to wrongdoers. After the offender accumulates several convictions,[34] the mitigation is used up and he or she is sentenced to the penalty which reflects the ceiling for the offence. Further transgressions are met with the same penalty. After the mitigation is used up, so the theory goes, it would be wrong to continue to impose increasingly severe penalties for each new offence, because this would give too much weight to persistence and violate the principle of proportionality. While the theory does not even purport to justify significantly sterner sanctions for repeat offenders (such as those found in three strikes laws), it nevertheless allows for more than a marginal degree of disparity for sentences between first timers and recidivists.

The form of the argument

There are several problems with this approach. First, there is the form of the argument itself. The argument attempts to circumvent an unpalatable consequence which follows from the theory (namely, that people should not be punished twice for the one offence) by urging that it is not that we are punishing repeat offenders more; rather we are going softer on first timers. Framing the issue in this manner makes the outcome far easier to sell. The claim that good folk should be given a second chance strikes an intuitive cord and is far less likely to come under close scrutiny than the contention that bad people should be subjected to additional punishment.

---

34 In terms of exactly how many prior convictions it takes to exhaust the mitigation, von Hirsch, 1985, frankly admits he has no answer: 'How may repetitions may occur before the discount is lost entirely? I have no ready answer, as this seems a matter of judgment even for everyday acts of censure.'

However, the approach is logically flawed. It attempts to invoke the perennial 'glass is half empty or half full' subterfuge, which normally leads to people aimlessly going around in ever increasing circles. It can be argued just as persuasively that 'surely, the corollary of allowing credit for good character should be the principle of punishing bad character'.[35] Thankfully, there is a solution to such dilemmas which prevents dizziness setting in: approach the issue from an objective standpoint. The correct question is: How much water is in the glass? And, to get to the crux of this matter, all that needs to be asked is: Do offenders with criminal records who commit identical offences to offenders without criminal records receive harsher sentences? With this behind us, we can now deal with the substantive issue. What is important is not the formal way in which the practice of punishing recidivists is sold, but the reasons that are advanced to justify this practice.

Substantive arguments

Andrew von Hirsch, the main proponent of the progressive loss of mitigation theory, claims that going soft on first timers is justified by the notion of lapse, which is supposedly part of our everyday moral judgments. He believes that this has its genesis in the fallibility of human nature and the view that a temporary breakdown of human control is the kind of frailty for which some understanding should be shown. von Hirsch notes that in sentencing, the lapse is an infringement of the criminal law, rather than a more commonplace moral failure, but argues that 'the logic of the first offender discount remains the same – that of dealing with a lapse more tolerantly'.[36]

Thus, the concept of lapse has the virtue of understanding or forgiveness at its core, and von Hirsch claims that this moral norm ought to be reflected in our sentencing system. Further, he believes that the practice of partial and temporary tolerance for human frailty is particularly appropriate in the area of criminal punishment due to the onerous nature of criminal sanctions and capacity for the law to formalise such judgments.[37] However, this argument fails for two reasons. First, it misrepresents the nature of tolerance and forgiveness for misdeeds. Secondly, such a virtue has no role in a system of law which aims to protect important human interests.

---

35 Henham, 1995, p 426.
36 Wasik and von Hirsch, 1994, p 410. The lapse argument is also made by von Hirsch, 1991, p 55; and von Hirsch and Ashworth, 1998, p 191.
37 von Hirsch, 1985, p 85.

Criticisms of the lapse theory

Forgiveness discretionary not mandatory

von Hirsch is right that we often accord some level of forgiveness to those who infrequently transgress. However, this is a discretionary, not a mandatory moral practice. People can seek forgiveness, but are never entitled to it. This is the reason that few would condemn the wife who leaves her husband after he has cheated on her 'only' once, and why those who break friendships following a single instance of betrayal are not criticised. The practice of forgiveness is simply not as pervasive or obligatory as von Hirsch suggests. In order for a moral norm to form the foundation of a legal *imperative* (such as, all first offenders should get a discount), it must first have almost universal acceptance in the moral domain. 'Virtues' that can be disregarded with total impunity are hardly the stuff that demand legal recognition. This is evident when the supposed ideal of tolerance for human frailty is compared to ideals such as respecting the property and freedom of others.[38]

No tolerance for serious offences

Even if one takes the view that, socially, forgiveness towards people who have not previously breached moral norms is widespread; this is generally only the case in relation to breaches of relatively minor prescriptions. The less serious the violation, the more likely it is that forgiveness will be forthcoming. People are rarely ostracised for their first white lie or breaking their first minor promise, but it can be quite a task breaking back into the group after being caught cheating in a serious card game or playing around with your friend's wife. And, the key distinction between criminal law prescriptions and moral prescriptions is precisely that the former relate to more important and precious human interests, such as the right to life, liberty and property. In the social sphere, where a friend intrudes on these rights he or she is unlikely to be showered with personal understanding. Why, then, should the law be *more* lenient? The reason that the State is justified in imposing the gross interventions that follow from breaches of the criminal law is because the criminal law is concerned with guarding important human concerns. Once this threshold has been crossed, there is no room for subjective judgments between the types of breach that are bad and those that are really bad. They are all *really* bad; if they are not, they should not be criminal offences. The opportunity of making such fine distinctions is lost in the decision to make certain conduct a crime.

---

38 An insistence that tolerance for human frailty is, indeed, a settled moral prescription would run head on into the objection that this entails that we are born with a certain amount of credit points which we progressively lose. If this was so, there is no logical reason why tolerance should only kick in at the sentencing stage. Surely, it would apply to give each of us immunity from prosecution and guilt in the first place.

In *Turner*, Lord Lane CJ stated that 'the fact that a man has not much of a criminal record, if any at all, is not a powerful factor to be taken into consideration when the court is dealing with cases of this gravity'.[39] This point is also endorsed by von Hirsch: '... where the gravity of the offence is great enough, even a first offence would seem to fall outside the scope of human frailty.'[40] Although these comments recognise that there should be no allowance for human frailty for serious missteps, they draw the line too far – all criminal offences are on the wrong side of the tolerance threshold. Of course there are less and more serious criminal offences, but this is irrelevant to the issue of where tolerance ceases. All criminal offences have in common the fact that they are thought to be sufficiently serious to violate (or threaten to infringe upon) an important personal or community interest and hence are more serious than the type of behaviour that commonly precludes forgiveness in other contexts, even for first timers.

Relational and infinite forgiveness

There are two further aspects regarding the notion of tolerance towards wrongdoers that militate against legal recognition of it (at least in the way von Hirsch suggests). First, tolerance is often motivated by relational ties: the closer the personal ties we have with the wrongdoer, the more likely that we are to make allowances for his or her human frailty. A practice which is so dependent in its observance on personal ties has no place in a system governed by law. Here, the rules must apply equally to all.

Also, the claim that forgiveness comes in limited doses is questionable. This is true for some people, but for many others it is not so finite. Many of us are taught to forgive and forget again and again, no matter how often we are wronged. If tolerance is used as the basis for a legal norm, it is unclear why the law should adopt the practice of limited forgiveness when it would seem that there is an equally strong moral case for infinite forgiveness.

Crimes under temptation/pressure and double dipping tolerance

In elaborating on the progressive loss of mitigation theory, von Hirsch argues that 'tolerance is granted on the grounds that some sympathy is due to human beings for their fallibility and their *exposure to pressures and temptations*' (emphasis added).[41] Thus, he claims that offenders who commit crimes under extreme or unusual circumstances (for example, where people steal owing to hunger or because they find a pile of money) are less culpable. However, this

---

39 (1975) 61 Cr App R 67, p 91. Here, the offence was armed robbery. See, also, *Billam* (1986) 82 Cr App R 347, p 349; *Bexley* (1993) 14 Cr App R(S) 462, p 465.

40 Wasik and von Hirsch, 1994, pp 415–16. See, also, von Hirsch, 1998a, p 196; von Hirsch, 1991, p 56.

41 von Hirsch, 1985, p 85. See, also, von Hirsch 1998a, pp 193–94; von Hirsch, 1991, p 55.

cannot be used as an argument to support tolerance in sentencing only towards first timers; a person who steals food out of hunger is worthy of mitigation no matter how many times he or she does it. And given that there is no evidence to suggest that first timers are more likely to commit crimes under temptation or pressure then recidivists, favourable treatment of first timers cannot be justified on this basis, because it is not a circumstance that is peculiarly applicable to all members of this class.[42]

Moreover, where it so happens that first timers are motivated by pressure or temptation to commit crime, there is no need for a first offence discount to mitigate their sentence. Human weakness is already catered for by the law of criminal defences (such as duress, provocation and necessity) and sentencing law and practice.[43] To extend additional mercy to first timers on top of this unjustifiably allows them to double (or triple) dip on account of their frailty.

Punishing bad character

Given the (apparent) failure of the progressive loss of mitigation theory, it seems that the practice of imposing heavier penalties on recidivists is objectionable because it, in fact, does amount to punishing people twice for the one offence. The only other way left to attempt to circumvent this conclusion is to argue that we are not punishing recidivists again for previous acts, but are punishing them for their (bad) *character*.[44] This gets to the bottom of why tolerance is shown to people who only infrequently violate moral norms: such behaviour is not 'truly' reflective of their character. The converse also applies: at the core of the impulse to punish recidivists more harshly is the sentiment that bad people deserve to suffer. In our daily lives, we often view character as being inherently worthy of praise or blame and make judgments and decisions in accordance with this. It is generally the dominant consideration in determining whom we befriend, marry, be nice to or choose to ignore or try to avoid. In assessing character, we give weight not only to past deeds, but also to the values and norms which a person holds. von Hirsch

---

42 In von Hirsch, 1998a, p 196, he touches on this issue by stating that 'arguably, there might' be a case for increasing the number of lapses in situations of reduced culpability. He uses the examples of repeat offenders who have limited intelligence and recidivists who are socially deprived, but indicates that greater tolerance in the latter case is more questionable: see, also, von Hirsch, 1991, p 56.

43 Offences which are committed impulsively, suddenly or opportunistically are treated less seriously than those which are planned and premeditated: see Ashworth, 1995, pp 134–35; Fox and Freiberg, 1999, pp 248–49. Offences committed under exceptional stress or emotional pressure are also regarded as being less serious: Ashworth, p 135.

44 von Hirsch makes a similar point: punishing recidivists more severely does not amount to penalising them twice for their past crimes if 'some feature of having being previously convicted affects the basis of [their] present punishment': 1998a, p 191; von Hirsch, 1991, p 2. Once the principle of lapse is excluded, logically, there is only one other distinguishing feature between recidivists and first timers: their previous convictions evince a character defect.

thinks that it is right to extrapolate such sentiments into legal standards: '... one visits censure or reproof on people, not acts – and it is this feature that makes prior misconduct relevant to an actor's desert.'[45]

In some Australian jurisdictions, character is expressly declared by statute to be relevant to the determination of the appropriate sentence.[46] In determining character, the court can consider not only prior convictions, but other matters including the offender's reputation and contributions that he or she has made to the community.[47] In the UK, the courts have a wide discretion regarding the types of factors that are relevant to sentence mitigation,[48] and good character is one such factor.[49]

However, under a system of punishment governed by law, there is no basis for ascribing weight to character. People should be punished only for what they do; not according to the type of people we think they are. To do otherwise 'assume[s] a superhuman level of insight into the individual'.[50] In a community governed by the rule of law, terms such as goodness and badness must be defined. And they are, in the only verifiable way possible: people are judged by their actions, not their values or beliefs; and the only relevant actions are those that infringe legal proscriptions. To punish character is to engage in 'moral book-keeping ... using previous records as an index of total moral worth'.[51]

Even if character could be accurately evaluated, it is still not a proper basis for the infliction of punishment. Mental states, such as values, beliefs, and desires, are not intrinsically good or bad. On the scale of pain or inconvenience to others, the net result of a million bad thoughts is zero. No matter how determinedly wicked and evil people are, the State has no authority to punish them unless and until their thoughts manifest into deeds and even then, they should only be punished for those deeds.

The criminal justice system already goes a long way towards accepting this view. People are never punished *solely* for their character. Until a crime is committed, the law permits people to be as nasty, offensive and wicked as they wish with total impunity. However, as the law currently stands, one misstep can serve as the catalyst for turning an immaterial consideration into momentous one. There is no logical reason for this. The only thing that has

---

45 von Hirsch, 1985, p 82. Although later, he suggests that the progressive loss of mitigation theory does not call into question the offender's entire career or character; see p 83.

46 Eg, Sentencing Act (1991) Vic, s 5(2)(f); Penalties and Sentences Act 1992 (Qld), s 9(2)(f).

47 Sentencing Act (1991) Vic, s 6; Penalties and Sentences Act 1992 (Qld), s 11 (general reputation is not expressly listed).

48 Criminal Justice Act 1991 (UK), s 28(1).

49 See, eg, Ashworth, 1995, p 135.

50 Walker, 1985, pp 138–39.

51 *Ibid*, p 127.

changed after the misstep is the misstep and it is for this only that punishment should be imposed: the reasons that previously existed for not punishing character remain unaltered.

Intentions/bad character analogy

It could be countered that punishing recidivists more harshly does not amount to punishing them for their character simply on the basis that we now see their acts as more than simply lapses. This, it might be argued, changes the quality or criminality (though not necessarily the harmfulness) of the act, in much the same way as intentional crimes are considered graver than ones committed recklessly or negligently.[52] This is probably the strongest argument in favour of imposing heavier penalties on recidivists. However, ultimately, the analogy (or link) between character and broader notions of criminal culpability breaks down.

The gravity of a criminal *act* is not affected by the offender's *general* moral outlook or character – an *intentional* killing by Mother Theresa is no less serious than one by Charles Manson. This is not to deny the relevance of broader notions of criminal responsibility to the assessment of offence gravity. Although intentions (which are at the top of the *mens rea* hierarchy) and other mental states are of no intrinsic moral relevance, we generally view them as worthy of praise or blame because there is a close connection between intentions and consequences. This link arises because most of us have sufficient factual knowledge about the empirical processes in the world to set in train the appropriate causal processes to achieve our intentions. But our general character is not the dominant consideration regarding the intentions that we may form. Character is a tendency to think or feel, but not necessarily to act, in a particular way on continuous occasions. It is not the case that poor character will necessarily (or even commonly) manifest itself as an intention to engage in criminal conduct. There are many other variables apart from character that appear to be relevant to the manner in which one decides to act. Perhaps the most important is one's social position and opportunities. That is why there are many 'scoundrels' in privileged positions who never commit crimes and many honourable poor people in jail. Intentions are the product of a complex mix of variables, only one of which is character. Accordingly, denying the relevance of character to the issue of how much to punish does not logically commit one to abandoning broader notions of criminal responsibility and adopting a strict liability system of criminal law and punishment. Character is simply too far removed from the stimulus that results in criminal conduct to enter properly into the assessment of criminal culpability.

---

52 I thank John Kleinig for raising this point.

This response could be criticised on the basis that although character is not the *only* thing relevant to the formation of criminally liable mental states, it is *one* consideration and, hence, should not be totally ignored at the sentencing stage.[53] However, although there is some connection between character and intentions, there is probably an even closer link between intentions and (say) social opportunity and, given that we do not view the latter as being a proper object of punishment, the same ought to apply regarding character.

Further, if character is regarded as being in some way relevant to the *mens rea* of an offence and for this reason it is felt that it is justifiable to punish recidivists more severely, this would amount to giving double weight to the culpability component of crime. Intentional acts, for example, are already punished most severely, and to then add a premium on top of the penalty on account of bad character (which is supposedly disclosed by the intentions of the offender) entails that an offender's degree of culpability is factored in twice in the determination of how much to punish – it is the converse of double dipping tolerance.

The capacity for people to respond to censure

There is a second limb to the progressive loss of mitigation theory. It is suggested that we should give first timers a discount because criminal punishment should recognise the capacity of people to respond to censure (the blame conveyed by criminal guilt and criminal sanctions) and to change their behaviour in response to this.[54] A repeat offender, on this view, loses the discount because he 'has chosen to disregard the disapproval visited on him through his punishment, and thus seems not to have made the requisite additional effort required at self-restraint'.[55]

However, even if we accept, as von Hirsch claims, that the principal justification for punishment is censure and that punishment addresses offenders as moral agents, thereby giving them the *opportunity* to respond by acknowledging their wrongdoing and showing greater self-restraint in the future, it does not follow that the failure to grasp this *opportunity* provides a basis for treating recidivists more severely. In order for us to be justified in mistreating others (or, as is the case here, treating them more harshly), a necessary condition[56] is that they have violated some duty or obligation – be it legal or moral. A mere failure to avail oneself of an opportunity may inspire others to pity or even mock us for failing to seize our chance, but it cannot justify them harming us.

---

53 Again, I wish to thank John Kleinig for this point.

54 von Hirsch, 1985, p 84; von Hirsch and Wasik, 1994, p 410.

55 von Hirsch, 1998a, p 195. See, also, von Hirsch, 1985, p 84; *ibid*, von Hirsch and Wasik, p 410.

56 Though utilitarians would argue that this is not a sufficient condition.

It could be countered that punishment *aims* to elicit moral reform,[57] hence offenders are expected to make stronger efforts at self-restraint.[58] But, this argument is not open to von Hirsch, since reliance on such an overtly consequentialist objective as rehabilitation would threaten to destabilise his account of punishment. Indeed, he is careful to point out that punishment 'gives the actor the opportunity for ... responding [in a morally appropriate manner], but it is not a technique for *evoking* specified sentiments' (emphasis added).[59] At one point, he does flirt with the notion that offenders are obliged to respond positively to punishment: '*perhaps* ... the offender has a duty to attend to the censure [of punishment] and make extra efforts at self-restraint' (emphasis added).[60] von Hirsch denies that this makes him a rehabilitationist because the first offender discount is not aimed at inducing future compliance: 'instead [it reflects] an *ethical* judgment: it is a way of showing respect for any person's capacity, as a moral agent, for attending to the censure in punishment' (emphasis added).[61] The discount is lost only because subsequent offending reveals that the offender does not 'take condemnation of [his or her] acts seriously'.[62] However, this turns the debate full circle. If morality requires that people ought to be given a chance to learn from their errors in response to condemnation, why should this opportunity be confined to only their first transgression? Sure, repeated wrongdoing may reveal deep rooted attitudinal defects, but the notion of lapse is not a stand alone moral prescription; it, supposedly, has the virtue of forgiveness at its core and we are still not told why this should be conferred in limited doses.

Retributivism and proportionality and the relevance of prior convictions

On a more fundamental level, von Hirsch's progressive loss of mitigation theory fails because it is inconsistent with the overarching retributive theory within which it operates. As we have seen, a key hallmark of most retributive theories is that the justification of punishment does not depend on the possible attainment of consequential goals. Retributive theories are backward looking – punishment is an appropriate response to a past offence, irrespective of any incidental effects of punishment. The cornerstone of many retributive theories, especially von Hirsch's just deserts theory, is that the

---

57 Although, as is stated in Chapter 6, this objective is misguided.

58 See Chapter 4, where I argue that expectations, as opposed to hopes, are grounded in obligations, which in turn are derived from (voluntary or inadvertent) participation in goal-orientated practices or transactions. Obligations occur because they are necessary to facilitate the objectives of the relevant practice or transaction. Thus, if punishment does not aim to reform, there can be no expectation that offenders should show greater restraint after being subjected to it.

59 von Hirsch, 1993, p 10.

60 von Hirsch, 1998a, p 196.

61 *Ibid*, p 193.

62 *Ibid*, pp 195–96.

amount of punishment should be in proportion to the severity of *the* offence. It has proved remarkably difficult to identify exactly what factors are relevant to gauging offence severity. But, as we have seen, broadly there are two: the harm caused by the offence and the culpability of the offender.

Prior convictions are obviously not relevant to the harm component: one hundred burglaries committed by a single offender cause exactly the same amount of harm as one hundred first timers committing a burglary each.

There is also no place for previous criminal history in the culpability variable. It is untenable to claim that the principle of proportionality means the punishment should be commensurate with the seriousness of *the offence* and then to allow considerations external to the offence to have a role in determining how much punishment is appropriate. Once the inquiry extends to matters not even remotely connected with the crime, such as the offender's upbringing or previous convictions, the parameters of *the offence* have been clearly exhausted.[63]

Further, as was discussed in Chapter 7, by allowing considerations such as criminal record a look in, much of the appeal of the principle of proportionality dissipates. To determine how much to punish, the concept of looking only at the *objective* seriousness of the offence is abandoned and the inquiry must move elsewhere (and, indeed, everywhere).[64] If the objective seriousness of the offence is such an amorphous concept that it includes considerations as remote as what an offender got up to 20, 30 or 40 years ago, there is no logical way to exclude any consideration as being irrelevant. This would readily make the principle of proportionality redundant.

Accordingly, a consistent retributivist is committed to ignoring prior convictions in determining penalty, since they have no bearing on the seriousness of the instant offence.

This leads us to an examination of the utilitarian reasons for punishing recidivists more harshly.

10.3.2 Utilitarian arguments – incapacitation and deterrence

The utilitarian is able to provide a far more coherent and straightforward account of why repeat offenders should receive heavier penalties. Put simply, the good consequences, in the form of incapacitation and deterrence, of imposing sterner punishment on recidivists outweigh the extra hardship endured by them.

---

63 von Hirsch, at one point (see von Hirsch, 1985, Chapter 7) argued that the fact of a prior conviction or convictions increases the culpability of the current offence (on the basis that the offender can no longer plead ignorance as a partial excuse), but he has subsequently resiled from this view: see 1998a, pp 192–93; von Hirsch, 1991, pp 2, 55.

64 The principle would need to be so extensive to include all of the 300 or so factors that the courts have recognised as being relevant sentencing considerations.

As is evident from the passage in *Veen (No 2)*, cited earlier, these goals are commonly endorsed by the courts to justify heavier sentences for recidivists. In *Hindle*, the Victorian Court of Criminal Appeal stated that 'a court can do little more than treat a ... [recidivist] as a public nuisance and remove him from circulation so that he ceases to prey upon his fellow citizens as long as is reasonably possible'.[65] Similar sentiments were expressed in the UK by the Court of Appeal in *Gilbertson*: '... one thing is for certain, if she goes on committing offences, the periods of imprisonment which will be imposed on her, merely to protect the shopkeepers, will become longer and longer.'[66]

The utilitarian argument in favour of sentencing recidivists more harshly, potentially justifies according far more weight to prior convictions than the progressive loss of mitigation theory. Under the utilitarian model, there is no ceiling to cap the importance that should be attributed to previous convictions, hence there is nothing to stop a cumulative principle being invoked. Indeed, the mandatory sentencing and three strikes laws in the US are founded on the incapacitative ideal.

Although the utilitarian argument is logically valid, it fails because, as we have seen, the available empirical evidence does not support the view that either incapacitation or deterrence are effective sentencing objectives, at least from the perspective of justifying harsher sentences.

Although deterrence does work, as was discussed in Chapter 6, the evidence suggests that it is only in the limited form of there being a direct connection between crime and some penalty; not a connection between crime and penalty level. Accordingly, deterrence cannot be used to justify heavier penalties *per se*, let alone for repeat offenders.

10.4 PROPER APPROACH TO PRIOR CONVICTIONS

It follows that no use should be made of prior convictions in sentencing. It might trouble our sensibilities to punish the career burglar who is up for the hundredth time in the same fashion as the first time burglar. But, intuition is never a good guide to policy, and in any event, our sensibilities in this respect are calmed by the realisation that we should not punish people for their character and that there is no verifiable good which stems from punishing recidivists more sternly. Further, a more lateral consideration of the workings of the criminal justice system reveals that ignoring prior convictions is in keeping with the way that most offences are already handled.

---

65 Cited in Fox and Freiberg, 1999, p 271. This passage is also approved of in *Bernes* (1998) unreported, Supreme Court of Tasmania, 2 April.

66 (1980) 2 Cr App R(S) 312, p 313. See, also, Ashworth, 1995, pp 153–54.

On the spot fines

In the UK, US and Australia, there is a growing trend towards the disposition of criminal matters by way of on the spot fine.[67] This involves serving a notice on the offender which sets a fixed penalty, normally in the form of a monetary fine. Payment of the fine within the prescribed time expiates the offence and this effectively finalises the matter. Notably, in all but a few instances,[68] the penalty that is imposed is identical for all offenders. Criminal history has no bearing on this. The practice is so widespread, that, for example, in Victoria over 85% of criminal offences are dealt with on the spot.[69]

This form of disposition is mainly reserved for minor offences and is motivated largely by expedience, owing to the cost involved in prosecuting such matters via traditional methods. However, the important point is that for the vast majority of criminal offences, prior convictions are irrelevant to sentencing and this has not resulted in adverse side effects (such as an increase in crime) and, at the theoretical level, has gone by without significant adverse comment. Arguably, this implies a rejection of the progressive loss of mitigation theory. If leniency to first timers is a credible principle, one would expect it to be most abundant in relation to the least serious types of criminal offences.

The reason why the impulse to impose sterner punishment on those who repeatedly commit offences punishable by way of the spot fine offender is absent is because such offenders do not infringe upon what are normally regarded as important human concerns, such as physical integrity or property interests, and hence such offenders are not regarded as being of bad character. However, once it is accepted that character is not punishable, the door is open for an extension of this approach to dealing with prior convictions to all criminal offences.[70]

10.5 ADVANTAGES OF FLAT RATE SENTENCING – UNJUST SOCIETY CONCERNS

There are also significant practical advantages to ignoring previous convictions. Given the difficulties involved in defining the ceiling for an offence and the size of the first offender discount, it would lead to far greater

---

67 For a comprehensive discussion regarding the use of on the spot fines, see Fox, 1995.

68 Eg, the UK and Victoria have a penalty point system for traffic offenders; when they accumulate 12 points a licence cancellation many follow: *ibid*, Fox; Ashworth, 1995, p 154.

69 See Bagaric, 1998.

70 Indeed, in Western Australia, it is legislatively prescribed that prior convictions are not aggravating: Sentencing Act 1995 (WA), s 7(2)(b).

consistency in sentencing. But, even more importantly, it would go a long way toward resolving the dilemma of what to do with offenders from deprived social backgrounds.

The problem of disadvantaged offenders is one of the most perplexing in sentencing. It is a worldwide phenomenon that people from poor and disadvantaged backgrounds commit far more crime than other citizens.[71] Compliance with legal standards that preserve and entrench existing social institutions and practices is much more difficult for those who are not flourishing under the status quo. Social disadvantage not only prompts rebellion, but people from such groups have less to lose from being sentenced to custody, and hence the fear of imprisonment is not as great.[72] By punishing people from deprived backgrounds more severely on their next (inevitable) conviction, despite the fact that the reasons for their predicament are largely not of their doing, sentencing law and practice perpetuates the social injustices that such people endure.

The unfair manner in which the criminal 'justice' system works against offenders from deprived backgrounds has led to some of the most eminent commentators on punishment to retract or rethink their theories of punishment.[73] For example, it led both Murphy and von Hirsch to abandon the unfair advantage theory of punishment.

von Hirsch accepted that the theory requires:

> ... a heroic belief in the justice of the underlying social arrangements. Unless it is in fact true that our social and political systems have succeeded in providing for mutual benefits for all members including any criminal offender, then the offender has not necessarily gained from other's law abiding behaviour.[74]

Murphy stated that punishment on this model was not justified until 'we have restructured society in such a way that criminals genuinely do correspond to the only model that will render punishment permissible – that is, make sure that they are autonomous and that they do benefit in the requisite sense'.[75]

---

71 See, eg, Box, 1987, p 96, who after reviewing 16 major studies between income inequality and crime concluded that income inequality is strongly related to crime; Carlen, 1994, p 309. The link between crime and social disadvantage is to some extent speculative, relying on data concerning the background of offenders who are actually apprehended. Another tenable explanation for this link is that the poor are simply more likely to be detected – perhaps police simply target people from poor backgrounds. This is not an issue which can be decisively resolved – there are (obviously) no data that record the identity of offenders who commit offences that are *not* cleared up. However, irrespective of the reason for the link, the problem for the socially deprived is just as acute.

72 See, eg, Burnett, 1994.

73 The same observation is made by Tonry, 1996, pp 17–18.

74 von Hirsch, 1985, p 58. For other reasons as to why von Hirsch abandoned the theory, see pp 57–60.

75 Murphy, 1973, p 243.

HLA Hart suggests that, although there should not be a general defence of economic temptation, 'for those who are below a minimum level of economic prosperity ... [perhaps] we should incorporate as a further excusing condition the pressure of gross forms of economic necessity'.[76] As we saw in Chapter 4, Duff accepts that his theory of punishment is not suitable in our present inequitable world. 'Punishment is not justifiable within our present legal system; it will not be justifiable unless and until we have brought about deep and far-reaching social, political, legal and moral changes in ourselves and our society.'[77] Duff believes that our failure to accord all citizens the concern and respect that they deserve provides disadvantaged offenders the strongest moral basis for resisting punishment: '... not because their actions are justified, not because they ought to be excused, but because we lack the moral standing to condemn them.'[78]

There is no ready solution to what ought to be done to remedy the problem of offenders from deprived backgrounds. Given that the underprivileged do not choose poverty or social deprivation, and the enormous efforts that are required to rise out of their predicament, there are extremely powerful arguments for treating disadvantaged offenders more leniently.[79] This could be done by making social deprivation a defence or perhaps a concrete mitigating factor at sentencing. Legislators and courts traditionally balk at such solutions,[80] either for fear that they would result in an escalation in the crime rate or because of the difficulty in determining the level of deprivation that would be sufficient to warrant a sentencing discount.[81] von Hirsch also suggests that socially disadvantaged offenders may be better off not getting a discount due to some notion of diminished responsibility because 'persons deemed incapable of responsibility for their actions tend to be seen as less than fully adult, and can become the target of proactive forms of State intervention that may be still more intrusive than the criminal law'.[82] Thus, there may be some pragmatic considerations which militate against positively implementing measures in the criminal justice system to claw back some of the disadvantages experienced by such offenders.[83]

---

76 Hart, 1968, p 51.

77 Duff, 1986, p 294.

78 Duff, 1996, pp 17, 23, fn 17.

79 The argument that social deprivation should not be a defence, because there are many people from such backgrounds who lead law abiding lives (hence, there is supposedly no necessary link between poverty and crime), is as barren as the view that the fact that there are many people who do not experience health problems from smoking, shows that there is no necessary link between smoking and bad health.

80 Eg, in Australia, coming from a disadvantaged background is not itself a mitigatory factor: *Neal* (1982) 149 CLR 305, p 326; *E (A Child)* (1993) 66 A Crim R 14, pp 30–32.

81 For an argument in favour of a defence of economic duress, see Hudson, 1998, p 205.

82 von Hirsch, 1990, p 409.

83 *Ibid*, p 397.

But, irrespective of the merits of the arguments that have been made against treating offenders from deprived social backgrounds more lightly, it has never been persuasively argued that rotten social background should serve as an aggravating factor in sentencing. Yet, this is precisely the perverse outcome that follows as a result of giving weight to prior convictions in the sentencing calculus. Socially disadvantaged offenders are far more likely to have prior convictions,[84] and it is they who overwhelmingly bear the brunt of the extra punishment that is meted out for previous misdeeds. For example, an analysis of Californian correctional statistics found a significant racial disparity in sentencing, with African Americans being sent to prison more than 13 times as often as whites.[85] And, despite the fact that African Americans comprise only 7% of California's population, they represent almost half (43%) of third strike inmates.[86] Similar figures come from Washington,[87] where African Americans account for about 13% of the State's population, yet they represent about 40% of three strikes casualties.[88]

Thus, the way that previous convictions are now treated causes the sentencing system to operate in a discriminatory fashion against disadvantaged offenders. Such offenders are more likely to have prior convictions and, on the basis of this irrelevant consideration, are sentenced more severely. Disregarding prior convictions will not cure the ills that make it more likely that offenders from deprived social backgrounds will commit crime, but the advantage of ignoring prior convictions is that it will ensure that every time such offenders are sentenced, their punishment will be no more than that imposed on the affluent offender who has committed the same crime. Disadvantaged offenders will still appear in court more frequently than

---

84 There is no direct evidence that the poor have more prior convictions. However, given that they are convicted of more crime, the corollary of this is that they must, on average, have more prior convictions.

85 This is even higher than the normal gross overrepresentation of African Americans in US prisons. In 1991, they comprised 49% of the country's prison population, and only 6% of the general population: Mauer, 1991.

86 McMurry, 1997, pp 12–13.

87 However, the number of people sentenced under three strikes laws is significantly less in Washington (79) than in California (15,000 – for second or third strike offences).

88 McMurry, 1997, p 13. It has also been forecast that the introduction of cumulative sentencing regimes in the UK, discussed earlier, will increase the already disproportionate representation of black and Asian offenders in English jails: Henham, 1997a, p 278, where he draws on prison population data from Hood, 1992. At present, in the UK, the proportion of black males in prison is around six times higher than in the general population: Ashworth, 1995, pp 186, 233. In Australia, a like picture emerges. In 1999, Western Australia had an indigenous rate of imprisonment 22 times the non-indigenous rate. The figures in other States were more 'moderate', but nevertheless inordinately high. Eg, in Victoria, indigenous people had a 12-fold higher rate of incarceration than the rest of the community, while in the Northern Territory the indigenous rate of imprisonment was 10 times the non-indigenous rate: see Australian Bureau of Statistics, *Australia Now*: Prisoners in Australia (2000) at http://www.abs.gov.au.

other offenders, but their sentence will now be determined on the basis of the instant offence, not according to other factors. In some jurisdictions, this will often mean the difference between life imprisonment and a small fine.

10.6 CONCLUSION

There is no sound doctrinal basis for giving weight to prior convictions in determining how much to punish. The progressive loss of mitigation theory involves a flawed conception of the virtue of tolerance and forgiveness towards human frailty. Moreover, it is inappropriate to give legal recognition to such an ill-defined principle.

While utilitarian arguments for punishing offenders are logically sound, they are empirically flawed. Incapacitation does not work due to our inability to accurately distinguish those offenders who will re-offend from those who will not. There is also no evidence to show that specific deterrence works. General deterrence works, but only to the extent of there being a general connection between the level of crime and the existence of punishment. Hence, given that there is no evidence to suggest a linear connection between crime rate and penalty level, there is no justification for the imposition of harsher penalties upon anyone, let alone recidivists.

Punishing recidivists more severely is repugnant because it violates the proscription against punishing twice for the one offence or involves punishing people for their character, not their acts. In a system governed by the rule of law, there is no rationale for invoking such an arbitrary and nebulous notion as character as a criterion for criminal punishment.

It has been argued that it would be wrong to disregard prior convictions in sentencing, because this would fail to show 'an element of tolerance to citizens on their first "lapse"'.[89] In fact, the opposite is true. Ignoring prior convictions shows the appropriate level of tolerance for *all* lapses and, in doing so, ensures that all offenders, even those from deprived backgrounds, are punished no more than is commensurate with the seriousness of the offence.

---

89 Ashworth, 1995, p 181.

CHAPTER 11

CONSISTENCY AND FAIRNESS IN SENTENCING – THE SPLENDOUR OF FIXED PENALTIES

11.1 INTRODUCTION

This chapter takes us back to the start of the book. At the outset, it was noted that there is a need to curtail judicial sentencing discretion to make the sentencing process fairer and more consistent. In light of the discussion regarding why we should punish, I consider whether fixed penalties are the way forward.

The need to curtail judicial sentencing discretion

Perhaps the most controversial area of sentencing law and practice is fitting the punishment to the crime. As was noted in Chapters 1 and 2, judges in Australia and the UK generally enjoy a wide discretion regarding the punishment that should be imposed in any particular case, owing to the enormous number and range of aggravating and mitigating circumstances that have been held to be relevant to sentencing. This has resulted in a large amount of disparity in sentencing, with the rule of law virtues of consistency and fairness being trumped by the idiosyncratic intuitions of sentencers. The unprincipled nature of sentencing practice is such that one eminent commentator on sentencing has noted that 'sentences sometimes reveal more about judges than about offenders'.[1] The most obvious solution to curbing judicial discretion is to introduce mandatory or fixed penalties.

As sentencing law currently stands, a wide ranging fixed penalty system is not feasible. There are simply too many variables which are 'relevant' to the sentencing calculus. As was noted at the outset of this book, two separate studies determined that there were over 200 factors that were relevant to sentencing. No guideline system could hope to be sufficiently flexible or sensitive to incorporate even a fraction of these.

But, if a primary rationale for punishment is adopted, it would facilitate a far more coherent and exacting approach to sentencing which, along the way, would provide a basis for distinguishing real from illusory sentencing considerations. This, in turn, may open the way for a broad based fixed penalty regime. In this chapter, it is argued that if a utilitarian theory is adopted, most of the sentencing considerations which we now perceive as important, become redundant, and a fixed penalty system is not only plausible, but also desirable.

---

1 Tonry, 1995, pp 266, 268.

Overview of criticisms of fixed penalties

Fixed penalties are widely despised. This is especially so in Australia and the UK, where judges 'in some sense [feel that they] own sentencing and that legislative encumbrances on that ownership are inherently inappropriate'.[2] In the US, the introduction of mandatory penalties has been the main reform to sentencing over the past two decades, and judges have become accustomed to the notion that sentencing should be governed by rules.[3] One of the main catalysts for fixed sentencing in the US was the stinging book by federal trial judge, Marven Frankel, who believed that the range of choice available to sentencers was 'unthinkable in a "government of laws, not of men"'.[4] However, fixed penalties are still spurned by leading American sentencing commentators. Michael Tonry notes that:

> The greatest gap between knowledge and policy in American sentencing concerns mandatory penalties. Experienced practitioners and social science researchers have long agreed, for practical and policy reasons ... that mandatory penalties are a bad idea.[5]

It appears that such sentiments are widely held. In a recent forum devoted to the concept of mandatory sentencing legislation in a leading Australian law journal,[6] there were eight separate papers on the topic, and there was not a single nice word to be had for mandatory sentences. More recently, the Northern Territory (and Western Australian) three strikes laws have been subjected to intense criticism following the suicide of a 15 year old Aboriginal boy in a Darwin prison while serving time under the mandatory sentencing provisions for the theft of paint and stationery valued at $90.[7] The intensity of the criticism was heightened when, several days later, an offender was sentenced to one year in jail for stealing $23 worth of biscuits.[8] The former chief justice of the High Court, Sir Gerard Brennan, condemned the three strikes laws as being immoral.[9] The United Nations Human Rights Committee has called for a reassessment of the mandatory sentencing laws.[10]

---

2 Tonry, 1995, p 269.

3 *Ibid*, p 274. Although, on the whole, they are still not supportive of the provisions: Tonry, 1996, p 152.

4 Frankel, 1973, p 5.

5 Tonry, 1996, p 134.

6 (1999) 22(1) University of New South Wales LJ.

7 Schulz, D, 'Outcry as boy dies in NT jail' (2000) *The Age*, 11 February, p 1. The boy was found hanged in his cell on 10 February 2000.

8 McDonald, J, 'Jail for stealing biscuits' (2000) *The Age*, 17 February, pp 1, 6.

9 *Ibid*.

10 Taylor, R, 'Canberra opposes UN rights report' (2000) *The Age*, 30 July, p 2. See, also, Daley, P, 'UN to vet jailing laws' (2000) *The Age*, 22 February, p 5. It is possible that the laws breach the United Nations Convention of the Rights of the Child which Australia ratified on 16 January 1991. Article 37(b) of the Convention provides that the detention of a child shall be used only as a measure of last resort (see, also, Art 40(1)).

The depth of feeling against these mandatory laws was at one point so high that thousands of people were moved to demonstrate in Melbourne against them. The Northern Territory and Western Australian provisions have been subject to several criticisms. The most perplexing aspect of them is that what amount to the sternest sentencing provisions in Australia are targeted at property offences, as opposed to offences against the person.[11] This chapter, while not seeking to defend the Northern Territory or Western Australian laws (which are quite simply too harsh), presents the other side of the argument so far as mandatory penalties in general are concerned.

Apart from the objection that fixed penalties are unfair, because they cannot incorporate all of the relevant sentencing variables, the other main criticisms of fixed penalties is that they are too tough. It is argued that this latter objection can also be met. It is not so much a criticism of the concept of fixed penalties *per se*, but more so of the harsh level at which such penalties are normally set. If softer fixed penalties were set, this, and many other, criticisms of fixed penalties can be circumvented. The objections against fixed penalties are discussed at length in the next part of this chapter. In the third section, the essential features of a workable fixed penalty system are outlined. In light of this, in the final section, other objections that could be made against the proposed system are considered.

Definitions – mandatory penalties and presumptive systems

Before turning to substantive matters, some definitional matters need to be cleared up. Fixed sentencing involves prescribing standard penalties to offences or instances of particular offences. Broadly, there are two different types of fixed sentencing options: mandatory penalties and presumptive penalties.

Mandatory sentences describe the situation where the sentencer strictly has only one option. Few jurisdictions employ such mechanisms. Even in jurisdictions which have mandatory life sentences for murder, there is generally an executive mechanism for mitigating the length of the sentence.[12] The more common variant of mandatory sentences are mandatory minimum penalties. This is where the legislature sets a minimum threshold beyond which the court cannot fall, but leaves the court room to impose a harsher sanction where it deems appropriate. Strictly, the fact that an offence has a level beyond which the penalty cannot fall does not make it a mandatory sentence. This penalty structure is simply the converse of mandatory maximum penalties, which accompany all offences. However, offences carrying mandatory minimum sentences have aroused far more discussion

---

11 This appears to infringe the principle of ordinal proportionality – see Chapter 7.
12 See Spears, 1999, p 304.

than the concept of 'mandatory maximums' and, in keeping with accepted nomenclature, for present purposes, mandatory penalties also include regimes which impose mandatory minimum terms. An example of a mandatory minimum term is the 'three strikes' law in the Northern Territory which prescribes harsh minimum gaol terms for certain property offences. Despite the harshness of these provisions, they only serve as minimum terms; sentencers are free to impose heavier penalties where this is thought appropriate.

Presumptive sentences refer to the situation where a standard penalty is fixed and must be imposed unless there is a demonstrable reason not to do so. Thus, there is a rebuttable presumption that the fixed penalty is appropriate. Two of the most widely publicised presumptive penalty systems are the grid guideline systems operating in Minnesota (see Chapter 10) and the US Federal Jurisdiction. In Minnesota, a judge can only depart from the presumptive sentence where there are substantial and compelling reasons for doing so. The guidelines provide a non-exhaustive list of factors which may or may not be used as a basis for departure. The Federal Sentencing Guidelines provide that departure from the nominated penalty can only occur where the court finds an aggravating or mitigating circumstance of a kind or to a degree not adequately taken into consideration in formulating the guidelines that justifies a sentence different to that prescribed.[13] In determining whether a factor was taken into account in setting the standard penalty, the court is directed to look only at material related to the drafting of the guidelines.

Throughout this chapter, the term fixed penalties refers to both mandatory and presumptive penalties, unless expressly indicated to the contrary.

Numerous objections have been levelled at fixed penalty regimes; however, as is discussed below, in the end they amount to two discrete criticisms. First, that they are too tough. Secondly, that they lead to unfairness. The persuasiveness of these criticisms is now considered.

11.2 CRITICISMS OF FIXED PENALTIES

11.2.1 Penalties too severe

The most common criticism of fixed penalties is that they are too severe. Fixed penalties are invariably introduced as part of a 'get tough on crime' political agenda,[14] and thus it is not surprising that such an objection would be forthcoming. The harshness of fixed penalty systems has resulted in several law reform bodies, and the like, coming down firmly against introducing

---

13 For a discussion of such considerations, see Doob, 1995, p 199.
14 See Morgan, 1999, p 270.

fixed penalties.[15] The claim that many fixed penalty regimes are too harsh is well founded. A good example is the three strikes law in California, outlined in Chapter 6, which provides for draconian penalties for repeat offenders.

The criticism that fixed penalties are too severe has been advanced in several different ways. While these are normally put forward as discrete reasons for rejecting fixed penalties, in effect they are no more than an elucidation of the undesirable consequences that follow when unduly harsh criminal sanctions (fixed or not) are imposed.

Perverse verdicts and more not guilty pleas

Two reasons that led the Australian Law Reform Commission to reject fixed penalties were that they tend to encourage technical defences and invite perverse verdicts.[16] These views were adopted by the New South Wales Law Reform Commission in its Discussion Paper about a decade later.[17] Although neither of these bodies invoked any empirical data supporting these contentions, it does appear that there is some basis for their concerns. Research evidence regarding trial rates in the US Federal Jurisdiction shows that, in response to the severe Federal Sentencing Guidelines, 'nearly 30% of those convicted of offenses bearing mandatory minimums were convicted at trial, a rate two and a half times the overall trial rate for federal criminal defendants'.[18] There is also evidence that juries in England in the 18th century would refuse to convict offenders who were 'guilty' of offences carrying a mandatory death penalty.[19]

More trials and incongruous jury verdicts are no doubt undesirable, but they are not unavoidable side effects of fixed sentences. The only reason that offenders may be disposed to resist more strenuously offences which carry mandatory sanctions, and juries may try harder to acquit accused charged with such offences, is that the stakes are high – and, indeed, too high. If fixed penalties were set at more moderate levels, the motivation for both of these side effects would dissipate.[20]

---

15 See Australian Law Reform Commission, 1988, p 29; New South Wales Law Reform Commission, 1996a, p 258.

16 *Ibid*, Australian Law Reform Commission, p 29. See *ibid*, New South Wales Law Reform Commission, p 258.

17 See *ibid*, New South Wales Law Reform Commission.

18 Tonry, 1996, p 150.

19 *Ibid*, pp 142–44. For further examples, see Morgan, 1999, pp 277–78.

20 The evidence certainly favours such a view. Where fixed penalties are not unduly severe there is no research or empirical evidence to support such matters. For example, there is nothing to suggest that the mandatory minimum penalties for drink driving, which are present in most Australian jurisdictions, have resulted in longer or more not guilty pleas.

Evasion of fixed penalties and shift in discretion

Another objection to fixed penalties is that they lead to surreptitious avoidance tactics by criminal justice officials. There is evidence that in jurisdictions where harsh fixed penalties apply, police, prosecutors and judges devise all sorts of innovative ways to avoid the operation of such laws.[21] For example, it has been established that prosecutors in the US circumvent the application of severe mandatory minimum sentences prescribed by the Federal Sentencing Guidelines, by charging offenders with different, but roughly similar, offences which are not subject to mandatory penalties.[22] Where offenders are charged under these provisions, judges sometimes sidestep the mandatory minimums by techniques such as refusing to find facts (such as the use of a firearm) which would trigger their operation; or simply not invoking the applicable penalties on the assumption that neither of the parties will appeal the sentence.[23] There is also strong evidence that prosecutors use mandatory provisions in order to exert pressure on accused to plead guilty to similar offences to those charged, but which do not carry a mandatory sentence.[24] As a result, there is a significant shift in discretion from judges to prosecutors.

Again, these problems are no more than a rehash of the more fundamental objection that some fixed penalties are too tough. If the legislature does not go over the top in prescribing the penalty, and gets it about right in terms of equating the level of the penalty to the seriousness of the offence, prosecutors could not use the threat of mandatory penalties as a weapon to coerce guilty pleas, and it is unlikely that criminal justice officials would seek to circumvent the operation of such laws – there would simply be no reason to do so.

Fixing the problem of harsh penalties

If a fixed penalty system is founded on a coherent rationale and proportionate penalties are set, the contrast between the experiences in the US Federal System and Minnesota shows that all the above problems (and others) can be avoided. The Federal Sentencing Guidelines were implemented without a primary rationale. The only discernible policy was to get tough on criminals. This it has done, but in a manner where the costs clearly outweigh the benefits. In addition to the problems discussed above, there is little evidence that the guidelines have led to increased uniformity in sentencing (owing to the complexity of the guidelines and avoidance techniques by criminal justice officials),[25] and the federal prison population has exploded since their

---

21 Tonry, 1995, pp 147, 150.

22 *Ibid.*

23 Nagel and Schulhofer, 1992, p 501; *ibid*, p 272.

24 *Ibid*, Tonry, pp 150, 151.

25 *Ibid*, pp 150–52.

introduction.[26] Not surprisingly, the system has proved largely unworkable and has been labelled as the 'most controversial and reviled sentencing reform initiative in US history'.[27]

A different picture emerges in relation to the Minnesota system, which is built on the core principles of proportionality and restraint in the use of prison; including a shift in the use of imprisonment towards only the more serious crimes – primarily, crimes against the person. Although the principle of proportionality is not rigorously applied, owing to the undue weight given to prior convictions, the grid system has on the whole operated successfully. Following an extensive evaluation of the system, Frase states that:

> The Minnesota Sentencing guidelines have, with varying degrees of success, achieved all of the principal goals of this reform. More violent offenders, and fewer property offenders, were sent to prison (although these shifts were not as dramatic as [the drafters of the guidelines] intended). Sentencing has become more uniform and racial disparities have been reduced.[28]

The level at which fixed penalties should be set – the principle of proportionality

Thus, the criticism that fixed penalties are too tough and lead to undesirable side effects can be answered if more 'lenient' fixed penalties are set. However, setting lower penalties simply in order to avoid the undesirable consequences which flow from harsh fixed penalties is not appropriate. The harm caused to the community by letting criminals off too lightly may outweigh any benefits flowing from improvements in the efficiency and consistency of the sentencing system. 'Softer' penalties should only be fixed if they are justifiable on the basis of more general criteria.

This is clearly the case. The concept of leniency is relative, and thus far it has been used by way of contrast to fixed penalty regimes which have been criticised for their harshness. In order for sanctions to be lenient compared to these systems, they would merely need to be proportionate to the severity of the offence. The question then is, whether there is a justification for matching the severity of the punishment to the seriousness of the crime. The answer is obvious: as was discussed in Chapter 7, the proportionality principle should be the dominant consideration in setting penalty levels.

---

26 Doob, 1995, pp 239–41. Although this may not be necessarily viewed as a failing of the system, given the objective to get tough on crime.

27 Tonry, 1992, p 139.

28 Frase, 1995, pp 169, 196. Minnesota has a significantly lower prison rate than the US as a whole; see p 177.

It follows that the starting point is that fixed penalties (and, in fact, all penalties) should be set at the level which is proportionate to the objective seriousness of the offence. In a utilitarian ethic, the principle of proportionality, like all principles, is not absolute and can be trumped by other considerations if this would maximise happiness. Thus, there may yet be a case for the imposition of severe fixed penalties.

Justifications for departure from proportionate sentences

There have been two main reasons advanced in favour of disproportionate punishments: incapacitation and general deterrence. It has been argued that the imposition of harsh penalties will reduce the crime rate by confining likely offenders who have already offended and will dissuade would-be offenders from offending in the first place. However, as we have seen, there is insufficient empirical evidence to support this view.

It follows that if fixed penalties are set for criminal offences, they should not be set at a harsh or draconian level. The principle of proportionality should be observed in setting the penalties. This being so, all of the above objections to fixed penalties can be met.

11.2.2 Inability to accommodate sentencing variables

The other main criticism of fixed penalties is that they are not sufficiently flexible to accommodate the full ambit of relevant sentencing variables, and as a result different cases are not treated differently. This violates what Tonry believes is the paramount objective of sentencing: fairness. Fixed sentences, he believes, are well equipped to achieve one aspect of the fairness equation – treating like cases alike – but are unable to deal adequately with the other limb: treating different cases differently.[29] In a similar vein, the New South Wales Law Reform Commission rejected fixed penalties partly because it believed they provide limited opportunity for addressing the subjective features of the offender or the offence, hence leading to injustice.[30]

A more sophisticated fixed penalty system

One way to respond to this criticism is to increase the number of variables that are relevant to the determination of the standard penalty. Fixed penalty systems can be as crude or as complex, in terms of the number of variables which are taken into account, as is thought appropriate. At its simplest, a standard penalty, say a fine of $1,000, is set for all breaches of a particular

---

29 See, eg, Tonry, 1995, p 273.
30 New South Wales Law Reform Commission, 1996a, p 257.

offence, such as drink driving, and there is no variation or allowance made for the offender's personal circumstances (such as prior criminal history) or the seriousness of the particular offence compared to other offences of that type.

A more sophisticated system would be sensitive to at least some aspects of both the personal circumstances of the offender and the relative seriousness of the offence compared to other offences of that type. An example of such a system is the Minnesota grid system. As we saw in the previous chapter, the two main variables which are relevant to the determination of the penalty are the severity of the offence and the offender's prior criminal record.

Obviously, even more complex systems could be constructed. For example, using the Minnesota model as a base, the presumptive sentence could be reduced, by say one-third, where the offender pleads guilty. A practical example of a more sophisticated fixed penalty system is the US Federal Sentencing Guidelines. Like the Minnesota guidelines, the Federal guidelines also utilise a sentencing grid. On one axis, there are 43 offence levels (as opposed to 10 in Minnesota) and on the other, there are six criminal history categories. For each type of offence the guidelines stipulate a 'base level' penalty. The sensitivity of the system is greatly increased by the fact that there are also adjustments which can increase or decrease the penalty level. The types of consideration which will result in an increased penalty include where the crime involves an abuse of a position of trust, or targets a vulnerable victim or a law enforcement officer. The base penalty is reduced where, for example, the offender's role in the offence is minor or the offender is clearly remorseful. A consideration of all these factors leads to the appropriate cell in the sentencing grid, where the penalty is stipulated within a relatively narrow range.

While, theoretically, there is no end to the range of variables which could be included in the mix, pragmatically, the fewer the better, otherwise some of the main advantages of a fixed penalty system (its simplicity and efficiency) will be overly compromised. Another governing consideration in designing a fixed penalty system is that the variables adopted should be as readily ascertainable as possible. Considerations such as the offender's criminal history, the level of injury caused, and the value of the items stolen are suitable in this regard, but the time and resources spent in determining subjective considerations such as whether the offender is remorseful may cut too deeply across the simplicity and efficiency of the system.[31] Thus, while the unfairness criticism can, to some extent, be offset by increasing the number of factors that go to setting the fixed penalty, this is at best only part of the answer.

---

31 As a general rule, considerations relating to the seriousness of the offence are easier to determine than factors involving the personal circumstances of the offender.

A more fundamental approach – distinguishing genuine sentencing considerations

A more wholesome response involves challenging the relevance of many of the factors which are now assumed to be an integral part of the sentencing inquiry. If there are only a small number of considerations that are properly relevant to the sentencing calculus, a fixed penalty system becomes far more tenable.

To ascertain which considerations are properly relevant to the determination of how much to punish, we need to go back to the rationale for punishing in the first place. The only verifiable good from punishment is that it deters a great many people from committing crime. It follows that sentencing practices and rules aimed at securing other objectives should be discarded. We should forget about punishing offenders for the purposes of rehabilitation, specific deterrence and incapacitation. Accordingly, all sentencing considerations which are primarily directed towards assessing the need and relevance of such objectives should be disregarded.

This makes redundant many considerations which are currently thought to be relevant to sentencing. The most obvious 'relevant' sentencing variable which now becomes irrelevant is previous criminal record. The courts normally place enormous weight on an offender's previous history as being relevant to specific deterrence, the prospects of rehabilitation and the need for incapacitation. However, as we saw in the last chapter, given that these are all flawed sentencing rationales, prior convictions fall along with them.

There are numerous other sentencing considerations which also fall by the wayside. Some of them are as entrenched as prior criminal history. For example, an offender's prospects of rehabilitation are clearly immaterial. An inquiry into whether an offender is remorseful or not is also irrelevant. A remorseful offender is supposedly in less need of specific deterrence and rehabilitation and less likely to engage in criminal conduct again, thereby diminishing the need for incapacitation. However, given that none of these are appropriate objectives of sentencing, the inquiry into remorse is superfluous.

Rather than going through each of the assumed relevant sentencing variables and picking them off incrementally,[32] it is far quicker to approach the issue from the other end – positively stating the factors which are properly relevant to the sentencing calculus.

---

32 Which would, in any event, be an almost impossible task, given the enormous number of such considerations.

Interlude – sentencing considerations already irrelevant to most offences

But first, a brief interlude. The contention that age old sentencing vestiges such as previous convictions and remorse are irrelevant to the sentencing calculus may, for some, seem so revisionary to be implausible. But a broader look at the way in which most criminal offences are currently dealt with reveals that this proposal is in keeping with the way most offences are presently treated. What is being proposed here is not a revolution, but a call for uniformity.

As was discussed in the previous chapter, there is a growing trend towards the disposition of criminal matters by way of on the spot fine. A notable feature of on the spot treatment of criminal offences is that the penalty imposed in most instances is identical for all offenders. Considerations such an offender's criminal history or whether he or she regrets the incident are irrelevant to the amount of punishment. The amount of punishment is determined solely by the objective features of the offence – considerations personal to the offender are totally irrelevant. This is despite the fact that based on contemporary sentencing practices, there is considerable scope for different treatment of the types of offences which are typically dealt with on the spot.

It could be argued that the on the spot analogy is weak because such treatment is normally reserved for minor offences which do not require a *mens rea*. However, this overstates the importance of *mens rea* in the *sentencing* calculus. Broadly, there are three different levels of culpability recognised by the criminal law: intention, recklessness and negligence. Generally, the different levels of culpability reflected in these mental states are incorporated into the definition of a particular offence or the maximum penalty for the offence. For example, the maximum penalty for intentional homicides is greater than that for negligent killings. The offender's *mens rea* is not, however, an important part of the sentencing inquiry; otherwise double weight would be attributed to this consideration. Accordingly, for the purpose of this discussion, there is no relevant distinction between more serious offences and the type of offences which are normally dealt with on the spot.

The analogy could also be criticised on the grounds that most on the spot penalties are not fixed, because the offender normally has the option to proceed to a court hearing, in which case the sentencer has a discretion regarding the appropriate penalty. However, for the most part, this is a distinction in theory only. Practical realities associated with the time and cost of taking such matters to court militate heavily against this form of disposition.

11.3   OUTLINE OF FIXED PENALTY REGIME

I now consider the essential features of a fixed penalty system. The starting point is to determine which factors are properly relevant to sentencing. This requires clarity concerning what justifies the practice of State imposed punishment. As we saw earlier, criminal punishment is justified because it deters many people from engaging in criminal conduct. Although there is a connection between criminal sanctions and crime rate, there is no link between increased penalties and crime rate. Thus, the objective of general deterrence does not justify imposing harsher penalties; only some type of harm in the form of State imposed sanctions. The level at which criminal sanctions should be set is governed by the principle of proportionality. This has two components: the harm caused by the offence and the offender's level of culpability. Considerations which do not affect either of these two matters are, therefore, irrelevant to sentencing.

Proportionality – the harm component

The factors that are relevant to determining how much harm has been caused by an offence are straightforward. This is determined by assessing the degree of unhappiness typically caused to the victim as a direct result of the offence. Each of us is different: thus, there is no objective measure of the standard degree of suffering caused by, say, a burglary, and one might think that this militates against the prospect of standard penalties. However, all legal standards and norms apply universally, hence, by their very nature, involve generalisations and approximations about human nature. It is for this reason that the concept of maximum penalties is unobjectionable. One can imagine an extreme case where a minor assault may cause long term fear and paranoia, totally impairing the victim's capacity to flourish and lead a productive life. Even if the offender was sentenced to the maximum term of imprisonment available for this offence (which is three months in Victoria and six months in England), one might be left with the feeling that the punishment was still far too soft.

This, however, does not reveal a defect in the rule. Given that legal rules must apply generally, extreme situations must be ignored in their development, otherwise we open the way for bad law. The same types of generalisation involved in setting maximum penalties should be used in determining the harm caused by each particular offence.

Proportionality – the culpability component

The other consideration that is relevant to the seriousness of an offence is the culpability of the offender. The central consideration here is whether the crime was committed intentionally or recklessly (or, in some cases, negligently). For most offences, this will be obvious after the finding of guilt. For those where it is not, different penalties could be set. Thus, a murder committed recklessly would have a fixed penalty, say, 20% less than an intentional killing.

In determining how much to punish, there would not appear to be any other general considerations which are *obviously* relevant. This makes for a small list. Not only is it small, but each of the factors can be determined quite easily from the objective circumstances pertaining to the offence. This makes it possible to develop a fixed penalty system which is not only consistent, but fair.

Presumptive or mandatory?

There remains the difficult question of whether fixed penalties should be mandatory or presumptive. Human foresight has its limits and, accordingly, a mandatory system, no matter how well designed, will at times lead to unfairness. However, the danger with making the guidelines presumptive, and incorporating a clause along the lines that the fixed penalty must be imposed unless 'exceptional' or 'special' circumstances exist, is that this leaves the door ajar for the splendour of a fixed penalty regime to be readily diminished, as more and more supposedly rare circumstances are discovered.

A compromise is the best solution to this dilemma. Where the fixed penalty does not involve a term of imprisonment, it should be mandatory.[33] No doubt, this will at times mean that offenders will be dealt with too severely, and on other occasions too leniently, but this is not too high a price, given that the sanctions involved (for example, a fine or licence disqualification) are not inherently overly oppressive. The costs in the form of unfitting sanctions[34] are likely to be outweighed by the advantages stemming from a more efficient sentencing process; one which will avoid the time consuming and expensive exercise of discovering every possible minute detail relating to the offender and the offence. This balancing process seems to accord with prevailing sentiment. For example, in most Australian jurisdictions, motorists detected with a blood alcohol content beyond a certain limit (in Victoria, the level is 0.1%) face a mandatory loss of licence. It could be argued that a 40 year old career taxi driver with three children who is the sole bread winner detected for drink driving should be treated differently from the 25 year old who exceeds the blood alcohol limit by the same amount, but who has no dependants, works from home and uses the car only to get around at weekends. Despite this, legislatures (and apparently the community) have

---

33   I have also argued that offences which do not carry the risk of imprisonment should be dealt with on the spot: Bagaric, 1998.

34   This assumes that if, in fact, a fixed penalty approach is adopted, it will result in an increased number of unfitting sanctions. However, given the unprincipled state of current sentencing practice, this is unlikely.

accepted that matters extraneous to the seriousness of the offence are irrelevant to the question of how much to punish such offenders.

However, where the fixed penalty involves a period of incarceration (however short), the penalty should only be presumptive. It is one matter to fine a person or take away his or her privilege to drive, but a far greater evil to tamper with his or her freedom of movement. Imprisonment is the most oppressive measure that the State utilises against its citizens – with the obvious exception of many parts of the US. It is fitting that, in determining the appropriateness or the length of a prison term, some concession should be made for the limits of human foresight. There will be (albeit rare) cases where even serious offences deserve little, if any, punishment. These will be confined to circumstances where no good will arise from meting out punishment. Good in this context refers to the ideals of general deterrence and proportionality. An example of a situation where a serious offence may not call for any punishment is the recent case of the Melbourne mother who left her child unattended in her car in a suburban hotel car park for about three hours. As a result of the hot weather, the child fell into a coma and died several days later. The mother has been charged with manslaughter by criminal negligence and, if convicted, faces the prospect of a significant gaol term.[35] Given the devastating loss and inevitable enormous feelings of guilt that the mother has already experienced, it is questionable whether meting out further pain to her will result in any good consequences. General deterrence in such circumstances seems misguided. The prospect of a stint in prison is hardly likely to provide a meaningful additional reason for desistence beyond the loss of a child. Further, it is unquestionable that the mother has already suffered sufficiently as a direct result of the crime.[36]

Making terms of imprisonment presumptive also gives the sentencer the opportunity to obtain information regarding the personal circumstances of the offender to ascertain whether an employment or education sanction is appropriate.

The above model merely spells out some essential characteristics of a wide ranging fixed penalty system. Given that this chapter is primarily concerned with the threshold issue of the desirability of a fixed penalty system, the precise mechanics of such a system are somewhat peripheral to the purpose at hand. However, for the sake of completeness, some of the finer features of such a scheme are now discussed.

---

35 For details regarding this incident, see Douez, S, 'Three hours in hot car: boy in coma' (2000) *The Age*, 19 February, p 5; Cant, S, 'Mother charged over child' (2000) *The Age*, 24 February, p 1. The maximum penalty she faces is 20 years' imprisonment.

36 In *Barci* (1994) 76 A Crim R 103, it was recognised that in some circumstances where the accused suffers as result of the offence, this may justify a lower penalty.

The level at which fixed penalties should be set

The main issue in any fixed system is the level at which the penalties should be set. As was discussed earlier, the harshness of the penalty should be proportionate to the gravity of the offence. There are numerous methods that could be employed to determine either the harshness of the penalty, the seriousness of the crime or the punishment that fits the crime. One method is simply to adopt current sentencing tariffs.[37]

This is similar to the approach taken by the New South Wales Court of Appeal in *Henry*, where a benchmark period of 4–5 years' imprisonment was set for the type of robbery under consideration. This seems harsh. But, in any event, once such a point is fixed, the standard penalty for other offences then becomes easier to set, given that there is now a point of reference. For example, burglary and theft are not as serious as armed robbery, and hence should be treated more leniently. Murder and rape, however, should be treated more seriously.

Fox and Freiberg suggest numerous other ways in which offence severity could be determined. The same approaches could also be used to determine penalty harshness or to directly match the penalty to the offence. These include everyday common sense judgments, public opinion research, and surveying professional opinion.[38] As was discussed in Chapter 7, the seriousness of the offence and the severity of the sanction should both be determined by reference to the one common variable, happiness. For present purposes, the relevant point is that irrespective of which criterion is adopted, it is clear that if a deliberative systematic measure is used, pre-determined penalties could be set for all criminal offences.

However, an important aspect of any fixed penalty regime is that it does not simply adopt pre-existing offence classifications. Owing to the broadness with which most criminal offences are defined, offences should be fragmented in order to distinguish more and less serious instances of the same offence and treat them accordingly.

In essence, the fixed penalty system should be structured along the lines of the Federal Sentencing Guidelines in the US to the extent that offences are compartmentalised into more and less serious instances of each type of offence. However, two significant departures should be made from this system:

(a) The level at which the penalties are set should be significantly reduced. The weight of empirical evidence does not support the efficacy of punishment to attain the objectives that are typically invoked to justify

---

37 See, eg, the approach by the New South Wales Court of Appeal in *Henry* [1999] NSWCCA 111, 12 May, discussed in Chapter 2.

38 See Fox and Freiberg, 1990, p 166.

disproportionate penalties, such as incarceration and marginal general deterrence. von Hirsch's suggestion that incarceration should be limited to serious offences (such as violent crimes and serious white collar crimes) and that the duration of confinement for these offences should not be longer than three years, except for homicide, where the duration should be up to five years,[39] appears to be far closer to the mark than the draconian penalties that are employed in many parts of the US, although, in my view, few (if any) property offences should result in imprisonment, and homicide offences committed intentionally or recklessly should normally be punished by a period of incarceration extending well beyond five years.

Recently, the English Court of Criminal Appeal has attempted to provide some guidance on the issue of when an offence is so serious that only a custodial sentence is appropriate. In *Howells*, it was held that while a court cannot lay down prescriptive rules governing the exercise of this judgment, it is helpful to begin by considering the nature and extent of any injury or damage caused to the victim and the nature and extent of the accused's criminal intention. Other important considerations are criminal history and a plea of guilty, especially where it is indicative of remorse. Where the offending has been fuelled by alcohol or drugs, the courts look more favourably on accused who have demonstrated a determination to address the addiction. Family responsibilities and physical or mental disability are also relevant in some circumstances. However, this list is too expansive to provide even general guidance to sentencers. A further problem is that the court did not provide examples of when the custody threshold is passed and when it is not.[40]

(b) Considerations relating to the personal circumstances of the offender should be ignored. This includes the offender's previous criminal history.

Examples

A few brief examples will assist to clarify the above model. The offence of theft encompasses the spur of the moment taking of a chocolate bar from a shop to the well planned dishonest appropriation of millions of pounds from one's employer. There is normally a very close correlation between the harm caused by the offence and the value of property involved. Thus, the offence should be compartmentalised according to the sum involved. For example, levels could be set at £50, £500, £2,500, £10,000 and £100,000 – with penalty

---

39 von Hirsch, 1976, Chapter 16; von Hirsch, 1993, p 43.

40 However, following *AG's Reference Nos 59, 60 and 63 of 1998 (Goodwin)* (5 December 1998), it appears that it will be uncommon for an offence of wounding with intent to cause grievous bodily harm or causing grievous bodily harm with intent, not to result in a custodial sentence, even where the offender is under the age of 18. For a discussion of this case, see 'Sentencing' [1999] Crim LR 341–43.

levels increasing accordingly. Where the sum involved is between, say, £50 and £500, the standard penalty should be a fine in the order of £1,000. This penalty should be applied irrespective of whether the offence concerns an impulsive decision to steal property from a shop, a well planned embezzlement from one's employer, or the pickpocketing of an unwary train passenger.

In the case of murder, the real evil in the crime stems from the deliberate destruction of a human life. There are many variables which, according to current sentencing practice, are relevant to determining how much to punish murderers. At one end of the spectrum is the 'hit man' who stalks a prominent public official for several weeks and kills for money. At the other is the jealous wife, who kills her husband in a fit of rage (in circumstances where the test for provocation is not satisfied) after she catches him cheating on her. The hit man has a page of prior convictions for serious offences against the person. The wife is a first offender and is genuinely sorry for her actions. Unlike theft, there would not appear to be any scope for distinguishing between different types of murder according to the level of harm caused. All human life is equal, thus it is irrelevant whether the victim is an eminent public official or a normal member of the community. In both cases, the same penalty of, say, 10 years' imprisonment should be imposed.

As I have noted above, these examples are merely intended to illustrate the core features of the proposed fixed penalty system. There is room for the incorporation of other variables into the sentencing chart. Penalty reductions may be appropriate in certain circumstances and increases in others; the important point being that any departures from the standard sentences should be made where there is a demonstrable reason for doing so. A demonstrable reason is not uninformed community outrage or a judicial hunch. It must relate to (a) the justification for punishing wrongdoers or (b) the seriousness of the offence.

It is tempting to follow one's intuition and impose a longer sentence on the hit man on the rationale that a very strong message needs to be conveyed to the community that professional killing is abhorrent and that there is a particularly strong need to rehabilitate and deter the hit man. However, this impulse must be resisted. As we have seen, there is simply insufficient evidence to support the view that punishment is able to achieve the goals of marginal general deterrence, rehabilitation or specific deterrence.

It may well be that there are some considerations which generally affect offence seriousness. For example, it is assumed that an offence is aggravated where it involves a breach of trust, or is well planned as opposed to being committed on the spur of the moment. If these considerations are relevant, then they could quite readily be incorporated into the sentencing chart. For example, the sentence could be increased by 10% where either of these considerations is relevant (and 20% where both are applicable). However, before attaching such premiums, it must first be established that the considerations are *properly* relevant to offence seriousness. This requires evidence that premeditated offences and those involving a breach of trust tend to cause more harm to victims (and the community in general) than similar offences where these factors are absent. This should be tested according to the criteria discussed above – such as public opinion research. Until such evidence is forthcoming, so called aggravating factors should be excluded from the sentencing chart.

11.4 OTHER OBJECTIONS TO FIXED PENALTIES

In light of the above discussion, it is opportune to consider briefly some further objections which may be levelled at the proposed scheme.

Whether fixed penalties violate judicial independence

Another criticism of fixed penalties is that they violate the independence of the judiciary:

> That persons are deprived of their liberty only in a public process by an officer of the State conducting himself or herself independently and able to bring an objective and disinterested judgment to bear on the facts free of political pressure seems ... to be the very essence of the rule of law.[41]

There are two possible parts to this argument. The first is the assertion that it *is* unlawful for parliament to prescribe fixed penalties. This has been flatly rejected by the courts. In *Palling v Corfield*, Barwick CJ stated that while it is usual and desirable for the courts to be vested with a discretion regarding the punishment to be imposed:

> It is beyond question that the parliament can prescribe such penalty as it thinks fit for the offences which it creates. It may make the penalty absolute in the sense that there is but one penalty which the court is empowered to impose and, in my opinion, it may lay an unqualified duty on the court to impose that penalty.[42]

The second is the normative argument that Parliament *should* not be permitted to tamper with the sentencing discretion of the court because this violates judicial independence. This, however, exaggerates the parameters of judicial independence. As Ashworth points out, the principle of judicial independence protects the impartiality of judges and their freedom from influence and

---

41 Adams, 1999, p 260.

42 (1970) 123 CLR 52, p 58. See, also, *Re S (A Child)* (1995) 12 WAR 392.

pressure; it does not confer supremacy on sentencing matters.[43] Tonry, who labels as 'silly' the view that it is an unjustifiable incursion into the independence of the judiciary to limit judicial sentencing discretion,[44] makes the further point that if judicial independence equated to sentencing supremacy, it would apply equally to impugn legislative codification of other bodies of law that evolved under the common law, such as torts and contract.

What if the utilitarian theory of punishment is not adopted

The utilitarian theory of punishment has been used as the backdrop to the proposed fixed penalty system, not because of its inherent amenability to such a system, but because, in my view, it is the soundest justificatory theory of punishment. It should be noted, however, that the retributive theory of punishment also provides a foundation for the imposition of standard penalties. Indeed, some would argue that it is even more compatible with such a system. As we have seen, the key features of a justifiable fixed penalty system are that the penalty should be commensurate with the seriousness of the offence and there is a sound basis for disregarding factors personal to the offender in the sentencing calculus. As pointed out previously, due to the wide diversity of retributive theories, it is questionable whether there is a single unifying principle which they share. However, a key hallmark of most retributive theories is that the justification of punishment does not depend on the possible attainment of consequential goals. Retributive theories are backward looking – punishing criminals is itself just. Considerations relating to why an offender commits an offence are at best remotely relevant; the emphasis being on the commission of the crime itself. Moreover, the cornerstone of many retributive theories, especially von Hirsch's just deserts theory, is that the amount of punishment should be in proportion to the severity of *the* offence. It is not surprising, then, that the Minnesota matrix is founded on a retributive ideal.

It follows that the arguments made in favour of fixed penalties cannot be sidestepped by simply rejecting the utilitarian theory. Fixed penalties present as a desirable sentencing reform, in the context of most top down approaches to sentencing, which search for a coherent justification of punishment and critically evaluate the proper relevance of existing sentencing considerations.

---

43 Ashworth, 1995, pp 44–47; Ashworth, 1997.
44 Tonry, 1996, p 181.

11.5 CONCLUSION

Two central objections have been made against fixed penalties. The first is that they are too severe. Secondly, it has been argued that they lead to unfairness because they cannot incorporate all the relevant sentencing variables. Upon adopting a utilitarian ethic as the primary rationale for punishment, both these problems are readily circumvented.

There is no utilitarian justification for disproportionate punishment, hence penalties should not be set which exceed the seriousness of the offence. Further, there is no foundation for most of the sentencing considerations which are commonly regarded as sacrosanct. Upon disregarding the irrelevant considerations, the ones remaining can readily be incorporated into a fixed penalty system. Accordingly, there is no merit in the claim that fixed penalties lead to unfairness.

This leaves the way open for a coherent sentencing law system: one where criminal justice is governed by predetermined rules and principles, as opposed to the mysterious idiosyncratic intuitions of sentencers.

CHAPTER 12

CONCLUSION

As was noted at the start of this book, nearly three decades ago sentencing law was described as a wasteland in the law.[1] Unfortunately, not much has changed. The rudimentary state of sentencing law is reflected by the fact that jurisdictions such as Australia and the UK pursue a contradictory mix of objectives, without attempting to prioritise them. Many parts of the US adopt a far more pointed approach to sentencing. However, this is generally result driven (with the aim being simply to imprison more offenders for longer periods), as opposed to being guided by a rationale for sentencing. The reason for this unsatisfactory state of affairs is the failure of legislatures and courts to adopt a coherent justification for punishment.

In order to develop a coherent sentencing system, the logical starting point is to determine the justification and purpose of imposing pain on wrongdoers. Once this is ascertained, the objectives of sentencing readily fall into line.

This book has evaluated the two main rival theories of punishment: retributivism and utilitarianism. In the philosophical domain, retributivism has represented the orthodoxy of punishment for the past two decades or so. To some extent, this has trickled down to sentencing law. However, even in jurisdictions which ostensibly adopt a retributive rationale, the theory is corrupted by practice. In Minnesota, for example, undue weight is accorded to prior convictions and in the UK, sentencers refuse to let go of utilitarian favourites such as general deterrence.

I have argued that retributivism cannot justify punishment. The most pervasive flaw with retributive theories is that they cannot justify the need for punitive measures without resort to consequential considerations. This expedient reliance on consequences undercuts the stability of many retributive theories. Retributive theories which do not incorporate consequentialist considerations are flawed because they lead to the unacceptable view that we should punish even if no good comes from it.

Utilitarianism is the most persuasive justificatory theory of punishment. All of the main objections that have been levelled against utilitarianism and have been responsible for its demise can be met. At the theoretical level, it has been suggested that punishing the innocent is not an insurmountable problem, since it is no different from other judgments we make in extreme circumstances. The more general criticism, that utilitarianism is inconsistent with the notion of rights, has been addressed by arguing that in fact it is only

---

1   Frankel, 1973.

in the context of a utilitarian ethic that rights have a coherent foundation. The pragmatic objection, that punishment is unable to achieve the utilitarian goals of rehabilitation, incapacitation and deterrence has been shown to be only partly right. There is no evidence showing that incarcerating high numbers of offenders results in less crime and there are no punitive measures which have been shown to reduce recidivism. However, punishment does result in much good: it deters many people from committing crime. Absent the threat of criminal sanctions, it is likely that there would be an enormous increase in the crime rate. The efficacy of punishment to attain absolute general deterrence justifies punishment. On the other hand, marginal deterrence appears to be a fiction. Given the failure of incapacitation and marginal general deterrence, there is no justification for the imposition of sentences which are disproportionate to the severity of the offence. The trend in most jurisdictions to tougher penalties should be stopped – and, indeed, reversed; no good has been shown to come from punishing offenders too severely.

It follows that the reason that we should punish offenders is because the good consequences in the form of deterring others from engaging in crime outweigh the pain inflicted through punishment on the offender. To make sentencing law and practice more coherent, principles and practices should be adopted which are consistent with this rationale. Although utilitarianism is, in my view, the soundest rationale for punishment, the implications that this has for sentencing practice differ from that traditionally associated with utilitarianism. The three traditional utilitarian pillars of rehabilitation, incapacitation and deterrence collapse into one: general deterrence. And indeed, only a limited form of general deterrence – absolute general deterrence, not marginal general deterrence. It is for this reason that the theory of punishment advanced in this book is best described as a modern utilitarian theory of punishment.

This theory makes for a vastly different sentencing system from that at present. The only objective that a sentencer would be driven by is to mete out punishment that will deter others from committing crime. This is best done by imposing a penalty that hurts the offender. It has been argued that some penalties that are presently widely employed are inadequate to this end. For example, the suspended sentence does not inflict any discernible pain and should be discarded as a sentencing option. The prime human interests which are targeted by criminal sanctions in most jurisdictions are freedom and material wealth. Not all crimes can be adequately dealt with by deprivations of these interests. Many middle range offenders should be dealt with by new sanctions which target employment and educational interests.

On the basis of a utilitarian ethic, the sentencing inquiry becomes far simpler than is presently the case. For example, considerations which are personal to the offender, such as previous convictions and remorse, are irrelevant. The only relevant consideration is the seriousness of the offence. If offences are compartmentalised into more and serious instances, this leaves the way open for a widespread fixed penalty regime. Fixed penalty systems have been widely criticised on the basis that they are too tough and cannot do justice in individual cases. However, these objections can be overcome by the introduction of proportionate fixed penalties and by rejecting the relevance of many supposedly central sentencing considerations. A fixed penalty system is the best way forward to a fair and consistent sentencing system.

One perhaps somewhat ironic aspect of this book is that, despite being at loggerheads with Andrew von Hirsch for much of the discussion, the position I arrive at, in terms of what I believe to be the most appropriate model for sentencing reform, is broadly similar to that which he proposes. We both believe that the objective of absolute general deterrence justifies the practice of imposing criminal sanctions and that the principle of proportionality is paramount in determining how much to punish. The main advantage of my theory, however, is that it is built on the bedrock of a utilitarian ethic. Von Hirsch, on the other hand, does not endorse a particular moral theory and his theory of punishment and sentencing is ultimately lacking at the justificatory level.

Further, many of the conclusions that I have reached concerning desirable sentencing reforms, such as the irrelevance of sentencing considerations, including specific deterrence, rehabilitation and prior convictions; the need for a greater range of criminal sanctions; and the desirability of a fixed penalty system, apply irrespective of which of the two theories of punishment examined in book is adopted. Even if the utilitarian theory of punishment is not adopted, hopefully, this book has demonstrated why sentencing law must be developed in a far more intellectually rigorous and exacting manner, whereby the focus is firmly kept on the justification for punishment and what is sought to be achieved by harming offenders.

BIBLIOGRAPHY

Adams, D, 'Fitting punishment to crime' (1996) 15 Law and Philosophy 407

Adams, M, 'Launch of UNSW Law Journal Forum' (1999) 22(1) University of New South Wales LJ 257

Advisory Council on the Penal System, *Sentences of Imprisonment: A Review of Maximum Penalties*, 1978, London: HMSO

Ancel, M, *Suspended Sentences*, 1971, London: Heinemann

Anderson, J, 'Reciprocity as a justification for retributivism' (1997) 16 Criminal Justice Ethics 13

Argyle, M, *The Psychology of Happiness*, 1987, London: Routledge

Armstrong, KG, 'The retributivist hits back', in Grupp, SE (ed), *Theories of Punishment*, 1971, Ontario: Indiana UP

Ashworth, A, 'Criminal justice and deserved sentences' [1989] Crim LR 340

Ashworth, A, *Sentencing and Criminal Justice*, 2nd edn, 1995, London: Butterworths

Ashworth, A, 'Changes in sentencing law' [1997] Crim LR 1

Ashworth, A, 'Four techniques for reducing disparity', in von Hirsch, A and Ashworth, A (eds), *Principled Sentencing*, 2nd edn, 1998, Oxford: Hart

Ashworth, A [1998a], 'Deterrence', in von Hirsch, A and Ashworth, A (eds), *Principled Sentencing*, 2nd edn, 1998, Oxford: Hart

Ashworth, A and Hough, M, 'Sentencing and the climate of opinion' [1996] Crim LR 776

Ashworth, A and von Hirsch, A, 'Not just deserts: a response to Braithwaite and Pettit' (1992) 12 OJLS 83

Ashworth, A and von Hirsch, A, 'Recognising elephants: the problem of the custody threshold' [1997] Crim LR 187

Ashworth, A and Player, E, 'Sentencing, equal treatment, and the impact of sanctions', in Ashworth, A and Wasik, M (eds), *Fundamentals of Sentencing Theory*, 1998, Oxford: Clarendon

Ashworth, A and von Hirsch, A, 'Desert and the three Rs', in von Hirsch, A and Ashworth, A (eds), *Principled Sentencing*, 2nd edn, 1998, Oxford, Hart

Aungles, A, *The Prison and the Home: A Study of the Relationship Between Domesticity and Penalty*, 1994, Sydney: Australian Institute of Criminology, Monograph Series No 5

Austin, J *et al*, 'The impact of "three strikes and you're out"' (2000) 1 Punishment & Society 131

Austin, J and Krisberg, B, 'The unmet promise of alternatives to incarceration' (1982) 28 Crime and Delinquency 374

Australian Law Reform Commission, *Sentencing of Federal Offenders*, Report No 15, 1980, Canberra

Australian Law Reform Commission, *Sentencing: Penalties*, Discussion Paper No 30, 1987, Canberra

Australian Law Reform Commission, *Sentencing*, Report No 44, 1988, Canberra

Ayer, AJ, *Language, Truth and Logic*, 1936, London: Gollancz

Bagaric, M, [1997a] 'The disunity of confiscation and sentencing' (1997) 21 Crim LJ 191

Bagaric, M, [1997b] 'The diminishing 'right' of silence' (1997) 19(3) Sydney L Rev 266

Bagaric, M, [1997c] 'Active and passive euthanasia: is there a moral distinction and should there be a legal difference?' (1997) 5 J Law and Medicine 143

Bagaric, M, 'Instant justice: the desirability of expanding the range of criminal offences dealt with on the spot' (1998) 24(2) Monash University L Rev 231

Bagaric, M and Lakic, T, 'Victorian sentencing turns retrospective: the constitutional validity of retrospective criminal legislation after *Kable*' (1999) 23(3) Crim LJ 145

Ball, RA *et al*, *House Arrest and Correctional Policy*, 1988, California: Sage

Ball, C, 'Part 1: a significant move towards restorative justice, or a recipe for unintended consequences' [2000] Crim LR 211

Barclay, GC and Travis, C, *International Comparison of Criminal Justice Statistics*, 1998 (Home Office Statistical Bulletin, No 2 of 2000)

Benn, SI, 'Rights', in Edwards, P (ed), *Encyclopedia of Philosophy*, 1967, New York: Collier-Macmillan, Vol 7, p 196

Benn, SI, 'Punishment', in Murphy, JG (ed), *Punishment and Rehabilitation*, 1973, Belmont: Wadsworth

Benn, SI, 'Human rights – for whom and for what?', in Kamenka, E and Tay, AE (eds), *Human Rights*, 1978, Melbourne: Edward Arnold

Benn, SI and Peters, RS, *Social Principles and the Democratic State*, 1959, London: Allen & Unwin, pp 175–76

Bentham, J, 'Anarchical fallacies: being an examination of the declaration of rights issued during the French Revolution' (1824), in Bowring, J (ed), *The Works of Jeremy Bentham*, 1962, New York: Russell and Russell, Vol 2

Bentham, J, 'Principles of morals and legislation', in Burns, JH and Hart, HLA (eds), *An Introduction to the Principles of Morals and Legislation*, 1970, London: Athlone

Bentham, J, 'The principles of penal law', in Bowring, J (ed), *The Works of Jeremy Bentham, 1838–43*, 1962, New York: Russell & Russell

Beres, LS and Griffith, TD, 'Do three strikes laws make sense? Habitual offender statutes and criminal incapacitation' (1998) 87 Georgetown L Rev 103

Beyleveld, D, 'Deterrence research as a basis for deterrence policies' (1979) 18 Howard Journal of Criminal Justice 135

Bianchi, H, 'Abolition: assensus and sanctuary', in Duff, RA and Garland, D (eds), *A Reader on Punishment*, 1994, Oxford: OUP

Blackburn, 'Reply: rule-following and moral realism', in Holtzman, SH and Leich, CM (eds), *Wittgenstein: To Follow a Rule*, 1981, London: Routledge & Kegan Paul

Blackburn, S, *Spreading the Word, Groundings in the Philosophy of Language*, 1984, Oxford: Clarendon

Blumstein, A, 'US criminal justice conundrum: rising prison populations and stable crime rates' (1998) 44(1) Crime and Delinquency 127

Blumstein, A *et al* (eds), *Deterrence and Incapacitation: Estimating the Effects of Criminal Sanctions on Crime Rates*, 1978, Washington: National Research Council

Blumstein, A, Cohen, J and Visher, C, *Criminal Careers and 'Career Criminals'*, 1986, Washington: National Academy

Bottoms, AE, 'Reflections of the renaissance of dangerousness' (1977) 16(2) Howard LJ 70

Bottoms, AE [1979a], 'The advisory council and the suspended sentence' [1979] Crim LR 437

Bottoms, AE [1979b], *The Suspended Sentence After Ten Years: A Review and Reassessment*, 1979, Leeds: Leeds UP

Bottoms, AE, 'The suspended sentence in England 1967–1981' (1981) 21 British Journal of Criminology 1

Bottoms, AE, 'Five puzzles in von Hirsch's theory of punishment', in Ashworth, A and Wasik, M (eds), *Fundamentals of Sentencing Theory*, 1998, Oxford: Clarendon

Bottoms, AE and Brownsword, R, 'The dangerousness debate after the Floud Report' (1982) 22 British Journal of Criminology 229

Box, S, *Recession, Crime and Punishment*, 1987, London: Macmillan

Braithwaite, J and Pettit, D, *Not Just Deserts*, 1990, Oxford: Clarendon

Braithwaite, J and Pettit, D, 'Not just deserts, even in sentencing' (1993) 4(3) Current Issues in Criminal Justice 225

Brink, D, *Moral Realism and The Foundations of Ethics*, 1989, Cambridge: CUP

Broadhurst, R and Loh, N, 'Selective incapacitation and the phantom of deterrence', in Harding, R (ed), *Repeat Juvenile Offenders: The Failure of Selective Incapacitation in Western Australia*, 2nd edn, 1995, Perth: Crime Research Centre, UWA

Brody, S, 'How effective are penal treatments?', in von Hirsch, A and Ashworth, A (eds), *Principled Sentencing*, 2nd edn, 1998, Oxford: Hart

Brody, SR and Tarling, R, *Taking Offenders Out of Circulation*, Research Study No 64, 1981, London: HMSO

Brown, A, *Modern Political Philosophy*, 1986, London: Penguin

Brown, M, 'Serious violence and dilemmas of sentencing: a comparison of three incapacitation policies' [1998] Crim LR 710

Burgh, RW, 'Do the guilty deserve punishment?' (1982) 79 Journal of Philosophy 209

Burnett, R, 'Recidivism and imprisonment', in Home Office Research Bulletin No 36, Special Edition: Prisons and Prisoners, 1994, London: Home Office Research and Planning Unit

Campbell, JQ, 'A sentencer's lament on the imminent death of the suspended sentence' [1995] Crim LR 293

Campbell, T, *Justice*, 1988, London: Macmillan

Campbell, T (ed), *Law and Enlightenment in Britain*, 1990, Aberdeen: Aberdeen UP

Campbell, T, 'Democracy, human rights and positive law' (1994) 16 Sydney L Rev 195

Campbell, T [1996a], *The Legal Theory of Ethical Positivism*, 1996, Aldershot: Dartmouth

Campbell, T [1996b], 'Realizing human rights', in Campbell, T *et al* (eds), *Human Rights: From Rhetoric to Reality*, 1996, Oxford: Blackwell

Campbell, T [1996c], 'The rights of the mentally ill', in Campbell, T *et al* (eds), *Human Rights: From Rhetoric to Reality*, 1996, Oxford: Blackwell

Campbell, T, 'The point of legal positivism', in Campbell, T (ed), *Legal Positivism*, 1999, Aldershot: Dartmouth

Canadian Sentencing Commission, *Sentencing Reform: A Canadian Approach*, 1987, Ottawa: Canadian Government Publishing Centre

Carlen, P, 'Crime, inequality and sentencing', in Duff, RA and Garland, D (eds), *A Reader on Punishment*, 1994, Oxford: OUP

Cavadino, M and Dignan, J, 'Reparation, retribution and rights' (1997) 4 International Review of Victimology 233

Christie, N, 'Conflicts as property' (1977) 17 British Journal of Criminology 1

Christie, N, *Limits of Pain*, 1981, London: Martin Robertson

Clear, TR and Hardyman, PL, 'The new intensive supervision movement' (1990) 36 Crime and Delinquency 42

Cohen, J, 'The incapacitative effect of imprisonment: a critical review of the literature', in Blumstein, A, Cohen, J and Nagin, J (eds), *Deterrence and Incapacitation: Estimating the Effects of Criminal Sanctions on Crime Rates*, 1978, Washington: National Academy of Sciences

Cole, D, *No Equal Justice: Race and Class in the American Justice System*, 1999, New York: New Press

Cottingham, J, 'Varieties of retributivism' (1979) 29 Philosophical Quarterly 238

Cragg, AW, 'Hume on punishment', in Campbell, T (ed), *Law and Enlightenment in Britain*, 1990, Aberdeen: Aberdeen UP

Dancy, J, 'Intuitionism', in Singer, P (ed), *A Companion to Ethics*, 1991, Oxford: Blackwell

Dignan, J, 'The Crime and Disorder Act and the prospects for restorative justice' [1999] Crim L Rev 48

Dolinko, D, 'Some thoughts about retributivism' (1991) 101 Ethics 537

Dolinko, D, 'Retributivism, consequentialism, and the intrinsic goodness of punishment' (1997) 16 Law and Philosophy 507

Doob, AN, 'The United States Sentencing Commission Guidelines: if you don't know where you are going, you might not get there', in Clarkson, C and Morgan, R (eds), *The Politics of Sentencing Reform*, 1995, Oxford: Clarendon

Douglas, R, *Guilty Your Worship*, 1980, Melbourne: LaTrobe University

Duff, RA, *Trials and Punishments*, 1986, Cambridge: CUP

Duff, RA, 'Punishment, citizenship and responsibility', in Tam, H (ed), *Punishment, Excuses and Moral Development*, 1996, Aldershot: Avebury

Duff, RA, 'Desert and penance', in von Hirsch, A and Ashworth, A (eds), *Principled Sentencing*, 1998, Oxford: Hart

Duff, RA, and Garland, D, 'Introduction: thinking about punishment', in Duff, RA and Garland, D (eds), *A Reader on Punishment*, 1994, Oxford: OUP

Duff, RA, and von Hirsch, A, 'Responsibility, retribution and the "voluntary": a response to Williams' [1997] CLJ 103

Dworkin, R, *Taking Rights Seriously*, 4th edn, 1977, Cambridge, Mass: Harvard UP

Dworkin, R, 'Liberalism', in Hampshire, S (ed), *Public and Private Morality*, 1979, Cambridge: CUP

Dworkin, R, *Law's Empire* 1986, London: Fontana

Ehrlich, I, 'Participation in illegitimate activities: a theoretical and empirical investigation' (1973) 81 Journal of Political Economy 521

Engelhardt, HT and Kenny, J, 'Principle of double effect', in Brody, B and Engelhardt, HT (eds), *Bioethics*, 1987, New Jersey: Prentice Hall

Ewing, AC, *The Morality of Punishment and Some Suggestions for a General Theory of Ethics*, 1929, London: Kegan Paul

Ezorsky, G, 'The ethics of punishment', in Ezorsky, G (ed), *Philosophical Perspectives on Punishment*, 1972, Albany: NY State UP

Fagan, J, 'Social and legal policy dimensions of violent juvenile crime' (1990) 17 Crime Justice and Behaviour 93

Fairall, PA, 'Violent offenders and community protection in Victoria – the Gary David experience' (1993) 17 Criminal LJ 40

Farrell, DM, 'The justification of general deterrence' (1985) XCIV The Philosophical Review 367

Farrington, D, 'Age and crime', in Tonry, M and Morris, N (eds), *Crime and Justice: An Annual Review of Research*, 1986, Chicago: Chicago UP

Findlay, M, Odgers, S and Yeo, S, *Australian Criminal Justice*, 2nd edn, 1999, Melbourne: OUP

Finnis, J, *Natural Law and Natural Rights*, 1980, Oxford: Clarendon

Floud, J, 'Dangerousness and criminal justice' (1982) 22 British Journal of Criminology 213

Flynn, M, 'One strike and you're out' (1997) 22 Alternative LJ 72

Flynn, M, 'Fixing a sentence: are there any constitutional limits?' (1999) 22(1) University of New South Wales LJ 280

Focault, M, *Discipline and Punish: the Birth of Prison*, 1977, London: Allen Lane

Foot, P, *Virtues and Vices*, 1978, Oxford: Blackwell

Fox, RG, 'Controlling sentencers' (1987) 20 Australian and New Zealand Journal of Criminology 218

Fox, RG, 'Dr Scwitzbegel's machine revisited: electronic monitoring of offenders' (1987) 20 Australia and New Zealand Journal of Criminology 131

Fox, RG, 'The killings of Bobby Veen: the High Court on proportion in sentencing' (1988) 12 Criminal LJ 339

Fox, RG, 'The meaning of proportionality in sentencing' (1994) 19 Melbourne UL Rev 489

Fox, RG, *Criminal Justice on the Spot*, 1995, Canberra: Australian Institute of Criminology

Fox, RG and Freiberg, A, *Sentencing: State and Federal Law in Victoria*, 1985, Melbourne, OUP

Fox, RG and Freiberg, A, 'Sentences without conviction: from status to contract in sentencing' (1989) 13 Criminal LJ 297

Fox, RG and Freiberg, A, 'Ranking offence seriousness' (1990) 23 Australia and New Zealand Journal of Criminology 165

Fox, RG and Freiberg, A, *Sentencing: State and Federal Offenders*, 2nd edn, 1999, Melbourne: OUP

Frankel, M, *Criminal Sentences: Law Without Order*, 1973, New York, Hill & Wang

Frase, RS, 'Sentencing guidelines in Minnesota and other American States: a progress report', in Clarkson, C and Morgan, R (eds), *The Politics of Sentencing Reform*, 1995, Oxford: Clarendon

Freckelton, I, 'Masochism, self mutilation and the limits of consent' (1994) 2 Journal of Law and Medicine 48

Freckelton, I, 'Introduction: criminal sentencing', in *The Laws of Australia*, 1996, Sydney: Law Book Co

Freiberg, A, 'Sentencing reform in Victoria', in Clarkson, C and Morgan, R (eds), *The Politics of Sentencing Reform*, 1995, Oxford: Clarendon

Freiberg, A, *Sentencing: State and Federal Offenders*, 2nd edn, 1999, Melbourne: OUP

Freiberg, A, and Fox, RG, 'Sentencing structures and sanction hierarchies' (1986) 10 Criminal LJ 216

Freiberg, A and Ross, S, *Sentencing Reform and Penal Change: The Victorian Experience*, 1999, Sydney: Federation

Galligan, DJ, 'The right to silence reconsidered' (1988) Current Legal Problems 69

Garland, D, *Punishment and Modern Society*, 1990, Chicago: Chicago UP

Gewirth, A, *Human Rights: Essays on Justification and Applications*, 1982, Chicago: Chicago UP

Gewirth, A, 'Epistemology of human rights', in Pojman, LP (ed), *Ethical Theory*, 2nd edn, 1995, Belmont: Wadsworth

Ghosh, E, 'Applying Pettit's republican liberty to criminal justice and judicial-making' (1999) 22(1) University of New South Wales LJ 122

Gibbs, J, *Race and Justice*, 1996, San Francisco: Jossey Bass

Glover, J, *Causing Deaths and Saving Lives*, 1977, London: Pelican

Goldman, AH, 'The paradox of punishment' (1979) 9 Philosophy and Public Affairs 42

Goldsworthy, J, 'Externalism, internalism and moral scepticism' (1992) Australasian Journal of Philosophy 40

Grabosky, PN, 'Zero tolerance policing' (1999) 102 Australian Institute of Criminology: Trends and Issues in Crime and Criminal Justice 1

Great Britain, Home Office, White Paper, *Crime, Justice and Protecting the Public*, 1990, London: HMSO

Grebing, G, *The Fine in Comparative Law: A Survey of 21 Countries*, 1982, Cambridge: University of Cambridge, Institute of Criminology

Greene, J, 'The unit fine: monetary sanctions apportioned to income', in von Hirsch, A and Ashworth, A (eds), *Principled Sentencing*, 2nd edn, 1998, Oxford: Hart

Greenwood, P, *Selective Incapacitation: Report Prepared for the National Institute of Justice*, 1982, California: RAND Corp

Greenwood, PE *et al*, *Three Strikes and You're Out: Estimated Benefits and Costs of California's New Mandatory Sentencing Law*, 1994, Santa Monica: RAND Corp

Greig, D, 'The politics of dangerousness', in Gerull, S and Lucas, W (eds), *Serious Violent Offenders: Sentencing, Psychiatry and Law Reform, Conference Proceedings* (1993) 47 Australian Institute of Criminology

Gross, H, 'Proportional punishment and justifiable sentences', in Gross, H and von Hirsch, A (eds), *Sentencing*, 1981, Oxford: OUP

Hancock, RN, *Twentieth Century Ethics*, 1974, New York: Columbia UP

Harding, C and Ireland, RW, *Punishment: Rule, Rhetoric and Practice*, 1989, London: Routledge

Harding, R, 'Rationale-choice gun use in armed robbery' (1990) 1 Criminal Law Forum 427

Hare, RM, *Moral Thinking: Its Levels, Methods and Point*, 1981, Oxford: Clarendon

Harel, A, 'What demands are rights? An investigation into the relation between rights and reasons' (1997) 17(1) OJLS 101

Hart, HLA, Are there any natural rights?' (1955) LXIV Philosophical Review Quarterly 175

Hart, HLA, *The Concept of Law*, 1961, Oxford: OUP

Hart, HLA, *Punishment and Responsibility*, 1968, Oxford: Clarendon

Hart, HLA, *Essays in Jurisprudence and Philosophy*, 1983, Oxford: Clarendon

Hawkin, DJB, 'Punishment and moral responsibility', in Grupp, SE (ed), *Theories of Punishment*, 1971, Ontario: Indiana UP

Henham, R, 'Cumulative sentencing and penal policy' (1995) 59(4) Journal of Criminal Law 420

Henham, R [1997a], 'Anglo-American approaches to cumulative sentencing and implications for UK sentencing policy' (1997) 36(3) Howard LJ 263

Henham, R [1997b], 'Dangerousness, rationality and sentencing policy' (1997) 26(4) Anglo-Am L Rev 493

Henham, R, 'Making sense of the Crime Sentences Act 1997' (1998) 61 MLR 223

Hobbes, T, *Leviathan*, 1968 edn, Harmondsworth: Penguin

Hogg, R, 'Mandatory sentencing laws and the symbolic politics of law and order' (1999) 22(1) University of New South Wales LJ 262

Hohfeld, WN (1919), *Fundamental Legal Conceptions*, 1964, London: Greenwood

Hood, R, *Race and Sentencing: A Study in the Crown Court*, 1992, Oxford: Clarendon

Hood, R, *The Death Penalty: A World Wide Perspective*, 1996, Oxford: Clarendon

Honderich, T, *Punishment: The Supposed Justifications*, 1984, Harmondsworth: Penguin

Howells, K and Day, A, 'The rehabilitation of offenders: international perspectives applied to Australian correctional systems' (1999) 112 Australian Institute of Criminology: Trends and Issues in Crime and Criminal Justice 1

Hudson, BA, 'Mitigation for socially deprived offenders', in von Hirsch, A and Ashworth, A (eds), *Principled Sentencing*, 1998, Oxford: Hart

Hume, D, *A Treatise of Human Nature* (1738), 1978 edn, Oxford: Clarendon

Hunt, D, 'Criminal law update – Court of Criminal Appeal' (1997) 3 The Judicial Review 115

Husak, D, 'Why punish the deserving?' (1992) 26 Nous 447

Jareborg, N, 'The Swedish sentencing reform', in Clarkson, C and Morgan, R (eds), *The Politics of Sentencing Reform*, 1995 Oxford: Clarendon

Jones, E, 'The failure of the "Get Tough" crime policy' (1995) 20 University of Daytona L Rev 803

Kapardis, A and Farrington, DP, 'An experimental study of sentencing by magistrates' (1981) 5 Law and Human Behaviour 107

Kleinig, J, *Punishment and Desert*, 1973, The Hague: Martinus Nijhoff

Kleinig, J, 'Human rights, legal rights and social change', in Kamenka, E and Tay, AE (eds), *Human Rights*, 1978, Melbourne: Edward Arnold

Kleinig, J, 'The hardness of hard treatment', in Ashworth, A and Wasik, M (eds), *Fundamentals of Sentencing Theory*, 1998, Oxford: Clarendon

Kozol, K, 'Dangerousness in society and law' (1982) 13 University of Toledo L Rev 241

Krisberg, B, 'The unmet promise of alternatives to incarceration' (1982) Crime and Delinquency 374

Lappi-Seppala, T, 'Regulating the prison population: experiences from a long-term policy in Finland' (1998) paper delivered at the Back to Beyond Prisons Symposium (Canada)

Lewis, CS, 'The humanitarian theory of punishment', in Grupp, SE (ed), *Theories of Punishment*, 1971, Ontario: Indiana UP

Lovegrove, A, 'Judicial sentencing policy, criminological expertise and public opinion' (1998) 31 Australian and New Zealand Journal of Criminology 287

McCloskey, HJ, 'A non-utilitarian approach to punishment' (1965) 8 Inquiry 239

McCloskey, HJ, *Meta-Ethics and Normative Ethics*, 1969, The Hague: Martinus Nijhoff

McCloskey, HJ, 'Rights: some conceptual issues' (1976) 54 Australian Journal of Philosophy 99

McIvor, G, *Sentenced to Serve: Evaluative Studies in Social Work*, 1992, Aldershot: Avebury

McKie, J, *Active Voluntary Euthanasia: The Current Issues*, 1994, Melbourne: Centre for Bioethics, Monash University

McMurry, K, 'Three-strikes laws proving more show than go' [1997] Trial 12

Mabbott, JD, 'Punishment', in Grupp, SE (ed), *Theories of Punishment*, 1971, Ontario: Indiana UP

MacIntyre, A, 'A critique of Gewirth and the notion of rights', in Pojman, LP (ed), *Ethical Theory*, 2nd edn, 1995, Belmont: Wadsworth

Mackie, JL, *Ethics: Inventing Right and Wrong*, 1977, London: Penguin

Mackie, JL, 'Morality and retributive emotions' (1982) 1 Criminal Justice Ethics 3

Marmor, A, 'On the limits of rights' (1997) 16 Law and Philosophy 1

Marshall, G, 'Rights, options and entitlements', in Simpson, AWB (ed), *Oxford Essays in Jurisprudence*, 1973, Oxford: Clarendon

Martinson, R, 'What works? – questions and answers about prison reform' (1974) 35 The Public Interest 22

Martinson, R, 'New findings, new views: a note of caution regarding sentencing reforms' (1979) 7 Hofstra L Rev 243

Mathiesen, T, *Prison on Trial*, 1990, London: Sage

Mathiesen, T, 'General prevention as communication', in Duff, RA and Garland, D (eds), *A Reader on Punishment*, 1994, Oxford: OUP

Mauer, M, *Americans Behind Bars: A Comparison of International Rates of Incarceration*, 1991, Washington DC: The Sentencing Project

Mill, JS, *Utilitarianism*, 1986 (Warnock, M (ed)), Glasgow: Fontana

Milte, KL and Weber, TA, *Police in Australia*, 1977, Melbourne: Butterworths

Monahan, J, 'The prediction of violent behaviour: toward a second generation of theory and policy' (1984) 141 American Journal of Psychiatry 10

Moore, M, 'Justifying retributivism' (1993) 27 Israel L Rev 15

Moore, M, 'The moral worth of retribution', in von Hirsch, A and Ashworth, A (eds), *Principled Sentencing*, 1998, Oxford: Hart

Morgan, N, 'Capturing crimes or capturing votes? The aims and effects of mandatories' (1999) 22(1) University of New South Wales LJ 267

Morris, H, 'Persons and punishment', in Grupp, SE (ed) *Theories of Punishment*, 1971, London: Indiana UP

Morris, H, 'Persons and punishment', in Murphy, JG (ed), *Punishment and Rehabilitation*, 1973, Belmont: Wadsworth

Morris, H, 'A paternalistic theory of punishment', in Duff, RA and Garland, D (eds), *A Reader on Punishment*, 1994, Oxford: OUP

Morris, N, *Madness and the Criminal Law*, 1982, Chicago: Chicago UP

Morris, N, 'Dangerousness and incapacitation', in Duff, RA and Garland, D (eds), *A Reader on Punishment*, 1994, Oxford: OUP

Morris, N, 'Desert as a limiting principle', in von Hirsch, A and Ashworth, A (eds), *Principled Sentencing*, 1998, Oxford: Hart

Morris, N and Tonry, M, *Between Prison and Probation: Intermediate Punishment in a Rational Sentencing System*, 1990, New York: OUP

Moxon, D, *Sentencing Practices in the Crown Court*, Study No 103, 1988, London: HMSO

Mullen, P, 'Mental disorder and dangerousness' (1984) 18 Australia and New Zealand Journal of Psychiatry 8

Murphy, JG 'Marxism and retribution' (1973) 2 Philosophy and Public Affairs 217

Murphy, JG, *Retribution, Justice and Therapy*, 1979, Kluwer: Dordrecht

Murphy, JG, 'Retributivism, moral education and the liberal State' (1985) 4 Criminal Justice Ethics 3

Murphy, JG, 'Marxism and retribution', in Duff, RA and Garland, D (eds), *A Reader on Punishment*, 1994, Oxford: OUP

Nagel, I and Schulhofer, S, 'A tale of three cities: an empirical study of charging and bargaining practices under the Federal Sentencing Guidelines' (1992) 66 Southern California L Rev 501

Nagel, T, *The View From Nowhere*, 1986, New York: OUP

Nagin, D, Farrington, D and Moffitt, T, 'Life course trajectories of different type of offenders' (1995) 33 Criminology 111

Nagin, D, 'Criminal deterrence research at the outset of the twenty-first century' (1998) 23 Crime and Justice 1

Nagle, JF, 'Punishment, parliament and the people' (1998) 10(3) Judicial Officers' Bulletin 17

Narayan, U, 'Appropriate responses and preventive benefits: justifying censure and hard treatment in legal punishment' (1993) 13 OJLS 166

New South Wales Law Reform Commission [1996a], *Sentencing*, 1996, Discussion Paper No 33

New South Wales Law Reform Commission [1996b], *Sentencing*, 1996, Report No 79

Newman, G, *Just and Painful*, 1983, London: Macmillan

Nozick, R, *Anarchy, State and Utopia*, 1974, Oxford: Blackwell

Nozick, R, *Philosophical Explanations*, 1981, Cambridge, Mass: Harvard UP

O'Connor, D and Fairfall, PA, *Criminal Defences*, 3rd edn, 1996, Sydney: Butterworths

Ovey, C, 'The European Convention on Human Rights and the criminal lawyer: an introduction' [1998] Crim L Rev 4

Owens, MW, 'California's three strikes laws: desperate times require desperate measures – but will it work?' (1995) 26 Pacific LJ 881

Packer, HL, 'Theories of punishment and correction: what is the function of prison?', in Orland, L (ed), *Justice, Punishment, Treatment: The Correctional Process*, 1973, New York: Free Press

Palmer, T, 'The effectiveness of intervention: recent trends and current issues' (1991) 37 Crime and Delinquency 330

Parke, J and Mason, B, 'The Queen of Hearts in Queensland: a critique of Part 10 of the Penalties and Sentences Act 1992 (Qld)' (1995) 19 Criminal LJ 312

Philpotts, GJO and Lancucki, LB, *Previous Convictions, Sentence and Reconvictions*, Home Office Research Study No 53, 1979, London: HMSO

Pigden, CR, 'Naturalism', in Singer, P (ed), *A Companion to Ethics*, 1991, Oxford: Blackwell

Pratt, J, *Governing the Dangerous: Dangerousness, Law and Social Change*, 1997, Sydney: Federation

Pratt, J, 'Towards the "decivilizing" of punishment?' (1998) 7(4) Social and Legal Studies 487

Posner, R, *Economic Analysis of Law*, 2nd edn, 1997, New York: Aspen Law & Business

Quinton, AM, 'On punishment' (1954) 14 Analysis 512

Raphael, D, *Moral Philosophy*, 1981, Oxford: OUP

Rawls, J, 'Outline of a decision procedure in ethics' (1951) 60 The Philosophical Rev 177

Rawls, J, 'Two concepts of rules' (1955) 64 The Philosophical Rev 3

Rawls, J, *A Theory of Justice*, 1971, Cambridge, Mass: Belknap

Raz, J, *The Authority of Law*, 1979, Oxford: OUP

Raz, J, *Morality of Freedom*, 1986, Oxford: OUP

Rex, S, 'A new form of rehabilitation', in von Hirsch, A and Ashworth, A, *Principled Sentencing*, 2nd edn, 1998, Oxford: Hart

Riley, D, *Drink Driving: The Effects of Enforcement*, 1991, Home Office Research Study No 121, London: HMSO

Rosen, F, 'Utilitarianism and the punishment of the innocent' (1997) 9 Utilitas 23

Ross, HL, 'Law, science and accidents: the British Road Safety Act of 1967' (1973) 2 Journal of Legal Studies 1

Ruby, CC, *Sentencing*, 4th edn, 1994, Toronto: Butterworths

Sadurski, W, *Giving Desert its Due*, 1985, Kluwer: Dordrecht

Schedler, G, 'Can retributivists support legal punishment?' (1980) 63 The Monist 185

Schwartz, GE, 'Executing the innocent' (1998) 34 Criminal Law Bulletin 328

Scott, P, 'Assessing dangerousness in criminals' (1977) 131 British Journal of Psychiatry 140

Sebba, L, 'Some explorations in the scaling of penalties' (1978) 15 Journal of Research in Crime and Delinquency 247

Sebba, L and Nathan, G, 'Further explorations in the scaling of penalties' (1984) 24 British Journal of Criminology 221

Shapland, J, *Between Conviction and Sentence*, 1981, London: Routledge & Kegan Paul

Sher, G, *Desert*, 1987, Princeton: Princeton UP

Sher, G, *Approximate Justice, Studies in Non-Ideal Theory*, 1997, London: Rowman and Littlefield

Shklar, J, *Ordinary Vices*, 1984, Cambridge, Mass, Harvard UP

Singer, P, 'All animals are equal', in Singer, P (ed), *Applied Ethics*, 1986, Oxford: OUP

Singer, P, *Practical Ethics*, 2nd edn, 1993, Cambridge: CUP

Small, R, 'Ressentiment, revenge and punishment: origins of the Nietzschean critique' (1997) 9 Utilitas 39

Smart, JCC, 'An outline of a system of utilitarian ethics' in Smart, JCC and Williams, B (eds), *Utilitarianism: For and Against*, 1973, London: CUP

Smith, J, 'Clothing the emperor: towards a jurisprudence of sentencing' (1997) 30 Australian and New Zealand Journal of Criminology 168

Smith, M, 'Realism', in Singer, P (ed), *A Companion to Ethics*, 1991, Oxford: Blackwell

Smith, M, 'Valuing: desiring or believing?', in Charles, D and Lennon, C (eds), *Reduction, Explanation and Realism*, 1992, Oxford: Clarendon

Sparks, RF, 'The use of suspended sentences' [1971] Crim LR 384

Spears, D, 'Structuring discretion: sentencing in the Jurisic Age' (1999) 22 University of New South Wales LJ 295

Spigelman, J, 'Sentencing guideline judgments' (1999) 73 Australian LJ 876

Sprigge, TLS, 'A utilitarian reply to Dr McCloskey' (1965) 8 Inquiry 272

Sprigge, TLS, *The Rational Foundation Of Ethics*, 1987, London: Routledge

Stolzenberg, L and d'Alessio, SJ, 'Three strikes and you're out: the impact of California's new mandatory sentencing law on serious crime rates' (1997) 43(4) Crime and Delinquency 457

Sumner, LW, *The Moral Foundation of Rights*, 1987, Oxford: Clarendon

Taifa, N, '"Three strikes – and – you're – out" – mandatory life imprisonment for third time felons' (1995) 20 University of Daytona L Rev 717

Tait, D, 'The invisible sanction: suspended sentences in Victoria 1985–1991' (1995) 28(2) Australia and New Zealand Journal of Criminology 143

Tata, C and Hutton, N, 'What "rules" in sentencing? Consistency and disparity in the absence of rules' (1998) 26 International Journal of the Sociology of Law 33

Taylor (Lord) 'Judges and sentencing' (1993) Journal of the Law Society of Scotland 129

Ten, CL, *Crime, Guilt and Punishment*, 1987, Oxford: Clarendon

Ten, CL, 'Positive retributivism' (1990) 7(2) Social Philosophy and Policy 194

Ten, CL [1991a], 'Crime and punishment', in Singer, P (ed), *A Companion to Ethics*, 1991, Oxford: Blackwell

Ten, CL [1991b], 'Dominion as the target of criminal justice' (1991) 10(2) Criminal Justice Ethics 40

Thomas, DA, *Principles of Sentencing*, 2nd edn, 1979, London: Heinemann

Thomas, DA, 'Sentencing reform: England and Wales', in Clarkson, C and Morgan, R (eds), *The Politics of Sentencing Reform*, 1995, Oxford: Clarendon

Thomas, DA, 'The Crime (Sentences) Act 1997' [1998] Crim LR 83

Tonry, M, 'Judges and sentencing policy – the American experience', in Munro, C and Wasik, M (eds), *Sentencing, Judicial Discretion and Training*, 1992, London: Sweet & Maxwell

Tonry, M, 'Sentencing reform across national boundaries', in Clarkson, C and Morgan, R (eds), *The Politics of Sentencing Reform*, 1995, Oxford: Clarendon

Tonry, M, *Sentencing Matters*, 1996, New York: OUP

Tonry, M, 'Interchangeability, desert limits and equivalence of function', in von Hirsch, A and Ashworth, A (eds), *Principled Sentencing*, 2nd edn, 1998, Oxford: Hart

Tyler, T, *Why People Obey the Law*, 1990, New Haven: Yale UP

Velasquez, M and Rostankowski, C, *Ethics: Theory and Practice*, 1985, New Jersey: Prentice Hall

Victorian Sentencing Committee, *Sentencing*, 1988, Melbourne: Victorian Attorney General's Department

Victorian Sentencing Task Force (authored by Fox, R and Freiberg, A), *Review of Statutory Maximum Penalties in Victoria*, 1989, Melbourne, Victorian Attorney-General's Department

von Hirsch, A, *Doing Justice: The Choice of Punishments*, 1976, New York: Hill and Wang

von Hirsch, A, *Past or Future Crimes*, 1985, New Jersey: Rutgers UP

von Hirsch, A, 'Criminal record rides again' (1991) 10(2) Criminal Justice Ethics 2 von Hirsch, A, *Censure and Sanctions*, 1993, Oxford: Clarendon

von Hirsch, A, 'Censure and proportionality', in Duff, RA and Garland, D (eds), *A Reader on Punishment*, 1994, Oxford: OUP

von Hirsch, A, 'Proportionality and parsimony in American sentencing guidelines: the Minnesota and Oregon standards', in Clarkson, C and Morgan, R (eds), *The Politics of Sentencing Reform*, 1995, Oxford: Clarendon

von Hirsch, A [1998a], 'Desert and previous convictions', in von Hirsch, A and Ashworth, A (eds), *Principled Sentencing*, 2nd edn, 1998, Oxford: Hart

von Hirsch, A [1998b], 'Proportionate sentences: a desert perspective', in von Hirsch, A and Ashworth, A (eds), *Principled Sentencing*, 2nd edn, 1998, Oxford: Hart

von Hirsch, A [1998c], 'Rehabilitation', in von Hirsch, A and Ashworth, A (eds), *Principled Sentencing*, 2nd edn, 1998, Oxford: Hart

von Hirsch, A, 'The politics of "just deserts"' (1990) 32 Canadian Journal of Criminology 397

von Hirsch, A *et al*, *Criminal Deterrence and Sentence Severity*, 1999, Oxford: Hart

von Hirsch, A and Ashworth, A, 'Not just deserts: a response to Braithwaite and Pettit' (1992) OJLS 83

von Hirsch, A and Ashworth, A, 'Protective sentencing under s 2(2)(b): the criteria for dangerousness' [1996] Crim LR 175

von Hirsch, A and Ashworth, A (eds), *Principled Sentencing*, 2nd edn, 1998, Oxford: Hart

von Hirsch, A and Jareborg, N, 'Gauging criminal harm: a living standard analysis' (1991) 11 OJLS 1

von Hirsch, A and Jareborg, N, 'The Swedish sentencing law', in von Hirsch, A and Ashworth, A (eds), *Principled Sentencing*, 2nd edn, 1998, Oxford: Hart

von Hirsch, A and Maher, L [1998a], 'Should penal rehabilitation be revived', in von Hirsch, A and Ashworth, A (eds), *Principled Sentencing*, 2nd edn, 1998, Oxford: Hart

von Hirsch, A and Maher, L [1998b], 'Rehabilitation', in von Hirsch, A and Ashworth, A (eds), *Principled Sentencing*, 2nd edn, 1998, Oxford: Hart

von Hirsch, A, Wasik, M and Greene, J, 'Punishments in the community and the principles of desert' (1989) 20 Rutgers LJ 595

Waldron, J, *The Right to Private Property*, 1988, Oxford: Clarendon

Walker, N, *Sentencing in a Rational Society*, 1969, London: Penguin

Walker, N, *Punishment, Danger and Stigma*, 1985, Oxford: Blackwell

Walker, N, *Sentencing: Theory, Law and Practice*, 1986, London: Butterworths

Walker, N, *Why Punish?*, 1991, Oxford: OUP

Walker, N and Marsh, C, 'Do sentences affect public disapproval?' (1984) 24 British Journal of Criminology 27

Walker, N and Padfield, N, *Sentencing: Theory, Law and Practice*, 2nd edn, 1996, London: Butterworths

Warner, K, 'Sentencing review 1997' (1998) 22 Criminal Law Journal 282

Warnock, GL, *Contemporary Moral Philosophy*, 1982, Hampshire: Macmillan

Wasik, M, 'The suspended sentence: "exceptional circumstances"' (1998) 162 Justice of the Peace 176

Wasik, M and von Hirsch, A, 'Section 29 revised: previous convictions in sentencing' (1994) Crim LR 408

Wasik, M and von Hirsch, A, 'Non-custodial penalties and the principle of proportionality', in von Hirsch, A and Ashworth, A (eds), *Principled Sentencing*, 2nd edn, 1998, Oxford: Hart

Wasik, M, 'Reparation: sentencing and the victim' [1999] Crim LR 470

Wasserstrom, R, 'Why punish the guilty?', in Ezorsky, G (ed), *Philosophical Perspectives of Punishment*, 1972, Albany: NY State UP

Weinstock, D and Schwartz, GE, 'Executing the innocent' (1998) Criminal Law Bulletin 330

Williams, B, 'A critique of utilitarianism', in Smart, JCC and Williams, B (eds), *Utilitarianism: For and Against*, 1973, Cambridge: CUP

Williams, CR, 'Psychopathy, mental illness and preventive detention: issues arising from the Garry David case' (1990) 16 Monash UL Rev 161

Wilson, JQ, 'Penalties and opportunities', in Duff, RA and Garland, D (eds), *A Reader on Punishment*, 1994, Oxford: OUP

Wilson, JQ and Kelling, G, 'Broken windows' (1982) 3 Atlantic Monthly 29

Wolpin, W, 'An economic analysis of crime and punishment in England and Wales, 1894–1967' (1978) Journal of Political Economy 815

Wood, D, 'Dangerous offenders, and the morality of protective sentencing' [1988] Crim LR 424

Wood, D, 'Dangerous offenders and civil detention' (1989) 13 Criminal Law Journal 324

Wood, D, 'A one man dangerous offenders' statute – the Community Protection Act 1990 (Vic)' (1990) 17 Monash UL Rev 497

Wootton, B, *Crime and the Criminal Law*, 2nd edn, 1981, London: Stevens

Zender, L, 'Reparation and retribution: are they reconcilable?' (1994) 57 MLR 228

Zimring, FE and Hawkins, GJ, *Deterrence: The Legal Threat in Crime Control*, 1973, Chicago: Chicago UP

Zimring, FE and Hawkins, GJ, *Incapacitation*, 1995, New York: OUP

INDEX